PRINCES

OF THE

RENAISSANCE

Mary Hollingsworth

PRINCES
OF THE
RENAISSANCE

PEGASUS BOOKS
NEW YORK LONDON

PRINCES OF THE RENAISSANCE

Pegasus Books, Ltd.
148 West 37th Street, 13th Floor
New York, NY 10018

First Pegasus Books cloth edition March 2021

ISBN: 978-1-64313-546-5

10 9 8 7 6 5 4 3 2 1

Printed in the United States of America
Distributed by Simon & Schuster
www.pegasusbooks.com

previous page
Agnolo Bronzino, *Duke Cosimo I*, 1543–4
(Florence, Uffizi). The ideal Renaissance
prince was a wise ruler, generous patron
of the arts and, above all, a hero on the
battlefield.

To John and Elisabeth

Ducats, Scudi & Florins:

A NOTE ON MONEY

Money was a complex business in Renaissance Italy. Each of the peninsula's many states had its own silver-based currency as well as its own system of weights and measures. Large states also issued internationally recognized gold currencies such the Venetian ducat and the Florentine florin; there was also a Roman ducat, which was replaced by the gold *scudo* (pl: *scudi*) in 1530. For the purposes of this book, they were all were all broadly similar in value.

INTRODUCTION

AN ITALIAN IDENTITY

I t is unlikely that the Renaissance would have happened without the humanists – the term derives from a *humanista*, Renaissance student slang for the university lecturer who taught their general arts courses (*studia humanitatis*), based on the study of classical texts on history, poetry, grammar, rhetoric and moral philosophy. This revival of interest in the culture of antiquity had its origins in late thirteenth-century Padua, where a small group of literate lawyers discovered the joys of the Latin poets and historians.

It was Petrarch (1304–74), living in Padua after a career at the papal court in Avignon, who transformed humanism into a movement that spread rapidly across Italy. His attempts to revive the ideals of ancient Rome were an inspiration to many who followed his example by searching the monastic libraries of western Europe for the lost manuscripts of ancient authors, collecting the antique coins churned up by farmers ploughing their fields and, above all, emulating his literary efforts with their own verse, histories and learned treatises, all written in correct Ciceronian Latin or, later, in ancient Greek. By the 1450s – less than a century after Petrarch's death – humanism had become the dominant intellectual force in Italy.

Humanism fostered the sense of a uniquely Italian cultural identity, one that was distinct from that of nations beyond the Alps. It was a message that spoke eloquently to Italy's princely rulers; even more so when Rome once again became the centre of the Christian world and the papacy increasingly Italian. For much of the fourteenth century the papacy had been the puppet of Europe's secular monarchs, initially resident in Avignon under the protection of the French crown and then split by the Great Schism – in the end there were three popes, each supported by a different bloc of rulers and each claiming to be the rightful heir to St Peter. With the credibility of the papacy at stake, in 1417 the Council of Constance ended the Schism by electing its own pope, Martin V, and his return to Rome three years later marked the point at which Renaissance Italy began to emerge as a powerful economic, political and cultural force in Europe.

From a Roman baronial family himself, it was Martin V who took the first steps to free the papacy from foreign interference, a policy that was continued by his successors, who filled the College of Cardinals with Italians. Having restored their authority in the Papal States, which had disintegrated during the absence of the papacy in Avignon, they became central figures in the politics of the peninsula, manipulating alliances between rival rulers for their own ends. They were to have a significant impact – for good, and for bad – on the fortunes of all the princes in this book, as well as providing them with opportunities for employment in the wars that plagued Italy throughout most of the fifteenth and sixteenth centuries.

As heirs to the mighty empire of ancient Rome, the Italians were immensely proud of their past. They could read about it in histories, and they could see it in the great ruins that were visible across the peninsula, above all in Rome itself. But it was not just Rome that could boast an imperial heritage. Mantua was the birthplace of the poet Virgil, while Catullus and Pliny the Elder both came from Verona, as did Vitruvius, whose treatise on architecture was to have such a profound impact on the visual appearance of the cities of the Renaissance princes. Padua, which had been home to the historian Livy, claimed that it had been founded by Antenor after the Trojan Wars. Julius Caesar crossed the Rubicon which still flows into the Adriatic just north of Rimini, a port which boasted an Arch of Augustus and an ancient Roman bridge. The bay of Naples had once been the playground of rich patricians and powerful emperors, while Milan was the city where Emperor Constantine signed the edict that established Christianity as an official religion in his empire.

Italy may have been a geographical unit but it was not a political one. While its citizens shared memories of a golden age gone by, they did not dream of that past being reborn into a glorious future of a united Italy. On the contrary, the peninsula was divided into many independent states, each with its own strong sense of individual identity – and each with its own system of currency, weights and measures, its own taxes, dialect, culinary specialities and patron saint. In the aftermath of the collapse of the Roman empire, Italy had been invaded by many armies: the Lombards, the Byzantines, Charlemagne and the Franks, and so on. Above all, it had been the arena for the power

Rimini, Arch of Augustus, 27 BC: built by Emperor Augustus
to commemorate the restoration of the Via Flaminia
which connected Rome with northern Italy.

struggle between Charlemagne's successors as Holy Roman Emperors and an increasingly powerful papacy.

The small states of northern Italy emerged during the twelfth century, when pope and emperor agreed their independence in the Peace of Constance (1183), while Rome acquired its own area of secular authority in the old Byzantine lands of central Italy, the so-called Papal States; and south of Rome, where the Holy Roman Emperors held sway, became the kingdom of Naples. One of the results of this carving up of the old empire was to have a significant impact on the politics of Renaissance Italy: Milan, Mantua, Modena and Reggio were all imperial fiefs, owing their allegiance to the emperor north of the Alps; by contrast, Ferrara, Rimini, Urbino, Pesaro and Naples were all papal fiefs, technically part of the Papal States.

Initially these independent city-states set up communal governments but during the thirteenth and fourteenth centuries they were taken over, one by one, by powerful families who installed themselves as dynastic rulers: the della Scala in Verona (1262), the Este in Ferrara (1274) and Modena (1288), the Visconti in Milan (1277), the Carrara in Padua (1318) and the Gonzaga in Mantua (1328). By contrast, in Genoa and Venice a sort of semi-seigneurial rule evolved under the leadership of an elected duke (dialect: *doge*) chosen from the wealthy mercantile classes, while in Florence and other Tuscan city-states traders set up their own republics ruled by elected committees of guildsmen.

The relative merits of princely versus republican government was a hot topic of debate in the 1430s. And this contemporary issue was debated in terms of its classical antecedents: the morality of the Roman republic of Cicero versus the flowering of culture in the empire under the Caesars. For the humanists employed at the princely courts, it was Julius Caesar and his successors, the emperors of ancient Rome, who were the heroes. By contrast, Florentine humanists promoted the republican Scipio Africanus as the ideal statesman and judged the emperors of ancient Rome to have been decadent. The debate was not just political but extended to the relative merits of their contributions to culture and science – the arguments in defence of Caesar included not only his skills as a historian and orator in his own right, but also his generous patronage of literary talent.

In an audacious and imaginative move, Renaissance princes, encouraged by their humanists, adopted the cultural language of their

previous pages   Verona, Porta Borsari, *c*.AD 75. Originally one of the city's gates, this double arch was incorporated into the medieval fabric of Verona, its Roman origins clearly visible in the classical lettering of the inscription.

forebears. Imperial Rome could provide flattering models for tyrants, usurpers, warriors and enlightened princes alike – though not for the Florentine republic, where any association with absolute rule was anathema. The nobility educated its sons and daughters in the culture of antiquity: they employed humanists to teach them classical history, oratory, poetry, ethics and mathematics, as well as experts in the more traditional aristocratic pursuits of horsemanship and the martial arts. Like their forebears, Renaissance princes knew the value of the arts as propaganda. Humanists promoted the power and authority of their masters in biographies and histories that exploited the themes of classical rhetoric and its tradition of lavish praise. Fifteenth-century cities adopted pagan figures to add ancient lustre to the Christian saints who were their traditional protectors. New *all'antica* images – images inspired by the remains of ancient Roman art – emerged to change both the style and content of sculpture and painting. One notable Renaissance invention was the portrait medal, developed by humanists inspired by the coins of ancient Rome. In the past, significantly, the use of portraits on coins had been restricted to the emperor, and their

View of the Roman Forum in the late sixteenth century showing the ruins of the Temple of Antoninus and Faustina and the Temple of Vespasian, from Étienne Dupérac's engravings of Roman monuments (1575).

revival at the courts of fifteenth-century Italy was a visible attempt to draw parallels with the ancient world. And, most conspicuously, these princes commissioned palaces, villas and churches all ornamented with the columns, capitals and other details inspired by the architectural language of ancient Rome.

The world of the Renaissance prince was essentially a world of war. Many of them started their careers as mercenary soldiers. Some seized their titles by force, but the talents that won victory on the battlefield did not necessarily translate into the wise statecraft required in the palace. Not all were cruel, immoral or greedy but they were ambitious. And their survival depended on their ability to exchange their military prowess for the more subtle and devious skills required to prosper on the highly competitive stage of Italian politics – not least to negotiate the often conflicting ambitions of popes, kings and emperors, the ultimate arbiters of power on the peninsula.

Off the battlefield it was a world of luxury and leisure: in the woods and marshes hunting wild animals with dogs and falcons; in the lists competing in tournaments; at the dining table for great banquets and theatrical entertainments; at the card table to win or lose large sums of money; and, in all parts of the palaces and villas, that great staple of court life, gossip. Aristocratic women did not fight but they certainly enjoyed hunting and feasting. Key to our understanding of Renaissance princes is the fact that they were all closely related, by blood or marriage, creating a complex web of alliances and rivalries, and an endless cycle of war and diplomacy. Husbands, wives, mistresses, mothers-in-law, cousins, brothers and sisters, their relationships illustrate how this network acted as the glue holding Renaissance society together but could also spark the feuds that regularly threatened to tear it apart.

Renaissance princes and their courts were peripatetic, rarely spending more than a month in each place. They might travel to visit friends and relatives, to make trips to Rome for jubilee celebrations or to attend a papal coronation, or to go shopping in Venice, but mostly they moved between their palaces, castles and villas, exchanging their main residence for those in the smaller towns of their state, or to their country houses to hunt, fish or escape the summer heat. They travelled by road, with carriages provided for ladies and for the infirm, though plenty of women and most men rode everywhere. This way of life involved an enormous amount of work for the household staff, who had to pack all the chests containing the clothes, furniture, silver and hangings which were then loaded on to mules. One of the advantages of tapestry was that it was relatively easy to transport, rolled into custom-made leather travelling bags – and the rich hangings could transform the most unpromising space into a luxurious room with just a few nails.

Travel was more luxurious at the courts of northern Italy where they could take advantage of the network of waterways that linked Milan to Venice, along the Po, its tributaries and canals, that provided essential arteries of trade transporting merchandise, building materials and crops across the Lombard plain – and river barges were much easier to load than mules. The princes of Milan, Ferrara and Mantua all travelled on their own *bucintoro*, a ceremonial barge which provided a much more comfortable, though slower, mode of travel than the unmetalled surfaces of the peninsula's roads. The *bucintoro* could be sailed but was more often manned by oarsmen and pulled by horses on narrow stretches of water. They could be huge structures, with a hull as much as 60 feet long supporting a superstructure of rooms, which were elaborately decorated with gilded ceilings and tapestries.[1] The tapestries were often specially made to fit these spaces which had much lower ceilings that their palace halls; and, with glass in the windows and stoves in the rooms, they were warm and cosy in damp winter weather.

Above all, the courtly society of Renaissance Italy was Christian, and religion played a dominant role in the lives of ordinary people as well as those of princes. The rhythm of court life revolved around the calendar of the Christian year. Easter, the major feast, was celebrated with solemn Masses but also theatrical performances of the story of the Crucifixion; some princes held Maundy Day ceremonies in imitation of Christ and the Last Supper, hosting a meal for poor men, washing their feet and giving them money and clothes. There were more festivities to celebrate Corpus Christi and the Assumption of the Virgin, and often traditional presents for hard-working courtiers on quarter days, such as the goose at Michaelmas. Most princes celebrated Christmas and New Year – the twelve days of Christmas – at their principal residences. January was the season for feasting; traditional cycles of the months carved in panels on cathedrals depicted this month with a peasant holding a flagon, seated at a table heaped with food, or dancing. And

overleaf Pisanello, *Vision of St Eustace*, c.1438–42 (London, National Gallery). The painter has included detailed portraits of the many breeds of hunting dogs owned, and loved, by the princes of the Renaissance.

the feasting usually lasted into Carnival, before the onset of Lent and the return of meat to the dining table to celebrate Easter again.

There were also the annual feast days of each city's patron saint, which in many places was celebrated with a horse race: racing, then as now, was the sport of princes and many Renaissance princes bred their own racehorses. Other, less regular, festivities were held to mark the visits of diginitaries or the entry of a bride. One of the most important rituals of courtly society, weddings were invariably accompanied by several days of feasting, as well as jousts and mock battles, theatrical performances, archery contests and hunting expeditions. It was a holiday for ordinary people too, with shops and businesses closed, allowing everyone to gather along the processional route to watch the cavalcade. The streets were hung with colourful garlands of greenery and flowers, and splendidly ornamented with temporary arches decorated with dynastic details that proclaimed the status of the visitor or, in the case of a wedding, the links between the two houses.

The court provided plenty of work for craftsmen and suppliers. There were temporary wooden stands to erect for guests viewing the races and temporary arches to design and build for bridal entries. The arches were often decorated with reliefs that had been painted to look like marble and terracotta statues coloured to resemble bronze. Spice merchants not only supplied pigments for painters but also edible colourings for the cooks who created the elaborate dishes or sugar sculptures that displayed the coats-of-arms and emblems of the two families. Painters did not only decorate walls with fresco cycles and panel paintings; they were employed on a whole raft of items from banners displaying heraldic devices to wedding chests, bedheads and birth trays. The births of children, especially heirs, were celebrated with bonfires, church bells, fireworks, even free wine.

Extravagance was a duty expected of the rich and powerful in Renaissance Italy. As one humanist praised his noble patron:

> You have not spared yourself from great expense in… the
> magnificence, the glories, the triumphs of arms, of the jousts and
> tournaments that you have prepared more readily to honour others
> and to give pleasure to your much loved subjects and to your splendid
> court, than for your own delight.[2]

Conspicuous consumption was the hallmark of aristocratic display in Renaissance society: how much you spent on your palaces and villas, your jewellery and clothes, your horses, your furnishings, the dishes you served at table, your tournaments and other leisure pursuits, all were indicators of your wealth and status. The details that were of special interest to the chroniclers recording the official entries of visitors in Renaissance Italy were essentially the opulence on show – the expensive Arabs, gold chains, damask and velvet dresses, even the number of pack mules bringing up the rear of the cavalcade. Tapestry in particular was one of the most important hallmarks of the rich: while plain wool hangings were only marginally more expensive than fresco, those made with silk and high-quality wool were five times more expensive, and the elaborate designs using gold and silver thread added significantly to the price.[3]

Renaissance princes developed new fashions to add to the list, notably collections of ancient statues and elaborate gardens, both of which derived from the habits of their imperial forebears. Above all, it was these princes who were responsible for the development of the art and architecture for which the Renaissance is justly famous. It was their leadership that enabled the creation of a new language for the display of the status and power of Italy's aristocratic elite – with such success that it would also be adopted by rulers across Europe.

ALFONSO OF ARAGON (1396–1458)
King of Aragon, Catalonia, Sardinia and Sicily

FRANCESCO SFORZA (1401–66)
Mercenary soldier

René, Duke of Anjou
and rightful heir to the kingdom of Naples

Alonso Borja
King Alfonso's elderly chief advisor

Filippo Maria Visconti, Duke of Milan
Jailer of King Alfonso and prospective father-in-law of Francesco Sforza

Bianca Maria Visconti
Duke Filippo Maria's daughter

USURPERS

Alfonso of Aragon

Francesco Sforza

The sea was calm on 5 August 1435 when Alfonso V of Aragon set sail along the southern Italian coast in search of a small Genoese fleet which, according to his spies, was in the area. He was expecting an easy victory, a boost to his campaign to capture the kingdom of Naples. The Genoese were sighted off the isle of Ponza and the king was encouraged to see three of their galleys, apparently too cowardly to fight, head out into the Mediterranean. Alfonso should have been more wary: the Genoese were seasoned fighters and skilled in the art of naval warfare. The rest of the fleet suddenly tacked and, hurling torches of boiling oil and quicklime, rammed into the royal armada. And just when Alfonso thought that the Genoese were beginning to tire, those three galleys sailed back to give renewed energy to the assault. His seasick Spanish knights were no match for the Genoese sailors, who had been trained to fight on a pitching deck; the king was made a prisoner along with over 400 Spanish nobles.[1] A Neapolitan, celebrating his country's narrow escape from foreign conquest, joyfully recorded: 'No net cast in the sea has ever caught so many fish at once.'[2] Astonishingly, within weeks, Alfonso V had transformed this naval disaster into a diplomatic triumph, turning his jailer Filippo Maria Visconti, Duke of Milan, into his ally. Alfonso V's move was one that would herald regime change not only in Naples but also in Milan, and significantly alter the political map of the peninsula.

Naples was eventually conquered by Alfonso V in 1442 after a lengthy war of attrition, fought mostly on land, while Milan fell to the mercenary captain Francesco Sforza in 1450 after a short but vicious siege. Both victors were usurpers, though that was about all they had in common. One was a king, descended from the ancient Castilian house of Trastamare; the other, Francesco Sforza, was the bastard son of an unlettered mercenary soldier. Duke Filippo Maria, who played a key role in both their stories, contrasted the characters of the two men: the king, he thought, was a 'lord by nature' but Sforza was definitely not.[3] Though Sforza certainly had talent, as recognized by Enea Silvio Piccolomini, whose memoirs are a key contemporary source for this period: 'The destiny of man delights in changing the lowest to the highest but rarely has any man climbed from a cottage to a throne without ability.'[4] Intriguingly, the stories of these two usurpers are

Pisanello, *Alfonso of Aragon*, 1449 (New York, Metropolitan Museum of Art).
The helmet and the royal crown testify to Alfonso's role as conqueror of Naples.
Pisanello, *Francesco Sforza*, c.1441 (New York, Metropolitan Museum of Art).
As the inscription makes clear, Sforza owed his position
to his father-in-law, Duke Filippo Maria Visconti.

closely intertwined – and they serve to remind us that the background to the Renaissance lay as much in the feats of men-at-arms as of those of men of letters.

Alfonso had inherited the throne of Aragon from his father on 2 April 1416 at the age of nineteen. Aragon had been a major power in the Mediterranean since 1100 – his full title was King of Aragon, Valencia, Catalonia, Majorca, Sicily, Sardinia and Corsica, with the courtesy titles of Duke of Athens and King of Jerusalem. He had been married the year before to his cousin Maria of Castile (the granddaughter of John of Gaunt). Educated in the art of war by courtiers and in the medieval Latin of the prayer book by priests, he was assiduous in carrying out his religious duties as monarch: he heard Mass several times a day and each Maundy Thursday he washed the feet of many paupers, serving them dinner while standing 'at the table with a napkin round his neck'.[5] Although very conscious of his rank, he was polite, friendly and generous; he rarely lost his temper and had a good sense of humour. He dressed plainly in expensive but not ostentatious clothes, favouring black velvet doublet and hose, tastefully embroidered with gold and pearls.[6] By all accounts he was a quiet, serious man, whose passions included history, music and hunting – as a youth he had enjoyed gambling but had given up this vice after losing the huge sum of 5,000 florins in a single session.[7]

Alfonso spent four years consolidating his position in Spain before turning his attention to his more distant Mediterranean possessions. In May 1420, leaving Maria of Castile in charge in Barcelona, he set sail at the head of a large fleet carrying the huge royal entourage of courtiers, secretaries and servants as well as soldiers, horses and artillery, even his musicians and hunting dogs. Having secured possession of Sardinia in June, he then attempted to do the same at Corsica, but here his efforts were frustrated by the Genoese, who were determined to protect their commercial interests from interference from Spain.

However, Alfonso's fortunes were about to change in a very un-expected manner. Early in 1421 envoys arrived from Queen Joanna II of Naples inviting the king to her court and offering to name him as her heir. The throne of Naples had been a dream long-cherished by the rulers of Aragon, who had been expelled from that kingdom back in the thirteenth century when the French dynasty of Anjou seized power. Joanna II, now aged fifty and childless, was the last of this Angevin dynasty. The royal council in Barcelona presciently warned Alfonso that this was an enterprise fraught with danger, though, according to one of his courtiers, he responded with characteristic vigour: 'No one has ever won glory yet without danger and difficulty.'[8]

However optimistic Alfonso appeared, the difficulties were very real. Joanna II's prevarication about naming an heir had caused alarm in Italy. In November 1420, without consulting the queen, Pope Martin V had taken the unilateral decision to proclaim her distant cousin Louis III, Duke of Anjou, as her successor. The queen's spirited response to this had been to name Alfonso as her heir, deliberately stirring up trouble by transferring her allegiance to the house of Aragon, the traditional rival to that of Anjou. Louis had retaliated by persuading the commander of Joanna II's army to defect, giving him the prize of Muzio Attendolo, one of Italy's foremost mercenary soldiers, as leader of his own troops.

Nevertheless, despite the danger, Alfonso of Aragon made his formal entry into Naples on 5 July 1421. The queen welcomed him with a mock sea battle and publicly invested him as Duke of Calabria, the title traditionally reserved for the heir to the Neapolitan throne. He set up court at Castel Nuovo, one of several royal castles in the city, and enjoyed plenty of hunting and jousting, but he chafed at the queen's refusal to allow him any share in the government. Worse, scheming courtiers and the notoriously factional Neapolitan barons who preferred the Anjou option fuelled the quarrels between the sovereign and her adopted son. And more opposition began to emerge on the wider political stage as several Italian states followed Martin V in voicing their support for Louis of Anjou. In particular Filippo Maria Visconti worried that a hostile ruler in Naples would directly threaten the economy of his client state Genoa; while fears about the safety of their galleys trading in the Mediterranean also turned both Florence and Venice against the Aragon claim.

Under pressure from both inside and outside her realm, Joanna II was forced to revoke her decision; on 14 September 1423 she dropped Alfonso V, declaring him a public enemy, and pronounced Louis of Anjou to be the new Duke of Calabria. Alfonso prepared to put up a fight but Louis of Anjou's army, led by Muzio Attendolo, forced him to flee. The king sailed back to Spain and, in retaliation, launched an attack on Marseilles, where he stole the body of St Louis of Toulouse, the pious grandson of the first Angevin king of Naples. The Spanish troops were given royal permission to loot the city, but the king issued an order forbidding rape and he arranged for the women to be moved to the safety of the city's churches under guard.[9]

Muzio Attendolo – whose nickname was Sforza, or 'strongman' – had earned his formidable reputation in the service of Milan, Florence and Ferrara before moving to Naples in 1412 to fight for King Ladislas, Joanna II's predecessor. And joining him that year was his eleven-year-old bastard son, Francesco, the other protagonist of this chapter; as a mark of favour to his mercenary captain, the king gave the boy the title of Count of Tricarico. After Ladislas's death in 1414, Joanna II continued to employ Muzio and rewarded him for his loyal military service with land and titles in the kingdom.

Warfare was endemic in Renaissance Italy – the jousts, tournaments and hunts that were such favourite sports among the nobility were excellent training for the battlefield. At the beginning of the fifteenth century war was waged not by professional armies but by troops of mercenary soldiers (*condottieri*) fighting under their captain who each signed a contract (*condotta*) promising to provide his employer with a quantity of lances to fight for a specified period. Muzio's *condotta* with Ladislas, for example, was for 830 lances – one lance unit consisted of a soldier in full armour, a lightly armoured squire, a servant and five or six horses.[10]

War was also a seasonal affair and fighting usually halted in winter when the weather made many roads impassable. Just how dangerous conditions could be was evident in January 1424 when, after forcing Alfonso of Aragon to flee Naples, Muzio and Francesco were fighting on the northern borders of the kingdom. While crossing the river Pescara swollen by heavy rain, Muzio's horse accidentally lost its footing and the soldier, in full armour, was dragged into the floodwaters and drowned. Francesco, aged just twenty-three, now took over the *condotta*. A promising fighter, as handsome and swaggering as his father, he adopted Muzio's nickname 'Sforza' as his own surname. And the queen confirmed his right to inherit his father's feudal possessions in the kingdom, which now included Benevento, Troia and Manfredonia, making the young soldier one of the leading feudal landowners in the kingdom.

Now that Alfonso of Aragon had been expelled from Naples and the succession secured on Louis of Anjou, Joanna II had no need of Sforza's services and gave him permission to fight for Duke Filippo Maria in the ongoing war between Milan and Venice. In December 1427 the duke sent him to Genoa where rebels were threatening to expel the Milanese from the city and, unfortunately, he was caught in a surprise ambush. He was lucky not to have been killed but the incident infuriated the famously touchy Filippo Maria; it was not until 1429 that he gave Sforza another *condotta*, this time to fight with the army he had sent to Tuscany to defend Lucca against the Florentines. Fortunately for his future prospects, this expedition was highly successful – not only did he win a decisive victory in Lucca in July 1430, he also managed to secure 50,000 florins that the Florentines still owed his father.

Sforza's reward was a stroke of excellent fortune, and one that had a surprising parallel in events in the life of his rival, Alfonso of Aragon. Stunned by the unexpected defection of one of his commanders, the duke decided to secure the loyalty of this talented *condottiere* by offering Sforza his own illegitimate daughter Bianca Maria as a bride. The betrothal took place on 23 February 1432; Sforza was thirty-one years old and his fiancée just six, too young for marriage itself, but the important subtext of the contract was that, as Filippo Maria had no son, Sforza himself would become the duke's heir. He would have to be patient – not one of the soldier's most notable virtues – and careful not to offend his tricky future father-in-law. However his luck held and the following year the duke, seizing the advantage of a pope preoccupied with his own affairs, encouraged Sforza to invade the Papal States. Presented with a fait accompli, Eugene IV had been obliged to cede the soldier the titles to Ancona and Fermo on the northern borders of Naples.

While Sforza was building up his reputation and power base in Italy, Alfonso V was biding his time in Spain – and making overtures to his most powerful enemies in Italy, notably to Duke Filippo Maria and Martin V, whose support would be essential if he were to relaunch his bid for Naples. An astute politician, the king had the gift of patience. First he negotiated a secret deal with Filippo Maria, relinquishing his claim to Corsica in exchange for ports on the Ligurian coast south

overleaf Milan, Duomo, begun 1386. A visible statement of the power and prestige of Giangaleazzo Visconti's court, which rivalled those of Burgundy and France and provided a model for his Sforza descendants.

of Genoa. Currying favour with the pope was more complicated as Alfonso had been a supporter of the Spanish anti-pope Clement VIII. Now, on the advice of his chief councillor Alonso Borja, he swapped sides to play a key role in securing the abdication of the anti-pope and thus bringing the Great Schism, which had divided Christian Europe for a century, to an end. Martin V rewarded chief councillor Borja with the prestigious bishopric of Valencia but unfortunately the king's anticipated political rewards were not forthcoming as the pope died in February 1431. It was a decisive moment: the new pope Eugene IV was Venetian and highly unlikely to support the Aragon claim to Naples but Joanna II was getting older – she had her sixtieth birthday in June that year. Alfonso V decided to gamble and, taking advantage of Eugene IV's temporary difficulties like Filippo Maria, made his plans to return to Italy.

Alfonso left Barcelona later that year for Sicily, setting up his court at Messina, just across the strait from the mainland. He equipped a powerful fleet which he used to great success against pirates in Tunisia and it was this display of naval power so close to her realm that persuaded Queen Joanna that perhaps the future of Naples might indeed be safer under Alfonso. So she rewrote the succession, again, this time dropping Louis of Anjou in favour of the Spanish king – but their reconciliation would prove shortlived. When Louis died in November 1434 Joanna changed her will yet again, this time to favour Louis's brother, René of Anjou. And then Joanna herself died on 2 February 1435. Ignoring the new will, Alfonso styled himself Alfonso I of Naples from the date of Joanna II's death, and made plans to seize his kingdom by force. Fortunately for him René of Anjou was a prisoner of the Duke of Burgundy, who was married to Alfonso's sister-in-law. But it was a very modest advantage – he faced almost universal hostility from Italy's rulers who now lined up to create a formidable coalition on behalf of René: the new Venetian pope Eugene IV; Duke Filippo Maria of Milan; Florence, which was traditionally pro-France; and Venice and Genoa, both protecting their commercial interests.

As we know, Alfonso's first bid for power resulted in his spectacular defeat at the Battle of Ponza in August 1435 and his capture by the Genoese, who sent their royal prisoner into the custody of their overlord, Duke Filippo Maria. Arriving in Milan on 15 September, the king was received with every courtesy and the two men apparently spent their first meeting discussing hunting. However, the talk soon turned to politics and Alfonso's persuasive arguments convinced the duke that a French dynasty in Naples was a far greater threat to Visconti Milan than the Aragonese. It was true Charles VII's wife was an Angevin princess but, more unsettling, his cousin, the Duke of Orléans, was Filippo Maria's nephew – the son of his sister Valentina – and as such a legitimate descendant who would have a better claim to Milan than Filippo Maria's own illegitimate daughter Bianca Maria. The two men agreed, somewhat arrogantly, to divide Italy into two spheres of influence and the duke pledged to support Alfonso's campaign to seize Naples 'in every possible way'.[11] There was no question of this alliance being made public so, on 21 September, Filippo Maria made a public show of his alliance with René of Anjou and then released Alfonso who, so he claimed, had been rescued from the Genoese 'with great difficulty and expense'.[12]

Significantly, another clause in the secret treaty pitted Alfonso I directly against Francesco Sforza. The *condottiere* had fallen out with his future father-in-law, who had cancelled the betrothal to Bianca Maria, and had signed a *condotta* with Eugene IV, Venice and Florence for 1,000 lances.[13] For a time it looked as if the king and the duke were about to go to war not only against Sforza but also against the pope and the two republics, but Filippo Maria changed his mind again and offered to reinstate the betrothal provided Sforza changed his loyalty back to the Milanese side. In the meantime, however, Sforza was showing signs of political skill. He had found himself another patron: the wealthy and wily Florentine banker, Cosimo de' Medici. Aware of the advantages of making an ally of Milan after decades of enmity between the duchy and Florence, the banker had agreed to open a new branch of his bank in Ancona to provide financial backing to Sforza's bid for power.[14] The nature of their financial relationship had to remain top secret but, on Cosimo's advice, Sforza accepted Filippo Maria's offer: the new betrothal was signed on 28 March 1438 and Bianca Maria, now twelve years of age, was to receive the substantial dowry of 100,000 florins and the lordships of Asti and Tortona.

Meanwhile the war for Naples was gaining momentum. René of Anjou's wife Isabelle of Lorraine had set up court in the city itself, where her husband joined her in 1438 after the large ransom demanded by the Duke of Burgundy had been paid. Alfonso had settled at Gaeta, a port on the northern borders of the kingdom, which he had conquered in 1435 soon after his release by Filippo Maria. He had begun the transformation of the castle at Gaeta into a royal residence for himself, his court and, importantly, his family. Alfonso had three children, Maria, Eleonora and Ferrante, all bastards – Queen Maria, an able partner to her husband in the business of government, had sadly proved unable to bear children. Although illegitimacy was no bar to inheritance at the Italian courts, it was more of a problem outside Italy so, while Alfonso could designate his son Ferrante as heir to Naples, he had to appoint his brother Juan to succeed as king of his Spanish possessions.

Alfonso's priority was his campaign for Naples and he appointed a treasurer to take charge of raising the necessary funds in Spain.[15] Fighting was expensive. The king bought African gold coins which were melted down to make Venetian ducats, and used the treasured relic of the Holy Grail in Valencia Cathedral as security to finance loans.[16] He ordered artillery and other vital supplies in Spain – on one occasion Queen Maria was asked to find 500 crossbowmen for the army – and fleets of ships were used to transport them across the Mediterranean.[17] Alfonso also planned for victory, evidence of self-confidence, perhaps, but also of a pragmatic approach to the real difficulties he would face once in power. Soon after taking Gaeta he dispossessed all the Angevin feudatories of their estates and nominated loyal Castilian and Catalan nobles in their place.[18] This was a statement of intent, as he still had to establish his own authority in the kingdom, but he must have been cheered by the steady stream of Angevin supporters arriving at Gaeta to request favours. His judicious grants of posts, titles, privileges and revenues wooed more to his side: Diomede Carafa, for example, scion of a prominent Neapolitan baronial clan, was an early convert to Alfonso's cause and was rewarded with a position in Ferrante's household, the only Italian among the prince's otherwise Catalan court.

Among those angered by Alfonso's peremptory 'confiscation' of their Neapolitan estates was Francesco Sforza, who had no intention of forging ties with the king. He believed that he could best protect his interests by securing the throne for René of Anjou. In July 1438, just four months after his second betrothal to Bianca Maria Visconti, he took the decisive step of invading the northern borders of Naples to seize land on the Adriatic coast adjoining his fief of Ancona. He then took up the post of Captain-General of René's army, another overtly public statement of hostility towards Alfonso.[19] Unfortunately for Sforza, the balance of power had begun to shift inexorably towards an Aragonese victory and Alfonso's army finally defeated Sforza's troops near Troia in June 1441. But Sforza still had two assets: the backing of the Medici bank and his marriage to Bianca Maria Visconti, which had taken place that October in Cremona, a city which now came to him as part of her dowry.

Alfonso finally reached the city of Naples itself in May 1442; he was able to avoid the horrors of a siege after a workman informed him of a disused drainage channel, part of an ancient Roman aqueduct, that gave direct access into the city. Late on 1 June, under cover of darkness, he sent Diomede Carafa with 200 soldiers through the ditch to open the gates for the men camped outside the walls – the king's humanists were delighted to draw the parallel with Belisarius, the Byzantine general who had used the same method to capture Naples from the Ostrogoths in the sixth century.[20] And Alfonso, who regularly beheaded soldiers found guilty of rape, gained much support among the Neapolitans themselves after he ordered his soldiers, on pain of the gallows, to refrain from sacking the city.[21]

With the acquisition of the huge kingdom of Naples, which comprised most of Italy south of Rome, Alfonso had a realm as large as that of the King of France and he celebrated his conquest with a formal entry into his capital city on 26 February 1433. This carefully choreographed event was witnessed by one of his Catalan subjects, who sent a report back to Barcelona describing the splendid cavalcade.[22] Led by a group of royal trumpeters announcing his arrival, the king was borne aloft on a carriage pulled by four magnificent greys. Holding his orb and sceptre, he was seated under a canopy of gold brocade, 'which cost 4,000 ducats', carried by the leading lords of his realm. His chair, covered in the same expensive gold brocade, had particular meaning: as the Catalan pointed out, this was the Siege Perilous of Arthurian legend and 'no other king, prince or lord was worthy enough to sit in it except this lord who had defeated and gained possession of this kingdom'. It was an appropriate emblem with which to mark his conquest.

The entry was not a coronation – Alfonso had already been

crowned in Barcelona in 1416 – but a 'triumph', the ancient imperial Roman custom of awarding victorious military generals the honour of a procession through Rome. Deliberately revived for this occasion, it was the first of its kind in Renaissance Italy. The 'emperor' who greeted Alfonso in 1443 was Julius Caesar, one of the king's heroes, who presented him with the throne and crown of his new kingdom. In one important respect, however, it differed from its ancient model: the procession that wound its noisy way through the streets of Naples did not include the human spoils of war. One of Alfonso's first acts after taking Naples had been to issue an amnesty for all Angevin supporters and, as one of his propagandists explained, the Neapolitan lords and nobles who followed his procession were 'the liberated nobility, they were not dragged like bound barbarians but as citizens celebrating their liberation from shackles'.[23]

There was soon more tangible evidence of the conquest. Alfonso improved life for ordinary Neapolitans with a campaign of urban renewal aimed at repairing the infrastructure of the dilapidated city with an extension to the port facilities together with new aqueducts and fountains to improve the water supply. He made major changes to the way royal authority was exercised, sweeping away the inefficient Angevin system of government and radically reforming the economy. He imposed a new hearth tax to replace the old system of levies. He introduced merino sheep from Spain and made far-reaching changes to the system of renting out winter grazing rights on the lowland plains, enabling these rents to be collected by the crown – one royal commissioner reported a five-fold increase in rents, which rose from 18,868 ducats in 1443–4 to 103,011 ducats six years later.[24] His most important change was to establish a centralized bureaucracy at the heart of government, manned with professional, salaried staff.

Above all, builders began work on Castel Nuovo, transforming this old Angevin fortress by the harbour into the king's official residence. Castles were the focus of sovereignty for early Renaissance princes, the prime image of their authority over their subjects inside the city walls but also of their power to defend these subjects from external enemies. As one architect of the period put it: 'The castle is the key element of the city, just as the head is the key organ of the body – if the head is lost, then so is the body, and in the same way whoever loses his castle also loses his power over the city.'[25] Appropriately dedicated by the king to St Michael, the Archangel who forced the rebel angels out of Heaven, the new Castel Nuovo was a huge, imposing edifice, boasting up-to-date defensive features including a double moat and five massive circular towers, and cost the substantial sum of 250,000 ducats.[26]

The entrance gateway, sandwiched between two of the towers, was also innovative, in a very different way. Recognizably *all'antica* in style, it had fluted Corinthian columns flanking the entrance and support-ing a frieze which bore an inscription describing Alfonso as 'pious, merciful and undefeated' – PIUS CLEMENS INVICTUS – carved in conspicuously classical lettering.[27] A contemporary humanist lik-ened it to the arches of Septimius Severus and Titus in Rome, while the Milanese ambassador described it as 'a marble arch sculpted and worked in the antique style'.[28] Its central section depicted Alfonso's triumphal entry into Naples and showed the king seated in the Siege Perilous carried on a horse-drawn cart and accompanied by the royal trumpeters, soldiers and courtiers. And the style of the carving was strongly resonant of sculptural decoration on ancient Roman trium-phal arches, while the empty arch above was intended to contain an-other piece of imperial propaganda, an equestrian statue of the king.

Behind the walls were elegant gardens planted with apricot seed-lings and other fruit trees imported from Spain, as well as a riding school, a jousting court and the royal hunting park.[29] In the summer of 1443 work started on the acqueduct to supply water to the palace – the aqueduct also supplied a flour mill, which had to stop working for four months each year as all the water was needed for the royal fountains![30] The costs rose inexorably: monthly expenses, which were around 500 ducats in 1443, doubled to 1,000 ducats the following year and had reached over 2,000 ducats by the end of 1446.[31] In 1455 the Milanese ambassador reported that Alfonso was spending 3,000 duc-ats a month on the castle: 'It is a magnificent and imposing work and nothing is allowed to interfere with the work on Castel Nuovo, either inside or outside.'[32]

Inside the palace Alfonso chose to give visual expression to his royal authority not in the *all'antica* language of the exterior but in definitively Spanish style. He replaced the Angevin great hall with a much larger room, the Sala dei Baroni, measuring 85 by 85 feet, which was accessible inside from the royal apartments and, for visitors, by a staircase leading up from the central court. In the contract signed with the Majorcan builder, Guillem Sagrera, Alfonso agreed to use local stone from Pozzuoli but also to ship supplies from Majorca to provide stone for the decorative details that was easy to carve.[33] The ceiling was manifestly Gothic with elegantly ribbed vaults ornamented with gilded bosses displaying the coats-of-arms of Alfonso's Spanish territories. There were balconies for his musicians to perform during banquets, and the dining room even had its own organ.[34] Most striking was the elaborate floor, laid with tiles ornamented with the royal coat-of-arms and Alfonso's personal emblems, including the Siege Perilous, which the king had specially made at Valencia and then shipped at considerable expense to Naples.[35]

The walls of the Sala dei Baroni were hung with tapestries, as were all the important chambers in the castle. Alfonso owned a set of six that had once belonged to Joanna II, depicting scenes of the story of Solomon and the Queen of Sheba.[36] He spent 5,000 ducats on a series depicting the Passion of Christ, designed by the Flemish painter Roger van der Weyden, which his agents bought in Flanders along with others depicting the Old Testament stories of Nebuchadnezzar and Ahasuerus.[37] Alfonso had close connections with Burgundy, which facilitated his business there. Duke Philip II was married to the king's sister-in-law, and he made Alfonso a Knight of the Golden Fleece,

the chivalric order he had founded in 1429 and the first foreigner he had invested with this coveted honour.[38] Alfonso regularly sent ships north from Naples carrying cargoes of sugar from Sicily, which could be traded for goods in Bruges. On one occasion his purchases were dispatched from Flanders in a Burgundian whaler, which the harbour authorities in Barcelona mistook for an enemy ship – it was attacked when it docked and much of the merchandise stolen.[39] Alfonso was furious and issued an inventory of the items he wanted returned, which included ten bales containing bolts of red, black, green, grey and violet cloth, a selection of black hats, ten silver candelabra, silver bowls, quantities of bedcovers and bed hangings, equipment for his falcons and, of course, many tapestries.

Alfonso's tastes were expensive. He spent 745 ducats on a single piece of gold brocade, paid a Genoese merchant 5,610 ducats for jewels, bought 580 marten furs for 1,160 ducats and spent 12,000 ducats on four silver items including a gilded cross and a salt cellar set with diamonds, pearls and rubies; the treasury was housed in one of the towers of Castel Nuovo, appropriately named the Torre d'Oro (Tower of Gold).[40] He had an impressive library in the castle, where he employed an army of librarians, copyists, illuminators and skilled leather-workers from Granada and Cordoba to do the bookbinding.[41] He bought paintings, favouring Flemish artists – among the pictures bought by his agents were a St George and the Dragon and the so-called Lomellini triptych, both lost works by Jan van Eyck, who also worked for Duke Philip of Burgundy.[42]

Inspired by the activities of his son-in-law, Leonello d'Este (see Chapter 2), Alfonso became a great collector of ancient coins 'of the illustrious emperors but especially [Julius] Caesar' and was inspired to virtue and glory, so he told one of his humanists, by seeing a gold coin of Nero which had just been found near Naples at Pozzuoli, an important port in Roman times.[43] He commissioned the Italian artist Pisanello to do designs for silverware and embroidery, as well as for all'antica medals, drawings for three of which have survived.[44] Ornamented with the profile portrait of their patron, the imagery praised him for his liberality, for his status as both warrior and peacemaker, his love of scholarship and, above all, as heir to the emperors of ancient Rome.[45]

Alfonso's court was one of the most splendid in early Renaissance Europe and, like his castle, a distinctive mixture of Italianate and

Naples, Castel Nuovo, Arch of Alfonso, begun 1452. The decoration of the arch deliberately invoked classical reliefs showing the triumphal processions accorded to victorious generals of the Roman empire.

Spanish traditions. The language of the court was Castilian, though the inner circle of courtiers and chamber servants who had close access to the king included both Castilians and Catalonians, many of whom had fought alongside Alfonso during the war for Naples.[46] Most of his 108 huntsmen and 100 falconers were Italian, though the masters in charge of the hunting, the dogs and the mews were invariably Spaniards.[47] A noted patron of musicians, Alfonso employed harpists and lutenists to accompany singers of secular music and dancing though most of his musicians were attached to the royal chapel, which contained a few Italian but mostly Spanish singers – he sent the Spanish master of his choirboys back to Spain to recruit boy sopranos, paying him 960 ducats to cover the cost of his trip.[48] Both in size and quality, his chapel was one of the grandest of the period with twenty-four singers, not including his boy sopranos or organists; by contrast, the papal chapel in Rome had only eighteen singers and Duke Philip II of Burgundy twenty-one, though Henry VI of England apparently had thirty-six singers in his chapel.[49]

The Spanish domination of Alfonso's court also extended into the political realm. While the old aristocratic families of the kingdom were initially flattered to have been appointed to the six traditional Angevin offices of state – admiral, seneschal, chancellor and so on – it was soon clear that these posts were now mere sinecures and that real power lay with the Spanish heads of the departments of the Aragonese system of government which Alfonso had imposed on the kingdom.[50] In an attempt to placate the barons, he betrothed his daughter Eleonora to Marino Marzano, heir to the Duke of Sessa, and arranged the marriage of his son Ferrante to Isabella di Chiaramonte, niece and heiress to the childless Prince of Taranto, the premier noble in Naples; he had also conferred titles on several others who had been loyal to his cause.[51] But these gestures were not adequate to make up for their exclusion from real power, a grievance that was to have disastrous consequences (Chapter 4).

There was one area, however, where Alfonso very conspicuously favoured Italians – the humanists he employed as propagandists, secretaries, diplomats and bureaucrats in his regime. And it was the king's patronage of humanism that brought lasting fame to his court. His love of ancient history was widely known – he set aside an hour each day to listen to his humanists, the so-called *ora del libro*, or book hour, even when in camp with the army; one of them read a biography of Alexander the Great while the king convalesced after a serious illness.[52] He loved books: one of his emblems was an open book with the punning motto 'Liber sum' (liber could be 'book' or 'free'), while his favourite author was Livy and he boasted an arm bone of the historian among his more conventional relics.[53] As the Roman humanist Flavio Biondo explained in a letter to Alfonso in 1443, written shortly after the king's conquest of Naples, the reason for the lasting fame of Emperors Augustus, Trajan and Hadrian (the last two, conveniently, Spanish-born) was precisely because they had cultivated men of letters.[54]

Many scholars dedicated their works to Alfonso in the hope of a court position – among these works were translations of famous Greek texts such as Homer's *Iliad*, commentaries on Roman and Greek historians and, at a more practical level, treatises on military subjects.[55] Exploiting the language of classical rhetoric to promote their patron as heir to the emperors of ancient Rome, Alfonso's humanists left copious accounts of his reign based on classical models that glorified the conqueror and legitimized his new dynasty. But it was not just their scholarship that appealed to Alfonso – he also appreciated the political and diplomatic skills that educated men could bring to his court and he set up a school for promising students.[56] Among Alfonso's humanists were many famous names: Giannozzo Manetti, who undertook several diplomatic missions for Alfonso I; Giovanni Pontano and Porcellio Pandoni, who were both employed as royal secretaries. Pandoni, in particular, flattered the king by drawing parallels between his patron and Julius Caesar, while promoting Naples as the new Rome. Naples also attracted several Greek humanists, notably George of Trebizond and Theodore Gaza.

Among Alfonso's most famous appointments were Antonio Beccadelli, better known as Panormita (nicknamed for his birthplace, Palermo), Lorenzo Valla and Bartolomeo Facio. Panormita gained fame in 1425 after publishing *Hermaphroditus*, a collection of pornographic verses recounting his sexual escapades while studying law at Bologna university.[57] He joined Alfonso in 1434, after a less-than-satisfactory period as Duke Filippo Maria's court poet: the king gave him several important positions in the new bureaucracy, and sent him on diplomatic missions abroad. His book on Alfonso's sayings and deeds (*De dictis et factis Alphonsi*, 1455), based on Xenophon's anecdotal life of Socrates, tells us much about the character of the king – or, at least, about his public image.[58] Lorenzo Valla was one of the king's secretaries on a salary of 350 ducats a year, substantially more than the 200 he would have earned elsewhere, though less than the 600 ducats the king paid his doctor and astrologer.[59] Valla's works included a commentary on Livy, as well as philosophical and religious treatises, and a history of the reign of Alfonso's father.[60] Bartolomeo Facio, a protégé of Panormita, started his Neapolitan career as tutor to the young Ferrante and was appointed royal historian to write a history of Alfonso's military and political achievements (*De rebus gestis Alphonso primo*).[61]

Meanwhile Alfonso I needed papal approval to secure his throne. Naples was a papal fief, part of the territory widely believed to have been granted to the papacy in perpetuity by Emperor Constantine as a reward to Pope Silvester I (314–335) who miraculously cured him of leprosy. The official document detailing this gift – the Donation of Constantine – was exposed by Valla as an eighth-century forgery, which it was.[62] But, while Eugene IV was able to dismiss the intellectual argument as irrelevant, he could not ignore the fact that there were cogent political arguments in favour of making peace with the king. Indeed, rumours had begun to circulate in 1442 of a powerful new alliance being planned between Naples, Rome and Milan with the aim of bringing about the downfall of Francesco Sforza. The ambitious mercenary, who continued to plot with René of Anjou, was a problem for all three rulers: his raids in the Abruzzi threatened the northern borders of Alfonso's kingdom; his refusal to relinquish the papal fief of Ancona challenged Eugene IV's authority in the Papal States; and now that he had married Bianca Maria, he no longer needed the support of Duke Filippo Maria Visconti.

That summer relations between Alfonso I and Sforza deteriorated significantly – not only had the king deprived this proud soldier of his Neapolitan possessions, but he now chose to humiliate him. At the end of July Alfonso offered Sforza a five-year *condotta* for 4,000 cavalry and 1,000 infantry; the terms were attractive, and the soldier accepted, but he should have been more wary.[63] The contract, it turned out, was a ruse whereby the king hoped to force Sforza's rival Niccolò Piccinino to accept a lower price for his services the coming season. The ruse worked: the king promptly dropped Sforza, claiming that his *condotta* had been negotiated without royal permission, and signed with Piccinino instead, on exactly the terms that he had offered to Sforza. Understandably furious and resentful, Sforza wrote after Alfonso I's death:

> He was the most presumptuous man and considered no one his social equal; his arrogance and his pride were such that he believed not only that he was honoured amongst men but that he was also adored by the gods; he thought that even the trees and the walls bowed down to do him honour... with him it was impossible to establish any sort of common interests or friendship.[64]

Negotiations between Eugene IV and Alfonso I began in earnest in early 1443. The pope, who had been forced to escape Rome in 1434 disguised as a monk after the city rebelled against papal rule, had set up his court in Florence, where news that he was planning a rapprochement with both Milan and Naples was viewed with alarm – when his presence at the negotiating table was required in early March 1443, he was forced to travel secretly to Siena.[65] The main negotiations opened in April at Terracina, a city in the Papal States near the border with Naples, between the king's trusted councillor Alonso Borja, bishop of Valencia, and Cardinal Ludovico Trevisan, patriarch of Aquileia – this bellicose cardinal, nicknamed the 'Angel of Peace', had been given his red hat by Eugene IV as a reward for his success on the battlefield as commander of the papal armies.[66] The treaty, which was signed on 14 June, promised papal recognition of Alfonso's rights to the throne of Naples, and a red hat for Alonso Borja, in return for the king's support for Eugene IV's struggle with the Council of Basle and for his impending crusade. More significantly for our story, Alfonso also promised to assist in the military campaign to remove Sforza from the papal territory of Ancona.

The campaign against Sforza now started in earnest, and by mid-August Alfonso I and his army had joined up with Piccinino at Norcia in the mountains north-east of Rome. Two weeks after leaving Norcia they were camped outside Iesi, which they took on 2/3 September. During that fortnight they had marched 120 miles over mountain roads and forced Sforza's troops out of San Severino, Tolentino and Macerata.[67] By the end of September they were beseiging Fermo, where Panormita continued his daily readings from Livy's *Histories*, 'and all the gentlemen in the army would attend these meetings'.[68] It was while they were outside Fermo that a royal herald recognized one of Sforza's servants walking through the camp and had him arrested. A search revealed that the servant was carrying a letter from his master to the captains who had surrendered Iesi to the king and were now part of Alfonso's army. The surrender, it turned out, had been a sham, a way of getting the captains into the enemy camp, and the letter now ordered them to capture Alfonso, killing him if necessary, so that Sforza could take Naples by force and install himself as king. It was a bold plan and might have worked but for the sheer chance that the herald spotted the servant among the hordes of camp followers. Or was that also a ruse? When accused of plotting the assassination, Sforza denied all knowledge of the plan, insisting that he had deliberately forged the letters to punish his captains for betraying him at Iesi.[69] Whatever the truth of the story, the commanders were arrested and sent to Valencia, where they were imprisoned in the Borja castle at Játiva.

In the end, the siege of Fermo failed and, with winter fast approaching, Alfonso withdrew his troops, satisfied that he had achieved his immediate aim of securing his own northern border against Sforza – though, at a cost of 800,000 ducats, the six-month campaign had proved very expensive.[70] And, unfortunately for Alfonso, his alliance with Eugene IV and Filippo Maria Visconti was also beginning to unravel thanks to Sforza's machinations. On 24 January 1444 Bianca Maria gave birth to a healthy son, and her father agreed to a reconciliation with her husband. Filippo Maria now signed an alliance with Venice and Florence to limit Alfonso's ambitions in Italy. The king responded by ordering Queen Maria to seize all cash and merchandise belonging to Venetians and Florentines trading in his Spanish possessions.[71] Borso d'Este, in Naples as a guest of Alfonso in 1444–5, wrote a report that exposed the weakness of the Neapolitan economy and warned the king that all Italy – Eugene IV, Duke Filippo Maria, Venice, Florence and Francesco Sforza – considered him to be their enemy.[72]

Over the next few years the pattern of alliances shifted again and again until the death of Eugene IV in February 1447 brought a new pope and a new political agenda. The year was to prove an eventful one in Italian politics. That August, Duke Filippo Maria also died and the succession in Milan was to prove far more complicated. It was Sforza's chance for real power. However, he was not the only claimant: in his memoirs Enea Silvio Piccolomini, now secretary to Emperor Frederick III, recorded that the duke 'died of dysentery, having publicly proclaimed King Alfonso as his heir'.[73] And there were others with a close interest in the succession, notably Piccolomini's patron, who claimed the duchy as an imperial fief; and the French claim, mentioned above, now became a possibility through Duke Charles of Orléans, whose mother, Valentina, was half-sister to Filippo Maria.

In the event, however, it was the Milanese themselves who seized the initiative. Within hours of Filippo Maria's death a group of patricians had taken power in the name of the Ambrosian republic, so named after Milan's patron saint, St Ambrose.[74] A rampaging mob of citizens vented their hatred of the Visconti duke by destroying the Castello di Porta Giovia, the huge castle that had been the symbol of the duke's authority in the city. But the new regime was also unpopular: the subject cities rebelled against domination by Milan, causing the city's income to plummet, and Venice moved into the vacuum. Francesco Sforza was faced with two options, neither very palatable: to serve with the republic against Venice, or vice versa. In the end he opted to fight for Milan but there was not enough money in the coffers to pay his wages. When the patricians who headed the republic offered to make Bianca Maria ruler of Milan, he refused point blank to accept the secondary role as consort – especially now that his success in recovering Milanese cities from the Venetians had begun to improve his own popularity in the duchy.[75] His methods were not pretty. He launched a particularly vicious attack on Piacenza: 'All the churches were robbed of their relics, crosses, and chalices… all the women, virgins, wives, widows, nuns, all of them were dishonoured and abused… all the men were taken prisoner and each saw his own wife, his own daughters shamed.'[76]

Milan itself, however, remained elusive. And Sforza's priorities now changed – on the advice of his wily banker, Cosimo de' Medici – from loyalty to the republic to an attack on the republic itself. In October 1448 he horrified the Milanese by agreeing a treaty with the Venetians for their assistance in the conquest of the city in return for territories in the east of the duchy. It was a truly Machiavellian plot: as Niccolò Machiavelli himself later put it, 'the Venetians knew that the Milanese did not trust Sforza, and that Sforza wanted to be duke of Milan rather than its captain-general', so they 'decided to make peace with Sforza and offered him aid to conquer Milan, knowing that when the Milanese saw how Sforza had deceived them, they would be so furious that they would prefer anyone rather than him'.[77]

As the Venetians predicted, the Milanese were indeed appalled by Sforza's treachery and resolutely continued to resist his assault. But Sforza slowly tightened his noose around the city. By the summer of 1449 food supplies could not get through the blockade and in September his troops were camped outside the city gates. In a last, desperate attempt to outmanoeuvre Sforza, the Ambrosian republic signed a separate peace deal with Venice. However, it was Sforza who had the upper hand and it was now that his partnership with Cosimo de' Medici began to pay real dividends. Thanks to the unlimited resources of the Medici bank he was able to continue the siege and by February 1450 the Milanese were desperate. A chronicler described people 'dying on the streets like dogs and because there was no bread, they were eating horses, dogs, cats, and mice'.[78] By the end of the month a starving mob opened the gates to Sforza's troops. Francesco Sforza made his entry into Milan on the afternoon of 26 February, the day after the capitulation, but it was no triumphal affair – thre was no parade and he scornfully refused to sign a petition offered to him by a group of leading citizens, leaving after an hour to return to the army camp. It took a month of negotiations before the ceremony could take place in the cathedral investing him with the symbols of his office.

Sforza's brutal conquest of the duchy had been recognized with a considerable degree of reluctance – he had much to do in order to be accepted. The new duke chose to justify his position by emphasizing his ties to the Visconti regime. Initially at least, his privy council was largely made up of men who had served in that role under Duke Filippo Maria.[79] He forged a deed purporting to show that his father-in-law had made him his heir and he adopted the Visconti viper as his emblem.* Each of his children were christened with the second name 'Maria', a Visconti tradition and, even more strikingly, they were

---

* The snake is still visible in Milan on the Alfa Romeo logo.

ordered to sign all their correspondence using their mother's surname Visconti – though his illegitimate children, who were also living at the court, were expected to use Sforza.[80]

Above all, Francesco used the visual language of art and architecture to underline the message of continuity. He restarted work on several Visconti projects, notably the Duomo in Milan and the Certosa at Pavia. At the Visconti castle in Pavia, instead of replacing the dilapidated, old-fashioned frescoes of hunting and jousting in the great hall which had been commissioned by Duke Giangaleazzo in the late fourteenth century, he took the unusual step of having these restored.[81] In Milan itself, however, he had to be more careful. Filippo Maria had been highly unpopular in his capital city where he had spent the last years of his life inside the protective walls of the Castello di Porta Giovia* – and the castle, the prime symbol of his hated regime, had been destroyed by the mob after his death. Sforza wisely chose not to restore it as his residence, but he did rebuild the fortress as part of the city's defences, spending the enormous sum of 300,000 ducats on the project.[82]

The new dynasty's official residence in Milan was the Corte Arengo, the old ducal palace beside the cathedral, though the family spent most of their time in Pavia, where the children received a humanist education like other members of the aristocratic elite to which they now belonged. Francesco was to prove more fortunate than Alfonso I in his marriage. Imperial secretary Piccolomini was a fan of Bianca Maria: 'A woman of high spirit and extraordinary wisdom,' he recorded in his memoirs.[83] She gave birth to nine children, all but one of whom survived into adulthood: Galeazzo (born 1444), Ippolita (1445), Filippo (1449), Sforza (1451), Ludovico (1452), Ascanio (1455), Elisabetta (1456) and Ottaviano (1458). There was no shortage of legitimate heirs for the new dynasty – and there were at least four of Francesco's bastards being brought up at court with their half-siblings.

It is difficult to overstate the importance of Cosimo de' Medici's backing for the survival of the new regime. The limitless coffers of the Medici bank ensured its financial security for the new regime. Cosimo provided funds for Francesco by opening a new branch of the bank in Milan in 1452; it was more a political investment than a commercial

---

* Large parts of the present castle, known as the Castello Sforzesco, were extensively rebuilt in the nineteenth century.

venture, though the careful banker was often critical of his client's extravagance. Above all, Cosimo offered Sforza valuable political advice – twelve years younger than his mentor, the new duke often called him 'father' in their correspondence – and played a key role in assisting him in his transformation from soldier on the battlefield to statesman in the council chamber.[84]

The new government set up by Duke Francesco was substantially different from that of the old Visconti regime. Typical of the soldier, his approach was businesslike and efficient. Taking firm control of the reins of power, he appointed professional councillors, bureaucrats and lawyers. Above all, he established his new ducal chancery as the 'nerve centre' of his regime. Its key functions were to see that the duke's orders were carried out properly and that the duke himself kept fully informed of affairs.[85] Head of the chancery was Cicco Simonetta, whose family had been in service with Sforza since the early days in Naples. The duke set great store by loyalty, preferring his old comrades-in-arms for positions of trust in his regime: the men serving as diplomats at foreign courts, the castellans of his border fortresses and even the paymaster handling the temptingly large sums of money involved in his building projects, were all ex-soldiers.[86]

Francesco's court in Milan was never a glittering affair like that of Alfonso I in Naples. Unlike the king, Francesco was not a cultured man – his education had been in the arts of modern warfare rather than the battles of classical history. However, he did employ humanists, many of whom had been part of Duke Filippo Maria's court. One of these was Francesco Filelfo, who, rather harshly, judged the duke to be 'an ignoramus about literature of any sophistication and the arts'.[87] It was Filelfo who was given the task of writing a biography of the duke, undoubtedly inspired by those that were being written in Naples in praise of the duke's rival, Alfonso I.[88]

Filelfo charted Francesco's rise to power in an epic poem, the *Sforziade*, which was based on Virgil's *Aeneid* (itself based on Homer's *Iliad*). More a showcase for Filelfo's literary talents than propaganda for the new Sforza dynasty, it wrapped the facts lavishly in ancient Greek style, complete with a chorus of grieving women and a portrait of Duchess Bianca Maria as the ancient female warrior Camilla.[89] It was certainly not what the duke wanted and he ordered Cicco Simonetta to draw up a blueprint for a more flattering history. The project was

One of the towers of the Castello Sforzesco, Milan, built in the 1450s on the remains of a fortification erected by the Visconti family. This earlier castle was largely destroyed in the siege of 1450 and rebuilt not as a palace but as part of the city's defences.

eventually completed by Cicco's younger brother Giovanni, a chancery secretary, whose account of Sforza's rise to power (*Francisci Sfortiae commentarii*) suggests that Giovanni was more conscious of the political importance of the book.[90] Based on Caesar's *Commentaries*, a typically flattering classical precedent to justify a soldier's actions, Simonetta's text was not so much a panegyric to Sforza as a sanitized version of events that would create a suitably positive account of his rise to power. The two authors gave very different accounts of the wholesale rape of the women of Piacenza that had taken place in 1447 when Francesco sacked the city. While Simonetta claimed that Sforza had imprisoned the women in order to protect them from 'injury and abuse', in Filelfo's narrative Sforza did not issue this order until after the abuse had taken place – and he has the injured women sing a long lament, in the style of Euripides, from their jail.[91]

'Do you prefer perhaps to be feared rather than loved?', Filelfo wrote in an epistle to Sforza: 'You will never be esteemed unless you prove yourself just and generous.'[92] The early years of Francesco's reign were dogged with problems. There was a serious outbreak of bubonic plague in Milan during the summer of 1451 that killed as many as 60,000 people.[93] And the Venetians continued to harry the eastern borders of the duchy, causing problems for Cicco Simonetta, who had to ensure that the duke was kept fully informed of political developments elsewhere on the peninsula while absent from Milan with his army. There was also the problem of the lack of recognition from foreign rulers. Although the propaganda campaign spearheaded from the ducal chancery did much to legitimize Sforza's position among Italian princes, Emperor Frederick III refused to recognize his claim. Milan was an imperial fief, a fact that the emperor rather callously underlined when he came to Italy in 1452 for his coronation in St Peter's and also for his marriage to the sixteen-year-old princess Eleonora of Portugal. Once again Alfonso I was able to upstage the parvenu duke: the bride was his niece and it was his royal galleys that transported the bridal party across the Mediterranean to Livorno.[94]

The emperor had refused to visit Milan on his journey south but on 19 January he stopped off in Ferrara, where Marquis Borso d'Este hosted pageants, banquets and tournaments to entertain his honoured guest. Four days later there were unexpected visitors: Galeazzo Maria, Duke Francesco's eldest son, and his uncle Alessandro. Having been effectively ambushed by the duke, the emperor had no option but to give Galeazzo Maria an audience the following day (24 January, the boy's eighth birthday) and listen to a speech that apparently amazed all who heard it: 'It was like listening to an experienced orator of thirty,' Alessandro informed his brother; 'everybody marvelled at the child and the Emperor himself expressed his satisfaction'.[95] However, Frederick III remained intransigent and politely declined the boy's invitation to visit Milan on his return journey – and he continued to refuse to recognize Sforza as duke. In Florence, where he also spent a few days, Francesco commissioned his ambassador to repeat the invitation – but this time Frederick III refused even to receive the diplomat.

After the formal ceremonial of the marriage and the coronation in St Peter's in Rome, Frederick III and his bride travelled south to Naples as guests of Alfonso I. The king gave the couple a magnificent reception, staging a display of naval power with thirty galleys, the crews in royal livery, in the harbour at Naples.[96] There were banquets every evening in the great hall of Castel Nuovo, accompanied by music, singing and dancing. There was a tournament on the street outside the castle, with fountains spouting red and white wine at each end – the king's expenses in April 1452 mounted to 100,000 ducats.[97] The king put on hunting expeditions with falconers and a superb hunt in the royal park, which began with a feast lasting three hours.[98] The park had been filled with wild goats, stags, deer, boars, hares and porcupines which the huntsmen, led by Alfonso's heir Ferrante, pursued with the help of the royal hunting dogs, while Eleonora and her ladies watched the hunt from the safety of a covered platform.

Being excluded from Frederick III's itinerary was a deliberate snub – and Francesco must have been even more peeved that May when he heard that the emperor had given Borso d'Este the title of Duke of Modena. Worse, his agents must have informed him that Alfonso I and Frederick III had held private discussions on the future of Milan, and that the king had offered his support to Frederick III if the emperor took the decision to remove Sforza from the duchy by force. However, Alfonso I was no longer the political force he had once been. In the summer of 1449 he had become infatuated with the nineteen-year-old Lucrezia d'Alagno, and she was now his publicly acknowledged mistress, treated as his queen and seated at his side to celebrate court festivities. He showered her with gifts and favours – posts for her brothers and cousins, prestigious marriages for her sisters, and so on.[99] 'Whoever wanted a favour from the king went to Madama Lucrezia and she made a lot of money', recorded one shocked chronicler, while Piccolomini, now bishop of Trieste, lamented the fall of 'a great king… who had conquered so many provinces of Italy and had defeated the most powerful generals in battle, and was finally conquered himself by love to become the slave of a woman'.[100]

Meanwhile the wars between Naples and Florence and between Milan and Venice were creating major financial headaches for both Alfonso I and Duke Francesco. War was expensive: Venice was spending 1 million ducats a year fighting in Lombardy, while Sforza's costs amounted to half the total revenues of his duchy.[101] It was unfortunate for the duke that Bianca Maria's expenses had to be settled before he could pay his soldiers, and that his armourers were refusing to supply anything more without payment of his outstanding bills.[102] There were political ramifications too. In May 1453 Constantinople fell to the Turks, but when Pope Nicholas V called for a crusade to recover this ancient Christian city he found it impossible to unite the Italian powers, so he invited Alfonso I, Francesco Sforza and the republics of Florence and Venice to send delegates to a peace conference in Rome. The negotiations went badly from the outset: each power demanded ridiculously large reparations as its price for peace while Sforza refused to send an envoy at all, on the grounds that Venice was offering 100,000 ducats as the price for his assassination.[103]

Although the Roman conference ended in failure, it was the prelude to the Peace of Lodi, a treaty signed in April 1454 between all five powers, who had been forced to the table under the threat of impending financial disaster. Above all, the treaty marked the end of the long struggle between Alfonso and Francesco. It was cemented the following year with a double betrothal: the king's grandson, Alfonso of Aragon, three months short of his sixth birthday, was to marry Ippolita, Francesco's nine-year-old daughter, while the king's granddaughter Eleonora of Aragon, aged five, was to be the bride of Sforza Maria, the duke's three-year-old son.

Nicholas V died in March 1455 and, much to everyone's surprise, his successor was the seventy-six-year-old Alonso Borja, Alfonso I's trusted councillor who had been made a cardinal by Eugene IV in 1443. Those who feared that this foreign pope would put Neapolitan or Spanish interests at the forefront of his agenda need not have worried: the new pope, Calixtus III, had but one overwhelming priority – a crusade for the reconquest of Constantinople. And Alfonso I's hopes for favours from his old advisor were soon dashed when Calixtus refused to grant him special powers over the church in the kingdom. He did give a red hat to Lucrezia d'Alagno's uncle, Rainaldo Piscicello, Archbishop of Naples, but he refused her request to grant the king a divorce from Maria of Aragon. However, he did receive Lucrezia at the Vatican, a gesture that shocked many – notably Piccolomini, who had just received his red hat from the new pope, 'who considered it inappropriate that a royal mistress should be so acclaimed by His Holiness', and he made his displeasure public by refusing to pay her the courtesy of a formal visit while she was in Rome.[104] And when Calixtus III refused to nominate Alfonso I's candidate for a bishopric in the kingdom, he warned the king: 'know your Majesty that the pope can depose kings.'[105] The king replied tartly, 'know your Holiness that a king, if he so desires, can find a way to depose the pope.' A year later in June 1458 Alfonso I was dead: according to Cardinal Piccolomini, Calixtus III 'held back neither his tears nor his laughter, weeping with sadness for the fragility of life and with joy for the removal of his enemy'.[106] Just over a month later the pope too died – and his successor was to be Cardinal Piccolomini, who chose the name Pius II.

Meanwhile, Duke Francesco had become increasingly confident: the Peace of Lodi had largely removed the threats posed by Alfonso I and Venice to his borders and, although Frederick III still refused to recognize his claim to the title of Duke of Milan, there was no sign that the Emperor intended to remove him by force. It was a mark of how much more secure he felt that he allowed his children to use his surname, Sforza, to sign their correspondence rather than the Visconti name of their mother.[107] With more funds at his disposal, he embarked on a campaign of urban renewal, improving the canal system to bring economic benefits to the city. He commissioned a huge hospital, the Ospedale Maggiore (begun 1456), and built several new churches in the city, all of which were assigned to new branches of the religious orders associated with the growing movement for church reform.

overleaf Milan, Santa Maria Incoronata, begun 1451. Built by Duchess Bianca Maria for the Augustinian Hermits, part of this church was dedicated to St Nicholas of Tolentino, the order's first saint who was canonised in 1446.

prinapiare pche furono tante lepietre diqueste rune chetutti isondamenti dun
partita cioe della croce della parte deglhuomini furono fatti fino alpian tereño

SIche essendo disegnato illuogho doue far sidoueua questo spedale alnome di
Cristo & della anuntiata fu ordinata una solenne procassione collo arcaue=
scouo & contutta lachereia Elducha Francesco sforza insieme colla illustrissi
ma biancha Maria Ilconte Galeazzo & madonna Ipolita & Filippo maria
& altri suoi figliuoli compiu altri Signori intraquali uisu ilsignore Marche
se diMantoua el Signore Guglielmo dimon ferrato furu ancora due inboscia
dori del Re alfonso diRagona Ilnome deluno fu ilconte di Santo angelo
laltro fu uno gentile huomo napoletano furu ancora el Signore Taddeo daInf
la & piu & piu huomini degni iquali colpopolo di Milano uennono colla detta
procassione alluogho diputati & disegnato doue chelaprima pietra sidoueua
collocare & gunti alluogho predetto io insieme con uno diquegli diputati fu po
ta lapietra laquale era istituita adouere mettere nelfondamento sopra laqua
le era scripto ilmillesimo & ancora ildi elmese ilquale millesimo correua 1457
adi 4 daprile & cosi certe altre arimone lequali erano queste cioe prima fu
tre uasi diuetro Vno pieno dacqua laltro di uino laltro dolio & Lo giordinai
uno uaso diterra nelquale era una cassetta dipiombo doue era piu cose intra
laltre uera certe memorie diteste scolpite di alcuni huomini degni difama &
apresentare queste cose doue lacима era stata pdouerla mettere & iui cantato
certo husicio elSignore insieme colpontefice & io insieme colloro collocamo que
sta pietra collaltre sopradette cose pdare inquesto luogho una dimostrazione alle
psone ghisu fatto come adire uno segno o uoi dire termine ghisu fatto come
adire una colonna, o uoi dire uno pilastro nelquale fu scripto uno pigramo
fatto p messer Tommaxo darieti & diceua inquesta forma cioe ꞏ
FRANCISCVS · SFORTIA · DVX · IIII · SED · Q · VIAMISSVM · PER · P · PRAECESSO
RVM · OBITVM · VRBIS · IMPERIVM · RECVPERAVIT · HOC · MVNVS · CRISTI
PAVPERIBVS · DEDIT · FVNDAVIT · Q VE · M · CCCC · LVII · DIE · D · XII · APRILIS
SI che tutte queste cose uolle che fussono dipinte nelportico & commemorate fare pri
mo dibuoni maestri imodo era degnia cosa auedere Era ancora sopra alla po
ta delmezzo uno pigramo fatto plodegnio poheta philelfo come dinanzi e scrip
to & diceua cosi uolle questo nostro Signore chesidipigniessi inquesto della nostra
nuoua citta & cosi innanzi alla porta fu fatto uno diquesti termini maquesto
fu fatto dbellissimo marmo & fu scolpito intorno didegnie cose intralaltre ghisu
scolpito la immagine delsignore Come egli misse & colloco laprima pietra &an
cora lania & alcune altre degne memorie Et disopra nella sommita uno be
llo fiorimento colla immagine della annuntiata Disopra uera scolpito ancora
iquanti tempi dellanno & tutto ledisitio come sifaceua & piu gentilezze lequa
li dilonedra credo glipiacera come piace adni uede quello dimilano Siche for
nito questo spedale ilquale allui somamente piacque Et intrallalre cose de
ome quando alcuno forestiere lauesse uicitato facena uedere questo p uno de
degni hedisitii chonella terra sua fusse ꞏ

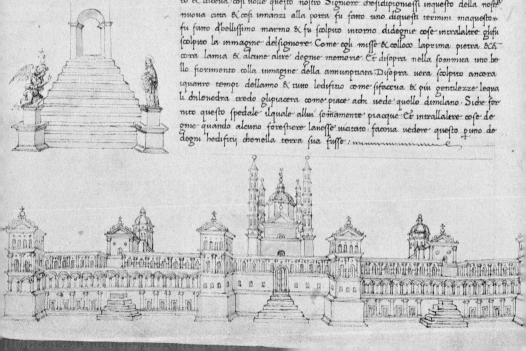

One of them, Santa Maria Incoronata, was actually a joint project between Francesco and Bianca Maria. The church, which belonged to the Observant Augustinians, had a particularly unusual form, with a double facade, two naves and two altars, with the duke's side dedicated to the Virgin and the duchess's to St Nicholas of Tolentino, who had only been canonized in 1446. Significantly, all the churches as well as the hospital were conspicuously Gothic, the style of Sforza's Visconti predecessors and prominently visible in their major projects, notably the Duomo.

Interestingly, however, there is evidence that efforts were underway to persuade Duke Francesco to adopt the classical style that was becoming high fashion at the other courts of northern Italy (see Chapters 2 and 3). Antonio Filarete, the mason in charge of building the Ospedale Maggiore, wrote a treatise on architecture which he dedicated to the duke. This was not a technical manual, but a highly imaginative account, based on Plato's dialogues, of how the patron and his architect built two cities. Filarete used some intriguing metaphors to describe the process of patronage. A patron, he considered, was like a man in love, not caring how much he spent; but both patron and the architect were essential to the process of design, the patron as its father, the architect as its mother and it was she who gave birth to the building, their child.[108] Many details link the treatise to the Sforza court in Milan. The names of the architect and the court scholar who assists him were anagrams of Filarete and Filelfo, while one of the cities is actually named Sforzinda with its gates named after Duchess Bianca Maria and their children. Above all, it was the story of how an architect taught his patron about the advantages of the classical language of architecture, and in particular how this could be used to denote the distinctions in rank that were so important at the Milanese court.[109]

Rank mattered to Francesco – he had fought for it all his life – and now as ruler of one of Italy's largest states he finally earned the respect he craved from his fellow princes. His status on the Italian political stage rose dramatically in the aftermath of the Peace of Lodi. His statesmanship was praised fulsomely in 1462 by Cosimo de' Medici, who was not alone in holding him in high regard: 'Very rarely, indeed almost never, have you taken a decision that has not been beneficial for yourself and your friends but also for all Italy.'[110] His close ties with Cosimo de' Medici created an alliance between Milan and

Filarete, design for the prince's palace, c.1460 (Florence, Biblioteca Nazionale Centrale). Filarete's imaginary city of Sforzinda also included residences for the poor, artisans, merchants and bishops, each graded by size and ornamentation according to rank.

Florence that provided the core strength enabling the survival of the delicate balance of power established at Lodi. One of Francesco's innovations was to install resident diplomats to report on events at the major Italian capitals, above all at Rome, the capital of the Christian world. Reliable news was a valuable commodity, and not easy to find in the rumour-fuelled courts of fifteenth-century Italy, so the often lengthy reports from Renaissance ambassadors charting the minutuae of day-to-day routines, great events and, above all, the gossip were of enormous help in determining foreign policy – and still make fascinating reading today.

Previously ambassadors had been appointed for specific purposes only and the introduction of permanent embassies was a costly process. It was to prove worth the outlay – by the end of the century the policy of having agents resident at foreign courts would become standard throughout Europe. Cosimo himself had initially considered them an expensive luxury but he too had to change his mind.[111] The Medici themselves had reason to be grateful to Duke Francesco's ambassador Nicodemo Tranchedini when Cosimo died in 1464; first, for easing the succession of his son Piero to his father's position at the head of the republic – not a very republican gesture, it must be said – and again two years later when the ambassador played an active role in quelling a violent uprising against the family. Duke Francesco's statesmanship was also evident after the death of his old enemy King Alfonso in 1458 when he put old quarrels aside and did much to assist Alfonso's illegitimate son Ferrante in putting down a rebellion so that the new king could inherit his throne (see Chapter 4).

Francesco outlived his rival by just eight years, dying on 8 March 1466 after an attack of dropsy. Despite unpromising beginnings, and the enmity between them which had on occasion threatened to derail both campaigns, they had established their dynasties as ruling houses in Italy's princely states – though, in the absence of a legitimate son, Alfonso I had been obliged to leave his Spanish possessions to his brother. However, the rivalry between their successors, which certainly Duke Francesco had worked hard to circumvent, would live on to dictate Italian politics for the rest of the fifteenth century.

Francesco Sforza, Duke of Milan, *condottiere* and founder of the Sforza dynasty, depicted *c*.1460 by Bonifacio Bembo (Milan, Pinacoteca di Brera).

LEONELLO D'ESTE (1407–50)
Marquis of Ferrara

SIGISMONDO MALATESTA (1417–68)
Lord of Rimini

Nicolò III, Marquis of Ferrara, *Father of Leonello*

Ginevra d'Este, *Wife of Sigismondo and Leonello's sister*

Isotta degli Atti, *Sigismondo's mistress*

Leon Battista Alberti, *Papal abbreviator*

Eugene IV, *Pope*

KNIGHTS AND HUMANISTS

Leonello d'Este

&

Sigismondo Malatesta

Di quà e là del Po,
Tutti figli di Nicolò

(On this side and the other side of the Po,
all are sons of Nicolò)[1]

This popular ditty boasting the virility of the first fifteenth-century marquis of Ferrara was not entirely without foundation. Nicolò III sired over thirty children: he was married three times and had scores of mistresses – aristocrats and commoners alike, including the wife of his farrier and even his maidservants. Illegitimate himself, he had at least six bastard sons before his first legitimate child, a daughter, and several more before the birth of a legitimate male heir.[2] Moreover, he made little effort to hide them and, in keeping with the chivalric culture of the period, named many after the knights and ladies of Arthurian romance, such as Leonello (Sir Lionel), Borso (Sir Bors), Ginevra (Guinevere) and Isotta (Isolde/Iseult).

Illegitimacy was common among the princes of fifteenth-century Italy: a French visitor remarked, with some surprise, that 'they make no great distinction at the Italian courts between a bastard child and a legitimate one'.[3] Illegitimate children were frequently brought up at court with their legitimate half-siblings and had useful roles to play in the dynastic game: the sons could fight as soldiers or gain valuable influence in Rome via careers in the church, while daughters were handy as brides to cement alliances with other princely families. Nor were their mothers forgotten but regularly rewarded with land or gifts and, if single, given a dowry and married off to a respectable man. And, while illegitimacy was technically a barrier to inheritance, it could easily be rectified by papal favour. However, a gang of illegitimate sons on the scale of that of Nicolò was a potential source of instability, as were resentful mothers.

This chapter is a story of bastards and mistresses told through the fortunes of two illegitimate princes: Leonello d'Este, Marquis of Ferrara, who was one of Nicolò's sons, and Sigismondo Malatesta, Lord of Rimini, whose cousin Parisina was Nicolò's second wife and who was himself to be married to Nicolò's daughter Ginevra. As younger sons, they had both been apprenticed at a young age to leading *condottieri* of the day and had inherited their titles after the death of an elder sibling, coming to power during a period of major political instability. As personalities, however, they could hardly have been more unalike. Leonello was an intellectual, a gentle man who Eugene IV thought would have made a good priest; Sigismondo, by contrast, was a fearless, aggressive soldier who had few scruples about putting personal gain before loyalty. But these two princes were also pioneers of the Renaissance, reviving the culture of ancient Rome to create two of the most sophisticated courts of the period – and their stories are a chilling reminder that, however beautiful the art, Renaissance society was essentially violent.

The Este and the Malatesta families belonged to the close-knit elite of *condottieri* dynasties who ruled the fiefs in the Papal States in north-eastern Italy – the courts of Ferrara and Rimini were just 20 miles apart, a gentle day's ride. The Este had been landowners in the fertile Po plain since the tenth century, becoming lords of Ferrara in 1264 and of the imperial fief of Modena in 1288. They were rich, their authority extending across some of the best agricultural land in Europe, and they were less reliant on an income from soldiering than their neighbours, the Malatesta. The Malatesta had been rulers of Rimini since 1280 and over the following century had extended their influence down the Adriatic coast with the addition of the cities of Pesaro, Fano and Cesena as well as many smaller communes such as Senigallia, Fossombrone, Mondavio and Mondolfo. Famous for their forbidding castles and military skills, but above all for their violent rivalries, the Malatesta inheritance was divided between different branches of the family by 1400 while that of the Este remained intact, and was enlarged by Nicolò III in 1409 with the city of Reggio Emilia.

Despite the excesses of his private life, Nicolò III was an astute politician, gifted with foresight and patience, and his reign of forty-eight years would see Ferrara established as an influential power on the peninsula. His first three sons were all born to his favourite mistress, the Sienese aristocrat Stella dell'Assassino – when she died in 1419 she

was buried in the Este family burial chapel in San Francesco, even though Nicolò had married his second wife Parisina Malatesta, a cousin of Sigismondo, the previous year. The marquis championed Stella's sons from the start. Having had the eldest, Ugo, legitimized by the pope so that he could be named as heir, and set one younger brother, Meliaduse, on a career in the church, Nicolò dispatched their third son, Leonello, to learn the soldier's craft with the famous *condottiere* Braccio da Montone. But Leonello's military career came to an abrupt end in May 1425 when Nicolò discovered Ugo in bed with his wife Parisina and he had them both beheaded: 'The head of Ugo, son of the illustrious marquis Nicolò, was cut off and that of madonna Parisina who was the stepmother of the said Ugo,' a local briefly recorded in his chronicle – but the scandal was headline news across Italy.[4] This brutal end to a forbidden romance was an indication of Nicolò's fury but also of the double standards of the period: although adultery was against the law in Renaissance Ferrara, needless to say none of the marquis's own married mistresses was punished for this crime. And, on a rather tragic note, the copious ledgers in the Este archives reveal that two years earlier Parisina herself had bought a copy of the romance of the star-crossed lovers Tristan and Isolde, whose adulterous affair also ended in death.[5]

For reasons that are not entirely clear, Nicolò decided to name Leonello rather than Meliaduse as his heir: in his will he made special mention of Leonello's 'piety, justice and wisdom', suggesting that he had more trust in his third son's political skills.[6] The 1420s and 1430s were difficult years in Italy, not only because of the war for succession in Naples but also due to the struggle between Milan and the Venetian republic for control of the Lombard plain. Nicolò III's own state shared borders with both Milan and Venice and he was very aware that involvement on either side would in all likelihood see Ferrara taken over by one rival or the other. So he went out of his way to cultivate a reputation for neutrality and maintained good relations with both powers. He also understood the importance of instructing his heir in the devious arts of diplomacy and involved Leonello directly in the business of government.

Leonello was widely liked: 'Gracious in speech and easily approachable, with an attractive face,' was typical of contemporary descriptions of the prince.[7] In 1429, at the age of twenty-two, he was betrothed to

Pisanello, *Leonello d'Este, c.*1441 (Bergamo, Accademia Carrara).
A princely image of a ruler who preferred scholarly pursuits
to a career as a soldier.

Margherita, the young daughter of Gianfrancesco Gonzaga, Marquis of Mantua. The marriage finally took place in 1435 when Margherita had her seventeenth birthday and the marquis staged lavish entertainments and decorations, funded by a special tax on his subjects, to welcome her to Ferrara. But the bride's father had insisted on several conditions before agreeing to the match: not only must his future son-in-law be legitimized but also Nicolò III must make a public declaration naming Leonello as his heir. Nicolò had no hesitation in complying with Gianfrancesco's requests; nor did he change his mind about the succession when his third wife, Rizzarda, the daughter of the Marquis of Saluzzo, gave birth to a legitimate heir, Ercole, in 1431, followed by Sigismondo, the spare, a year later.

Interestingly, the Marquis of Mantua had another, less direct influence on Leonello's future. Inspired by Gianfrancesco Gonzaga's boldly innovative decision to open a humanist school in Mantua for the education of his own children (see Chapter 3), Nicolò III invited the humanist Guarino da Verona to Ferrara in 1429 to serve as his son's tutor, with a handsome salary of 350 ducats a year.[8] Old enough to appreciate the curriculum of classical texts, Leonello revelled in his late schooling, and Guarino must have enjoyed teaching this enthusiastic pupil. One of their key texts was Julius Caesar's *Commentaries on the Gallic Wars*, which Guarino used as a manual to teach Leonello about the ideal statesman-warrior – when Leonello asked his tutor's opinion of swimming, Guarino replied that it was a healthy occupation, and that Caesar himself had enjoyed it.[9]

Meanwhile, Sigismondo was on the road towards power. His father died in 1427, when he was just ten years old, leaving his elder half-brother Galeazzo Roberto – also illegitimate but with a different mother – as the new lord of Fano. The links between the Malatesta and the Este were further strengthened that year by the marriage of the sixteen-year-old lord of Fano to Margherita, one of Nicolò III's illegitimate daughters. Sigismondo and his younger brother Domenico moved to the court of their uncle Carlo Malatesta, Lord of Rimini, who was childless and adopted all three brothers as his heirs – he persuaded Martin V to legitimize Sigismondo the following year. In 1429 Carlo died, leaving Galeazzo Roberto as Lord of Rimini, Cesena and Fano, and Sigismondo as his heir until he had a son.

Sigismondo now embarked on his military career, apparently

leading his own troops into battle in 1430, at the age of just thirteen; the following year he helped Galeazzo Roberto repulse an attack on Rimini. In November 1431, in a bid to improve relations between the Malatesta and Venice, Sigismondo was betrothed to the daughter of the republic's captain-general, the famous *condottiere* Francesco Bussone, Count of Carmagnola – but he broke off the engagement when Carmagnola was executed for treason six months later, though he refused to return the dowry. By now it must have been evident to all that Galeazzo Roberto was dying and that Sigismondo would soon inherit Rimini. Known for his exceptional piety, Galeazzo Roberto reputedly never consummated his marriage, preferring, with the approval of his wife, to devote himself to a life of asceticism. Emaciated by perpetual fasting, his body covered with weeping sores, he died on 10 October 1432 at the age of just twenty-one. Considering himself unworthy of burial inside the church of San Francesco, the traditional site of Malatesta tombs, he asked to be interred in a grave in the piazza outside, which soon became the focus of a local miracle-working cult.

So, Sigismondo became lord of Rimini and Fano at the age of just fifteen (Cesena went to his brother Domenico). Nicolò III decided to maintain the alliance between their families and in May 1433 betrothed his daughter Ginevra, Leonello's legitimate half-sister, to the young firebrand. Sigismondo staged a magnificent reception for the entry of his bride into Rimini the following February, ordering all shops and businesses to close for three days so that his subjects could watch the entertainments, which included a mock battle on a 'castle' erected in the main square. Sigismondo's military career took off over the next few years: he was appointed captain-general of Eugene IV's army in 1435, signed a *condotta* with Venice in 1437 and by 1439 had begun to enlarge the Malatesta state by seizing eight castles belonging to his neighbours, the Montefeltro family (see Chapter 4). He had begun to build a fearsome repuion on and off the battlefield – his favourite emblem was an elephant, the symbol of military victory.

Nicolò III, too, was cultivating good relations with the Venetian republic and the papacy. His success with Martin V and Eugene IV – and the value that an independent Ferrara represented to the papacy – was measured financially by the dramatic drop in the size of the annual census charged by Rome on this papal fief, which fell from 10,000 florins in 1400 to 4,000 florins thirty years later.[10] Moreover, when Eugene IV decided to host a meeting to negotiate a union between the western and eastern Orthodox churches, he chose Ferrara as the site for this prestigious ecumenical council. The council, which opened on 9 April 1438, was attended by three important figures: the pope, who arrived in Ferrara in January 1438; the Greek patriarch, Joseph II; and Emperor John VIII Paleologus, who travelled by sea from Constantinople to Venice, where he was met by Nicolò III and his sons Leonello and Borso. Travelling with these potentates were huge entourages, which included Italian humanists, Greek scholars and theologians from both churches, whose heated debates over the nature of the Holy Spirit were interspersed with hunting parties and banquets. Although an outbreak of the plague in July forced Eugene IV to move the council from Ferrara to Florence,* Leonello in particular must have enjoyed this unparalleled opportunity to discuss intellectual ideas with the leading scholars of his day.

Ferrara, unlike its neighbours such as Padua, Mantua and Rimini, could not boast a Roman past. Situated on the north bank of a navigable branch of the Po, it had grown prosperous during the Middle Ages and possessed a fine Romanesque cathedral, begun in 1135. By 1400 the city's skyline was dominated by symbols of Este power: the Palazzo di Corte (begun 1243), the family residence that faced the cathedral across the central market place; the Castello Vecchio, a massive unadorned fortress that had been begun in 1385 in the aftermath of an uprising against Nicolò III's uncle, Nicolò II, as a deterrent to further rebellion; and Castello Tedaldo (begun 1395) and Castel Novo (begun 1425), two more large fortresses built by Nicolò III at either end of the wharves to protect against an attack by water. There were also country palaces and hunting lodges, notably Belfiore and Belreguardo, both of which had been built by Nicolò III.

Leonello became Marquis of Ferrara after the death of his father on 26 December 1441. The succession, so carefully planned by Nicolò, proved straightforward despite the attempts of Rizzarda of Saluzzo to claim the title for her ten-year-old son Ercole. With Leonello firmly in control,

---

* It is therefore often referred to by historians as the Council of Ferrara-Florence.

Piero della Francesca, *Sigismondo Malatesta*, c.1450 (Paris, Louvre). Most images of Sigismondo emphasise his military achievements but this, imitating the profile images on ancient Roman coins, records his interest in the culture of antiquity.

and his younger brother Borso acting as chief advisor, the widow was obliged to leave Ferrara the following year. Private by nature, Leonello continued his father's policy of maintaining a balance of power between Milan and Venice and throughout his reign he sought to avoid involvement on the political stage – the one exception to this rule occurred in the summer of 1442 when he astutely decided to recognize Alfonso V of Aragon as the rightful claimant to the throne of Naples. Leonello's first wife Margherita Gonzaga having died in 1439, the alliance between the king and the marquis was cemented by the latter's betrothal to Maria of Aragon, the king's illegitimate daughter, which was signed on 1 April 1443. In Naples it was considered an excellent match, 'a grand and fine marriage, as he is lord of a very rich city', as one of Alfonso's Catalan agents rated Leonello in a report to Spain.[11] The links between Naples and Ferrara were further cemented by Borso, who spent several months in Naples in 1445–6, and by Leonello's young half-brothers, Ercole and Sigismondo, who were sent to the royal court to be educated by Alfonso's humanists and to master the skills of a chivalric knight as well as the more brutal ways of the professional solder. A clever move on Leonello's part, it was designed to minimize the risks of either of Nicolò's legitimate sons becoming the focus of opposition at home.

The marriage between the thirty-seven-year-old Leonello and the teenage Maria took place in 1444 and no expense was spared in entertaining the guests, who included the royal courtiers of the bridal party from Naples as well as ambassadors from Italy's other princely states. The revels went on for two weeks – banquets, jousts, tournaments and a hunting spectacular at Leonello's country palace of Belfiore, where the bride and groom watched hunters killing a large quantity of wild animals.[12] According to one chronicler the wedding party consumed 15,000 sweetmeats, 80,000 chickens, 4,000 beef cattle, 'pheasants and doves without number' and 20,000 casks of wine.[13]

Leonello proudly commemorated the event by commissioning a portrait medal with an inscription that boasted his status not only as Marquis of Ferrara but also as King Alfonso's son-in-law.[14] Portrait medals were high fashion in the 1440s. One of the first patrons of this genre, Leonello had commissioned a medal to commemorate his accession as ruler of Ferrara, Modena and Reggio in 1441 and his example did much to popularize the medal at other princely courts in Italy. The portrait medal derived from the coins of rulers of antiquity that were

Pisanello, *Leonello d'Este*, after 1441 (Bergamo, Accademia Carrara).
One of six medals known to have been cast by Pisanello for the marquis, all of which testify to his patron's enthusiasm for the culture of antiquity.

eagerly collected by Petrarch and other fourteenth-century humanists, and by the marquis himself. And the profile heads of Renaissance
princes on their own medals underlined the image of the prince as heir
to the imperial traditions of ancient Rome. In 1435, on the occasion
of his first marriage, Leonello was given a portrait of his hero Julius
Caesar by the court artist Pisanello, who was rewarded with the sum
of 2 gold ducats.[15] It is not clear whether this image was a painting
or a medal – Pisanello's earliest medal is generally thought to be that
of Emperor John VIII Paleologus, who was briefly in Ferrara in 1438
to attend the council.[16] Six of Pisanello's portrait medals of Leonello
have survived, their reverses ornamented with erudite classical imagery
that still baffles scholars today – though the charming reverse of the
marriage medal mentioned above, which shows Cupid teaching a lion
(Leonello) to sing, is perhaps more self-explanatory.[17]

In view of the cultural relationships that developed between
Ferrara and Naples, the imagery of the medal was particularly apposite.
While Alfonso of Aragon was quick to adopt his son-in-law's passion
for Pisanello's portrait medals (see Chapter 1), Leonello for his part was
inspired by his father-in-law's love of music. Imitating what Alfonso
had done in Naples, Leonello became a leading patron of music, both
religious and secular, and he too added his own private chapel to his
palace at Ferrara, complete with an altarpiece and gilded silver vessels,
as well as singers imported from France.[18]

Above all, Leonello's court was a magnet for scholars and, thanks
to them, Ferrara became one of the leading centres of Renaissance
humanism. One of his first missions was to revive the *Studium*, the
university of Ferrara, which had been founded in 1391 but had all but
closed due to financial problems. It was evidently a major priority for
the learned Leonello: on 17 January 1442, just three weeks after his
father died, the new marquis reopened the *Studium* with new funding
and new teachers. It provided employment for the circle of humanists
and scholars surrounding Leonello, such as the Greek Theodor Gaza
and the Italian Basinio da Parma. Leonello's old tutor Guarino moved
out of the palace to become the new professor of rhetoric, though
he still acted as secretary and occasional diplomat for Leonello. The
numbers of students soared – in the 1430s there had been on average
just thirty-four students a year but a decade later this figure was 338.[19]

One of the humanists attracted to Ferrara was Angelo Decembrio, a doctor from Milan whose text, *De politia litteraria*, recounted a series of discussions between the marquis and his humanists on various topics, revealing much about the Ferrarese court and about Leonello himself. One of Decembrio's most telling comments concerned Leonello's appearance: 'In his style of dress he was not concerned with opulence and ostentation as are some other princes.'[20] Indeed, the overall impression given by Decembrio was not so much one of a prince but rather a modest, learned man who was genuinely interested in classical scholarship, who enjoyed lively debates with his small circle of fellow humanists on the merits of ancient authors and who used his wealth and position to further scholarship rather than to boost his own personal status and prestige.

Leonello was not a patron on the grand scale of his contemporaries; yet, in his modest way he deserves to be remembered as one of the first patrons of the Renaissance. Unlike other princes of the period, he did not spend visibly on his castles, the conventional images of dynastic power. It is a revealing analogy that this prince, so determined to avoid political conflict abroad, should also prefer a more pacific image at home. His humanists promoted him as a knowledgeable connoisseur rather than a prolific builder of fortresses, the image preferred by other early Renaissance princes, notably Sigismondo Malatesta. Many of his commissions were private in nature, such as the expensive intarsia decoration and frescoes for the studios in his various residences, his collections of ancient coins, engraved gems and jewels, and his elegant but modest portraits by Pisanello and the Venetian Jacopo Bellini.

The Este library, which had numbered just 279 volumes in 1436, benefited in particular from Leonello's patronage of the humanists who flocked to Ferrara.[21] The marquis himself was rather dismissive of his father's taste for Arthurian romances, 'books which on winter nights we sometimes read to our wives and children'.[22] He substantially enlarged the collection with quantities of classical texts, including many translated by his humanists, and employed a staff of scribes and miniaturists to create and embellish the manuscripts. His interest in the culture of the ancient world was evident in his collections of gems and other valuables as well as Roman coins: 'I often take great pleasure in looking at the heads of the Caesars on bronze coins,' he is recorded saying, 'and they impress me no less than descriptions of their appearance in Suetonius and others.'[23]

Similarily, Leonello's desire to transform Ferrara into a humanist court was reflected in new attitudes to the decoration of his palaces and castles. Although he was highly critical of the artistic value of tapestries, he did admire the skill with which they were made: 'Certainly there is much skill in this kind of work but the weavers and designers are far more concerned with the opulence of colour and the frivolous charm of the tapestry than they are with the science of painting,' he was reported to have said.[24] Despite his low opinion of this staple of aristocratic display, Leonello added to his father's large collection of Flemish hangings. The new tapestries were mostly decorated with scenes of hunting or heraldic emblems but he also sent designs by his own painters to the weavers in Brussels, and in 1444 he persuaded two Flemish weavers to set up their own workshop in Ferrara, a novelty at the Italian courts.[25]

There were also new themes in the frescoes that ornamented the rooms of Leonello's residences. Instead of the chivalric romances preferred by his father, such as the story of Tristan and Isolde or Charlemagne's paladins, for example, or exotic Este heraldic devices like the elephant or the unicorn, Leonello's choices reflected the new Renaissance interests.[26] He commissioned a fresco cycle of the Sibyls, the famous prophetesses of the ancient world, for a room at his country palace at Belriguardo, and another depicting the Muses, the goddesses of the liberal arts, for his studio at Belfiore. Neither cycle has survived, but we do have a letter from Guarino to Leonello regarding the Belfiore frescoes in which the humanist used his knowledge of the culture of antiquity to give advice on how each of the Muses should be depicted.[27] Specialist advisors would play a significant role in the development of Renaissance art. As Leonello, inspired by his own reading of classical literature, explained, a painter was a craftsman who had the skill to copy what he saw but lacked the creativity to invent.[28]

Another humanist who offered specialist advice to Leonello was Leon Battista Alberti, the illegitimate son of an exiled Florentine noble, who was obliged to earn his living as an abbreviator, a high-ranking official in the papal chancery. It was in this capacity that Alberti had been in Ferrara with the papal court for the council in 1437–8 and had become good friends with Leonello. He dedicated several comedies to the marquis, whom he described as 'a prince and a most learned man'.[29] Alberti himself was also a scholar with a keen interest in the culture of

Pisanello, drawing of a horse, c.1434–45 (Paris, Louvre).
Pisanello's exquisite studies of birds and animals
illustrate his skills as a draughtsman and colourist.

ancient Rome, and had been a pioneer in the evolution of the portrait medal, commissioning his own oval plaquette around 1430.[30] He was to be author of several dialogues and treatises – he wrote on the family, on language, and even on ships (*Navis*, 1447), following his failed attempt to raise an ancient Roman galley from Lake Nemi in the Alban hills south of Rome.*[31] His literary fame rests on three artistic treatises, on painting (*De pictura*, 1435), sculpture (*De sculptura*, undated) and architecture (*De re aedificatoria*, 1452, first printed 1485). And Alberti himself claimed that he had written the treatise on architecture thanks to the enthusiastic encouragement of Leonello.[32]

In 1443 a competition was announced in Ferrara for a monument to Leonello's father, Nicolò III. The statue itself was to revive a particular genre of ancient sculpture, the equestrian monument. The custom of honouring military prowess with an equestrian statue was popular in northern Italy in the Middle Ages but these were mostly of wood – this would be the first life-size free-standing bronze of this type since antiquity. Alberti served on the judging panel for the competition and, inspired by the experience, wrote a treatise on horses (*De equo animante*, 1442), which he dedicated to Leonello. Based on classical texts, Alberti's treatise was a manual on the care of horses, their diseases and their training as racehorses, hunters, chargers for battle and other skills. More significantly Alberti was also involved with the design of the base for the equestrian monument.† Designed in the form of an arch and attached to the Palazzo di Corte, its elegant Composite capitals and fluted columns revealed the architect's close study of the remains of antiquity. It was the first known work by this humanist who, as we shall see, was to have such a powerful impact on the development of Renaissance architecture.

Meanwhile, Sigismondo was busy on the battlefield, pursuing his dream of uniting the Malatesta territories under his leadership and, early in 1444, he embarked on an attack to oust his cousin Galeazzo Malatesta from Pesaro and Fossombrone. Approaching his sixtieth birthday and

---

* A feat finally achieved in the twentieth century by Mussolini.
† Though the arch is still in situ in Ferrara, the equestrian monument itself was destroyed by rioters in 1796.

Ferrara, Arco del Cavallo, 1443. Probably designed by Leon Battista Alberti, the classical features of this arch reflect his scholarly study of the monuments of ancient Rome.

too old for the fight himself, Galeazzo had employed a local *condottiere*, Federigo da Montefeltro, Count of Urbino, who successfully repulsed Sigismondo's attack. The situation was still deadlocked at the end of the fighting season and both mercenaries signed lucrative new contracts for the following year: Sigismondo agreed to become captain-general of Eugene IV's army while Montefeltro entered the service of Count Francesco Sforza, who was currently fighting the pope and Alfonso of Aragon (see Chapter 1). And the wily Galeazzo, who had begun to tire of Sigismondo's belligerence, managed to outwit his cousin by selling his two fiefs to his allies: Montefeltro paid 13,000 ducats for Fossombrone, while Count Francesco Sforza bought Pesaro for 20,000 ducats and installed his brother Alessandro Sforza as ruler there.[33]

Sigismondo was furious: with his cousin, for the insult; with Federigo, whose small hilltop state of Urbino he coveted; and with Francesco Sforza, for not showing the loyalty that he felt was due to him as the count's son-in-law – Sigismondo had married Sforza's daughter Polissena in 1442, two years after the death of his first wife Ginevra d'Este. It is worth remembering that Sigismondo had become lord of Rimini at the age of fifteen, with little experience of government, without the restraining influence of the older generation and, moreover, he was impulsive and aggressive by nature. However, the smear campaign he launched against the ruler of Urbino was ill-advised to say the least. Writing to Francesco Sforza, he accused Federigo of cowardice and, more damagingly, challenged his right to the title of Lord of Urbino.[34] The ruler of Urbino, Oddantonio da Montefeltro, had been assassinated that summer (see Chapter 4) and, in the absence of a legitimate male heir, Sigismondo had claimed the state for his brother Domenico, who was married to Oddantonio's sister Violante. But, before Sigismondo had a chance to intervene, Federigo da Montefeltro himself had seized power, claiming that he was Oddantonio's illegitimate half-brother. Sigismondo insisted that this was untrue, that the new count was not a son, legitimate or otherwise, of Oddantonio's father – and there is some evidence to support this claim – but the accusation sparked a quarrel that was to have major repercussions for both Sigismondo and his rival Montefeltro (see Chapter 4).

Unfortuately for Sigismondo, the ferocity of Montefeltro's response to these accusations was disproportionate in the extreme – and the mud stuck. Not only did he challenge Sigismondo's own paternity, about which there was no doubt, but he then went on to hurl vicious insults, calling him a blind leper, a wife-beater, a wife-poisoner and a rapist, who 'had reduced the monastery of Fano to a whorehouse' and where 'eleven nuns were pregnant by him'.[35] 'You have spread slander about me at the papal court and caused ill to be spoken of me,' retorted Sigismondo; 'I am determined to show with my person against yours that I am a better man than you.'[36] The quarrel, as we shall see, was to have a lasting impact on Sigismondo's reputation.

Initially, at least, Sigismondo held the advantage. He held the influential position of captain-general of Eugene IV's army, and was able to curb Francesco Sforza's growing power in the Marche, returning much of the count's territory around Ancona to papal control. Moreover, Eugene IV was not a fan of Federigo da Montefeltro. Sigismondo must have been gratified when the pope not only refused to recognize Montefeltro as the legitimate ruler in Urbino but also excommunicated him for the purchase of the papal fief of Fossombrone. He also excommunicated Francesco and Alessandro Sforza, along with Sigismondo's cousin Galeazzo, and all four men were warned that they would be removed from their fiefs by force if they continued to oppose the pope's wishes. The Venetians took Sigismondo's side, warning Sforza that any attempt to challenge the Lord of Rimini's authority in his own fiefs would be unsuccessful: 'They are lands strongly and most affectionately bound to their lord.'[37]

Unfortunately for Sigismondo, his patron Eugene IV died on 23 February 1447 and the new pope, Nicholas V, as so often happened, took a very different view of the political situation. One of his first actions was to lift the four sentences of excommunication and, in return for a payment of 12,000 ducats, to recognize the rights of both Alessandro as ruler of Pesaro and Federigo as lord of Urbino and Fossombrone.[38] And Sigismondo's own actions did not help his cause: having signed a *condotta* with Alfonso of Aragon in the autumn of 1447, he not only reneged on the deal but, worse, infuriated the king by refusing to return the advance of 32,400 ducats that had already been paid.[39] The following spring Sigismondo joined the opposition to fight for the Florentine republic, which was busy defending its allies in the south of Tuscany who were under attack from Alfonso I. That autumn he was sent to the aid of the port of Piombino, which was under siege from land and sea by a formidable Neapolitan force of 6,000 troops, including 1,000 crack Spanish crossbowmen, as well as nineteen ships and galleys.[40] The encounter between the two armies was particularly bloody. With the Spanish trapped between the walls of Piombino and Sigismondo's men, over 1,000 of Alfonso I's army were killed: it was widely judged by his contemporaries to be Sigismondo's greatest victory.[41]

Back home in Rimini Sigismondo had other priorities, not least his beautiful mistress. He had fallen passionately in love with Isotta degli Atti, the daughter of a local wool merchant who had become his mistress in 1446, when she was just fourteen. The following May she had given birth to a son, who died soon afterwards and was buried in the Malatesta family chapel in San Francesco.[42] Sigismondo had certainly had other mistresses but Isotta was formally recognized as a favourite with a place at court and public positions for her family: her father became a member of Sigismondo's privy council and her brother was knighted. But not everyone was delighted, especially not Sigismondo's wife Polissena, nor her father Francesco Sforza. And his hostility towards Sigismondo increased in 1449 after Polissena died suddenly in mysterious circumstances – of the plague, explained Sigismondo, but Sforza had other ideas.

Inevitably, given the personalities involved, a very public argument ensued with Sigismondo and Sforza hurling insults at one another. Sforza insisted that his daughter had hidden herself in a convent to avoid the humiliation of encountering Isotta at court, and that she had then been murdered by Sigismondo – Sigismondo, in another of his ill-considered responses, accused Polissena of infidelity, though the priest whom he had paid to confirm the story refused to comply and was thrown into prison.[43] The truth of the matter remains unclear, though it is likely that Polissena did indeed die of the plague. What is remarkable about the story is that seven years later Sigismondo married Isotta, a rare union between a Renaissance prince and his concubine. The change in status brought new responsibilities for Isotta: as his wife she was now in charge of the upbringing not only of her own five children with Sigismondo (four sons and a daughter) but also of those born to his other wives and mistresses. Although the sons born to his first two wives had both died as babies, he did have a legitimate daughter and plenty of bastards born before, and after, his marriage to Isotta, several of whom were legitimized by Nicholas V.

Like many *condottieri* princes, though not Leonello, Sigismondo's real interest was military matters: he was 'most knowledgeable about war' and admitted how much pleasure he got from the hours he devoted to the study of the subject.[44] According to a chronicler he 'delighted in building', so it comes as no surprise to find that Sigismondo's first project was a military one.[45] In 1437 he began remodelling the old Malatesta family castle into a more potent symbol of his princely authority – unlike Leonello, he needed to give visual expression to his authority over both his enemies outside the walls and his subjects within. More surprising, however, is the medal he commissioned to commemorate the new edifice: this was the first Renaissance medal to celebrate a building rather than a person (although the fortress was named Castel Sismondo after himself). The castle was largely destroyed in the sixteenth century but its depiction on the medal suggests that it was a powerfully defensive stronghold with a crenellated keep surrounded by angled curtain walls reinforced at the corners by massive towers. Designed to withstand attack by cannon fire, it was extolled by a contemporary as one of the marvels of modern Italy on account of both its beauty and its strength.[46]

Sigismondo was an avid patron of portrait medals, undoubtedly inspired by the example of Leonello. He also chose several of the same artists as his ex-brother-in-law, notably Pisanello and Pisanello's pupil, Matteo de' Pasti, who made many of Sigismondo's medals including that of Castel Sismondo.[47] Among Pasti's first medals for Sigismondo was one of Isotta, her profile surrounded with the inscription 'To Isotta of Rimini, the ornament of Italy for beauty and virtue' – and on the reverse an elephant, Sigismondo's favourite emblem, the symbol of military strength and victory.

Almost uniquely among the fifteenth-century patrons of the new fashion for medals, Sigismondo was not overly interested in the esoteric imagery devised by humanists from their studies of the literary remains of classical antiquity. Indeed, the proud soldier's own medals, perhaps not unsurprisingly, were distinctive for their use of martial imagery. One of Pisanello's reverses showed a fully armed knight, in chain mail and a helmet, its visor closed for action, surrounded by Malatesta devices; another commemorated Sigismondo's appointment as Eugene IV's captain-general in 1445 with a knight astride his charger leading his army into battle on the reverse.[48] One of the few medals of Sigismondo without military imagery depicted him and Isotta facing each other

in profile, a design Matteo de' Pasti based on ancient Roman coins of the Emperor and his consort.[49] Sigismondo commissioned some fifteen different designs for medals of himself – a very large number by contemporary standards – and over 175 of these have been discovered in the foundations of his castles and other buildings, presumably only a small fraction of the total he buried.[50]

Rimini had an illustrious and ancient history: known as *Ariminum*, a port in Roman times, the Renaissance city still boasted a Roman arch built by Emperor Augustus and a massive Roman bridge; it was also just a few miles from the place where Julius Caesar crossed the Rubicon to start his historic march on Rome. In the 1450s it was one of the most cultured courts of Italy. Sigismondo and Isotta surrounded themselves with humanists and artists who celebrated Malatesta prestige in prose, poetry and art. He himself wrote poems, mostly in praise of Isotta, and even Pius II (who, as we shall see, did not have a very high opinion of Sigismondo) thought him 'eloquent', with 'a thorough knowledge of history and no small understanding of philosophy'.[51] Among the many humanists attracted to the court was Roberto Valturio, a papal abbreviator who became Sigismondo's secretary and wrote a treatise on military matters (*De re militari*, c.1450) in which his patron was the only modern soldier to be named alongside the great commanders of the past. Sigismondo sent expensively bound manuscript copies of this piece of undisguised flattery, along with a medal or two, as gifts to princes across Europe.[52]

Sigismondo's reputation as a formidable fighter was also a favourite topic with the humanist Basinio da Parma, who moved to Rimini from Leonello's court in Ferrara. He exalted his new patron's career in an epic poem *Hesperis* (early 1450s) which, like Filelfo's *Sforziad* for Francesco Sforza, was inspired by Virgil's *Aeneid*. The poem praised Sigismondo as the defender of the Latin people against invading barbarians, a thinly veiled reference to Alfonso I of Naples (Alfonso V of Aragon) whose ambitions to expand his authority into Italy had recently been checked by Sigismondo at the siege of Piombino; among the miniatures illustrating the text was a view of his camp at Piombino. Significantly, Basinio described how Jupiter had entrusted Sigismondo with the mission of expelling the barbarians from Italy – Basinio describes the Aragonese as 'Celts' – and so to bring peace to the Latin people.[53] And, as we shall see, Sigismondo certainly gave visual expression to this idea

Matteo de' Pasti, *Isotta degli Atti*, c.1449–52 (Washington, National Gallery).
The reverse of this image of the beautiful Isotta was ornamented with an elephant, the emblem of her lover Sigismondo.

by abandoning the Gothic style of European courts in favour of the classical Latin culture of imperial Rome.

Arguably Sigismondo's most important contribution to the development of Renaissance art was the church of San Francesco. Despite its more popular name, the Tempio Malatestiano,* the building was unambiguously Christian and had long been the site of Malatesta family tombs. In 1447 plans were begun to remodel two chapels in the church, one, dedicated to St Sigismund, for his own tomb, and the other, dedicated to St Michael, for that of Isotta.[54] In September Nicholas V issued a bull giving Isotta patronage rights over her chapel and permission to spend 500 florins on its remodelling. It is probable that the money came from Sigismondo: Isotta was just fifteen years old and had only been his mistress for a year, though they had buried their baby son in the church four months earlier.

The chapels were lavishly decorated. The entrance arch to Sigismondo's chapel rested on elegant Composite piers set on pairs of elephants carved in hard black marble. Isotta's tomb also rested, appropriately, on elephants. Inside, Piero della Francesca's votive fresco (dated 1451), set in fictive classical architecture, showed Sigismondo kneeling – not, for once, in armour – before St Sigismund with a roundel depicting his Castel Sismondo. The inclusion of the castle in a votive painting was unusual and suggests the importance that he attached to it as the pre-eminent symbol of his power. Even more unusual was a pair of greyhounds which, as one scholar has shown, may well be inspired by not by Sigismondo's hunting dogs but by his humanists and their interest in Anubis, the ancient Egyptian god of death.[55]

Three years later, Sigismondo decided on a more radical rebuilding of the interior of San Francesco, cladding the walls with coloured marbles: red from Verona and white from Carrara, transported across Italy from Carrara at considerable expense. The abbot of Sant'Apollinare in nearby Ravenna was severely reprimanded for allowing Sigismondo to take 100 carts of marble, serpentine and porphry from ancient churches in the area.[56] This second stage of the rebuilding project involved several new chapels, including one for the tombs of Sigismondo's first two wives, Ginevra d'Este and Polissena Sforza, and the so-called Chapel of the Planets (actually dedicated to St Jerome), ornamented with a

---

* The name 'Tempio Malatestiano' dates from the nineteenth century.

Rimini, San Francesco, begun c.1450. Designed by Alberti, the pioneer of Renaissance architectural style, it was originally planned to crown this church with a magnificent dome inspired by the Pantheon in Rome.

series of reliefs of the planets and signs of the zodiac – and Cancer, Sigismondo's birth sign embellished with a view of Rimini and the Castel Sismondo.

In 1450 Sigismondo embarked on his most innovative project: a new facade for the church, designed by Leon Battista Alberti, the leading expert on the culture of antiquity and friend of Leonello. It is difficult to overstate the importance of this landmark in architectural history – it was the first Renaissance building to adopt the architectural language of imperial Rome. The design of the facade, its three arches flanked by fluted Composite columns supporting a classical entablature, was evidently based in part on the Arch of Augustus in Rimini, which had been erected in 27 BC to commemorate the emperor's repairs to the Via Flaminia. Sigismondo's role as patron is recorded in an inscription in the frieze, written in elegant classical capitals. Built under the supervision of Matteo de' Pasti, who cast another medal to commemorate the project, there was also an illumination of the facade under construction in Sigismondo's manuscript of Basinio da Parma's

Hesperis.[57] The medal shows that the building was to be crowned with a huge hemispherical dome inspired by the Pantheon in Rome, though this was never completed. Along the sides of the church were a series of niches where Sigismondo placed the tombs of his humanists and courtiers, including both Valturio and Basinio, accompanying their patron in death as they had while alive.

The wealth of classical detail attracted much criticism, not least from Pius II, who described San Francesco as 'so full of pagan works of art that it seemed more a temple of heathen devil-worshippers than a Christian sanctuary'.[58] In fact, Sigismondo had been careful to ensure the church retained its Christian context. Inscriptions inside recorded that he had dedicated the building to God in honour of a vow he had made after surviving a particularly bloody battle: it finished with the words, 'and left behind him a monument both notable and holy'.[59] Moreover there were winged cherubs' heads, a conspicuously Christian detail, at the centre of each of the Composite capitals on the facade, and this motif was repeated in the entablature above.[60] In his *De re militari* Valturio was fulsome in his praise for this 'incomparable monument built in God's honour' and 'nothing in this most famous town is more truly ancient, nothing is considered a more worthwhile sight'.[61] He also predicted a glorious posthumous future for Sigismondo's reputation: 'Your praise will be sung in the Tuscan tongue, in French and in Spanish... and you will be celebrated for centuries to come.'[62]

Unfortunately that glorious future never materialized. Sigismondo's fortunes changed dramatically after 1458 and the election of Pius II, who was a close ally of two of his powerful enemies, Alfonso I of Naples and Federigo da Montefeltro. The pope decided to confiscate Senigallia, Mondavio and Mondolfo from Sigismondo and use them to ennoble and enrich members of his own family – and to justify this barely legal action Pius embarked on the political annihilation of Sigismondo, launching a vitriolic attack on the soldier. He outlined the evil nature of Sigismondo's character in his memoirs: 'His lust was so unbridled that he violated his daughters and his sons-in-law,' for example; 'he oppressed the poor, robbed the rich and spared neither widows nor orphans'; 'he hated priests and despised religion' and 'he killed his two wives one after the other with the sword or poison', and so on. The litany of accusations was suspiciously reminiscent of those insults hurled by Sigismondo's rival Federigo da Montefeltro back in the 1440s – it is worth repeating that they had little basis in fact.[63] The pope also deliberately insulted Isotta by calling her Sigismondo's concubine, despite the fact that the two had married in 1456.[64] In 1460 Pius II held a public consistory at which a papal lawyer accused Sigismondo of a terrible list of crimes – robbery, arson, massacre, debauchery, adultery, incest, murder, sacrilege, betrayal, treason and even heresy – and urged the pope 'to cleanse Italy at last of this foul and abominable monster'.[65] On 25 December Sigismondo was excommunicated and his possessions were declared forfeit to the church.[66] And the pope now took the unprecedented decision to condemn Sigismondo to Hell:

> Let him be enrolled a citizen of Hell. Sigismondo's crimes, unprecedented in our age, call for new and unprecedented procedure. No mortal heretofore has descended into Hell with the ceremony of canonization. Sigismondo shall be the first deemed worthy of such honour. By edict of the pope he shall be enrolled in the company of Hell as comrade of the devils and the damned.

Sigismondo was formally condemned in 1462: the Mantuan agent reported that 'on Tuesday 27th of this month [April] the cardinals assembled in the presence of Our Lord, the indictment against Lord Sigismondo Malatesta was published and the sentence given against him for blasphemy, theft, adultery, incest and heresy'.[67] Three life-size effigies of the prince were burned the following morning: one on the steps of St Peter's; another at the Capitol, the ancient centre of imperial Rome; and the third in Campo dei Fiori, the marketplace where common criminals were executed. Each bore the legend: 'This is Sigismondo Malatesta, king of traitors, enemy of God and man, condemned to the fire by the decision of the College of Cardinals.'[68]

That autumn, 1462, Pius II launched a military campaign against Sigismondo – Mondavio fell in the autumn, and the following spring there was a fierce fight for Fano; the Venetians sent galleys to aid Sigismondo but the port finally fell in September, followed immediately by Senigallia. Venice, which judiciously chose to support Sigismondo in order to protect its southern borders from papal ambitions, together with the support of Florence and Milan, forced Pius II to sign a truce with Sigismondo. But the peace terms offered by the pope were harsh:

Sigismondo was allowed to retain the city of Rimini and the land within a 5-mile circumference while his brother Domenico was allowed to retain Cesena on the same terms, though both fiefs were to revert to the church when the brothers died. When Sigismondo had come to power in 1432, the Malatesta had ruled the Adriatic coast from Cervia and Cesena almost as far south as Ancona – now they had lost almost all their territory and, moreover, had also lost their status as dynastic rulers.

Sigismondo responded to Pius II's animosity by looking for alliances with the pope's enemies. When the war of succession for the kingdom of Naples started in 1458 after the death of Alfonso I, Sigismondo was quick to offer his support to the Prince of Taranto, one of the Neapolitan barons who supported the claim of René of Anjou over that of the Aragon dynasty. The prince sent Sigismondo 16,000 ducats but could do little more after the Angevin army was defeated at Troia in the summer of 1462.[69] Sigismondo even sent an embassy to Sultan Mehmed II, sworn enemy of Christendom, who had asked if he could have the loan of the services of Matteo de' Pasti. The artist was dispatched to Constantinople with maps and books on military subjects, including Roberto Valturio's *De re militari* as presents for the Sultan.[70] Unfortunately he was arrested in Crete by the Venetian authorities and sent to Venice, where the Council of Ten accused him of spying – he was let off with a caution, but Sigismondo was warned not to make any attempt to contact the Sultan again.

Sigismondo's humiliation at the hands of Pius II was eloquently visible in Rimini, where work had to stop on the Tempio Malatestiano because of lack of funds – it was never finished though, fortunately for us, it was not destroyed like Castel Sismondo. Deprived of most of his territory, his state revenues had plummeted; and worse, his options for employment as a *condottiere* were severely limited. In March 1464 he decided to sign a *condotta* with Venice to fight the Turks in Morea,* leaving Isotta in charge as regent in Rimini, though even this job soured when the Venetian official in charge of the military campaign turned out to be the very jealous husband of one of Sigismondo's former mistresses.[71] He returned to Rimini in March 1466, broken in spirit and in health, and died there on 9 October 1468.

Sigismondo does not deserve his scandalous reputation – Pius II's

---

* The modern day Peloponnese in Greece.

very public condemnation of him was widely denounced at the time, even by his enemies. However, although it is possible to see him as the victim of the intrigues of two unscrupulous rulers, Pius II and Federigo da Montefeltro (see Chapter 4), this evidently talented fighter was certainly no politician, lacking prudence, patience and the ability to control his explosive temper. It was typical of Sigismondo that he left Rimini to Isotta and Sallustio, the third of his living sons, and the second of those born to Isotta – their daughter would be beheaded by her husband for adultery. Within months his eldest son Roberto had challenged Sallustio's position and, with the help of their father's old enemy, Federigo da Montefeltro, seized control of the state. Isotta was sidelined, while Sallustio and his younger brother Valerio were both murdered, and Roberto celebrated his achievement by marrying Federigo's daughter, Isabetta. Roberto died of malaria in 1482, leaving Rimini to his illegitimate son Pandolfo, another unpleasant character who seems to have murdered both his mother and his brother. Pandolfo lost Rimini to Cesare Borgia in 1500, and the family died out.

By contrast, Leonello made careful plans for the future of the Este dynasty. When he died in 1450, of a 'terrible headache', he ignored the claims of his own illegitimate son Francesco and instead left Ferrara to his brother Borso.[72] Borso had been a loyal and effective right-hand man to Leonello and he would prove a beneficial ruler, enhancing the family status with the titles of Duke of Modena (1452) and Duke of Ferrara (1471). Borso had no children and left the state to his younger brother Ercole, who was the legitimate son of Nicolò III and Rizzarda da Saluzzo and whose line continued unbroken through the sixteenth century (see Chapters 6 and 10).

Although very different characters, Leonello and Sigismondo share the accolade of being the first two patrons of the Italian Renaissance. They illustrate the flexibility of the image of imperial Rome to provide models for the learned connoisseur and the soldier-prince alike, though its promise of posthumous fame could never be guaranteed. What is surprising is that the very significant achievements of these two princes have indeed been forgotten, rarely remembered or recognized outside the world of academia. While Sigismondo's reputation is inevitably tarnished by the lurid accusations made by Pius II, Leonello's has slipped into obscurity, overshadowed by the attainments of his successors.

LUDOVICO GONZAGA (1412–78)
Marquis of Mantua

BARBARA OF BRANDENBURG (1422–81)
his wife

FRANCESCO GONZAGA (1444–83)
Cardinal, their son

Their other children:
Federigo, Gianfrancesco, Susanna, Dorotea,
Cecilia, Rodolfo, Barbarina, Ludovico and Paola

Pius II, *Pope*

Leon Battista Alberti, *Papal abbreviator*

Andrea Mantegna, *Painter*

A FAMILY MAN

Ludovico Gonzaga

&

Barbara of Brandenburg

The huge, colourful cavalcade that escorted Pius II through the narrow streets of Mantua on 27 May 1459 was designed to impress the crowds who had gathered to watch the procession, enjoying the unexpected bonus of a holiday outside the annual calendar of church feasts. A papal court on the move was quite a spectacle, and one that few of those jostling on the street would expect to see again in their lifetime. The leader of Christendom, the successor to St Peter, who had been chosen by Christ himself to lead the faithful, the pope's supreme spiritual authority over secular princes made him one of the most powerful figures on the European political stage. And, although Pius II's personal tastes were frugal, and he frequently found it necessary to require his cardinals to rein in their extravagant habits, as pope he was expected to travel in style:

> First came the servants of the Curia and the households of the cardinals, followed by the less important officials of the Curia; then twelve white horses with gold saddles and bridles... then three banners carried by nobles in armour riding gorgeously caparisoned horses... They were followed by the ambassadors of kings and princes, the subdeacons, auditors, scribes and lawyers of the papal palace under a golden cross... then a golden tabernacle containing the Eucharist borne on a white horse... then the venerable order of cardinals, and finally the pope himself, raised high on his throne, wearing his papal robes with his mitre blazing with precious gems... Behind him came the gentlemen of his bedchamber and his personal attendants, then the bishops, notaries, abbots and a great throng of prelates.[1]

This description, written by Pius II himself, reveals just how important appearances were at the princely courts of Renaissance Europe, where ostentatious display was the essential indicator of rank. And it was not just the enormous size of the papal entourage that would have impressed the crowds that day. It was also the wealth conspicuously on view: the gold collars and valuable jewels, the expensive velvets, silks and satins trimmed with costly fur, the liveried servants and, of particular interest to the Mantuans who were good judges of horseflesh, the expensive thoroughbred horses and mules ridden by many of guests.

Pius II was in Mantua to host an international congress to plan a crusade against the Turks. For the next six months this small city, and not Rome, would be the focus of the Christian world, crowded with red-robed cardinals and mitred bishops, with ambassadors from all the courts of Europe and with the bureaucrats of the Curia drawing up the bulls, dispensations, letters of appointment and spiritual favours granted to the faithful. It was a political coup for Ludovico Gonzaga, Marquis of Mantua – and there was also the financial bonus of profits to be made on the huge quantities of food for the guests as well as fodder for the horses, all of which had to be imported into the city.

For the rulers of the minor states of northern Italy, survival in the ruthless world of Italian politics was a matter of luck and judgement. Too small to rely on their own military strength to overcome the aggression of the major powers, they needed to develop more cunning strategies – not least shrewd diplomacy and fruitful family alliances – to outwit their enemies. This chapter will show how Ludovico Gonzaga and his family used these tactics to safeguard their tiny state. Above all, it will show how the papal congress spurred him to transform his provincial capital into a splendid Renaissance court, achieving a level of fame for Mantua that was out of all proportion to its size.

Mantua was one of the smallest of Italy's princely states, sandwiched on the Lombard plain between the rival powers of Milan and Venice. The city itself had grown up in the river Mincio at the point where travellers on the road north to Germany through the Brenner pass had to cross the waterway which flowed from Lake Garda to the Po. Built on islands in the river, it was surrounded by mosquito-infested swamps, cold and muddy in winter and unpleasantly humid in summer – or as the Roman poet Virgil, who had been born in Mantua around 70 BC, described in more lyrical fashion, 'where the great Mincius wanders in slow windings and fringes his banks with slender reeds'.[2] And, conveniently, the marshes also provided excellent opportunities for hunting and wildfowling, favourite pursuits of the Renaissance aristocrat.

The Gonzaga had become captains (*capitani*) of Mantua in 1328 after a particularly bloody revolt and they celebrated the anniversary of this rout every year on 16 August with church services, processions and the excitement of a horse race (*palio*) run through the city streets – as breeders of some of the best racehorses in Italy, the Gonzaga mounts often won first prize. They held another *palio* on 29 June staged as part

overleaf Mantua, Palazzo Ducale, begun late thirteenth century. Built by the Gonzaga as the prime image of their authority, this palace with its elegant arcade beside the cathedral was in marked contrast to the aggressively defensive strongholds built by the rulers of Naples, Milan and Rimini.

of the celebrations honouring Mantua's patron saint St Peter, which also included the more entertaining spectacle of races for asses, soldiers and prostitutes.[3] The city was also famous for its relic of the Holy Blood, which was kept in the church of Sant'Andrea and attracted crowds of pilgrims every year on the Feast of the Ascension when it was displayed in public. And it was as custodians of this treasured relic that the Gonzaga gave visible expression to their role as protectors of Mantua on the silver coins minted by Ludovico's father Gianfrancesco, which showed an allegorical view of the city with the reliquary at its centre.[4]

Gianfrancesco, like Nicolò III in nearby Ferrara, had been particularly vulnerable in the 1420s to the growing hostility between Milan and Venice and he too understood the importance of remaining outside this conflict. However, Gianfrancesco's options for dealing with the problem differed from those of Nicolò III. While Ferrara was a papal fief, the Gonzaga owed their loyalty to the Holy Roman Emperor, a link that Gianfrancesco was able to exploit. Having accepted the position of captain-general of the Venetian armies in 1433, the *capitano* balanced this favour by strengthening his links with his feudal lord, a clever move as Milan was also an imperial fief. That same year Emperor Sigismund gave a very public affirmation of his alliance with Gianfrancesco, investing him with the more prestigious title of Marquis and agreeing to a betrothal between Gianfrancesco's heir, Ludovico, and his own niece, Barbara von Hohenzollern, the daughter of the Margrave of Brandenburg.

The new marquis celebrated his promotion into Europe's aristocratic elite by decorating the great hall of his palace with frescoes by Pisanello depicting the knights of King Arthur's Round Table but he was also an early patron of humanism, collecting manuscripts of Cicero and other classical authors. In 1423, in an unprecedented contribution to the new learning, he invited the humanist Vittorino da Feltre to set up a school in Mantua. Known as the Ca' Zoiosa, it was the first of its kind in Renaissance Europe and was intended for the education of his six children, daughters as well as sons, and for girls and boys from families of courtiers and the local nobility. Vittorino was a dedicated teacher. He got up early, by candlelight on winter mornings, breakfasted with the children and attended Mass with them every day. In the morning they studied philosophy, history, rhetoric, poetry and other subjects from classical texts, both Latin and Greek; they also learned music and drawing. The afternoons were dedicated to physical exercise outdoors, whatever the weather, with ball games, fencing and riding, and in the summer they escaped the sultry heat with trips up into the cool air of the foothills of the Alps.

Vittorino's pupils varied in their academic prowess. Ludovico, the future marquis, was apparently rather plump and gauche as a boy and clumsy in his movements, but he was bright enough and had a love of learning. Under Vittorino's tutelage, he grew up to become a decent, honest, loyal and unusually cultured man. His brother Carlo was not so conscientious and more interested in sport than in his studies, though their youngest sister, Cecilia, was exceptionally clever and at the age of seven amazed the humanist Ambrogio Traversari with her knowledge of classical Greek.[5] She was betrothed to Oddantonio da Montefeltro, heir to the Count of Urbino, but was so shocked by rumours of his scandalous behaviour that she refused to marry him and entered a convent instead: 'Cecilia is not a business transaction like horses and other things,' Gianfrancesco informed the count when they were haggling over the dowry.[6] The youngest brother, Alessandro, suffered from a congenital deformity and was constantly ill, but he was also highly intelligent and Vittorino's favourite pupil – he became Ludovico's close confidante and aide.[7] Rather tragically, most of Ludovico's siblings died young: Margherita, who married Leonello d'Este, Marquis of Ferrara, was only twenty-one; Cecilia was twenty-five, as was Gianlucido, who was very clever and intended for a career in the church, while the lively Carlo died at thirty-nine, as did the chronically ill Alessandro. Luckily for the future of the Gonzaga dynasty, Ludovico himself was sixty-six years old when he died in 1478.

The Gonzaga dynasty was also particularly fortunate in the choice of Barbara von Hohenzollern as Ludovico's wife. When the couple were betrothed in July 1433, she was three months short of her eleventh birthday; she arrived in Mantua that Christmas, speaking no Italian and, on the orders of her in-laws, allowed only a very few servants from home, 'so that she will forget her German customs'.[8] A brave little girl, she adapted well to life in Mantua, joined her husband's younger siblings in the schoolroom at the Ca' Zoiosa, and the marriage was consummated the following year. Her first child, a son, was not born until around 1438, and he sadly died in infancy, as did her next two babies, both girls. However, by the time Ludovico became marquis in 1444, Barbara had given birth to both an heir and a spare – Federigo, aged three, and Francesco, a six-month-old baby. Over the next two decades she bore another nine children, four boys and five girls, only one of whom failed to survive the perils of childhood – quite an achievement given the high mortality rate among babies and toddlers in Renaissance Europe. Ludovico also had several bastard sons and daughters who, like his legitimate children, all attended the Ca' Zoiosa, where they received a humanist education from Vittorino, and from Vittorino's pupils after their master died in 1446.

Above all, Barbara proved to be an exceptionally competent consort. From the huge quantities of letters written and received by her that have survived in the Mantua archives, it is evident that she was much loved and trusted by her husband and the court. Clever and diligent, she had a shrewd understanding of political, diplomatic, financial and familial issues, and capably took charge of the affairs of state during the frequent absences of her husband as he fulfilled the contracts of his military career.

Meanwhile, relations between Ludovico and his father were proving fraught. The solidly competent Ludovico was a disappointment to Gianfrancesco, who far preferred his second son Carlo, a spirited and adventurous soldier – and it was Carlo who was usually chosen to join the marquis fighting as captain-general of Venice. In 1436, apparently desperate for his father's approval and denied the chance of proving himself in any other way, Ludovico signed a *condotta* for 300 lances with Duke Filippo Maria Visconti – in other words, against Venice, but the contract did include a clause stating that he would not fight against his father.[9] It was an extraordinary act of family disloyalty, and all the more astonishing in view of the fact that loyalty was to become one of Ludovico's key traits. Moreover, the motives behind this move are not entirely clear: maybe he was just jealous of his younger brother? Whatever the reason, the marquis was furious and showed his anger in a very public manner by banishing Ludovico from Mantua and taking the unusual step of getting imperial approval to change the succession and name Carlo as his heir. Two years later, however, Ludovico was reinstated when the marquis himself also 'defected' to Milan – and it is quite possible that Ludovico's defection had actually been part of a clever ruse to avoid upsetting the Venetians.

Ludovico became Marquis of Mantua on 23 September 1444 and his title was formally endorsed by Emperor Frederick III a year later. Like his father, Ludovico had to prioritize the protection of his borders during the ongoing war between Milan and Venice, and this task became increasingly complicated after the death of Duke Filippo Maria in 1447 and Francesco Sforza's pursuit of power in Milan. To balance Sforza's changes of allegiance Ludovico himself was obliged to make several tactical changes in order to preserve his independence, fighting in turn for Florence, Venice and Naples. The policy might have been a tactical success but it brought financial problems when the Florentine republic, notoriously bad at paying its mercenary soldiers, obliged him to 'agree' to donate the unpaid part of his contract to finance the rebuilding of a pilgrimage church in Florence, Santissima Annunziata.[10] It was not until 1450, once it began to look certain that Sforza would be the victor, that the marquis offered him his support.

The two men were very different characters. While the arrogant Sforza relished the drama of tactical changes of allegiance to gain advantage over his enemy, Ludovico was by nature prudent and placed a high value on honesty: 'We are neither the son nor friend of Fortune and we do not solely pursue profit… we are always the same Ludovico, made to the same model,' he wrote.[11] Sforza himself had considerable respect for Ludovico's quiet talent to get the best out of his men, but he was the better fighter.[12] In September 1448 Ludovico and his Venetian troops were routed by Sforza and the Milanese army at Caravaggio. Ludovico was lucky not to have been captured and forced to pay a ransom to regain his freedom. Instead he managed to borrow a horse and escape with two comrades, but he was injured and in some distress – he sent an urgent letter to Barbara, asking for a mule and some cushions, because he was 'greatly troubled in both body and mind'.[13]

After Sforza seized Milan in 1450, he persuaded Ludovico to sign a more permanent *condotta*, rather than the conventional military contract, and its clauses revealed just how important the marquis was as an ally to the new duke. To start with the duke agreed to the betrothal of his heir Galeazzo Maria to the marquis's eldest daughter Susanna, though this was more a statement of intent, as the girl was only three years old. There were also changes to the way Ludovico's wages were to be paid: he was to earn 82,000 ducats a year during wars but this was to drop to 47,000 ducats in peacetime.[14] Developed in response to the greater stability ushered in by the Peace of Lodi (1454), this variable rate of pay was a new development designed to retain the loyalty of the notoriously venal *condottieri* – and the definition of 'war' was an attack by over 4,000 men resulting in a struggle that lasted over three months.[15] Moreover, there was no reference to the number of lances Ludovico was expected to provide: instead the contract required him to pledge himself to the duke 'in person, with cavalry and infantry and with his state'. In other words this was more an alliance between heads of state than the traditional arrangement between a prince and his mercenary captain – and Duke Francesco continued regularly to renew his contract with Ludovico over the next decade. The marquis conscientiously fulfilled his role as loyal ally: when the duke fell seriously ill, Ludovico spent a month in Milan, only returning home once Sforza was fully recovered.[16]

Ludovico had his own problems at home – not least his younger brother Carlo, who coveted his title. The adventurous schemer hatched several plots to unseat his brother and in 1453, with the assistance of Venetian troops, launched an offensive against Mantua. Leading his own army against Carlo, Ludovico finally defeated his brother at the Battle of Goito and Carlo's death three years later put an end to the matter. There were financial problems too. Since the signing of the Peace of Lodi in 1454, Ludovico's income from Milan had dropped from 'war' to 'peace' rates and, moreover, Duke Francesco's own financial problems made it difficult to extract any cash from the Milanese coffers, so his wages were invariably paid considerably in arrears. When Pius II announced his intention of holding a congress to arrange a crusade against the Turks, Ludovico was quick to seize the opportunity to promote Mantua – close enough to Rome for the elderly pope, close enough to the borders of the empire for the imperial delegates – as the ideal location for the congress. Ludovico's agents had lobbied hard in Rome and Barbara had coaxed her German relatives into agreeing on Mantua. Their success was a very welcome boost to their finances, and the cause of jealousy elsewhere – as one rather sullen cardinal complained, the pope's decision would 'enrich foreigners while leaving his own [the Romans] in poverty'.[17]

Pius II, born Enea Silvio Piccolomini, had been elected in August

1458 at the age of fifty-two, comparatively young for a pope but he was in poor health, suffering from gout, kidney stones and a chronic cough. Famously the first humanist pope, he was the author of several literary works, including his memoirs, which are a fascinating source for the period. He was unusually well travelled for an Italian and had visited many parts of Europe as secretary first to Cardinal Domenico Capranica and then to Emperor Frederick III, who crowned him poet laureate. He had even visited Scotland, and endured a terrifying storm in the North Sea; 'the men are short and brave, the women fair', he noted, and 'there is nothing [they] like better than to hear abuse of the English'.[18] His journey north from Rome had started in January in the depths of winter – he had ordered just six cardinals to accompany him, giving the others permission to join the party in Siena, where he intended to celebrate Easter, by which time the weather would be warmer and the roads no longer blocked with ice and snow. By the time he reached Mantua in late May it was almost too hot to travel.

Marquis Ludovico met the papal party at the border with Ferrara near Revere, where Pius II transferred from the Marquis of Ferrara's ceremonial barge (bucintoro) on to Ludovico's own bucintoro for the last leg of his journey up the Mincio to Mantua. The congress finally opened on 1 June but, much to the disappointment of the pope, none of the expected delegates had arrived. Pius II, however, remained optimistic and insisted on staying in Mantua, obliging the papal court also to remain in the city. According to the pope, the cardinals were especially critical – 'the place was marshy and unhealthy, the heat was oppressive, the wine was undrinkable, the food was awful, most of them were unwell, many had the fever, nothing was to be heard except the frogs' – and they worried that they would all die of fever from the humid air.[19] Some were able to escape the heat in Ludovico's hunting lodges, where they could amuse themselves with hawking expeditions, though Ludovico complained to his gamekeeper that Cardinal Rodrigo Borgia was hunting 'with so many dogs and nets that he will ruin the whole countryside within a few days'.[20] Other cardinals amused themselves with boating parties, forcing an exasperated pope to scold them for this unseemly display, or so Barbara reported to her friend, Duchess Bianca Maria.[21]

Meanwhile, the need to assemble an army to stem the Turkish advance was growing increasingly urgent. By July delegations had begun to arrive from Rhodes, Cyprus, Albania, Bosnia, Hungary and other places directly under Turkish threat – but it was not until the middle of August that any of Europe's major powers made an effort to attend the congress. On 15 August an embassy arrived from Duke Philip of Burgundy, led by his nephew accompanied by 400 horsemen, but the party was hit by a severe fever and left after just three weeks. Duke Francesco Sforza and Marquis Borso d'Este had both promised to arrive in mid-August but as the date approached they began to prevaricate – it seems that they too worried about the ill effects of the heat. In the end Borso reneged on his promise to attend the congress in person, refusing to travel the 50 miles to Mantua because, as Pius II recorded with disgust, the marquis's astrologers had predicted that he would die if he did.[22]

It is unlikely to have been a coincidence that Duke Francesco judiciously waited until the worst of the summer heat was over before he made his entry into Mantua on 17 September. Sailing down the Po with an escort of forty-seven ships, he was met at the border by Ludovico and Barbara, who were accompanied by just twenty-two vessels, a neat definition of the rank of these two rulers. And now, as autumn advanced, delegations began to flood into Mantua from the other Italian states and, eventually, from France and Germany. Writing on 25 September, the Sienese envoy reported that 'Mantua is adorned with prelates, lords and ambassadors and with many courts and is very splendid'.[23]

Not surprisingly, given the number of rulers represented in Mantua, there were endless arguments over precedence, a prickly issue in Renaissance Europe. 'Kings would not give way to kings, nor dukes to dukes, each wanting superior status for himself,' Pius II recorded.[24] There were similar arguments between the bishops, who objected to the custom of giving way to lawyers of the Curia, a practice which the pope now banned, but he could not exercise the same absolute authority over secular princes. And negotiating a union between states with very different views on the Turkish question was never really a rational possibility, not least for the Venetians, whose trading links relied on access to the eastern Mediterranean and Constantinople: they were seeking, if not exactly friendship, then at least a working relationship with the Sultan and sent delegates to Mantua with the greatest reluctance.

Andrea Mantegna, *Francesco Gonzaga as a boy*, *c*.1460 (Naples, Museo di Capodimonte). Destined for the Church since birth, Francesco had been made an apostolic protonotary at the age of nine.

The congress finally closed in January 1460 and, while it was not the success Pius II had hoped, it had been a personal triumph for Ludovico – though exhausting enough for him to travel south in May to Petriolo near Siena to take a cure in the warm sulphur springs that Renaissance medics thought were so good for the health.[25] The rewards of the congress were not long in arriving. On 18 December 1461 Pius II announced in consistory that he was giving a cardinal's hat to Ludovico's second son Francesco. The youth was just seventeen years old, though the family had been careful to ensure that the pope was informed that he was, in fact, approaching his twenty-second birthday, the age at which, according to canon law, he could legally become a cardinal deacon.[26] Francesco had been destined for a career in the church from an early age: he had been appointed protonotary by Nicholas V when he was just nine years old. Even as a boy he does not seem to have been particularly well suited for the ecclesiastical life. His tutor, Bartolomeo Marasca, did not consider him very bright and complained to Barbara that he had 'a very poor memory' though he was benefitting from 'conversations in Latin two or three times a week'.[27] Indeed Francesco was apparently much keener on hunting than Latin or prayer – in September 1458 he wrote excitedly to his mother from the hunting lodge at Cavriana that 'today we caught two deer, a pheasant and a hare'.[28]

Francesco's new status as a prince of the Church was evident in March 1462 when he travelled south to Rome for the arcane ceremonies by which Pius II would make him a cardinal. He was accompanied by a large party that included his younger brother Gianfrancesco and his uncle, the crippled Alessandro. They stayed in Florence for three days and Barbara received letters from various members of the party: her sons managed rather short notes to their mother, while Francesco's secretary and majordomo both wrote longer letters, and she also received an immensely long screed from her brother-in-law. Alessandro listed in detail the presents Francesco had been given by the Florentine government as a mark of respect, including various types of candles, large marzipan cakes, ten large boxes of sweetmeats, two large silver bowls filled with lampreys and four 'very large' eels, 160 bottles of wine, half white Trebbiano and half red, and fifty sacks of spelt.[29]

Francesco's red hat was a key step in the evolution of the Renaissance cardinal. The Council of Basle fixed the number of cardinals at twenty-four, with the recommendation that they should be evenly distributed between the various Christian nations – France, Spain, England, Scotland, Germany and Italy, none of which should have more than a third of the total. Strictly speaking, Francesco's appointment was for Germany and had been made at the request of his uncle, Prince Elector Albrecht III of Brandenburg. However, Ludovico and Barbara had certainly been key figures in the negotiations with Rome, and the appointment would benefit Mantua far more than distant Brandenburg. It is worth underlining the scale of the marquis's achievement here: Francesco was the first member of an Italian Renaissance ruling dynasty to receive a red hat – neither the King of Naples, nor the Duke of Milan, nor any of the others, had been granted this signal favour. Above all this appointment set an important precedent: by the end of the century, almost all the Italian ruling dynasties would have a family member in the College of Cardinals. And, moreover, by 1500 the college would be dominated by Italians: in 1458 there were twenty-six cardinals, just nine of whom were Italian; by 1492 only six of the twenty-seven cardinals were foreigners.

Francesco's red hat was not the only benefit to emerge from the congress of Mantua. In the fifteen years he had been marquis, Ludovico had initiated only one major building project in his capital, a large hospital; though, at a more practical level, he had made substantial improvements to the network of waterways to benefit the transport of goods and agricultural produce around the state. But this reluctance to spend money on the embellishment of Mantua was about to change. Shortly after the congress closed, one of Ludovico's agents reported a conversation he had had with a member of the papal court about Mantua's muddy streets, so 'I replied to him that your excellency had begun paving the squares and planned to do the same all over the city'.[30] But Ludovico had a much more ambitious project underway – the redevelopment of the city centre. He had evidently been stung by the criticism that Mantua was an unimportant centre in contrast to the great European courts, such as Milan. Significantly he decided to assert his independence from Duke Francesco by rejecting the Gothic style preferred by the duke in favour of the cultural language of imperial Rome. And the catalyst for this was the humanist Leon Battista Alberti, the papal abbreviator who had met the marquis when he was in Mantua for the congress.

Alberti's reputation was growing thanks to his innovative architectural projects for Leonello d'Este and Sigismondo Malatesta (see Chapter 2) and, above all, to his treatise on architecture, the *De re aedificatoria* (1452, first printed 1485), which established him as an expert on classical architecture. Basing his own treatise on that written by the ancient Roman architect Vitruvius, Alberti showed fifteenth-century patrons how the architectural language of ancient Rome could be used for the design of their palaces, castles, churches and all the other grand buildings that were the essential features of a powerful city. It was a message that resonated with the marquis's ambitions. Above all, Alberti promoted himself as an architect, making a sharp division between the intellectual talents of the designer of a building and the manual skills of the craftsmen who built it. This was a key milestone in the evolution of the modern concept of the architect – the term had fallen out of use during the Middle Ages and this was something Alberti had learned from reading Vitruvius' text.[31]

The first we know of the relationship between Ludovico and Alberti dates from December 1459, shortly before the congress closed, when the marquis sent a messenger to Alberti asking him to return a copy of Vitruvius' treatise because Pius II wanted to borrow it: 'And if you have not taken it with you but have left it here please could you write to whoever has it, so that we may lend it to His Holiness; I would be very grateful if you could do this.'[32] We know nothing more about the manuscript but on 27 February 1460, a week after the pope left Mantua, Alberti wrote to Ludovico asking for the loan of the Gonzaga hunting lodge at Cavriano:

> Because I am feeling somewhat under the weather and some of my sensible friends have advised me to seek a change of air for a few days, so I asked Piero Spagnuolo, your secretary, if I could use one of your country palaces; he thought that Cavriana was the best place and I agreed.[33]

He closed the letter with the information that 'the models of San Sebastiano, San Lorenzo, the loggia and the Virgil are finished and I believe you will not dislike them'.

Leon Battista Alberti, self-portrait, *c*.1430–35 (Washington, National Gallery). The son of an exiled Florentine noble, Alberti had been fortunate to carve himself a career in the Church administration.

Ludovico's plan to remodel the centre of Mantua focused on the creation of an impressive area around the market square, Piazza delle Erbe, and the church of Sant'Andrea, where the treasured relic of the Holy Blood was kept. Three of Alberti's plans related to this project: the Romanesque church of San Lorenzo, the merchant's loggia and the town hall (the Palazzo del Podestà, nicknamed 'the Virgil' because of the statue of the poet on its facade). Unfortunately the project was beset by difficulties from the start, the main obstacle being Ludovico Nuvoloni, abbot of the monastery of Sant'Andrea, which owned many of the properties that Ludovico was hoping to demolish, or alter, including San Lorenzo. As early as July 1460 it was evident that Abbot Nuvoloni was implacably opposed to Ludovico's scheme: 'He has told us that he would not agree to it in a hundred years.'[34] So the marquis decided on the drastic step of closing the monastery and replacing it with a collegiate church, a new secular foundation over which he could exercise control and benefit from its income. However, he first had to get rid of the abbot – and this would require the approval of the pope.

Ludovico's first step in his efforts to have Abbot Nuvoloni removed from Sant'Andrea was to launch a smear campaign in order to discredit him at the papal court. Initially he accused Nuvoloni of being unfit for his position and, when that proved unsuccessful, of financial malpractice; finally he questioned the state of religious observance at the monastery, but to no avail.[35] The abbot, who was a lawyer by training and must have had his own network of support in Rome, steadfastly refused either to give permission for the demolition or to resign. In response he accused Ludovico of fraud: no, not fraud, the marquis insisted, 'we wanted to demolish these houses solely to embellish the area'. There was nothing the marquis could do except wait until the abbot died.

The fourth plan mentioned by Alberti in his letter of 27 February 1460 was for a new church dedicated to San Sebastiano. This project met with more success – a month later, in March, we have news that work had started on the foundations. The cult of St Sebastian as protector against the plague was popular in Renaissance Italy, and Ludovico may well have chosen this dedication in thanksgiving for his city being spared while Pius II and his court were in Mantua for the congress. Built beside the river bank at the edge of the city, the church was raised over a crypt to protect it from flooding. Visually it had

Mantua, Sant'Andrea, façade, begun 1460. Alberti's imposing façade combined elements of a Roman triumphal arch with a temple pediment.

little in common with the elegant Gothic arches of Sforza's Milan, or indeed medieval Mantua. The classical pediment split by an arch on its imposing facade, and the imposing barrel vaults covering the four arms of its Greek-cross plan were features that derived from ancient Rome. Unfortunately, the project later ran into difficulties and remained unfinished.* Cardinal Francesco, writing in 1473, commented that 'although built in the classical manner, not very different from the vision imagined by Messer Battista di Alberti, I still do not understand whether it is meant to be a church, a mosque or a synagogue'.[36]

Despite the difficulties with their projects, Ludovico's friendship with Alberti continued to prosper. The abbreviator was in Mantua again in late 1463 when the marquis sent him a basket of quails.[37] He also assisted Luca Fancelli, the foreman in charge of the construction at San Sebastiano, with advice: in December Fancelli wrote to Ludovico informing him that Alberti was 'very keen to lay down the whole pavement and has told me that we need a large supply of bricks; I estimate that 36,000 will be enough'.[38] As patron, Ludovico took an unusually close interest in all of his projects, replying promptly to Fancelli and the other foremen employed on his building sites with answers to their requests and, on occasion, advice on their personal problems; when Fancelli fell down and hurt a testicle, his master replied that 'God allows men to be punished in that place where they have sinned'.[39] Significantly the marquis addressed all these craftsmen in the second person singular whereas his courteous correspondence with Alberti was conducted entirely in the formal second person plural, clear evidence that the abbreviator was not an employee but a man of social status.

In 1464 Ludovico was quick to offer support to his friend when the new pope, Paul II, abruptly sacked all the abbreviators in early December. On 1 January he wrote to Paul recommending 'the most excellent Messer Battista degli Alberti who in recent years I have got to know well and who has often been a guest at my court and has never failed to offer me his time and services, for which I am very grateful'.[40] Five days later he wrote to his son Cardinal Francesco to ask him to do what he could in Rome for the unfortunate Alberti: 'You know how much Messer Battista has done for us recently not only in the design

---

* Its present appearance is the result of dubious restoration work carried out in the 1920s.

and construction of our San Sebastiano, and how much we are obliged to him and now he has written to us imploring us to recommend him to His Holiness,' he informed his son, 'and we would like you also, out of the respect you bear us, to recommend him as well, and to do every possible favour you can.'[41] On 11 January Ludovico wrote again to Alberti to let him know what action had been taken and 'if there is anything else we can do, we will be happy to oblige'.[42]

Meanwhile, the radical change of image that Ludovico had adopted was also evident inside the Palazzo Ducale, the seat of Gonzaga power in Mantua. He commissioned portrait medals of himself, his sister Cecilia, his father Gianfrancesco and his old tutor Vittorino da Feltre. Ludovico himself was depicted in profile wearing Roman armour on the obverse, and in tournament armour astride a great charger on the reverse; Cecilia was now a Clarissan nun and the reverse of her medal depicted, appropriately, a unicorn, the symbol of chastity.[43] Ludovico also began to collect antique texts: when the Sicilian humanist Giovanni Aurispa died in Ferrara in 1459, his agent spent 60 ducats on Greek manuscripts from the humanist's library, including a commentary on Homer.[44]

The congress had necessitated some changes to the domestic life of the Gonzaga court. In preparation for the arrival of the papal entourage, Ludovico and Barbara had vacated the old family palace opposite the cathedral so that it could be fitted out to accommodate Pius II and his household, and moved into the Castello San Giorgio, the fortified castle overlooking the Ponte San Giorgio, the covered causeway that crossed the artificial lakes created in the twelfth century to strengthen the city's defences. It had required considerable work to convert this fortress into living quarters for the family and court. Ludovico had been warned by an astrologer that it would be fatal to knock it down: 'We have no need of astrologers,' the marquis replied, 'and if you are the one who predicted to my illustrious father that the castle would collapse, you know nothing about divination, because we have demolished half of it.'[45]

Ludovico's new stylistic preferences were also visible in the decoration of the new apartments in Castel San Giorgio. His choice of artist was Andrea Mantegna, a young painter in his late twenties who was much favoured by scholarly patrons in Verona and Padua, the home of humanism. He had accepted the marquis's invitation to join the

Gonzaga court in 1457 but, despite Ludovico sending him 20 ducats to pay for the cost of moving to Mantua, he did not take up the post until 1460.[46] Keen to attract Mantegna to Mantua, Ludovico offered him very generous terms of employment: he was to be paid 180 ducats a year and given a house, together with grain to feed six people and firewood – the annual rent on a barber's shop in the city centre was just 9 ducats.[47] His job included a wide range of tasks. In addition to decorative work at the Palazzo Ducale and the various castles that Ludovico was repairing and embellishing at Goito, Cavriana, Saviola, Marmirolo and Gonzaga, Mantegna was also expected to provide designs for ephemeral decorations for weddings, church feasts and other pageants. One of his first works for the marquis was a portrait of the young Francesco (*c.*1460) painted before the boy received his red hat. Mantegna also painted a series of panels for the new chapel in Castel San Giorgio: the *Ascension of Christ*, the *Adoration of the Magi*, and the *Circumcision* (the so-called Uffizi triptych), and the *Death of the Virgin* (Madrid, Prado), with its view of boats in the river and the covered bridge, the Ponte San Giorgio, visible through the window in the background.

Mantegna's most famous work for his new patron was the decoration of the Camera Picta (begun 1465), Ludovico's bedroom and formal reception room.* Instead of the ideal of knightly chivalry at the court of King Arthur painted by Pisanello for his father some three decades earlier, Ludovico chose to display the prestige of his own court and its association with the tradition of imperial Rome. Mantegna's decoration of the room was a masterpiece of illusion: in the vaults, which were painted to look like *all'antica* stucco mouldings, were portrait medallions of the Emperors of ancient Rome, with fictive reliefs of stories from classical mythology in the lunettes. In the centre of the ceiling he created a fictive oculus, apparently open to the sky with a parapet around which court ladies giggled and gossiped, while a flower pot balanced precariously on its rim and a *putto* looks tempted to drop an apple into the room.

On the walls, set behind fictive curtains drawn back to reveal their scenes, were portraits of Ludovico, his family and his courtiers. In one the marquis holds a letter and talks earnestly to his secretary, with Barbara beside him dressed in a very expensive robe of cloth-of-gold – their status made evident by the fact that everyone else is standing

---

* Its modern name, the Camera degli Sposi (Room of the Newlyweds) is a seventeenth-century invention.

Andrea Mantegna, *Death of the Virgin*, *c.*1460 (Madrid, Prado). Through the window in the picture Mantegna included a view of the covered bridge: the Ponte San Giorgio.

– surrounded by their children, courtiers and the court dwarf. Dwarves were collectors' items at the Renaissance courts, prized above all for the bawdy entertainment they provided – and the hand gesture of this one can be seen as a deliberately coarse reference to the fruitfulness of Ludovico and Barbara's union. Under Ludovico's chair is his old dog, Rubino, who was devoted to his master: on one occasion when the marquis left on a trip, Barbara had found Rubino wandering through the palace, 'going from room to room in search of you'; and when the dog died Ludovico had him buried with a tombstone and epitaph in a spot he would have been able to see from his bedroom.[48] On another wall is a scene of huntsmen in Gonzaga livery and portraits of Ludovico's hunting dogs. In the third scene, with another of his dogs at his feet, he is welcoming Cardinal Francesco, with more family members, including Ludovico's two young grandsons and two rulers, Emperor Frederick III and Christian I, King of Denmark, who was married to Barbara's sister.[49]

Meanwhile, the plans Ludovico and Barbara had made for their children's futures had suffered a setback, which was to have political repercussions. In 1457 they discovered that their eldest daughter Susanna, then aged ten, was beginning to show signs of a spinal abnormality and her betrothal to Galeazzo Maria Sforza had to be annulled. Fortunately Duke Francesco agreed to the substitution of her younger sister Dorotea and continued to employ the marquis as commander of his army. In March 1463 Ludovico renewed his *condotta* with the duke as usual but, later that year, without warning, Duke Francesco announced that Galeazzo Maria's betrothal to Dorotea was cancelled and that his heir was to marry Bona of Savoy, sister-in-law to Louis XI of France, instead.[50] This was a deliberate insult and Ludovico was furious, even more so when Duke Francesco insulted him again by offering to reinstate the betrothal if Ludovico would agree to sign a lifelong contract with Milan, a move that would in effect have made Mantua a subject state of Milan.

For the next two years Ludovico refused to sign another *condotta* either with his old ally or with anyone else. But when Duke Francesco died suddenly on 8 March 1466, Ludovico, who was now fifty-four

Andrea Mantegna, ceiling oculus, 1465–74 (Mantua, Palazzo Ducale).
A master of *trompe l'oeil*, Mantegna decorated the ceiling of the Camera Picta with giggling ladies and putti precariously balanced on the fictive stonework.

years old, was suddenly in demand again – there were offers from King Ferrante of Naples and Francesco's widow Duchess Bianca Maria, while Venice bid the huge sum of 100,000 ducats for his services.[51] Rejecting both Venice and Milan, Ludovico signed a contract with Naples on 1 April – and he managed to negotiate a clause whereby he would not have to do any fighting himself, allowing him to spend the last twelve years of his life in relative leisure, much to the envy of his contemporaries.

In a tragic postscript to the jilting of Dorotea, the young girl died four years later in April 1467, at the age of just eighteen. The whole family were devastated. Cardinal Francesco, reported the Ferrarese ambassador in Rome, 'has said publicly that neither his father nor himself nor any of his brothers nor any member of the family wishes [Duke Galeazzo Maria] well… the death of Dorotea is entirely due to him and to no other cause'.[52] The marquis was more forgiving: when Galeazzo Maria was assassinated in 1477, Ludovico moved his troops to the Milanese border in case they were needed to guarantee the succession of the duke's young son Gianlaeazzo (see Chapter 5).

Fortunately, the marriages of Ludovico's other children were not dependent on Sforza favour. Ludovico had betrothed his heir, Federigo, to Margherita von Wittelsbach, sister of Duke Johann of Bavaria, and in July 1463 the marquis sent two of Federigo's brothers, Gianfrancesco and Rodolfo, to Innsbruck with the bridal party that was to escort Margherita back to Mantua. The seventeen-year-old Gianfrancesco was particularly impressed with the bride who was 'very lovely', he reported to his mother, 'though she is not very tall and is rather plump'.[53] And Ludovico reinforced his links with the imperial court by choosing German princes as husbands for his two youngest daughters: Barbara, affectionately known as Barbarina, was married to Eberhard I, Duke of Württemberg, in 1474 and Paola married Leonhard, Count of Gorizia, three years later. The Gonzaga dynasty was further strengthened in 1466 when Margherita gave birth to a son: he was portrayed by Mantegna in the Camera Picta as the taller of the two young boys in the meeting scene, standing between the marquis and Cardinal Francesco. In a letter to Barbara, Ludovico seemed almost blasé about the birth of Francesco (see Chapter 6), the first of five grandsons: 'The bonfires and the ringing of bells that our people did here are childish things,' he told Barbara:

It might have been alright when we were born but that was only because the illustrious lord our father of blessed memory was an only son and it seemed as if it could be the end of the dynasty but, thanks be to God, this is no longer the case.[54]

Meanwhile, Cardinal Francesco was establishing himself at the papal court. Barbara had taken charge of appointing trusted courtiers and servants to her son's new household, while Ludovico's agent in Rome, Bartolomeo Bonatto, looked for suitable accommodation for them. Given the importance of the size of one's household as one of the key indicators of rank in Renaissance Europe and the fact that as a cardinal Francesco's rank was significantly higher than it had been when he was merely the second son of a provincial prince, there was much discussion about the matter. Ludovico himself, unsure of what was involved, asked Bonatto for advice. Bonatto, in turn, asked several cardinals for their opinions: 'At most twenty squires, one prelate, six or eight chaplains, four grooms, then others including cooks, table-deckers, purveyors and stable boys, making a total of sixty mouths and, above all, to have a majordomo who must be a man of reputation,' was the recommendation.[55] Barbara must have decided that this figure was inadequate because she increased the size of Francesco's household to eighty-two mouths.[56] She also decided to offer the coveted post of majordomo to Francesco's old tutor, Bartolomeo Marasca; this was an odd choice because, although Marasca was a priest, strict and excessively pious, he was also the son of a fish weigher and decidedly not noble.[57] Nevertheless he was devoted to Francesco: indeed, in 1464 the twenty-year-old cardinal had to ask his mother to explain to Marasca that he no longer wanted to share his bed with the man as he had been obliged to do as a child – Barbara replied that his old tutor loved him like a baby, and begged him 'to try to show affection towards him'.[58]

By all accounts Cardinal Francesco enjoyed life at the papal court, performing the ceremonial and social duties required of the members of the college – though apparently his singing of the liturgy was bad enough to make Paul II giggle.[59] Key for his career was the favour of the pope and other important figures who were in a position to grant benefices and other sources of income. Marquis Ludovico had advised his son that 'we earn our livelihood as Marquis of Mantua and as a soldier, you must do this as a prelate'.[60] The cardinal followed his father's advice, giving an annual gift of sparrow-hawks to Rodrigo

Borgia, the powerful vice-chancellor. He also made a conspicuous point of supporting Pius II's crusade, commissioning a suit of armour and his own war galley to sail with the papal fleet – and the marquis presented his son with a pair of war horses for the fighting.[61] The fleet was about to sail from Ancona in August 1464 when Pius II died, obliging the cardinals to return to Rome to elect his successor. For Francesco, and for his colleagues, the whole ingratiating process now started again, juggling the often conflicting loyalties between their own interests, loyalty to their families and their positions at the papal court.

In time Francesco's career proved the value of having a family member at the heart of the papal court. He began to amass benefices which, although they were not necessarily very lucrative, did increase the control that Marquis Ludovico was able to exercise over the church in his territories. In 1460 the cardinal had been appointed as administrator of San Benedetto Polirone (familiarly, San Benedetto Po), an important Benedictine abbey outside Mantua, and once appointed as cardinal he had used his influence in papal consistories to gain positions in charge of other Benedictine houses in the area. In 1466 he was appointed Bishop of Mantua, a benefice that would remain in the family for the next century.

There was also the unfinished business of the church of Sant'Andrea and its stubborn Abbot Nuvoloni. Marquis Ludovico had planned to give this benefice to Francesco when the abbot finally died, so the cardinal was rather nettled to discover that his father had changed his mind and was now intending to give the position to his youngest son, Ludovico. In May 1469 Francesco wrote to his mother to say that he was glad to hear that the nine-year-old Ludovico had taken minor orders, but 'regarding the abbey of Sant'Andrea, I do not know what has persuaded the Illustrious Lord my father not to allow me to have it'.[62] As Francesco knew well, Barbara had better powers of persuasion over her husband, and so it proved.

In March 1470 Abbot Nuvoloni died and the marquis was finally able to put into action his plan for taking control of the monastery and its precious relic of the Holy Blood. Cardinal Francesco's help would be essential in Rome to institute both the religious reforms to the house and the long-cherished plan to rebuild the church. On 16 March Francesco reported to his father that he had officially asked Paul II if he himself could be appointed as abbot and this was confirmed a

overleaf Mantua, Sant'Andrea, interior, begun 1470. The monumental scale of the interior of this church, together with its coffered barrel vault, was inspired by the Basilica of Maxentius in Rome.

week later. On 21 April he wrote to his father again, thanking his parents for their offer to contribute 200 ducats a year to the building fund and promising to contribute the same sum himself.[63]

That autumn Alberti was in Mantua: 'I have also recently heard that Your Lordship and your citizens have been discussing building at Sant'Andrea and that your main aim was to create a large space so that the Blood of Christ can be seen by many,' he wrote to Marquis Ludovico.[64] He also outlined his design for the new church, 'which I am sending to you; it will be much more spacious, more eternal, more dignified and more cheerful and it will cost a lot less; this form of temple was known to the ancients as Sacred Etruscan and, if you like it, I will draw it up in a scaled plan'. Marquis Ludovico, who was at his castle at Gonzaga at the time, replied on 22 October that 'we have seen the design that you sent and like it but because we do not understand it very well we will wait until we are both in Mantua and then, once we have talked with you and told you our idea and also understood yours, we will see what is best'.[65] While it is impossible to know whose ideas won the marquis's approval, it is evident that the resulting building was a landmark in the revival of the architectural style of imperial Rome in both style and scale. Its imposing facade combining the classical motifs of a temple front and a triumphal arch dominates the piazza in front of the church; inside, the enormous space promised by Alberti was inspired directly by the Basilica of Maxentius in the Roman Forum.

The ruins of ancient Rome had long been of interest to Cardinal Francesco – soon after his arrival in the city in March 1462, his lawyer reported to Barbara that 'today he rode about Rome looking at some churches and many ancient buildings'.[66] He was impatient to get the building project at Sant'Andrea started as soon as possible. Even if the funding was not yet in place, he reasoned with his prudent father in January 1471, the project would attract offerings 'once work starts' – significantly, he used the example of Milan: 'I don't want it to be like the cathedral in Milan which has never been finished.'[67] But there was one more hurdle to pass: Sant'Andrea was still a Benedictine house and they needed papal permission to rebuild it. Unfortunately Paul II was withholding his agreement and it was not until the pope died in August 1471 that the project could finally begin.

Paul II's successor, Sixtus IV, was more amenable to Marquis Ludovico and Cardinal Francesco. Not only was he a client of the

Rome, Basilica of Maxentius, begun by Emperor Maxentius in AD 307 and completed by his successor Constantine, who famously defeated Maxentius with the sign of the Cross at the Battle of the Milvian Bridge (312).

Duke of Milan, he had been elected with the help of the cardinal and owed him a favour or two. The first came in autumn 1471 when little Ludovico was appointed a papal protonotary.[68] And on 15 January 1472 Cardinal Francesco was able to report to his father:

> Regarding what your Excellency asked me to do to get permission to demolish the church of Sant'Andrea and rebuild it, I spoke with His Holiness who is agreeable and so he has given his verbal consent that Your Lordship can have the church knocked down in part or wholly, whichever you prefer.[69]

Work began a month later and that June Sixtus IV issued the bull reforming the monastery into a collegiate church.

Meanwhile Cardinal Francesco continued to enjoy life at the papal court. Unusually good-looking, according to contemporary reports, he had an illegitimate son, apparently the result of an affair with one of his own Mantuan servants; the child, nicknamed the 'Cardinalino', or little cardinal, was initially cared for by the redoubtable Barbara and later legitimized.[70] Above all, Cardinal Francesco had become a patron of the arts in his own right. His interest in the culture of antiquity was soon evident in his palace in Rome where he displayed his growing collection of antique sculpture and coins, as well as medals, gems, cameos, tapestries, silver and curiosities.[71] He also owned some 200 manuscripts, including a sumptuous version of Homer's *Iliad* and the *Odyssey* in Greek and Latin parallel texts, known as the 'Vatican Homer'.[72] Majordomo Marasca was horrified at his extravagance and wrote several times to Barbara on the subject. 'In my last letter I begged you to write to [Francesco] on the importance of regulating his expenditure and of not giving in to desires, especially for items which are neither necessary nor very useful' – the frugal Marasca's complaint on this particular occasion concerned a gilded silver salt cellar in the form of an elephant carrying a castle on its back which had cost the cardinal the enormous sum of 400 ducats.[73] On another occasion Francesco sent his mother three camels, 'a husband, wife and little daughter' as he phrased it, and a Turkish slave, 'the slave is not baptized'.[74]

Cardinals were expected to display a level of ostentation appropriate to their status as princes of the church – and lavish expenditure was to become a key characteristic of all princely cardinals, along with a tendency to ignore the rules of celibacy. In Francesco's case his expenditure far exceeded his income and he was obliged to rely on bankers to fund his extravagant tastes. When they became too demanding, as the Medici bank did in 1466, he was forced to turn to his parents, to fellow cardinals and even to his younger brother Ludovico for funds to repay his debts. Among the creditors claiming money owed to them by the cardinal after his death were several members of his own household and a canon of Mantua cathedral, who was owed 500 ducats, as well as the Medici bank, who claimed 3,500 ducats from the estate.[75]

Marquis Ludovico died on 12 June 1478, followed three years later by Barbara and then the cardinal himself in October 1483. They had all played their part in the dramatic transformation of Mantua into one of Italy's premier Renaissance courts.

FERRANTE I OF ARAGON (1425–94)
King of Naples

FEDERIGO DA MONTEFELTRO (1422–82)
Duke of Urbino

Sixtus IV, *Pope*

Alfonso, *Duke of Calabria, heir to Ferrante I*

Girolamo Riario, *Lord of Imola, Sixtus IV's nephew*

Galeazzo Maria Sforza, *Duke of Milan*

Lorenzo de' Medici, *Banker*

CONSPIRACY AND GREED

Ferrante I of Naples

&

Federigo da Montefeltro

On 25 July 1478 Sixtus IV wrote to his army commander Federigo da Montefeltro explaining his reasons for the war he and his ally Ferrante I had launched earlier that month against the republic of Florence or, more precisely, against its *de facto* leader, Lorenzo de' Medici:

> We trust that God, whose honour and glory is at stake, will grant you victory in everything, especially as our intentions are straightforward and just. For we make war on no one save on that ungrateful, excommunicated and heretical Lorenzo de' Medici; and we pray to God to punish him for his evil acts, and to you as God's representative deputed to avenge the wrongs he has iniquitously and without cause committed against God and His Church with such ingratitude that the fountain of infinite love has been drained.[1]

For the pope, the wrongs that needed avenging were grievous indeed: two months earlier the Florentine authorities had very publicly executed five or six priests and an archbishop in direct contravention of the law that exempted the clergy from the jurisdiction of the secular authorities. The pope had taken his revenge for this crime by excommunicating Lorenzo in a bull entitled 'Son of Evil' (*Iniquitatis filius*) and declaring war on the city. The pope's self-righteous indignation, however, masked an uncomfortable truth: the churchmen had been executed for their part in a murderous attack on Lorenzo which, shockingly, had taken place in the sacred setting of Florence cathedral. The attack was the culmination of a five-year feud that had started as a mere squabble between Sixtus IV and the Medici before escalating into a conspiracy to force regime change in Florence. Under the direction of Girolamo Riario, the pope's devious nephew, the cast of characters grew to include some of Italy's most influential figures, not least Ferrante I and Federigo da Montefeltro, with the shadowy figure of Sixtus IV ever present in the background. And very likely it was embarrassment that the coup had failed, as much as anything else, that had roused the pope to such an extreme level of rage.

It is an unpleasant story of conspiracy and greed from which none of the characters emerges untarnished, not even the intended victims – certainly not the king, who hoped for allies to bolster his hold on power; nor the talented *condottiere* who, like Riario, craved social status;

nor even the pope himself, though he denied all knowledge of the plot. Above all, it shows how far these Renaissance princes were prepared to compromise in order to achieve social status, wealth and political power.

Ferrante I and Federigo da Montefeltro were old allies who, despite their difference in rank, had much in common, not least the insecurity of their position. One root cause of this was the fact that they were both bastards who had been officially legitimized by papal bull, but whose illegitimacy nevertheless still caused problems on their accession to power – bizarrely, they were also subject to assassinations plots involving their sisters. It was this insecurity that lured them into the 1478 plot, and the calculated and self-seeking solutions that resulted.

Federigo da Montefeltro had seized power in Urbino on 23 July 1444 after the assassination of his younger half-brother Duke Oddantonio. The seventeen-year-old, who was married to Isotta d'Este, the daughter of Nicolò III, had a reputation for extravagance and was colourfully described by a chronicler as a serial adulterer 'slain by his subjects because he had little respect for their wives by night or by day'.[2] It was rumoured that the duke had been found castrated with his penis stuffed into his mouth – and 'forthwith the people of Urbino unanimously called for Signor Federigo who at once took possession of the state'. Federigo, aged twenty-two, does seem to have been suspiciously well prepared to take over from Oddantonio, who had been promoted from Count to Duke of Urbino by Eugene IV the previous year. But, though there is no proof that he was directly involved in this conspiracy, rumours that he had been responsible for Oddantonio's death persisted: even Ferrante I's son Alfonso, in a moment of anger in the late 1470s, accused him of being a second Cain.[3]

More controversial at the time, however, was Federigo's claim to be Oddantonio's half-brother. Many, including Federigo's own chancellor, insisted that he was not the son, illegitimate or otherwise, of Count Guidantonio da Montefeltro but of Bernardino degli Ubaldini, commander of the count's army.[4] However, when Federigo's neighbour Sigismondo Malatesta, lord of Rimini, voiced these doubts, Federigo flew into a rage and hysterically accused Sigismondo of being a blind leper, a wife-poisoner, a rapist of nuns and so forth, a catalogue of crimes dreadful enough to disguise his own guilty conscience.[5] As we shall see, Federigo was to be fortunate that his preposterous accusations against Sigismondo would stick (see Chapter 2).

The first years of Federigo's rule were further marred by opposition from family, neighbours and, above all, from Rome. Eugene IV not only refused to grant Federigo the title of duke held by Oddantonio, but also withheld his formal approval to the succession itself. There were other claimants to Urbino, not least Domenico Malatesta, Sisigmondo's brother, whose wife Violante da Montefeltro was Oddantonio's sister. In March 1446 the count uncovered a plot involving Sigismondo and Violante's younger sister Sveva, who still lived at Urbino and was to provide the conspirators with access to the city – all the plotters in Urbino were executed, though Federigo refused to behead his sister.[6] It was not until 1447 and the election of Nicholas V that Federigo's title of Count of Urbino was confirmed, but the new pope refused to grant him the dynastic right to pass the state to his legitimate sons – and Oddantonio's title of duke was off the agenda.[7]

With his position in Urbino formally recognized, the doubts surrounding his parentage began to fade as Federigo established a formidable reputation on the battlefield. A clever politician, he was careful to weigh the advantages of any alliance; while financial rewards were important, his priority was securing Urbino from Sigismondo's ambitions. He signed his first *condotta* with Duke Filippo Maria Visconti at the age of sixteen, fighting for Milan for several seasons before changing his allegiance to Alfonso I in October 1442 – he may well have first met Ferrante when he visited Naples the following year.[8] In 1446 he signed a *condotta* with Francesco Sforza, an alliance that brought political benefits but personal disfigurement. During a joust he staged to celebrate Sforza's successful conquest of Milan in 1450, the lance belonging to his opponent smashed into his skull at the top of his nose, forcing his right eye out of its socket. It was a gruesome injury but remarkably, in an era when lesser wounds frequently proved fatal, Federigo survived – though he had to take sick leave in 1453 when an attack of malaria threatened the sight in his remaining eye.[9]

By 1451 Count Federigo was back in service with Alfonso I amid rumours that the Emperor planned to oust Sforza from Milan and enforce the terms of Duke Filippo Maria's will, which bequeathed the duchy to the king rather than to his son-in-law. The king paid well but, more importantly, specifically promised military aid to Federigo in the event of any attack on Urbino. When Federigo's fighting contract expired after the Peace of Lodi in 1454, the king rewarded him with a pension of 6,000 ducats a year; and in further marks of favour named him a royal councillor and promoted him to captain-general of the army.[10] Unlike other *condottiere*, who frequently changed sides to enhance their incomes, Count Federigo would remain a loyal ally of Naples for the rest of his life – and, as we shall see, was able to amass a fortune on the side.

When Ferrante inherited his father's throne on 27 June 1458 Federigo would have the opportunity to prove his worth as soldier, diplomat and friend. Relations between Naples and Rome had soured since the unexpected election of Calixtus III in 1455. The pope, who had been Alfonso I's chief minister and Prince Ferrante's tutor, now refused to recognize Ferrante as king and declared Naples to be a lapsed fief. Count Federigo, despite the danger of publicly opposing papal policy, sent his eldest son, Buonconte, to Naples to congratulate the new king, though tragically the boy caught the plague and died on his way home.[11]

Ferrante faced formidable problems – but fortunately he had been well trained. Alfonso had been diligent in preparing his son for political leadership and Ferrante's presence had been noted in council meetings and private audiences, silent but attentive. He was not an easy ally, often acting expediently and frequently devious: 'We learned from a good teacher,' he explained.[12] Hostility to his succession was not limited to Rome. René of Anjou, his father's old enemy, quickly seized this opportunity to renew his claim to Naples. It was soon evident that the Angevin cause had considerable support in the kingdom itself, setting off a rebellion led by two of Ferrante's own relations: Giovanni Antonio Orsini, Prince of Taranto, who was the uncle of Ferrante's queen, Isabella; and Marino Marzano, Prince of Rossano (Duke of Sessa), the husband of the king's half-sister Eleonora. Indeed Ferrante I was lucky to survive an attempt on his life when Marzano lured him to a meeting to discuss the possibility of a truce and attacked him with a dagger.

Ferrante I must have been very relieved when Calixtus III himself died just over a month after he had succeeded to the throne – and on 19 August came the welcome news that the conclave had elected Enea Silvio Piccolomini as Pius II. It was to prove an astonishing stroke of

good fortune for both Ferrante and Federigo. As usual, the election of a new pope brought a realignment of the political landscape, but Pius II was also a new type of pope, one with ambitions to use his influence to establish his impoverished Sienese relatives in the ranks of Italy's aristocratic elite. It was a significant moment in the history of the papacy – the introduction of what one historian has called a 'dynastic narrative in a papal context' would be exploited by the pope and his successors to dramatic effect.[13]

Pius II's agreement not only to reverse Calixtus III's ruling but also to support Ferrante I's war against the joint forces of René of Anjou and the rebel Neapolitan barons was directly linked to this novel policy. The pope's price reflected the dynastic ambitions he coveted for his family: his nephew Antonio Piccolomini was to become Duke of Amalfi, a prestigious title in the kingdom, with permission to quarter the royal coat-of-arms with his own; he was also betrothed to Maria of Aragon, the king's illegitimate daughter. By the end of the year 1458 Ferrante I's future no longer looked so bleak: his title had been secured with his coronation by the papal legate and he had signed an alliance with Pius II. Moreover, thanks to papal influence, he had also acquired the support of his father's old enemy Duke Francesco Sforza, who needed the support of the Emperor, who was Ferrante's cousin, to acquire the formal recognition of his own title (see Chapter 1).

Despite the military skills of Federigo da Montefeltro and Duke Francesco's brother Alessandro, lord of Pesaro, the war did not go well initially for Ferrante I. On 7 July 1460 he was heavily defeated at Sarno, just east of Mount Vesuvius, and a fortnight later Count Federigo was attacked at San Fabiano and forced to retire.[14] Remarkably Pius II remained firm in his support of Ferrante, even when the French king attempted to persuade the pope to switch sides by offering him a bribe of 70,000 soldiers to fight in the crusade, a project dear to Pius II's heart, in return for papal support for the Angevin cause.[15] It was not until August 1462, when the enemy was defeated at Troia, that the war turned decisively in the king's favour – and when the rebel Prince of Taranto judiciously changed sides a month later, it was evident that the king would be the victor. Finally, in July 1465, the Angevin fleet was defeated off Ischia and the king was able to return to his capital after an absence of seven years.

Ferrante I celebrated victory over his enemies by setting up his

Domenico Gagini, *Ferrante I* (Paris, Louvre). This style of portrait bust, inspired by Roman sculpture, reflects the king's importance as a patron of humanism.

overleaf Tavola Strozzi, *c.*1480 (Naples, Museo di Capodimonte). Celebrating Ferrante's victory in 1465, this painting shows Naples and its waterfront dominated by the massive ramparts of the royal palace of Castel Nuovo.

own chivalric order, that symbol of royal power that marked favoured status at courts across Europe. The Knights of the Ermine were inaugurated on 29 September 1465. The date was appropriate: it was the feast of Michaelmas. Just as his father had celebrated victory over the Angevins in 1442 by dedicating Castel Nuovo to St Michael, so Ferrante I dedicated his knights to the archangel in an obvious allusion to his own victory: 'And there was war in heaven: Michael and his angels fought against the dragon... and the great dragon was cast out, the old serpent called the Devil' (Revelations 12: 7–9).[16] The ceremonial associated with the order, which included a gold collar and a sumptuous ermine-lined red satin mantle, was suitably splendid.

Ferrante I now concentrated on strengthening his hold on power, using his children to establish a network of alliances across Italy and beyond the Alps. Fortunately Queen Isabella had secured the succession with four sons and two daughters – Alfonso (born 1448), Eleonora (1450), Federigo (1452), Giovanni (1456), Beatrice (1457), and Francesco (1461) – while the king also had over ten illegitimate offspring born to several different mistresses, who were also brought up at court. The alliance between Naples and Milan, the backbone of the Peace of Lodi, had been cemented with two Aragon–Sforza betrothals both signed in 1455: Ferrante's heir, Alfonso, Duke of Calabria (aged seven) to Francesco Sforza's daughter Ippolita (ten); and Eleonora of Aragon (five) to the duke's third son, Sforza Maria (four). The first marriage took place in 1465, soon after Ferrante I had regained his kingdom, but the second fell through and Eleonora was betrothed to Duke Ercole d'Este of Ferrara instead (see below) – the king, strapped for cash as usual, managed to save a third of the agreed dowry price of 60,000 ducats by promising to grant Ercole a fief in the kingdom, though he never did.[17] Plans to solidify Naples's defences against René of Anjou by marrying Federigo to the daughter of the Duke of Burgundy also fell through; he later married to Anne of Savoy, which further strengthened the links between Naples and Milan as she was the sister of Bona of Savoy, the wife of Duke Francesco's heir Galeazzo Maria, who was to become Duke of Milan in 1466.

A bigger headache for Ferrante I was his relations with the Neapolitan barons, who may have been beaten but were far from cowed. Surprisingly, less than 20 per cent of the towns and villages in the kingdom actually belonged to the crown, and in some provinces

Francesco Laurana, *Ippolita Sforza*, c.1472 (Washington, National Gallery).
Traditionally identified as Ippolita, this is one of several portraits
of ladies of the Neapolitan court sculpted by Laurana.

there were no crown lands at all so Ferrante decided to increase his authority by appointing members of his own family to titles he had confiscated from the rebels.[18] His second son, Federigo, for example, became Prince of Squillace, then Prince of Taranto and finally Prince of Altamura after his marriage to the daughter of the rebel who brought that title as part of her dowry; Francesco, his third son, became Duke of Sant'Angelo and later married the heiress to the Duke of Venosa; while the title of Duke of Sessa, which had belonged to Marino Marzano, Ferrante's would-be assassin, went to his son-in-law, Antonio Piccolomini. Unfortunately this deliberate undermining of baronial prestige would have disastrous consequences.

Above all, Ferrante I spent conspicuously on the prime symbol of his power, Castel Nuovo. It was a move designed to assert his authority in his capital city but also to disguise the fact that he was broke: without the resources of his father's Spanish kingdom, his options were severely limited – when Pius II tried to get hold of the substantial sum of 60,000 ducats that Alfonso I had willed to the crusade, the king delayed proceedings for six months and then only sent half the amount.[19] Embellishing the grounds with costly marble fountains, pavilions and an aviary, he demolished buildings at the front of the fortress to create an imposing piazza for the city facade and commissioned a hugely expensive set of bronze doors for the castle entrance.[20] The doors were cast by Fra Guglielmo da Perugia,* his master of artillery, who had made bells and clocks as well as cannons, bombards and other weapons for Alfonso I – Ferrante placed a high value on his services, and increased his salary from 400 ducats to 600 ducats a year.[21] Depicted on the castle doors was a graphic account of the recent campaign against the rebel barons and their Angevin allies.[22] The six scenes, all identified by explanatory inscriptions, included Marzano's attempted assassination of the king and the victory at Troia (18 August 1462), tagged by lines that drew a parallel between Ferrante's achievements and those of Julius Caesar. Above the doors was another expensive bronze relief showing his coronation by the papal legate, unmistakable evidence of his right to the throne.[23]

Ferrante I's court never enjoyed the same fame as that of his father, though Francesco Filelfo's compaint that hunting had now replaced

---

* He is sometimes mistakenly referred to as Fra Guillaume of Paris, a misreading of the Latin for Perugia (Perusinus).

scholarship at Naples was a little unfair.[24] Like Alfonso, Ferrante was a keen patron of music: he sent his Flemish composer Johannes Tinctoris to Flanders to recruit new singers for the royal chapel, giving him a substantial sum for expenses, warning him to 'take care to use the expenses judiciously'.[25] Ferrante was in fierce competition with Duke Galeazzo Maria Sforza, who repeatedly poached his singers from Naples, much to the king's outrage.[26]

Ferrante also shared his father's passion for books; he encouraged the new medium of printing and set up one of the first presses in Italy.[27] Many of Alfonso's humanists remained loyal through the war of succession: unable to pay his salary in cash, Ferrante rewarded Panormita with a garden he had confiscated from the rebel Marino Marzano and appointed him as tutor to his heir, Alfonso of Calabria.[28] Panormita's successor, Giovanni Pontano, served as royal secretary on a salary of 400 ducats, and wrote a history of the war (*De bello napoletano*) as well as a series of treatises on moral virtues such as obedience, fortitude and liberality.[29] He encouraged Ferrante's patronage with pamphlets on magnificence, which he defined as the duty of a ruler to make an appropriate and public display of his rank, and on splendour, the importance of appropriate display in private. 'Just as day-old soup does not go into a silver plate, so too a man of the first rank does not eat humble cabbage,' Pontano explained. 'Just as his table will shine with gold and silver, so too will it be splendid in its foods.'[30]

These concepts of 'magnificence' and 'splendour' were also evident at Urbino, where Count Federigo created a court to display his own rank and ambitions. His first wife, Gentile Brancaleoni, had died childless in 1457 and three years later, at the age of thirty-eight, he had married Battista, the fourteen-year-old daughter of his neighbour Alessandro Sforza, lord of Pesaro. Soon after the marriage Pius II granted Federigo the dynastic right to pass his title to his legitimate sons but, so far, Battista had only given birth to girls.[31] Unlike other princes of the period, Federigo did not surround himself with humanists – indeed many of those who wrote flattering biographies in the hope of employ-ment were disappointed. According to Vespasiano he liked to listen to Livy's *Histories* during meals, or a religious text during Lent, and

overleaf Piero della Francesca, *Federigo da Montefeltro and Battista Sforza*, 1472–74 (Florence, Uffizi). In this iconic double portrait, it is the duke's wealth that is on display in the duchess's priceless jewels and costly robe.

had plain tastes in food, avoiding sugary sweetmeats and, unusually, wine.[32] His court was relatively modest, with some 400 courtiers and staff – by contrast at Naples the royal huntsmen and falconers alone numbered over 200 men.[33] One scholar has described Federigo as a 'prima donna' and certainly he had his fussy side.[34] He drew up rules for his household: his doctor, for example, was not allowed to have his wife in his room in the palace as he was 'on duty day and night to serve his lord as required', while the bedchamber servants had to wash their hands and feet daily and cut their nails.[35]

What is remarkable about Federigo is the enormous amount of money he spent on buildings and their decoration. Indeed, it is estimated that he spent more on the arts than any other Renaissance prince – but then, of course, he had a lot more to prove.[36] His first wife's dowry had brought land to boost his original patrimony, the tiny hilltop citadel of Urbino, but (as with Ferrante I) it was the favour of Pius II that really transformed his fortunes. 'Proceed then,' the pope had ordered him in the autumn of 1462, in a distinctly bloodthirsty manner, to 'conquer, destroy and consume this accursed Sigismondo and in him neutralize the poison of Italy.'[37] One by one, the Malatesta fortresses fell into Federigo's hands: the inhabitants of Mondavio, for example, paid an indemnity of 3,000 ducats to avoid a sack.[38] Thanks to Pius II, Federigo acquired over fifty castles and towns which had been under Malatesta rule, in addition to his considerable income as a *condottiere*. It has been estimated that his total income for the years 1451–82 came to a total of 1,580,000 ducats and that at least 875,000 ducats of this was profit.[39]

Federigo built palaces in his subject towns and upgraded his fortresses and castles. Above all, he lavished money on Urbino, embellishing his capital with a new cathedral, churches, convents and the other hallmarks of a great Renaissance city. His most ambitious project was his palace, begun in 1468, which reputedly cost 200,000 ducats. As an inscription on the building claimed, he began it 'after overthrowing his enemies', a clear reference to his defeat of Sigismondo Malatesta. He himself explained that he wanted 'to build a residence in our city of Urbino as beautiful and dignified as befits the rank and praiseworthy fame of our ancestors' and significantly, 'our own status'.[40]

The palace was indeed impressive – built on the side of a hill, it had two contrasting facades, not unlike Castel Nuovo in Naples. Seen from the road through the mountains to the south, the massive walls, ramparts and turrets suggested a strongly fortified citadel; by contrast, the city facade was elegant and open, with large windows and doors decorated with elaborately carved detail opening on to the central piazza opposite the new cathedral. The palace was built around a splendid central courtyard surrounded by arcades supported on Composite columns, with Corinthian pilasters flanking the windows in the floor above. The combination of motifs did not strictly follow the rules of ancient Roman architecture and the courtyard is often judged as less 'classical' than Sigismondo Malatesta's San Francesco in Rimini, or Ludovico Gonzaga's Sant'Andrea in Mantua; however, the capitals themselves were based on ancient prototypes and so was the lettering of the inscription in the frieze.

The interior of the palace was also magnificent, with grand reception halls and audience chambers, private apartments for the family and their guests, a chapel, gardens and loggias as well as stables, kitchens, storerooms and cellars – there was even a place for storing snow and ice. Federigo reputedly spent 50,000 ducats on silver and furnishings – like other parvenus he had to buy his own trappings of aristocratic power.[41] One extravagance was a set of tapestries depicting the Trojan War, costing 2,557 ducats, which were woven by Jean Grenier of Tournai who had made a similar set for Duke Charles of Burgundy.[42] Another extravagance was his library. As a youth Federigo had briefly been a pupil at Vittoriano da Feltre's school and knew the importance of classical learning but, unlike his fellow princes, he had not inherited a family collection and so had to buy his own. With 1,100 volumes it was a substantial library for the period and contained rare classical works on agriculture and mathematics as well as more conventional texts on history and poetry. Many of the manuscripts were supplied by the Florentine bookseller Vespasiano da Bisticci, who estimated that the count spent 30,000 ducats on the project, though the quality of the copying and illumination suffered as the bookseller hurried to fulfil this lucrative commission.[43]

One of the books in the library was the first version of an architectural treatise by Francesco di Giorgio, a painter by training and an engineer by trade who would become one of the leading defence experts in late fifteenth-century Italy. The text (c.1475), dedicated to Federigo, contained a series of very precise drawings showing water mills, mining

overleaf Urbino, Palazzo Ducale, façade, c.1475. The defensive appearance of this façade is a reminder that Urbino was a strategic stronghold guarding the routes across the Apennines south to Rome and west to Florence.

equipment, cranes, pumps and, above all, designs relating to defence. The combination of Federigo's unparalleled knowledge of warfare and Francesco di Giorgio's technical expertise lay behind the development of innovative designs for his fortresses, which needed to be able to withstand the increasingly powerful siege guns that were being developed during this period. Under Federigo's descendants, Urbino would become the leading centre for innovation in the architecture of defence (see Chapter 7).

Federigo had come a long way since becoming Count of Urbino in 1444. Wealthy and powerful, with a reputation both as a formidable soldier and an astute politician, he would celebrate his fiftieth birthday in 1472, old age for a Renaissance prince. However, he still coveted one supreme ambition: the title of duke that had been enjoyed by his predecessor and that no pope, not even the indulgent Pius II, had been prepared to grant him.

News of the election of a new pope in August 1471 was greeted with enthusiasm across Italy – not least Urbino and Naples. Sixtus IV was an unusual choice: ex-minister-general of the Franciscan order with a reputation for morality and widely respected for his theological learning (these details are worth remembering, in view of later developments), he came from Liguria and had links with Milan but was otherwise a complete outsider at the papal court. Initially at least, he was disposed to grant favours to all Italy's rulers: 'This pope evidently wants to get on with everyone,' reported the Mantuan envoy in early September.[44] Within weeks there was evidence that the pope intended to grant substantial favours to Ferrante I. The king's fifteen-year-old son Giovanni was given the prestigious abbey of Montecassino and, following the precedent set by Marquis Ludovico Gonzaga a decade earlier (see Chapter 3), he would soon receive a red hat. The pope also cancelled the financial tribute due each year from Naples and even cancelled all Ferrante I's debts to the papacy.

The Naples–Rome alliance was celebrated very publicly at the papal court in June 1473 with a stupendous reception given to Ferrante's daughter Eleonora, who was on her way to Ferrara to marry Duke Ercole d'Este. Spending several days as the guest of the pope's nephew

athenoc

tyuoni le grand?

eneas

achilles

Dyomedes

thelamoala

PO
PUNIPS·TER

achilles

Interunt hnoinem achilles + Jagittarius fortiter certant

Cardinal Pietro Riario, she was showered with priceless gifts of jewels, silver and costly fabrics by the pope and his court: her seven ladies-in-waiting were given a diamond each.[45] The highlight of the visit was the banquet hosted by the cardinal, which was lavish in the extreme and was soon a byword for opulence.[46] Among the forty-four dishes served were a whole stag, suckling pigs, goats, capons, geese, roast eels and sturgeon; capons decorated with gilded pomegranate seeds; more capons in aspic in the pattern of the cardinal's coat-of-arms, which Eleonora much admired; sugar sculptures representing the Labours of Hercules – a direct allusion to her husband, Duke Ercole – and a 'ballet danced by five men and nine ladies during which some centaurs arrived and fought a delightful battle and were sent away by Hercules'. The banquet lasted six hours, with frequent breaks between the service of food with bowls of scented waters for the diners to rinse their hands or to listen to talented musicians and singers perform pieces inspired by classical mythology.

Sixtus IV, aware of the enmity between Naples and Milan, took care to balance his favours to both rulers. At one level he urged these old enemies to harmonize relations, though their rivalry continued to simmer just below the surface: in Naples, for example, the Milanese courtiers of Ippolita Sforza, Duchess of Calabria, were not popular at court, where their apparent loyalty to her family was the source of frequent rows between the duchess and her husband.[47] Behind the political bargaining, however, lay Sixtus IV's plans to install his family in Italy's ruling elite, much as Pius II had done but on a far grander scale.

Within months of the election Sixtus IV had given red hats to two nephews, Pietro Riario and Giuliano della Rovere. Thanks to their uncle's influence, both were Franciscan friars, though neither of them showed evidence of this: Giuliano, the future Julius II, acquired a mistress soon after his red hat, while Pietro, whose extravagance was legendary, died in January 1474 having spent 300,000 ducats in little over two years and built up debts of 60,000 ducats.[48] Three other nephews were destined for secular careers, for which the pope now sought the help of both Ferrante I and Duke Galeazzo Maria. Ferrante I agreed to the betrothal of Lionardo della Rovere to one of his illegitimate daughters and made his new son-in-law the Duke of Sora – and when Lionardo died without an heir in 1475, the title passed to his cousin, the fourteen-year-old Giovanni della Rovere, younger brother of Cardinal Giuliano. Meanwhile Cardinal Pietro was sent to Milan to negotiate a position for his brother Girolamo Riario. A grocer before Sixtus IV's election and his uncle's favourite after the death of Pietro, Girolamo was made Count of Bosco, a title bought from Duke Galeazzo Maria for 16,000 ducats in a transaction that was to be kept 'very secret', and the following year he was betrothed to the duke's illegitimate daughter Caterina – she was just ten, he was thirty.[49]

To finance his dynastic ambitions Sixtus IV hoped to rely on his banker Lorenzo de' Medici, and he oiled the machinery of their relationship with several significant favours. The twenty-two-year-old arrived in Rome as Florentine ambassador for the papal coronation, and he was welcomed by Sixtus IV, who bestowed many favours on Lorenzo and his family, including plenary indulgences (the forgiveness of all sins) and gave him valuable antiques from the papal collection, including a priceless cameo, the Tazza Farnese.[50] Lorenzo's relations with Ferrante I were not especially cordial – Naples had regularly provided a haven for enemies of the Medici over the past decades – but he had close ties to Count Federigo, who was not only his godfather but had also led the Florentine armies on several occasions. When Lorenzo's first son was born in February 1472 Count Federigo, whose wife had finally borne him a son a month earlier, sent a letter to congratulate him: 'Tell your wife she has done much better than my wife who made eight girls before she made my son.'[51] Later that year Lorenzo had the count appointed to lead the Florentine army in putting down an anti-Medicean rebellion in Volterra; it took twenty-five days of bombardment before the city was forced to capitulate. The victorious Federigo failed to stop his 5,000 soldiers indulging in twelve hours of vicious looting, rape and murder – Federigo himself acquired a valuable polyglot bible during the sack, which he placed in his own library.[52] Afterwards the count gave valuable advice to a government committee in Florence on building a fortress to deter further rebellion and he was rewarded for his victory by Lorenzo with a beautiful silver helmet, ornamented with the figure of Hercules triumphing over a griffon, the emblem of Volterra.[53] Relations between Florence and Rome were still cordial in July 1473 when Lorenzo agreed to the appointment of Cardinal Pietro Riario as Archbishop of Florence, staging lavish ceremonies to welcome the cardinal to his benefice the following month.

However, Sixtus IV's plans were upset in May 1473 when news arrived that Duke Galeazzo Maria had arranged with Lorenzo de' Medici to sell the papal fief of Imola to the Florentines for 100,000 ducats.[54] The pope objected to this extension of Florentine power across the Apennines and refused his consent. Moreover, he then persuaded Galeazzo Maria to accept the much lower figure of 40,000 ducats to install his nephew Girolamo Riario (the duke's son-in-law) as ruler, and asked his bankers to raise the necessary funds. Unfortunately Lorenzo put his personal feelings before business sense and, insulted by the way he had been treated, refused to agree to the loan – it was a decision that was to have major repercussions. The pope was furious and, to punish Lorenzo he turned to the Medici's rivals, the Pazzi, whose bank was happy to make the loan.

It was now Count Federigo's turn to benefit from Sixtus IV's machinations and make an alliance with the pope. That May he was in Rome as a guest of Cardinal Giuliano della Rovere at his grandiose palace attached to Santi Apostoli and it was noticed that the count had been conspicuously honoured by the papal master of ceremonies at a service; he had been assigned 'a place in the chapel on the benches of the College of Cardinals, so that he sat immediately below the last cardinal, an honour hitherto reserved for the eldest sons of kings'.[55] The reason behind this apparent rise in social status was evident when Federigo returned to Rome that summer: on 21 August he was installed as Duke of Urbino in the majestic setting of St Peter's, built by Emperor Constantine in the fourth century. It was the title he had coveted since succeeding to power in 1444 – and the first of several signs that marked the growing status of the Montefeltro family. The next day his daughter Giovanna was betrothed to the pope's nephew Giovanni della Rovere. In early September he was in Naples where, dressed in a scarlet satin mantle lined with ermine, he was installed as a Knight of the Ermine by Ferrante I in the chapel royal in Castel Nuovo, in gratitude for his help in countering the Angevin threat. More remarkably, later that month Federigo was also invested as a Knight of the Garter by representatives of Edward IV of England, an honour apparently given in recognition of his military reputation.

It should come as no surprise that Federigo was inordinately proud of his new status. He made sure that it was conspicuously on show throughout his new palace, where the windows in the courtyard and the mantelpieces around the fireplaces in the reception rooms upstairs were all emblazoned with the letters FE DUX (Federigo, Duke). It is also a striking fact that his taste for commissioning portraits of himself dates from after his nomination as duke in 1474, and they were filled with allusions to his elevated status. The various aspects of the ducal image were all on display in a portrait of Federigo and his son Guidobaldo, painted by the court artist Joos van Ghent: the talented soldier, dressed in armour with his helmet on the ground; the successful statesman, honoured with the gold chain of the Order of the Ermine hanging round his neck and the ermine-lined scarlet satin robe given to him by Ferrante I, while the badge of Edward IV's Order of the Garter was tied at his left knee; and the erudite scholar, reading from a leather-bound manuscript. Moreover, this dynastic double-portrait type was a major iconographic innovation of the period, depicting the founder of a new dynasty with its future, the young Guidobaldo, holding the ducal sceptre given to Federigo by Sixtus IV.[56]

Inside the palace Federigo started work on his exquisite *studiolo* around 1475, arguably the single most expensive room in the place and widely recognized as one of the jewels of Renaissance art. Measuring just 11.5 by 11.5 feet, its gilded coffered ceiling was studded with Federigo's devices and its walls were covered in intarsia panels, beautifully inlaid in wood in various shades of brown – walnut, spindlewood, pear and dark bog oak – to create a fictive study, with latticed cupboards, piles of books, musical instruments, an astrolabe, a basket of fruit, a parrot in a cage, a chessboard and a delightful little squirrel cracking a nut on a terrace with a view of the Apennines beyond. Above the intarsia were a series of portraits of famous men, including biblical figures such as Moses and Solomon; the philosophers of the ancient world, Plato and Aristotle; the fathers of the early Christian church, including St Ambrose and St Augustine, and the medieval heroes Dante and St Thomas Aquinas. And Federigo included the two popes who had played such as important role in his career to date: Pius II and Sixtus IV.

The year 1474 also marked the start of a dramatic downturn in relations between the pope and Lorenzo de' Medici. In July, to punish the

banker further for refusing to loan the money he needed to buy Imola for his nephew Girolamo Riario, Sixtus IV moved the lucrative papal account to the Pazzi bank. And, having inflicted a certain amount of financial hardship, he now began to undermine Lorenzo's political authority. In October 1474 he named Francesco Salviati, a cousin of the Pazzi, as Archbishop of Pisa, an appointment that Lorenzo refused to ratify. The relationship between the two leaders continued to deteriorate. That October the Florentines refused to pay the arrears of wages due to Duke Federigo, now overtly an ally of the pope; in December, when Lorenzo asked Federigo to lend him a favourite horse for a joust, the duke replied that he was unable to oblige because he had already loaned the charger in question to the Pazzi.[57] Meanwhile Ferrante too was showing signs of favouring enemies of the Medici, not least Florence's traditional rival, Siena; he also arranged the appointment of a member of the Pazzi family to the Neapolitan see of Sarno. Lorenzo was aware of the rift and its source: writing to Duke Galeazzo Maria he blamed the worsening situation on the Pazzi, who 'have been puffed up by his Majesty King Ferrante and the Duke of Urbino and are seeking to hurt me as much as they can'.[58]

In this increasingly hostile atmosphere, it was also evident that relations between Italy's major powers had begun to deteriorate. Duke Galeazzo Maria, in particular, distrusted the alliance developing between his own protégé Sixtus IV and the King of Naples – this was particularly galling as it had been the duke who had supported the pope's election in the first place. In November 1474 he signed an alliance with Lorenzo de' Medici (formally, with Florence) and Venice, inviting Sixtus IV to join the league. But the pope refused and summoned his own allies, Ferrante I and Federigo da Montefeltro, to Rome to discuss the situation. The year 1475 was a jubilee in Rome so the visits of the king and the duke were easily disguised as pious pilgrimages. Nevertheless, Sixtus IV went out of his way to show favour to Ferrante I by sending his nephew, Cardinal Giuliano della Rovere, and Rodrigo Borgia, the influential vice-chancellor, to the borders of the Papal States to escort the king to Rome. Ferrante was not intending to devote his time to piety; according to a contemporary witness, he brought so many falcons with him that the city's owl population vanished.[59] And for Duke Federigo there was not only the post of captain-general of the papal army but also the signal favour of the Golden Rose, a gilded

Urbino, Palazzo Ducale, studiolo, 1476. Designed to display Federigo's interest in learning, these fictive panels of intarsia woodwork show cupboards filled with books and scientific instruments.

spray of roses studded with precious jewels given by the pope each year during Lent in recognition of services to the church.

The church, all three rulers agreed, would form an alliance with Naples and Urbino against Milan, Florence and Venice. And Sixtus IV voiced his disapproval of Lorenzo's pretensions to power: 'We have to use our irons to help him see that he is a citizen and that we are the pope because it has thus pleased God.'[60] The precarious balance of power had shifted, and this came into sharper focus in December 1476 when Duke Galeazzo Maria, Lorenzo's closest ally, was assassinated, leaving the duchy in the hands of his widow Bona of Savoy acting as regent for their seven-year-old son Giangaleazzo (see Chapter 5). The pope is reported to have exclaimed 'The peace of Italy is at an end!' when he heard the news.[61] Prophetic words indeed.

Within a year the desire to humiliate the Medici had evolved into a conspiracy to force regime change in Florence and to murder the banker. The exact timescale of this is unclear: the plotting of such a sensational event was inevitably shrouded in secrecy. Much of what we know comes from the confession of Giovanni Battista, Count of Montesecco, a soldier of the Vatican guard – the confession, although extracted under torture by the Florentines, rings true and has been confirmed by other sources. Invited to a secret meeting in the Vatican with Francesco de' Pazzi, the head of the Rome branch of the Pazzi bank, and his cousin Francesco Salviati, Archbishop of Pisa, Montesecco was made to swear a vow of secrecy and then asked for his help in overthrowing the Medici regime. It was a conspiracy that involved the top echelons of power, notably Sixtus IV's nephew Girolamo Riario, Count of Imola: 'How could we get up to something like this without the Count's consent?', they reassured him.[62]

Indeed, Riario had the strongest reason for wanting regime change in Florence: he had made an enemy of Lorenzo, who had not only the will but also the political influence to deprive him of Imola after the death of his uncle. It was Riario who made the true extent of the plot clear to Montesecco: 'To cut Lorenzo and Giuliano to pieces, and to have soldiers ready to go into Florence.'[63] It would be Montesecco's job to lead these soldiers into the city to support the opponents of the Medici who, Riario and the Pazzi assumed, would rise up against the tyrants. Montesecco was apprehensive: 'Will all this please the Holy Father?' he asked. 'His Holiness hates Lorenzo, he wants this more than anyone else,' was the reply.[64] Later, Montesecco had an audience with Sixtus IV, at which the pope admitted to disliking Lorenzo and to wishing for a change of government in Florence, but he was absolutely insistent that he did not want anyone to be killed. A letter, in code, to Duke Federigo from his agent in Rome dated 6 February 1478 shows that, although the plans were well underway, Montesecco was having doubts: 'The Count [Riario] is uncertain about two things, one whether he agrees to the involvement of Montesecco who is very reluctant... the other whether to change the date to a day earlier'.[65]

Montesecco overcame his doubts and on 26 April, during Mass in Florence cathedral, Francesco de' Pazzi and two priests armed with daggers viciously attacked Lorenzo, who miraculously escaped, although his brother Giuliano was killed. And the plan to force regime change failed because the plotters had overestimated the level of anti-Medici sentiment in the city, where there was no appetite for a popular uprising.

Two days later the Milanese ambassador reported that the Venetian government 'is convinced, and says so in public, that King Ferrante has led this business of killing Lorenzo de' Medici through Count Girolamo Riario... and the duke [Federigo] is tightly linked to the king'.[66] The rewards for both men were clear: for Ferrante I the prize was acquiring ports on the coast of southern Tuscany, and even the city of Siena itself; for Federigo it was the price he was prepared to pay for loyalty to the king and gratitude to the pope for his coveted rank of duke. The Venetians were also convinced 'that the pope himself has agreed to it all', though whether Sixtus IV was actually complicit in the murder is open to debate – what is certain is that both Ferrante I and Federigo, as the king's chief military advisor, knew exactly what was being planned, even if they did not participate directly in the violence. Their responsibility was planning the war that would follow the assassinations, a war which did go ahead despite the failure of the coup.

The Florentines were quick to incriminate both Sixtus IV and Count Girolamo, and on 4 May they published Montesecco's confession as proof; remarkably, they redacted all references to the involvement of either Ferrante I or Duke Federigo, presumably to leave a loophole for future diplomatic efforts to negotiate peace. However, scholars at work in the archives have been able to fill in the gaps, and have unearthed evidence to show how Federigo contrived to hide his plans from the notoriously suspicious Lorenzo. As early as the autumn of 1477 Lorenzo was informed that the duke had sent Neapolitan soldiers into southern Tuscany: 'Five squadrons of the king's men have gone to the Maremma at the request of the Duke of Urbino.'[67] The duke could not hide the troop movements, so he pretended to change sides and made secret overtures to Milan to arrange a *condotta* for the following year, but then delayed signing the papers.[68] In December he suffered a wound to his leg, which affected his fitness to fight – according to a Mantuan envoy, he was 'badly cut in four or five places'; that same month Federigo's agent in Rome was informed that, on the contrary, the duke was in excellent health.[69] As the Milanese ambassador reported after the coup, the reasons behind 'the duke's pretended delay in signing the contract' were now abundantly clear.[70]

What took place in Florence on 26 April 1478 shocked all Europe. Within hours twenty corpses were dangling from the walls of the palace of the town hall, including Francesco de' Pazzi and Archbishop Francesco Salviati together with many of their relations and associates, while the two priests were found a few days later hiding in a monastery. Also hanged were the chaplains and boy sopranos belonging to the household of Sixtus IV's great-nephew, Cardinal Raffaello Riario, who had been attending Mass in the cathedral; a week short of his seventeenth birthday, he had been a cardinal for less than five months and was on his way to Rome to receive his red hat. As we have seen, Sixtus IV reacted robustly – some might say, overreacted – accusing the Florentines in general, and Lorenzo de' Medici in particular, of sacrilege, the brutal murder of churchmen and of the violation of ecclesiastical immunity, ending with the menacing threat that if Lorenzo were not sent to Rome for trial then the city would be placed under an interdict. Ferrante I sent envoys to Florence asking the government to banish Lorenzo or face outright war. The government ignored both requests.

Fighting started in early July when Duke Federigo and the papal army crossed into Florentine territory, armed with artillery pieces called Cruel, Desperate, Victory, Ruin and other warlike nicknames.[71] He was soon joined by Alfonso of Calabria and his Neapolitan troops and the two armies marched north unhindered. By August they had laid siege to Castellina and advanced to within 20 miles of the city walls before fighting stopped for the winter. The following April Sixtus IV offered to lift the interdict if Florence accepted his terms, but again his offer was rejected. The tide turned against Florence in early September 1479 when Alfonso of Calabria won a famous victory at Poggio Imperiale. With them on the battlefield was Francesco di Giorgio, Duke Federigo's fortifications expert, who earned an extra 3 ducats for a painting of the battle, which Alfonso sent to his father in Naples.[72]

By now the war had begun to cause real hardship in Florence – and it was Ferrante I, whose coffers had been almost emptied by the cost of the war, who gave the Medici the escape clause they so badly needed. The king, in search of allies wherever he could find them, had been a long-standing supporter of Ludovico Sforza, who that autumn had seized control of the regency council in Milan (see Chapter 5). Ferrante I informed him that he was willing to consider negotiating a separate peace with Florence and on 12 November Ludovico passed this information on to Lorenzo's agent in Milan, advising him to act immediately. Less than a month later Lorenzo left for Naples in a royal galley and the two men negotiated a peace treaty, which they signed on 13 March 1480. Sixtus IV was furious.

That July Ferrante I faced another disaster when over 150 Turkish ships carrying 18,000 armed soldiers seized the Neapolitan city of Otranto and savagely massacred its inhabitants – the archbishop and the governor were apparently both sawn in half, and many men were taken away into slavery.[73] Of a population of 22,000, over half were tortured and killed, including 813 who were executed for refusing to convert to Islam.* This was the first occasion on which the Turks had attacked the Italian mainland, and it was a profound shock. Alfonso of Calabria and the army left for the south, while his father, desperate for cash, arranged a loan of 38,000 ducats with the Florentine banker Battista Pandolfini, giving him ninety-nine manuscripts, forty-six printed books and a quantity of jewels as security – the contract specified that Pandolfini could sell any of the collateral that had not been redeemed within a year, but Ferrante made sure he had repaid the loan in time.[74]

Sixtus IV, although furious at Ferrante's betrayal, did much to assist in the recovery of Otranto, assembling a fleet which helped oust the Turks in September 1481. The contemporary historian Sigismondo de'

---

* The 813 were declared martyrs; they were beatified in 1771 and canonized in 2013 by Pope Francis I.

Conti recorded that the pope 'would have witnessed the misfortunes and loss of his faithless ally with great indifference, had Ferrante's enemy been anyone but the Sultan'.[75] The victory was celebrated in two medals, one for Sixtus IV and the other for Alfonso of Calabria – and both, rather inappropriately, had the same image on the reverse of a nude female figure of Constancy with a quotation from Virgil: 'To spare those who have been oppressed and to destroy the proud.'[76]

The peace agreed between Ferrante I and Lorenzo in March 1480 marked a realignment of the Italian political scene with the emergence of the so-called Triple Alliance between Ferrante I, Ludovico Sforza and Lorenzo de' Medici, judiciously oiled by funds from the Medici bank. Inevitably the alliance did not find favour in Rome, where Sixtus IV was determined to punish Ferrante I for his disloyalty and Girolamo Riario, who nursed a deep hatred for Lorenzo, hoped to profit from a further period of turmoil in Italy. It would take Lorenzo another eight years to wreak his revenge on Girolamo for the murder of his brother – he was finally able to celebrate after arranging for the brutal assassination of Girolamo by the count's own subjects of Forlì.[77]

Meanwhile, in September 1481 Girolamo arrived in Venice to negotiate an alliance with the republic – though he did nothing for his popularity in the city by failing to tip either the oarsmen of the state *bucintoro* which had ferried him across the lagoon, or the servants in the guests quarters of the ducal palace.[78] The league between the two states was ostensibly designed to secure the count's hold on Imola, as well as the much more prestigious fief of Forlì, which the pope had recently confiscated from its previous owners and given to his favourite nephew. In private, however, Sixtus IV and Girolamo aimed at a far more ambitious target – they wanted the assistance of the Venetian navy to seize the Neapolitan ports along the Adriatic coast, while its army was to help in the attack on the kingdom by land with the ultimate goal of ousting Ferrante from power. And in return, the pope would assist Venice in the conquest of Ferrara, where Ferrante I's daughter Eleonora was duchess. For the Venetians the prospect of acquiring control of the wealthy duchy of Ferrara was so tempting that they abandoned their usual caution, and the count returned to Rome in triumph.

Once again Italy was about to be split by war. This time Ferrante I was an ally of the Florentines and Duke Federigo was appointed as their captain-general, their involvement in the Pazzi conspiracy conveniently swept under the carpet. In late March 1482 envoys arrived in Urbino to get Federigo's signature on the contract but they had to wait until 15 April for a day to arrive that was acceptable to his astrologers.[79] War was finally declared in May; Alfonso of Calabria advanced into the Papal States at the head of his army. Unfortunately the Neapolitan army was humiliatingly defeated on 21 August by the Venetian captain-general Roberto Malatesta at the Battle of Campo Morto (the Field of Death), so named for the malaria that was endemic in this marshy area west of Rome.

News of the defeat reached Ferrara, where Duke Federigo himself was suffering from a bout of malaria. He was beset by the fear that his young son Guidobaldo, just ten years old, would lose Urbino to the victorious general Roberto Malatesta, who was not only the son of his old enemy Sigismondo but also married to his daughter (see Chapter 2) and would have no scruples about seizing Urbino in his absence.[80] Despite the danger to his health, he insisted on starting for home immediately, but before the party reached Bologna his condition had deteriorated so badly that they were forced to turn back. His half-sister Violante, the widow of Sigismondo's brother Pandolfo and now the abbess of Corpus Domini in Ferrara, left her convent to be with him on his deathbed. Federigo died in Ferrara on 10 September, racked by the fear that he had lost everything – all that he had gained from the Malatesta and all that he himself had achieved. He died not knowing that, by an extraordinary coincidence, Roberto too was fatally ill with the same disease; he died the day after his father-in-law. Federigo's coffin was taken back to Urbino, stopping each night at towns and cities en route – despite the war, his reputation was such that he was even honoured in Forlì.

In the end Guidobaldo's succession was peaceful and Urbino continued to be ruled by Duke Federigo's descendants into the seventeenth century (see Chapter 6). His heir built San Bernardino in Urbino as his father's burial place, and commissioned an altarpiece from Piero della Francesca, known as the Brera altarpiece, for the main altar of the church.[81] The painting celebrated Federigo's achievements: he was portrayed kneeling on the right of the painting, dressed in full armour

with his mangled helmet on the ground beside him – a symbol of his gratitude for his miraculous escape after his jousting accident in 1450 – and an ostrich egg hanging from the ceiling, a symbol of miraculous birth and another sign of gratitude to the Virgin, this time for the birth of his son. His own image as the ideal Renaissance prince lives on, encapsulated in an oration on his achievements delivered in 1477, which described him as 'arbitrator of Italy, defender of the Church of Rome, founder of the Latin peace, father of studies, guardian of the Italian race, you [Federigo] who can see farther with only one eye than others with the hundred eyes of Argos'.[82]

Ferrante I was not so lucky with his fate, nor with his posthumous image. When the war finally ended in August 1484, it was evident that Sixtus IV had had his revenge: although Venice did not acquire Ferrara and had to return all the ports seized from Naples, Ferrante I's coffers had been drained by the enormous expense of the war. Worse, within days of signing the peace treaty, Sixtus IV died and his successor, Innocent VIII, was from Genoa, a city with a long tradition of hostility towards Naples. Ferrante's position grew increasingly precarious. In order to raise money he increased taxes on hearths and salt by a massive 50 per cent, causing immense hardship and further antagonizing the barons who were already angry at the transfer of titles and estates to members of the royal family, or to members of nascent foreign papal dynasties; they accused Ferrante of putting pleasure before economic sense by wasting good agricultural land and using it for hunting parks; they also objected to the levies they had to pay in order to obtain royal permission for their marital alliances. Above all, they objected to Alfonso of Calabria, who was increasingly taking over the reins of power from his sixty-year-old father. A bully by nature, he exacerbated an already tense situation by unashamedly boasting that he planned to dispossess all those who held estates within a 30-mile radius of Naples and place this land directly under the control of the crown.

In October 1485 the barons rebelled again, this time with the support of Innocent VIII, sparking a civil war that Ferrante put down with the help of the armies of the Triple Alliance. In the peace treaty signed ten months later by both the king and the pope, Ferrante I agreed to pardon the rebels – but within days he reneged on his promise. Those guilty of treachery were punished without mercy; hundreds of barons, their wives and their children were thrown into the filthy

Guido Mazzoni, *Lamentation*, 1492 (Naples, Sant'Anna dei Lombardi). A detail of the eight life-size terracotta statues of the Christ and witnesses to his Crucifixion including Joseph of Arimathea, portrayed as Alfonso of Calabria.

cells in the bowels of Castel Nuovo and their property confiscated – one of the palaces was given as a present to Lorenzo de' Medici as a reward for his support.[83]

Once again, despite the lack of financial resources, the royal family celebrated its victory over the barons in Naples in a veritable orgy of building, masterminded this time not by Ferrante but by his heir. According to Joampiero Leostello, one of Alfonso's courtiers, the duke 'much enjoyed building' and 'made many poor men rich', especially 'very poor builders with four or five daughters who now found it easy to marry them off because of the money they earned being continually employed in building palaces and houses'.[84]

Alfonso of Calabria's fame as a patron rests on two elegant villas, La Duchesca and Poggioreale, both landmarks in the history of Renaissance architecture and, perhaps more illustrative of the duke's personality, decorated with scenes of his military victories. La Duchesca, built for Ippolita Sforza in the grounds of their official residence Castel Capuano, was ornamented with a charming fountain featuring a statue of Parthenope, the mythical founder of Naples, with water spouting from her nipples into the mouths of *putti* who then urinated it back into the fountain basin. In 1490 Alfonso converted a nearby nunnery into a memorial chapel for the martyrs of Otranto, moving the nuns elsewhere, and deposited ten cases of their bones in the chapel.[85] Much grander was the elegant Doric suburban villa at Poggioreale, just outside the city walls. With its sunken amphitheatre for theatrical performances and beautiful gardens with views of Vesuvius in the distance, it was a favourite venue for parties, music and evening dinner parties under the stars. He also planned an enormous office block in Naples, the Palazzo dei Tribunali, to house the departments of government which, with a ground plan covering over 500 feet square, would have been the largest civic building in Renaissance Italy. The project would have revealed much about Alfonso's belief in the status and power of the Aragonese dynasty; it is perhaps symbolic that it was never built.[86]

Alfonso's desire to display his royal status with due grandeur and magnificence cloaked the depressing reality that Naples and the Aragon dynasty were in terminal decline. The storm clouds were gathering. Ferrante I died suddenly on 25 January 1494 at the age of seventy. A pivotal figure in Italian politics since the 1450s and the latter years of his father's reign, he had survived two serious attacks on his throne, due in large part to his political skills. Unlike Federigo da Montefeltro, whose image as talented soldier, skilful statesman and erudite patron of the arts has endured, Ferrante's reputation has not. Even at the time there was no great outpouring of sadness at the death of this ruler who had dominated the political stage for decades. He died unshriven, according to Johannes Burchard, the papal master of ceremonies, 'without the light of grace, without the cross and without God'.[87] In Ferrara it was reported that Duke Ercole's father-in-law had sunk into a severe depression 'after hearing that King Charles of France was about to invade Italy with a great army to seize his throne' (see Chapter 5).[88]

When Alfonso of Calabria, now Alfonso II, heard the news, he 'boasted that he would fight with the king of the French in open battle... and more grandly... that he would not hide himself in a narrow pass or in some den in the woods after the manner of lowly beasts'.[89] Despite his swaggering manner, however, the new king was unable to face the reality of a French army at the borders of his realm and he abdicated on 23 January 1495 before sailing off to Sicily. His successor, his twenty-six-year-old son Ferrante II, put up little defence against the French and bided his time: the French army departed in May, leaving a garrison in the heavily fortified Castel Nuovo – and they too were driven out in November after the engineer Francesco di Giorgio exploded a mine in a tunnel dug under the citadel. Unfortunately Ferrante II died of sudden illness the following October, leaving the kingdom to Alfonso II's brother Federigo, Ferrante I's second son. But the political and economic problems faced by Naples, exacerbated by the instability of the Aragonese dynasty which had got through four kings in as many years, left it vulnerable. In the end it was the superior power of the monarchs of Spain, Ferdinand and Isabella, who won, and Ferdinand was able to evict the last of the illegitimate descendants of his uncle Alfonso of Aragon to seize Naples. In 1504 he installed a viceroy to rule the kingdom from Spain.

LUDOVICO SFORZA (1452–1508)
Ruler of Milan

ASCANIO SFORZA (1455–1505)
Cardinal, Ludovico's brother

GIANGALEAZZO SFORZA (1469–94)
Duke of Milan, their nephew

ISABELLA OF ARAGON (1470–1524)
Duchess of Milan, their niece

Giovanni Sforza, *Lord of Pesaro, their cousin*

Caterina Sforza, *Ruler of Forlì, their cousin*

Alexander VI, *Pope*

Cesare and Lucrezia Borgia, *The pope's children*

Charles VIII and Louis XII, *Kings of France*

Leonardo da Vinci, *Designer*

NEST OF VIPERS

Ludovico Sforza, Ascanio Sforza
&
Giangaleazzo Sforza

Giangaleazzo Sforza was just seven years old when he became Duke of Milan after the assassination of his father. Duke Galeazzo Maria's death, which occurred on 26 December 1476 during the annual season of feasting and fun that lasted for the twelve days of Christmas, had been heralded by several omens – a comet blazing across the sky, ravens behaving mysteriously, and so on. His murderers made their plans around his custom of attending Mass on the Feast of St Stephen at the church of Santo Stefano, where they waited, daggers hidden under their thick capes, and stopped the duke on the pretext of handing him a petition before stabbing him in the groin and the stomach. The thirty-two-year-old duke was dead before anyone could react.

Galeazzo Maria had not been popular. His widow Bona of Savoy worried that he had died unshriven and asked the pope to absolve him of his crimes – he had been, she listed:

> Versed in warfare, both lawful and unlawful; in pillage, robbery and devastation of the country; in extortion of subjects; in negligence of justice; in injustice knowingly committeed; in the imposition of new taxes which even included the clergy; in carnal vices; in notorious and scandalous simony and in various and innumerable other crimes.[1]

The assassins, three disgruntled patriots who had been inspired by the murders of tyrants in the ancient world, failed to destroy the authority which the Sforza dynasty exercised over the duchy of Milan. Giangaleazzo, who had been named after his great-grandfather Giangaleazzo Visconti, the first Duke of Milan, had a younger brother, Ermes (aged six), and two sisters, Bianca (five) and Anna (six months), as well as several illegitimate siblings. It was the new duke's misfortune that he also had five uncles, all sons of the adventurous *condottiere* Francesco Sforza, who had used his military talents to seize the duchy of Milan in 1450: Filippo (aged twenty-seven), Sforza (twenty-five), Ludovico (twenty-four), Ascanio (twenty-one) and Ottaviano (eighteen). More than one of them had inherited their father's courage and ambition.

This is the tragic story of the young duke and his villainous uncles – and of how they comprehensively destroyed the Sforza dynasty and its reputation for good government that had been so carefully built up by Duke Francesco. They were indeed a nest of vipers, the writhing snake that embellished the family coat-of-arms emblazoned on buildings throughout the duchy.

Later on the day of Galeazzo Maria's assassination, ducal authority transferred seamlessly to the regency council, which now proclaimed Giangaleazzo as duke with his mother Bona of Savoy as regent. Real power, however, lay in the hands of Cicco Simonetta, the able head of the ducal chancery and loyal right-hand man to both Francesco and Galeazzo Maria. It was Simonetta who decided to continue the dead duke's policy of barring his brothers from power and they were now also excluded from the regency council. While Filippo, the eldest, seems to have been content to live a quiet life in the duchy, and Ottaviano drowned in an accident in 1477, the other three all showed signs of sedition which Simonetta was quick to silence. Sforza, who had been made Duke of Bari in 1465 by Ferrante I, was exiled to his Neapolitan estates; Ludovico, who had already been caught in June 1476 plotting with Sforza to assassinate their eldest brother and had been exiled to France, was now sent to Pisa where he spent several idle years hunting. Ascanio was destined for a career in the church. At the age of ten had been given the abbey of Chiaravalle, the richest benefice in the duchy, by his father, and he was now sent to the university of Perugia to continue his studies, though it was soon evident that he too preferred hunting, hawking and gambling to learning.

Unfortunately, the precarious stability established by Simonetta was not destined to last. In April 1478 news of the coup to oust the Medici from Florence sent shockwaves across Italy – and nowhere more so than in Milan, Florence's closest ally. In the war that followed Simonetta remained loyal to the Medici, sending troops to aid the Florentines in their struggle against the combined armies of Sixtus IV and Naples. Sforza and Ludovico, however, seized the opportunity to side with the enemy against Simonetta and, with the assistance of Ferrante I, attacked the southern borders of Milan. The regency council declared them both rebels but they continued to receive support from the king, and when Sforza died unexpectedly in August 1479 the king transferred the duchy of Bari to Ludovico. A month later Ludovico forced Bona of Savoy's hand and returned in triumph to Milan – and that autumn he deftly outmanoeuvred both Bona of Savoy and Simonetta to seize control of the regency council. By November he had made his first decisive interference in Italian politics, infuriating Sixtus IV by brokering peace between Ferrante I and Lorenzo de' Medici (see Chapter 4).

Simonetta certainly knew what was in store: 'Most illustrious Duchess,' he informed Bona of Savoy, 'I shall lose my head and you, before long, will lose the state.'[2] Simonetta was imprisoned, his properties confiscated, and Ludovico executed him on 30 October 1480, a cruel end for an elderly man whose entire career had been devoted to the loyal service of the Sforza family. Ludovico now made life intolerable for Bona, separating her from her son Giangaleazzo by confining him to the inner apartments of Castello di Porta Giovia. She left Milan on 2 November 1480 but before she could cross the border into Savoy, she was detained and imprisoned at Abbiategrasso, 'deprived of our liberty and ill-treated,' she wrote in 1482, 'by that iniquitous and perfidious Lord Ludovico'.[3]

Ludovico had taken less than four years to become regent for his underage nephew and the manner in which this had been achieved betrayed a level of ruthlessness that impressed all Italy. More significantly he had established himself as the *de facto* ruler of Milan and it was not long before his name began to appear alongside that of the rightful duke in state papers. Outside Milan his status was widely recognized: in Rome the papal master of ceremonies, Johannes Burchard, recorded an audience given by the pope to the 'ambassadors of Giangaleazzo, Duke of Milan, and of Ludovico il Moro, Duke of Bari'.[4]

Ludovico had been nicknamed 'il Moro' (the Moor) by his father on account of his dark hair, eyes and complexion. A sickly child who had grown into a strong man, he was also astute enough to exploit the advantages of his moniker. Without the title of Duke of Milan, the nickname 'il Moro' was a distinctive and unusual identifier. He used a black face in profile with a white headband as his logo on his seals and documents – and he was often accompanied by a black page, his 'living emblem', as it were.[5] Bernardo Bellincioni, Ludovico's somewhat sycophantic court poet, praised his patron's political skills as combining the craftiness of the fox, the energy of the lion and the greed of a bird of prey – though Paolo Giovio, writing around 1530 with the benefit of hindsight, sarcastically described Ludovico as 'surpassing other princes in wisdom so long as his policies, whatever they were, were not thwarted by a hostile and changeable Fortune'.[6]

Having got rid of Simonetta, he also purged the court of others who might cause trouble: Cicco's brother Giovanni, a chancery scribe and author of the official biography of Francesco Sforza, was imprisoned and Captain-General Giangiacomo Trivulzio, a member of the old Milanese nobility, was unceremoniously sacked from his post, a move Ludovico would later come to regret. Indeed, the nobility in general found themselves sidelined from power as Ludovico surrounded himself with a close circle of loyal courtiers. It was soon evident that he had no intention of sharing power with anyone – above all, not with his nephew nor his younger brother. Ascanio was exiled first to Ferrara and then to Ferrante I's court at Naples, where he concocted many schemes to overthrow his brother. More suited to life as a soldier than a priest, Ascanio signed a *condotta* with Venice and was advancing on Brescia with a troop of 1,000 mounted soldiers in September 1482 when Ludovico offered him an olive branch and the two made an uneasy peace.[7] Ascanio's reward was to be a cardinal's hat, which he received in March 1484, and wealth from lucrative benefices in the duchy, which included the bishoprics of Novara and Cremona and the abbey of Sant'Ambrogio in Milan. But Ludovico made sure that his brother spent his time in Rome and it is difficult to escape the conclusion that Ascanio was effectively in exile from Milan.[8] However, as we shall see, Ascanio did not waste his time, becoming one of the most influential figures at the papal court and, in the end, an important source of support for Ludovico.

Ludovico spent lavishly on creating a court filled with artists, philosophers and poets that would provide evidence of his princely tastes, though he was less interested in music than Duke Galeazzo, whose famous chapel was largely disbanded. His poet Bernardo Bellincioni wrote a sonnet in praise of the four artistic stars at Ludovico's court: the historian and humanist Giorgio Merula; the goldsmith Caradosso; master Giannino, the artillery expert from Ferrara; and the Florentine artist, Leonardo da Vinci. Many – not least Bellicioni, Caradosso, Leonardo and Bramante, the architect of many of Ludovico's projects – belonged to the humanist academy in Milan, which was supported by Ludovico and consisted of an informal circle of courtiers, philosophers, musicians, poets and artists who met to debate and discuss, and on occasion, to contribute to the staging of theatrical entertainments.[9]

Il Moro himself had literary pretensions and planned to write a humanist history of the lives of famous men, including his own father. He idolized Duke Francesco, in direct contrast to Duke Galeazzo Maria, who had emphasized his Visconti heritage by adopting Visconti emblems and naming his heir Giangaleazzo after their great-grandfather, the first Visconti duke. Ludovico could hardly base his own claim to power on being the heir of the first Duke Giangaleazzo, with the second Duke Giangaleazzo alive in the Castello di Porta Giovia. But he did fancy himself as his father's rightful heir. So, when the manuscript of Giovanni Simonetta's biography of Francesco Sforza (*Francisci Sfortiae commentarii*, see Chapter 1) was found among the goods confiscated from the Simonetta brothers, Ludovico decided to publish it, with some judicious alterations.

In 1483 il Moro ordered the publication of 400 copies of the biography and this was followed by two more editions – Ludovico had several copies lavishly illuminated, with plenty of Moorish profiles ornamenting the margins.[10] Importantly, all three editions were prefaced by a eulogy on Ludovico's own talents, providing evidence that il Moro was the true heir to Duke Francesco's military and political skills. A similarily blatant gesture was Ludovico's plan to erect a 24 ft-high equestrian monument to his father, showing the duke astride a rearing horse. On 22 July 1489 it was reported that Ludovico was planning 'a grand tomb for his father and has already ordered Leonardo da Vinci to make the model, that is Duke Francesco in armour astride a colossal bronze horse', but this technically ambitous project was never cast.[11]

Leonardo, who became Ludovico's principal court artist, engineered his move to Milan largely as a result of his skills as a military designer. In a letter dated around 1486, he set out what skills he could offer, listing the ability to design portable bridges, siege machinery, naval weapons, mines, mortars and cannon before adding that 'in peace time I believe I can give the greatest satisfaction… in public and private buildings'.[12] He would have known the importance Ludovico attached to defence: 'Fortresses and soldiers,' il Moro wrote, are 'the most important things, for in these two lie the strength and conservation of states.'[13] Ludovico's agent in Florence also recommended the best

Leonardo da Vinci, study of a rearing horse, *c.*1485 (Royal Collection).
An early study for the bronze equestrian monument of
Francesco Sforza, showing him trampling a fallen enemy.

painters available in the city, who included Botticelli, Filippino Lippi, Perugino and Ghirlandaio, but it seems that none of them was to his taste. The other key artistic figure at Ludovico's court was the architect Donato Bramante, whose knowledge of Alberti's buildings in Rimini, Ferrara and Mantua had inspired his interest in the architectural language of classical antiquity.

Like his father, Ludovico understood the important role played by art and architecture in the creation of an image of power and authority. He made a point of continuing Duke Francesco's projects, notably the Duomo in Milan, the church of San Sigismondo in Cremona and the Cerosa, the Carthusian monastery at Pavia. For his own projects, however, he abandoned his father's preference for traditional Gothic in favour of the new fashion for *all'antica* design. Ludovico, who had more need than most Renaissance princes to assert his own authority, chose to adopt the image of imperial Rome to give visual expression to his status. And, although his book-keepers were careful to record transactions in the name of Duke Giangaleazzo, it was Ludovico's own name that was conspicuous in the inscriptions that were prominently placed on all his projects.

Ludovico started campaigns of urban renewal in all the major towns of the duchy. In Milan he removed porticoes and other obstructions, issued laws to encourage uniform heights for housing, and demolished buildings to create imposing squares in front of the Castello di Porta Giovia and the Duomo.[14] At Santa Maria presso San Satiro, where there was no space for a proper apse at the east end, Bramante faked one with a *trompe l'oeil* coffered barrel vault, inspired by ancient Roman prototypes. At the ancient basilica of Sant'Ambrogio, dedicated to St Ambrose, Milan's patron saint, Ludovico and Cardinal Ascanio enlarged the monastery, commissioning Bramante to design a Corinthian Canonica and two cloisters, one Ionic and the other Doric. Cardinal Ascanio too contributed to work on a new cathedral for Pavia, and Bramante based the design for the vaults for the crypt of this building on those he had seen in Emperor Hadrian's villa at Tivoli.[15] More privately, Leonardo frescoed a room at the Castello di Porta Giovia in imitation of an *al fresco* bower, based on literary descriptions of rooms in the imperial palaces of ancient Rome.

The new style was amply evident in Ludovico's most important project, the transformation of the small town of Vigevano – though

Milan, Santa Maria presso San Satiro, choir, begun 1478. Designed by Donato Bramante, this fictive coffered barrel-vaulted apse was commissioned to house a miracle-working painting of the Virgin.

his hopes that the pope would grant it civic status were not fulfilled, despite Cardinal Ascanio's lobbying at Rome. Ludovico was very fond of the area and its Visconti castle, where, it was noted, 'he much enjoyed staying not only for the healthy air but also for the hunting of all sorts of animals and birds'.[16] He invested heavily in the local economy, building new canals and making innovations to the agriculture of the area, notably mulberry trees, rice paddies and new breeds of sheep. He made sure that his enterprise was profitable by granting himself the privilege of not having to pay the customary tolls charged on all goods entering Milan and Pavia.[17] He remodelled the old Visconti castle into a luxurious villa, where he spent most of his time, with apartments for himself, his family and guests, grand reception rooms, gardens, a labyrinth, fishponds and dovecotes, an enormous mews for his falcons and stables for his horses, including those he bred for racing. And he transformed the old merchants' square into an enormous *all'antica* forum, surrounded by elegant arcades: it was, according to his own proclamation of 3 May 1492, 'to be grand enough to be suitable for the greatness and dignity of a prince'.[18]

Meanwhile Duke Giangaleazzo was inexorably approaching his majority but Ludovico was deliberately vague about the point at which this would be declared and kept him out of sight, under guard in the innermost fort of the Castello di Porta Giovia, officially to protect him from assassination. However, the situation was not entirely under il Moro's control. In 1472 Duke Galeazzo Maria had betrothed his three-year-old heir to his niece, Isabella of Aragon, the daughter of Alfonso, Duke of Calabria and Galeazzo Maria's sister, Ippolita. Ludovico had been obliged to confirm his nephew's betrothal to Isabella, who was the granddaughter of his ally Ferrante I, and the king had rewarded il Moro with the Order of the Ermine, another public token of the Sforza--Aragon alliance.

The wedding took place in great style in Milan in February 1489 – Giangaleazzo was now a few months short of his twentieth birthday, well past the normal age of majority for the period, and Isabella was a year younger. The city was decked out with temporary arches erected along the route, hung with traditional wedding greenery: ivy,

Vigevano, Palazzo Ducale, completed 1492. This splendid arcaded piazza adjoining the enormous ducal palace added grandeur to the modest town of Vigevano, though Sforza's attempts to give it civic status were less successful.

juniper, laurel, myrtle, which was sacred to Venus, and lemons, an emblem of fidelity.[19] In the great piazza at the Duomo was a huge arch, probably designed by Bramante, which was decorated with the deeds of Ludovico's revered father: Giangaleazzo himself described the canvases painted 'with all the victories and memorable deeds of the illustrious lord our grandfather'.[20] Surprisingly, the old hostility between Milan and Naples was also evident. The Ferrarese ambassador was not impressed by the bride, whom he thought 'dark skinned and not very pretty'.[21] And another observer noted scenes of the victories that Duke Francesco had won against Isabella's great-grandfather, Alfonso I of Naples: 'Every energetic campaign Francesco Sforza undertook against the Samnites [i.e. in southern Italy], all the brilliant operations against the Venetians and all the magnificent things he did for the Milanese.'[22]

The long weeks of wedding celebrations, which had started in Naples in December, were proving taxing for the new bride. The day after the proxy marriage at the royal court the Milanese representatives accused Ferrante I of paying part of the dowry of 100,000 ducats in underweight gold coins, very embarrassing all round.[23] On 30 December Isabella had boarded the royal galley and endured a dreadful voyage, beset by terrible winter storms, before finally arriving at Genoa on 18 January. Sick and exhausted, she had to rest before the journey to Milan. At Tortona she sat through an interminable banquet where each dish had been presented in the guise of an appropriate mythological story – Diana transforming her lover Actaeon into a stag for the venison, and so on – followed by a ballet of Orpheus and Euridice, staged by Ludovico's dancing master.[24]

On 28 January she arrived at the ducal villa at Vigevano, where she spent her first night with Giangaleazzo, but it was evident that her husband was either unwilling or unable to consummate the marriage. The Ferrarese ambassador thought that the nineteen-year-old duke was unusually immature for his age, appearing 'part boy part simpleton' because 'he fears being humiliated'.[25] And humiliated he certainly was by his uncle Ludovico, who was present as one of the official witnesses at the deflowering ceremony and had laughed derisively at his nephew's incompetence. Il Moro could be very cruel, and had evidently adopted a policy of coercive control to bully his nephew into submission.

Francesco Laurana, *Isabella of Aragon*, c.1490 (Vienna, Kunsthistorisches Museum). This unfortunate duchess was humiliated by her uncle, who seized power from her husband, poisoned him and removed her sons from her care.

Ludovico continued to intimidate Giangaleazzo and shame him in public whenever possible in the hope that his nephew would fail to sire an heir. The duke's impotence was the subject of much gossip. The court gossip at Naples was that 'the marriage could not in any way be consummated because of the illness of the most illustrious duke who is said to be wholly impotent'.[26] In Milan it was rumoured that il Moro had used witchcraft to put a spell on the couple to stop Isabella conceiving. Maybe the couple resorted to herbal remedies: Giangaleazzo's half-sister Caterina Sforza, Countess of Forlì, was the author of a book of recipes that included methods of determining virginity and how to counterfeit it (with a pessary of carnations powdered in wine), as well as cures for male impotence, which involved the use of satyrion root (orchid root), pepper and powdered lizard.[27] Isabella herself took more practical steps to redeem the situation, asking her family for help; two 'expert women' were sent from Naples to 'encourage the duchess to help the duke'.[28] As the Ferrarese ambassador judged, Isabella needed to 'make up for the duke's failings and tame him, for women must and will do anything in bed with their husbands'.[29] Remarkably, just over a year after the wedding, Isabella did become pregnant and gave birth to a son on 30 January 1491, named Francesco after Giangaleazzo's grandfather, followed by three daughters: Ippolita (born January 1493), Bona (February 1494) and Bianca (1495).

While Giangaleazzo had been a minor, Ludovico was able to present himself as protector of the boy, but this illusion became increasingly difficult to maintain as the duke grew up, and it became frankly impossible after the birth of Francesco. However, as the court poet Bellincioni cynically remarked, 'the Duke has consummated his marriage [but] il Moro is preserving his patrimony'.[30] Ludovico kept Giangaleazzo and Isabella out of the public eye as far as possible. Soon after Isabella's arrival in Milan Ludovico ordered them to move to the castle at Pavia, where they were to live on a measly allowance of 13,000 ducats a year – it was later raised to 15,000 ducats but the duchess had to justify every item of expenditure to Ludovico's treasurer in Milan. All the Neapolitans in the duchess's household were ordered to leave and were replaced with his own nominees. Isabella complained that her household was composed of 'men and women of no standing but slaves or people of little account' and that they behaved more like 'Ludovico's spies rather than her personal servants' – which, of course, they were.[31]

Criticizing Isabella's behaviour in public was another useful tool to belittle the duchess; apparently her tastes were too foreign, too indulgent (read, Neapolitan), such as her penchant for sweet drinks. But Isabella had a powerful tool of her own: her grandfather and father in Naples, King Ferrante and Alfonso of Calabria. When they demanded that Ludovico must show the duchess the respect that was her due, he responded by hosting a splendid party for the couple, the so-called Festa del Paradiso, a spectacular show with a set designed by Leonardo. However, the close friendship that had seen Ferrante I aid Ludovico's rise to power back in 1479 had begun to unravel.

Meanwhile, in 1490, with Isabella visibly pregnant, Ludovico's own dynastic plans took on a greater urgency. He had been betrothed to Beatrice d'Este, the five-year-old daughter of Duke Ercole of Ferrara, in 1480 and, with his bride now aged fifteen, it was time to celebrate the wedding – it is no coincidence that the celebrations were planned for the last weeks of January 1491, the date when Isabella was due to give birth. And Ludovico enhanced the maliciousness of his decision by arranging a double wedding celebration: his own to Beatrice and also that of Giangaleazzo's younger sister Anna to Beatrice's brother Alfonso, heir to Ferrara. Giangaleazzo and Isabella did not attend the lavish banquets, theatrical performances and other entertainments, which included a tournament at which one of il Moro's courtiers entered the lists with a team of twelve blacked-up 'moors' as a tribute to the groom.[32] One of the highlights was a visit to the ducal treasury, kept in the keep of Castello di Porta Giovia, where the guests marvelled at 'hundreds of thousands of gold ducats... indeed it was commonly said that there were around 800,000 ducats... and silver vessels, statues, jewels and gold medals'.[33]

By all accounts Beatrice was pretty and loved dancing, but she seems also to have been a very determined young lady with no intention of tolerating any rival, certainly not Isabella. The duchess was only five years older than the new bride – and, moreover, the two women were first cousins, the daughters of Alfonso of Calabria and Eleonora of Aragon – but their relationship grew increasingly acrimonious after Isabella gave birth to Francesco. Beatrice also had to cope with Ludovico's young mistress, Cecilia Gallerani, whose lovely portrait painted by Leonardo around 1490, when she was seventeen years old, makes a fascinating study in Renaissance iconography.[34]

Leonardo portrayed Cecilia holding an ermine, a weasel in its winter dress and a familiar symbol of purity. But there were other messages in the painting. The ermine could be a play on her name – the ancient Greek name for weasels was *galée*. Equally, the animal could refer to Ludovico, who was a member of the Neapolitan chivalric Order of the Ermine, making the portrait a very overt celebration of their relationship. Importantly, scholars have also interpreted the ermine as a symbol of pregnancy and we know that Cecilia bore Ludovico a son, Cesare, in May 1491, just months after his marriage to Beatrice. Although Ludovico sent Cecilia away from court, he did formally recognize her son and she continued as his mistress for several more years.

Meanwhile Cardinal Ascanio was using his 'enforced exile' at the papal court to good use. With a talent for politics, he had become an influential figure in the College of Cardinals. Choosing to oppose Innocent VIII's decision to back the Barons' Revolt against Ferrante I, he developed a close relationship with another pro-Aragon cardinal, the powerful vice-chancellor Rodrigo Borgia – though this policy earned them both, and Ludovico, the bitter enmity of Cardinal Giuliano della Rovere, their chief rival in the college. With a large income of 50–60,000 ducats a year , including a generous allowance of 13,500 ducats from the ducal treasury in Milan, Ascanio was one of the richest cardinals in Rome.[35] Indulging his tastes for hunting, hawking and gaming, he owned a parrot who could recite the Credo.[36] He was a generous patron of literature, music and the arts; he wrote poetry and employed Josquin des Prez and other musicians who had lost their jobs in the ducal chapel in Milan after the assassination of Duke Galeazzo Maria. Famous for his lavish display, he was the model for the ideal princely cardinal in Paolo Cortesi's treatise, published in 1510. In June 1492, when Alfonso of Calabria's eldest son Ferrante made an official visit to Rome, the Ferrarese ambassador reported that the cardinal 'staged an almost incredible theatrical performance to honour the said prince at his palace during a banquet that lasted all day'.[37]

1492 was to prove a watershed in the history of Europe: above all, it was the year that the Genoese adventurer Christopher Columbus made his journey across the Atlantic and found a continent that radically

Leonardo da Vinci, *Lady with an Ermine*, c.1490 (Kraków, National Museum). Ludovico's mistress, the seventeen-year-old Cecilia Gallerani, is seen accompanied by an ermine, a traditional symbol of purity.

altered the Eurocentric view of the world. The year had started in dramatic fashion when Ferdinand and Isabella of Spain made their entry into Granada to celebrate their victory over the Muslims, who were now expelled from their kingdom – the urbane vice-chancellor Cardinal Rodrigo Borgia celebrated the event in Rome by staging a bullfight at his palace. That April Lorenzo de' Medici died from the complications of gout, precipitating dramatic events that would change the map of Italy. He was credited with 'restraining the outbreaks of animosity and suspicion' between Ludovico Sforza and Ferrante I by the sixteenth-century historian Francesco Guicciardini, but without his guiding hand it was not long before this old rivalry degenerated into open hostility.[38]

Two months later Innocent VIII also died; the conclave assembled in the Vatican in the stifling heat of early August to elect his successor. Ascanio was one of the three front runners, along with Giuliano della Rovere and Rodrigo Borgia. According to a report sent to Ludovico by his agent in Rome, Ascanio could rely on seven votes with another four possibles, but not enough for the sixteen necessary to achieve the two-thirds majority.[39] Giuliano della Rovere, with nine firm supporters and the backing of Charles VIII of France, was the favourite but the Ferrarese envoy thought that Ascanio was ahead of Rodrigo Borgia, whose Spanish background made him unpopular – but he warned that the lucrative benefices, notably the coveted post of vice-chancellor, that Borgia would be able to distribute if elected made him potentially a serious candidate.[40] After four days of inconclusive voting Ascanio decided to play popemaker and put all his votes behind Borgia, who was elected on 11 August as Alexander VI.

The cardinals had chosen a worldly and astute politician with thirty-six years of experience in the notoriously corrupt papal court, highly skilled in the judicious exchange of favours needed to acquire wealth and power. What few realized was the extent to which Italian politics was about to be dominated by his ambitions for his children. Alexander VI had six children living in 1492, born to a series of mistresses: Pedro Luis (born 1462) had tragically died in 1488, while Isabella (1467) and Girolama (1469) were both married into the Roman nobility; the four younger children were Cesare (aged seventeen), Juan (sixteen), Lucrezia (twelve) and Jofrè (ten). While many of the Borgia pope's predecessors had had children, they usually disguised this flaunting of the rules of celibacy behind the title of 'nephew' (the Italian word, *nipote*, can mean both nephew and grandson). What shocked many was the way Alexander VI showed off his large brood of healthy children, all of whom had been born after he had been made a cardinal – and there would be another son born six years after he became pope.

It is no coincidence that one of Alexander VI's very few artistic projects was to celebrate his family in frescoes decorating his apartments in the Vatican. To underline his Spanish ancestry, the main room contained scenes of the life of St Catherine of Alexandria, on whose feast day, 25 November, Ferdinand and Isabella had defeated the Moors at Granada in 1491. The indulgent paterfamilias had himself portrayed in full pontifical robes kneeling before the Christ of the Resurrection, while his daughter Lucrezia was portrayed as St Catherine and his sons swaggered among the extravagantly dressed figures observing the scene. Most bizarrely, given the location of the room, its ceiling was decorated with stories of the ancient Egyptian deities Isis and Osiris – Osiris's emblem was a bull, like that of the Borgia family, and this link encouraged one of the pope's humanists to trace the pope's descent from this pagan god.

Alexander VI was widely accused of achieving his election through simony – and the principal beneficiary of his largesse was Cardinal Ascanio. The papal master of ceremonies recorded in his diary that:

> It was said that to gain the votes of Ascanio and others, before the conclave opened he had sent four mules to his palace, laden with silver which, it was said, would be safer there than in his own palace, but the silver was in fact given to Ascanio to obtain his votes.[41]

There is no evidence to prove or disprove this story – but the new pope did have a lot of favours to grant and it is a fact worth recording that only five cardinals received no favours at all: Giuliano della Rovere and his four closest supporters.

The favours rolled in for Ascanio. Alexander VI gave him apartments in the Vatican, making him a palatine cardinal, an honour reserved for specially favoured courtiers. By the end of the year he had acquired more lucrative benefices, including the prestigious Hungarian bishopric of Eger, and been appointed legate to Bologna. Above all, he was now vice-chancellor of the church, the most important figure at the papal court after the pope himself. Alexander VI also gave him the

grand palace he had built in Rome, known as the Cancelleria Vecchia,* the seat of the vice-chancellor – Ascanio in turn gave his own palace to the children of his illegitimate half-sister, Caterina Sforza, whose husband Girolamo Riario, Count of Imola, had been assassinated a few years earlier.[42]

Meanwhile, in Milan, Ludovico had much to celebrate, not least his own dynastic line. On 25 January 1493 Beatrice d'Este gave birth to a son, whom they named Ercole after Beatrice's father. He was born in a suite of rooms lavishly decorated for the occasion with furnishings of gold brocade and crimson velvet in the inner keep of the Castello di Porta Giovia, appropriately sited next to the ducal treasure chamber.[43] Ludovico ensured that Beatrice was surrounded by all possible luxury and skilled attendants, as well as her mother Eleonora of Aragon – he himself would prove a devoted father, later becoming 'much distressed' that the baby 'was not very well yesterday and today as he is teething'.[44] He had taken care, however, to ensure that the birth of Ercole took pride of place – there had been no special treatment and no visitors for Duchess Isabella when she gave birth to a daughter a day or two earlier.

The proud father was also looking forward to benefitting from his brother's success, and the fruits of Ascanio's political skills were soon apparent. Within months of his election Alexander VI proposed a marriage between his daughter Lucrezia and Giovanni Sforza, Lord of Pesaro – cousin to Ludovico and Ascanio, he was the grandson of Alessandro Sforza (see Chapter 2) and his first wife had recently died in childbirth. The couple were betrothed on 2 February 1493 with a dowry of 31,000 ducats and the marriage took place in June, celebrated with much pomp in the Vatican palace.[45] The bride, who was just thirteen years old, was accompanied by 150 Roman damsels including the pope's mistress, Giulia Farnese, and her train was carried by a young African girl. Burchard, the papal master of ceremonies, recorded in his diary that the banquet in the Vatican that evening 'went on until long after midnight, with bawdy comedies and tragedies which made everyone laugh'.[46]

Another bonus for Ludovico was the news that the close relationship that Alexander VI had enjoyed with Ferrante I while a cardinal was

---

* Now the Palazzo Sforza-Cesarini.

The *Pala Sforzesca*, 1495 (Milan, Pinacoteca di Brera). Ludovico commissioned this altarpiece shortly after the birth of his second son, shown here in swaddling clothes beside his mother; the eldest son is next to his father.

now souring after the king sided against the pope in an argument with Cardinal Giuliano della Rovere. Ludovico's own relationship with Ferrante was also deteriorating. Duchess Isabella was distraught at the way in which her son, the rightful heir to the duchy, had been eclipsed by the birth of baby Ercole, and begged her father for help: 'I would rather die by my own hands than bear this yoke of tyranny and suffer in a foreign country under the eyes of my rival,' she wrote.[47] Ludovico also took offence at the behaviour of one of Ferrante I's close allies, Piero de' Medici, now *de facto* head of the Florentine republic, whose wife was a Neapolitan aristocrat loyal to the king. Ludovico detested Piero: when Piero travelled to Rome to congratulate Alexander VI on his election, il Moro was furious to see the splendour of the clothes and jewels worn by the twenty-year-old because 'it looked as if Piero wanted to compete with him and that not only did he want to be an equal of him and the other princes of Italy, but even to surpass them'.[48] Evidently il Moro was rather sensitive about his status.

In April 1493 Alexander VI, with the connivance of Ludovico and Ascanio, signed an alliance with Milan, Venice, Mantua and Ferrara against Naples and Florence. Ferrante I and Alfonso of Calabria responded to this very public league against them with a gesture designed to remind Ludovico of just how precarious was his hold on power. They intimated to Louis, Duke of Orléans, who was the legitimate great-grandson of Giangaleazzo Visconti and his first wife Isabelle of Valois, that they would support any attempt on Louis's part to oust the Sforza from Milan. Ludovico's response was characteristically aggressive – he offered his support to Charles VIII of France, should the king decide to assert his claim to the throne of Naples. As we shall see, il Moro also put other plans in place for dealing with the 'disobedience' of his nephew and niece.

Meanwhile Alexander VI's policies, not least his close ties with the Sforza brothers, were beginning to cause alarm across Europe. Ferrante I was bitterly critical of the pope: 'He cares for nothing except for the ennobling of his children by whatever means,' he explained, and 'thinks of nothing but war and devastation, and his cousins are of the same mind, all they want to do is lord it over the papacy.'[49] But the

Sforza brothers could not satisfy all Alexander VI's dynastic ambitions. The pope needed the backing of Ferdinand and Isabella to further the career of his son Juan, Duke of Gandia. In May the pope issued his famous bull *Inter caetera* which divided the New World heavily in favour of Spain; he was rewarded that August when the king agreed to the marriage of Juan and a royal princess. Under pressure from the monarchs to make up his quarrel with Ferrante I, that month Alexander VI also signed an alliance with Naples, sealed with the betrothal of Jofrè Borgia and Sancia of Aragon, the illegitimate half-sister of Duchess Isabella; and the king gave the title of Prince of Squillace and an income of 40,000 ducats a year to his new son-in-law.

To negotiate alliances with both Ludovico Sforza and Ferrante I was no mean achievement and even the Milanese envoy in Rome was impressed:

> Many people think that the pope has lost his marbles since he was elected... [but] he has managed to marry his daughter to a Sforza... and has persuaded the king to provide a wife and a state for his son – I don't think these are the achievements of a man with no brains.[50]

But to maintain the two enemies as allies was a project fraught with difficulty. Initially the pope was careful to balance his favours. The month after Jofrè's betrothal he created twelve new cardinals: one was his own son, Cesare;, and another was Alessandro Farnese, the brother of his mistress Giulia; a third, a signal favour to Milan, was Beatrice's fifteen-year-old brother, Ippolito; the other nine were nominees of the rulers of the empire, France, Spain, England, Venice, even Poland; but there was none for Naples.

Ludovico certainly understood the implications of this renewal of close ties between the Borgia pope, Spain and Naples. The Sforza and Borgia agendas were about to diverge and in view of this uncertainty, il Moro needed to take steps to acquire other powerful allies to protect his fledgling dynasty. So that summer, after the death of Emperor Frederick III, he approached Maximilian I with a view to negotiating a marriage between the new emperor and Ludovico's niece Bianca Maria, the twenty-two-year-old sister of Duke Giangaleazzo. The proxy wedding took place on 30 November 1493 in Milan cathedral, ornamented for the occasion with a triumphal arch displaying the imperial and Sforza coats-of-arms, surmounted with 'an effigy of the late Duke Francesco on horseback', probably the clay model of the statue designed by Leonardo, and 'with the imperial insignia and the coat-of-arms of my husband underneath' as Beatrice informed her sister, Isabella d'Este, Marchioness of Mantua.[51]

This very ambitious match had been an equally expensive enterprise, a prize that had cost Ludovico the enormous sum of 500,000 ducats in cash, jewels and valuables as a dowry for his niece.[52] And there were other, more sycophantic gestures: Ludovico gave the name Massimiliano to his baby son Ercole, to underline the Emperor's role as protector of the Sforza regime. And the huge size of the bride price masked the extra cash demanded by Maximilian to secure imperial confirmation of the title of duke. Maximilian had issued a brief on 5 September naming Ludovico as duke on the bizarre grounds that il Moro had been the first child born to Francesco Sforza after he had been made duke – not surprisingly, the Emperor insisted that this document must be kept secret.[53]

In a move that was more overtly hostile to Ferrante I, Ludovico also negotiated an alliance with Charles VIII of France, promising his support for the king's desire to claim the Neapolitan throne. Rumours gathered pace at the Italian courts during the autumn of 1493 that Charles VIII was planning to invade Italy and that his principal backer was il Moro, who had lent the king 100,000 ducats for the enterprise.[54] Alexander VI avoided taking sides but the sudden death of Ferrante I in January 1494 forced him to take a position regarding the future of Naples – should he recognize Alfonso of Calabria as Ferrante's heir or accept the claim of the French king? Cardinal Ascanio led a majority of the college in trying to persuade the pope to choose the latter course but, after eight hours of heated debate, Alexander VI decided to support the Aragon claim. He appointed a legate to crown Alfonso II in May and then to preside over the nuptials of Jofrè Borgia and the new king's illegitimate daughter, Sancia.

Relations between Cardinal Ascanio and the pope were tense but not hostile. At Mass in Santa Maria sopra Minerva on 1 April the master of ceremonies overheard the two men making a joke about the situation: 'When the pope is in concord with the King of Naples he hears Mass celebrated by the Bishop of Concordia,' remarked the cardinal; to which the pope replied 'when there is peace between His Holiness and Ludovico Sforza he will have Mass celebrated by the

Bishop of Pace' (*pace* is Italian for 'peace' and also the Latin name of the Spanish see of Badajoz).[55]

Ludovico urgently needed to redress the balance of power and his ambassador in Rome had an ingenious suggestion: 'If we can persuade Cardinal Giuliano to change sides and support France,' he explained to il Moro, in code, 'we will have created a powerful weapon against the pope' – and against Ferrante, although this was left unsaid.[56] The ruse worked: on 23 April Giuliano della Rovere left Ostia by ship for France, where he proved a reliable ally of Ludovico and Ascanio, encouraging not only the French invasion of Naples but also, in the hope of forcing the pope himself to change sides, encouraging Charles VIII to issue repeated threats to call a council to depose Alexander VI. In July Louis of Orléans met Ludovico in Alessandria to collect the first tranche of the loan of 100,000 ducats.[57] And in Rome Ascanio was assisting the war effort by assembling a force of soldiers, bowmen and cavalry to block any advance made by the Neapolitan army to attack the French troops, when they arrived.

Over the summer reports about the French army massing on the borders of Savoy became increasingly alarming – what had been rumours about an unlikely worse-case scenario suddenly became stark reality when news was confirmed that Charles VIII had assembled 30,000 troops who would march into Italy and another 10,000 to sail on a fleet of 100 ships making for the coast of Naples.[58] It was far larger than anything the Italians had seen for centuries and it crossed the Alps in late August – by the middle of September there were French galleys at the mouth of the Tiber. On 9 September Charles VIII himself arrived at Asti, where he was welcomed by il Moro, Beatrice and her father Duke Ercole.

It was Ludovico who was widely blamed for the chaos that now ensued. His decision to back the king's claim to Naples as a means of settling an old score with his enemy, and to give himself the cachet of a royal ally, had been astonishingly short-sighted – he did not seem to realize that while he could encourage the French into Italy, he was not powerful enough to rescind the invitation without help. Giovio, harking back to the golden age of the fifteenth century, commented, 'we would be flourishing brilliantly now too had not everything been disrupted in deadly disorder,' and he laid the blame on four different rulers: Ludovico, who was 'provoked by the monstrous arrogance' of Alfonso II of Naples; and Alexander VI, 'the worst of men'; also culpable were the Venetians, 'more ambitious than was fitting'.[59]

Arguably the first casualty was Duke Giangaleazzo, who had been ill for several months and, no coincidence here, receiving treatment from il Moro's doctors. When Charles VIII went to Pavia in early October to visit his cousin – their mothers, Bona and Charlotte of Savoy, were sisters – he found Isabella 'in a pitiable state because her husband is so ill and is held in this castle under guard with his son and one or two daughters', as the elderly French statesman Philippe de Commynes recorded in his diary.[60] It cannot have come as much of a surprise when Giangaleazzo died on 21 October. Although the official cause of death was given as excessive sex (immoderate coitus), a final cruel jibe from his uncle, it is evident that he died of arsenic poisoning, the doses administered by Ludovico's doctors.[61] According to the Venetian diarist Domenico Malipiero, 'the Duke Zuan Galeazzo of Milan has died of the flux but it is the general opinion that Ludovico his uncle has had him poisoned'.[62] Despite the legal rights of her three-year-old son Francesco, Isabella was powerless to enforce the succession. Within hours of Giangaleazzo's death Ludovico had himself declared duke by the privy council. A month or so later he moved Isabella and her children into the security of the Castello di Porta Giovia.

Charles VIII and his army marched through the duchy towards the Florentine border, where Piero de' Medici unwisely surrendered Pisa, Livorno and other key fortresses in return for peace. Unfortunately he had done this without the permission of the city's elected government and when he returned to Florence the next day, instead of being hailed as a hero ('peace in our time') he and his family were exiled for exceeding their proper authority. It would be another eighteen years before they could return. Meanwhile, by Christmas Florence had elected a pro-French theocratic government under the leadership of a highly charismatic but fanatical Dominican friar, Girolamo Savonarola.

In Rome Alexander VI continued his policy of loyalty to Naples, despite the urgings of Cardinal Ascanio for him to take a neutral position in the conflict. On 9 December the pope ordered the arrest of all pro-French cardinals, though Ascanio was allowed to remain in the comfort of his Vatican apartments under guard. Burchard reported that he was soon back in favour: he attended Mass in the Sistine Chapel on the third Sunday of Advent (14 December), seated to the left of the pope who 'talked to him all through the service even during the raising of the Host'.[63] Leaving his decision to the eleventh hour, Alexander VI changed tack at the very last minute and agreed to talks with Charles VIII, who entered Rome on 31 December escorted by cardinals Ascanio and Giuliano della Rovere – the French army was so enormous that it six hours to enter the city.[64]

In early January it was decided that the king was to perform a public ceremony of obedience to the pope and in return would receive red hats for two of his bishops and the right of passsage through the Papal States for his army. Alfonso II was horrified at the news – and the king, who had once boasted that he would fight Charles VIII rather than 'hide in some den in the woods like a lowly beast' promptly abdicated, leaving the throne to his son Ferrante II.[65] In retrospect he would have been better advised to be patient, and to listen to the exceptionally evasive manner with which Alexander VI was dealing with Charles VIII's requests for the pope to invest him as King of Naples.

The French left Rome on 28 January 1495, much to the relief of its citizens, who had endured weeks of looting by unruly foreign soldiers. There was little opposition to Charles VIII's march on Naples and he was 'crowned' in Naples cathedral in May, though without papal approval it was not a valid coronation. Indeed, Alexander VI had been busy on the diplomatic front during the previous four months negotiating a Holy League against Charles VIII and had the agreement of Emperor Maximilian, Ferdinand and Isabella of Spain, Venice and even Ludovico, now officially the Duke of Milan – only Florence remained staunchly pro-France, with Savonarola preaching fiery sermons that savagely attacked the pope and his policies. Unwilling to confront the league, Charles VIII left Naples immediately after the coronation. He arrived in Rome on 1 June but Alexander VI had judiciously left to avoid meeting him. The city braced itself for the arrival of the soldiers – 'more silver and valuables have been removed from the city than at any time in the last hundred years', reported Ludovico's ambassador – but the king had banned his troops from another looting spree and all remained quiet.[66] Charles VIII and his army left Italy that summer, after a fierce battle with the new league at Fornovo (see Chapter 6).

Charles VIII's invasion was a watershed moment in Italian history in several ways. His campaign to seize Naples might have failed, but the peace that followed was to be of very brief duration – as we will see, the invasion would prove just the precursor to far more dramatic political change. The invasion also marked important changes in the nature of Renaissance warfare, as larger armies equipped with new, more vicious artillery ruthlessly sacked towns and murdered their inhabitants in cold blood. As one contemporary wrote, 'this way of making war, not having been common in Italy for centuries, made everyone absolutely terrified'.[67] Charles VIII's soldiers were a professional army and, at the time, the best equipped in Europe with lighter, bronze cannon which could be carried on horse-drawn gun carriages, unlike the cumbersome iron cannon pulled by oxen that were common in Italy.[68] The Italian troops were overwhelmed – and as war got bloodier, and more deadly with full-scale battles taking the place of the attritional sieges that had characterized earlier fifteenth-century warfare, it also got more expensive.[69]

One of the less familiar legacies of this French invasion was the epidemic of syphilis that had arrived in Italy with the French troops in 1494. 'The French call it the Neapolitan pox and the Italians name it the French disease,' recorded the historian Francesco Guicciardini, 'but it is clear that it came from those islands found by Christopher Columbus.'[70] Guicciardini may have been right; there are several theories about how syphilis was brought to Europe, and this was one of them. Having arrived, it spread astonishingly quickly into the general population, and one of its many victims was Ascanio Sforza, who had a serious attack at the beginning of 1497. In 1499 the master of ceremonies had to move Cardinal Bartolomé Marti from his proper seat to one at the end of a row for Easter Mass in St Peter's, because he was suffering so badly, while Cardinal Juan Borgia was unable to appear in public for two years because of it; Bartolomeo Lunate, castellan of Castel Sant'Angelo, died of the disease in 1497.[71]

The year 1497 was an *annus horribilis* for the Sforza family, and for the Borgias as well. On 3 January Beatrice d'Este died hours after giving birth to a stillborn son; the rumour in Rome was that she had 'given birth to a monster'.[72] It was her third son – a second had been born in February 1495 and named Francesco after his grandfather, no doubt deliberately to annoy Duchess Isabella. Ludovico seems to have been

genuinely devastated by the loss of his lively wife, who was only twenty-one years old: as he explained to his sister-in-law Isabella d'Este, 'I have lost the dearest thing I have in this world.'[73] The Venetian ambassador in Milan noticed that the duke suddenly became more devout, praying twice a day at Beatrice's tomb, and he stayed in Milan all through the long, hot summer to maintain this vigil.[74] He even insisted on paying the money that a pregnant Beatrice had promised to various churches dedicated to the Virgin in return for her safe confinement, a prayer that patently not been answered.

And, in a very cruel postscript to Beatrice's untimely death, Ludovico decided to separate the elder Francesco, now six years old, from his mother, moving Isabella into another palace in Milan so that he could start to exercise control over the upbringing of the boy. Despite imperial recognition of Ludovico's position as Duke of Milan, most Milanese continued to believe that Giangaleazzo's little son was the rightful ruler. Apparently il Moro had him confined to the Castello di Porta Giovia 'because once when he went out, more than a year ago, there was a cry of "Duca, Duca", and the Duke of Milan did not like this sound and ordered that he was not to leave the castle, where he stays with his mother and lovely sisters'.[75]

Ludovico placed Beatrice's tomb in the church of Santa Maria delle Grazie, where he commissioned a magnificent marble monument from

Leonardo da Vinci, *Last Supper*, 1498 (Milan, Santa Maria delle Grazie). Commissioned by Duke Ludovico for the refectory of the convent, this fresco is widely recognized as Leonardo's masterpiece.
overleaf detail Leonardo used gestures and expressions to convey the shock at the table when Christ announced that one of them would soon betray him.

the sculptor Cristoforo Solari. It was intended as a joint burial place for himself and his wife, and was surmounted with recumbent effigies of the two of them.* In the aftermath of her death, Ludovico spent liberally on this church, which had been built by his father, demolishing the Gothic apse of the old building to create a monumental tribune for the memorial chapel, topped by a vast dome, probably designed by Bramante and inspired by both the scale and the style of the architecture of antiquity. Although his plans to update the Gothic nave and facade were never realized, he rebuilt the cloisters and sacristy of the church and, most famously, commissioned Leonardo to paint the *Last Supper* (1496–7) for the refectory. Although Leonardo's experiments with oil for this fresco were unsuccessful and the painting soon began to deteriorate, his interpretation of the subject was strikingly innovative. Set beneath lunettes ornamented with ducal emblems, the fresco does not tell the story of the invention of the Eucharist but, unusually, the much more dramatic moment at that table, 'one of you will betray me', the event that foreshadowed the Crucifixion itself.

Meanwhile in June 1497, just six months after Beatrice's death, the body of Juan Borgia, Duke of Gandia and Alexander VI's favourite son, was found floating in the Tiber. There was no doubt that he had been murdered: he had been stabbed nine times. A wood merchant had seen five men throwing the corpse into the river at night but he could not, or would not, identify any of them. The Sforzas were high on the list of suspects, Ascanio and his cousin Giovanni in particular. The cardinal had had a violent argument with the duke a few days before and had failed to attend a public consistory immediately afterwards. His palace was searched but with no result, and Alexander VI insisted his friend was innocent: 'God forbid that I should have such terrible suspicions of someone I have always loved as a brother.'[76] Suspicions about Giovanni were based on the rumour that his marriage to Lucrezia Borgia was about to be dissolved – fortunately he had been in Milan at the time, discussing the rumour with il Moro, and his brother had not left Pesaro. 'Although it is unbelievable that either of them could be guilty of such a cruel act,' Ascanio wrote to his brother, 'I am glad Giovanni has been able to prove that he and his brother are innocent.'[77] The official investigation launched in Rome ended without an arrest but,

---

* The tomb is now in the Certosa at Pavia.

despite the lack of hard evidence, popular history has ascribed the crime to Juan's elder brother, Cesare – and Juan's widow certainly believed in Cesare's guilt, commissioning an altarpiece to show him in the act of cruelly stabbing Juan to death.

The murder added lurid colour to a court that was already riddled with abuse and corruption. In 1497 Giambattista Ferrari, Alexander VI's datary, was accused of throwing away supplications as if they were 'butchers' bills'.[78] That September his private secretary Bartolomeo Florès was arrested, accused of forging bulls and letters: 'They are speaking of around 3,000 fraudulent briefs,' recorded the master of ceremonies.[79] For a very brief period after Juan's murder, a penitent pope attempted to pass measures for reform but he soon returned to his dynastic agenda. And this agenda would soon engulf all Italy – including Ludovico and Ascanio – once again in chaos.

The rumours about the marriage of Giovanni and Lucrezia Borgia were, of course, true. On 20 December 1497 Alexander VI made the dissolution public and it was evident that he had exacted a humiliating price: Giovanni was forced to declare, in writing, that he had been unable to consummate the marriage and then to return Lucrezia's dowry of 31,000 ducats. Four days later Cardinal Ascanio attended a meeting in the Vatican at which the pope announced that Cesare Borgia intended to resign his cardinal's hat, 'and the pope wants to manage this so as to create as little scandal as possible'.[80] Cesare wanted the throne of Naples, and to get it he planned to marry Carlotta of Aragon, the only daughter of Federigo I, who had succeeded his nephew Ferrante II the previous year. The reasons for Lucrezia's divorce were becoming clearer: the pope wanted to reinforce the new Borgia–Aragon union with a double marriage. In June 1498 he announced Lucrezia's betrothal to Alfonso of Aragon, the illegitimate son of Alfonso II and half-brother of Sancia, her sister-in-law, to be followed by that of Cesare and Carlotta once the formalities had been completed to allow the groom to renounce his red hat. Unfortunately for everyone, the king recoiled in horror at the prospect of a Borgia son-in-law and refused to give his permission for the betrothal.

Meanwhile in France an event occured that would have serious implications for Italy and prove catastrophic for the Sforza family. On 7 April 1498 Charles VIII had accidentally hit his head on a door lintel and although initially he seemed unhurt, he collapsed a few hours later and died. He was just twenty-eight years old and had no legitimate heir. His wife of six years, Anne of Brittany, had given birth to a healthy son who had died of measles at the age of three; she had borne three more sons and three daughters, all of whom were tragically either stillborn or died shortly after birth. The crown now passed to Charles VIII's cousin Louis, Duke of Orléans, heir not only to the Angevin claim to the throne of Naples but also the duchy of Milan. Ludovico's response was to order portraits of Giangiacomo Trivulzio – the *condottiere* he had sacked when he first seized power and who was now commander of Louis XII's army – hanging by a foot, the customary Renaissance punishment for treachery, to be placed on street corners in Milan.[81]

With the resources of the French crown at his disposal, Louis XII intended to enforce his claims to both Milan and Naples. The implications of this would not have been lost on either Duke Ludovico or King Federigo, but it was the actions of Alexander VI that would effectively seal their fate. Once again Alexander VI prioritized his family interests in dealing with the political situation. Determined to secure Cesare's marriage to Carlotta, the pope offered the king a tempting favour. He knew that Louis XII wanted a divorce from his wife, Jeanne of Valois,* who had proved unable to bear children, so that he could marry Charles VIII's wealthy widow, Anne of Brittany. And it was an arrangement that suited the pope – Carlotta of Aragon was a lady-in-waiting at Anne's court. The basic terms of the alliance were made public on 17 August 1498 and it was viewed with alarm not only by Ludovico in Milan but also Federigo I in Naples and by Ferdinand and Isabella in Spain. In Rome Ascanio quarrelled with the pope and accused him of bringing disaster to Italy through his alliance with Louis XII: 'It was your brother,' retorted Alexander VI, 'who first invited the French into Italy.'[82] Ascanio tried to avert disaster by siding with Ferdinand and Isabella, whose ambassador had threatened Alexander VI with a council to depose him, but the pope was able to use his power to placate them with the title of 'Most Catholic Kings'

---

* Jeanne of France later founded an order of nuns dedicated to the Annunciation; she was canonized in 1950.

and the gift of increasing their authority over the church in Spain.

In January 1499 Louis XII and Anne of Brittany were married and, although they refused to give permission for the betrothal between Cesare and Carlotta of Aragon, they did agree to another 'Carlotta' – Charlotte d'Albret, sister of the King of Navarre – and the couple were married that May. Although Cesare had lost his chance to acquire the throne of Naples, his father had placated his ambitious son with promises of secular power in Italy. In July Alexander VI confiscated the papal fiefs of Imola, Faenza, Forlì, Cesena, Rimini, Pesaro, Urbino and Camerino on the spurious grounds of non-payment of dues. Taken together as a bloc, these eight states formed a substantial territory, which was to be known as the duchy of the Romagna, stretching from Ferrara down the Adriatic coast almost to the borders of Naples. And part of the deal was that Cesare would have French help to ensure an easy conquest of his new state.

During the summer of 1499 a second French army crossed the Alps into Italy, under the able command of Giangiacomo Trivulzio. Cardinal Ascanio fled Rome on 14 July, on the pretence of going hunting, carrying 200,000 ducats in valuables and cash, and took charge of the defence of the duchy. By mid-August, however, it was clear that Ludovico's allies were unable to help – the Emperor had more important tasks in hand and Federigo I of Naples was too weak. On 1 September, as Marshal Trivulzio and his soldiers pushed on relentlessly to Milan, il Moro fled over the Alps to the safety of the imperial court, and the cardinal soon followed.

On 6 September Trivulzio entered Milan, where he was handed the keys to the treasury of Castello di Porta Giovia, followed a month later by Louis XII, at the head of a superb cavalcade which included Cesare and representatives of his other allies, Ferrara, Savoy, Monferrat, Mantua, Ferrara, Florence and Venice. He viewed Leonardo's *Last Supper* and requisitioned Ludovico's hunting cheetahs, which he sent back to France for his own park at Amboise.[83] He rewarded Trivulzio with the title of Duke of Vigevano, together with Ludovico's treasured villa in the town. And, keeping the bargain that he had made with Alexander VI, the king sent some 6,000 cavalry and footsoldiers to assist Cesare in his conquest of the duchy of the Romagna.

The Romagna campaign had barely started, however, when the French troops had to return to counter an attack on Milan by the

Sforzas. Cardinal Ascanio, leading an army belatedly supplied by the Emperor, occupied Como on 1 February and two days later entered Milan, followed four days later by Ludovico. But the Sforza restoration did not last long. The French quickly regrouped and, reinforced by more troops sent from France, inflicted a crushing defeat at the Battle of Novara on 8 April. Ludovico was taken prisoner and although Ascanio escaped, he was taken by the French near Piacenza a few days later – when the news of the cardinal's capture arrived in Rome Alexander VI tipped the courier the very substantial sum of 100 ducats.[84] The brothers were both imprisoned in France. Louis XII, determined to humiliate Ludovico, made him enter Lyons on a mule surrounded by armed bowmen and dressed in a cloak of cheap woollen cloth.

Louis XII had been able to deprive Ludovico of his title and estates but Ascanio, appointed a prince of the church, had retained both his title and his status. He was freed in time to travel to Rome for the conclave following the death of his friend-turned-enemy, Alexander VI, on 18 August 1503. He entered Rome with several French cardinals late in the evening of 10 September to be met by crowds of people: 'All the houses were lit up with torches and candles and everywhere people were shouting "Ascanio! Ascanio! Sforza! Sforza!".'[85] Much had changed in the three years he had been away. Cesare Borgia had conquered his duchy of Romagna, by fair means and foul, with Alexander VI resorting to corruption on a massive scale to fund his son's ambitions. Milan was now under the control of Louis XII, while Naples, which the French had taken in 1501 before being decisively defeated in April 1503 at the Battle of Cerignola by the Spanish, now belonged to Ferdinand and Isabella, who had installed their talented general Gonsalvo de Cordoba as their viceroy in the kingdom.

At the conclave following the death of Alexander VI, which opened in the middle of September 1503, Ascanio had cast his votes against the favourite candidate, Cardinal Giuliano della Rovere, to engineer the election of the elderly Cardinal Piccolomini as Pius III. Unfortunately the new pope died after less than a month in office and the cardinals returned to the Vatican in late October. Once again Giuliano della Rovere was the favourite candidate and this time Ascanio decided to support him, despite their past enmity; della Rovere was duly elected Julius II after one of the shortest conclaves in history. One of his first acts was to dismantle Cesare Borgia's duchy of the Romagna (see Chapter

6) and when Ascanio died of the plague – some said syphilis – eighteen months later, it was Julius II who commissioned his tomb, prominently positioned in the choir of Santa Maria del Popolo in Rome.

Ludovico Sforza died in the castle of Loches in May 1508, still a prisoner of the French. Greedy and incompetent, he had squandered the legacy left to the family by his father Duke Francesco. Milan, for the time being, was French, with France now the dominant power in Italy – and it is difficult to escape the conclusion that this was very substantially Ludovico's fault.

ISABELLA D'ESTE (1474–1539)
Marchioness of Mantua

ALFONSO D'ESTE (1476–1534)
Duke of Ferrara

FRANCESCO GONZAGA (1466–1519)
Marquis of Mantua

LUCREZIA BORGIA (1480–1519)
Duchess of Ferrara

Ercole d'Este, *Duke of Ferrara, father of Isabella and Alfonso*

Julius II, Leo X and Clement·VII, *Popes*

Francis I, *King of France*

Charles V, *Emperor and King of Spain*

6

SURVIVORS

Isabella d'Este

&

Alfonso d'Este

It was the afternoon of Candlemas, 2 February 1502, when Lucrezia Borgia made her ceremonial entry into Ferrara as the bride of Alfonso d'Este. It was a magnificent procession, led by Alfonso himself with three squads of crossbowmen all dressed in his colours of red and white, which made its way slowly through the crowded torch-lit streets resounding with the sound of trumpets, church bells and cannon. The onlookers were eager to get a glimpse of Lucrezia, the infamous daughter of Pope Alexander VI; she had already had two husbands, and scandalmongers accused her of adultery and murder, even incest with her handsome brother. But they were surprised to see a pretty, blonde girl, aged just twenty-one – and they were quick to notice her superb cloth-of-gold and purple satin gown, the splendid caparisons of the horses, and the 'seventy-two mules laden with goods all belonging to the bride', as the the chronicler Bernardino Zambotti reported.[1] There was nearly a disaster by the church of San Giovanni when Lucrezia's horse was startled by the noise of a cannon and she fell off but, much to everyone's relief, she picked herself up cheerfully and continued on her way. The winter sun had almost set by the time the noisy cavalcade reached the ducal palace in the city centre opposite the cathedral, where Lucrezia dismounted and made her way up to the top of the ceremonial staircase to be welcomed formally by her new sister-in-law, Isabella d'Este. The two women were soon rivals, competing in fashionable clothes, hairstyles and musical tastes and, less frivolously, for the attentions of Isabella's husband – Isabella reminded herself that her own mother, Eleonora of Aragon, who had been dead for almost ten years, had been a royal princess while Lucrezia's was an innkeeper in Rome.

Marriage into one of Italy's oldest dynasties had been a major coup for the Borgias but an unappealing political compromise for the seventy-year-old Duke Ercole I, only eased by a large sum of money. The delicate balance of power in northern Italy that had been shaken by the invasions of Charles VIII and Louis XII (see Chapter 5), was about to be destroyed completely as war engulfed the Lombard plain. The first decades of the sixteenth century were turbulent times for the small courts of Ferrara and Mantua, their existence under threat from Julius II, the 'warrior' pope who led his own armies into battle; from two Medici popes, Leo X and Clement VII, who prioritized their own family over the church; and, above all, from the increasingly hostile rivalry between Francis I and Charles V.

This is the story of how two princely dynasties survived these difficult years: Alfonso I d'Este and Lucrezia Borgia in Ferrara, and his sister Isabella and her husband Marquis Francesco Gonzaga in Mantua. They were fortunate to have inherited considerable political nous from their parents, Duke Ercole I and Eleonora of Aragon – it would prove an invaluable asset in negotiating their paths through the increasingly murky political quagmire.

Traditionally Ferrara and Mantua took opposing sides on the European political stage: the Este were rulers of a papal fief and were traditionally loyal to France, while the Gonzaga owed their loyalty to the empire. The betrothal in 1480 between the marquis's fourteen-year-old heir Francesco and Duke Ercole's daughter Isabella, who was just short of her sixth birthday, was designed to strengthen links between these adjoining states, uncomfortably sandwiched between the rival powers of Milan and Venice. The marriage took place ten years later, by which time Francesco had become Marquis of Mantua. He had been assiduous in visiting his fiancée regularly over the past ten years, though she was not the only temptation in Ferrara: there was also Duke Ercole's park where guests could hunt with dogs or – a rare treat – with leopards, or watch horse races over the jump course the duke had designed, a novelty in Renaissance Italy.[2] Isabella made her entry into Mantua on 15 February 1490; she brought a dowry of 25,000 ducats and her baggage contained jewels worth 8,000 ducats, a silver dinner service valued at over 2,000 ducats, as well as clothing worth another 9,000 ducats, including 'many gowns of different coloured silks and gold and silver most beautifully worked' and 'numerous ornaments of diverse types'.[3]

The marriage proved fruitful – Isabella was lucky, and boasted that she gave birth 'without very great difficulty'.[4] Her first child, Eleonora, was born in 1493: Francesco was a doting father and sent Isabella reports of the baby's progress: 'We were pleased to see her happy and healthy and had her dressed in our presence in the white damask outfit

overleaf Pinturicchio, *Disputation of St Catherine of Alexandria*, begun 1493 (Vatican, Borgia apartments). The artist depicts portraits of members of Alexander VI's family and courtiers, including his daughter Lucrezia as St Catherine.

as you ordered and she looked very good in it.'⁵ Eleonora was followed by Margherita (1496), who sadly died after two months; Federigo (1500); Livia (1501), who died aged seven; Ippolita (1503); Ercole (1505); Ferrante (1507); and another Livia (1508) born shortly after the death of the first – with three sons, Isabella had done her duty.

Isabella was not conventionally pretty, rather plump and stouter with age, but she was an intelligent woman with a strong personality. Educated by humanists, she had a taste for classical literature, for beautiful things, for dancing and music. Traditionally Francesco has been presented as the boorish soldier, uninterested in the arts and the complete opposite to his highbrow, cultured wife. But neither of these images is correct: Isabella herself carefully crafted her image as an intellectual while Francesco's reputation as a cultural dinosaur was invented by modern scholars as a foil to his wife's talents.⁶ In fact, as we shall see, they were both important patrons of Renaissance art and amicable rivals in their projects. But most importantly, they were a political team: over 3,000 letters have survived to chart their close partnership. Although there were occasional differences of opinion, Francesco's energy and Isabella's intelligence enabled them not only to act effectively on the political front but also to achieve an impressive level of cultural prestige for their state that belied its modest size.

Like his grandfather Ludovico Gonzaga (see Chapter 3), Francesco relied on his career as a *condottiere* for financial security. In March 1489, five years after becoming marquis, he abandoned the Gonzaga tradition of military service with Milan and signed a *condotta* with Venice. There were good reasons for this: although Isabella's sister Beatrice was betrothed to Ludovico Sforza, family loyalty did not outweigh the fact that Sforza was heavily in debt; Venice, by contrast, was well known for paying its captains in full and on time. But the alliance had its drawbacks: he felt unable to attend the lavish party held in Milan in February 1491 to celebrate Beatrice's marriage, though he did don a disguise to take part in the jousting. Moreover, he was careful not to back Sforza's support for Charles VIII's invasion in 1494 and even turned down a tempting offer from the king to command the French army for the Naples campaign, preferring to display his loyalty to Venice.

One immediate result of this policy was Francesco's appointment in 1495 as captain-general of the league assembled by Alexander VI and Venice to drive Charles VIII out of Italy. Francesco and his men intercepted the French army as it marched homeward from Naples, fighting the Battle of Fornovo on 5–6 July by the banks of the river Taro near Parma. The horrific bloodbath was described by the Ferrarese chronicler Bernardino Zambotti and also by Alessandro Benedetti, the doctor treating the wounded. 'The horses got stuck in the mud as did the infantry,' recorded Zambotti, and the soldiers 'fought with great cruelty, slaughtering for a full two hours.'[7] Benedetti described how 'on every side the sky flashed repeatedly with fire and thundered with artillery... and iron, bronze and lead balls hissed past and the air was filled with wails and cries'.[8] The French army, which numbered 20,000 men plus camp followers and forty-two artillery pieces, suffered little damage: Zambotti thought 'around four thousand Italians were killed and not more than sixty Frenchmen, though many on both sides were wounded', and the chronicler judged it a French victory.[9]

However, Charles VIII was in such a hurry to return home that he ordered his troops to leave behind all the treasure pillaged from Naples. Benedetti estimated that the booty, which included silver, gold, carpets, tapestries and chests of clothing, was worth over 200,000 ducats.[10] Indeed, there was such a quantity of valuables that the Italians claimed victory – and indeed, if victory was assessed by financial profit then the Italians definitely were the winners. Venice rewarded Francesco by raising his annual pay, and with a present of 1,000 ducats for Isabella.[11] His 'victory' was also recognized by Alexander VI, who gave him the Golden Rose in March 1496, the prestigious honour handed out annually by the pope to ruling princes in high favour. He arrived back in Mantua with the tapestries that had decorated the French royal pavilion, as another present for his wife.[12]

Like other Renaissance princes, Francesco knew the value of the arts as propaganda. The battle was celebrated in epic poetry by his humanist Battista Spagnoli while he ordered two medals with inscriptions that proclaimed him as the 'liberator of Italy' and a bust of himself in Roman armour (c.1498). He also commissioned Mantegna's *Madonna della Vittoria* (the Virgin of the Victory), an enormous altarpiece some 9 feet high, with himself as donor, kneeling in armour at the feet of the Virgin with the warrior saints Michael and George. It was carried through the streets of Mantua on 6 July 1496 to celebrate the first anniversary of Fornovo: 'I remember the harsh and cruel day of the battle,' recalled his brother Sigismondo in a letter that described how

a friar had exhorted the large crowds 'to remember that it was [the Virgin] who had freed your excellency from danger on that day'.[13]

Although Francesco and Isabella had kept out of the political controversy surrounding the French invasion of Italy in 1494, they could not ignore Louis XII's claim to Milan, which threatened Isabella's brother-in-law, though they disagreed on what to do. Paying scant attention to warnings not to deal with the king, Francesco attempted to obtain his favour with presents, including a painting by Mantegna and carp from Lake Garda. The Venetians were furious and accused him of treason, 'plotting to ally with the king of France', as they put it, and sacked him as captain-general. It was a blow to his pride, but more especially to the state coffers. In November he signed a *condotta* with Louis XII and when the king invaded Milan in 1499 did nothing to help Ludovico Sforza, despite Isabella's open support of her brother-in-law and the duke's tempting offers of border towns to add to the Mantuan dominion. In spite of urgent appeals from Isabella, he remained adamant when the duke reconquered Milan in February 1500 with the help of imperial troops – fortunately, as it turned out, in view of the massive defeat inflicted on Ludovico at the Battle of Novara that April.

In May, however, there were signs that Francesco was tiring of his alliance with Louis XII. He asked Emperor Maximilian to be god-father to his son Federigo; he seems to have been hedging his bets, as the other godparent was Cesare Borgia. In September 1501 he was nominated captain-general of the imperial army. Neither Louis XII nor Maximilian paid well, and the loss of the lucrative Venice contract had left Francesco seriously short of funds, obliging him to ask Isabella to pawn her jewels. This was quite a regular event: she once had to remind her husband that all but four gems were already pledged.[14] But she was pragmatic: 'People like us should not keep jewels except as a supply of goods to serve our needs… and therefore I willingly send your excellency what you have asked me.'

Renaissance nobles had extravagant and exotic tastes, and Isabella was no exception. She owned domestic cats – a hobby she shared with her father, who installed special cat flaps in the heavy wooden doors of the ducal palace in Ferrara – but she also bought civet cats to supply musk for her cosmetics.[15] At 200–250 ducats each, five times the price of a cheetah, these cats were incredibly expensive, though she hoped to economize by breeding them with her brother's civets in Ferrara. She

Andrea Mantegna, *Madonna della Vittoria*, 1495–6 (Paris, Louvre), an enormous altarpiece commissioned to celebrate Marquis Francesco's victory over the French at the Battle of Fornovo.

also kept black African girls as servants, who were becoming as fashionable in elite households as males: 'We could not be more pleased with our black girl,' she wrote, 'and we think she will make the best buffoon in the world.'

Isabella had inherited a taste for beautiful things from her mother Eleonora of Aragon – as a baby she had slept under a coverlet made of white damask and taffeta, fringed with gold and silk, bought specially by the princess.[16] As an adult her real extravagance was her clothes, and her desire to have all the latest fashions. Her dresses were made from rolls of expensive fabrics bought from shops in Venice, Italy's centre of international trade, which had excellent transport links with Mantua along the network of rivers and canals of the Po plain. She seized any opportunity to ask favours of family courtiers travelling abroad. In April 1491, for instance, she sent a shopping list and 100 ducats to Girolamo Zigliolo, the master of her mother's wardrobe who was about to leave for France on business for Duke Ercole.[17] She wanted engraved amethysts, rosaries and blue cloth, 'even if it costs 10 ducats a yard' and she did not mind if he overspent: 'I would prefer to be in your debt so long as you get me the latest fashions.'[18] She placed great emphasis on quality: 'If it is not the most beautiful,' she wrote to another agent about buying silk, 'then it is not worth anything.'[19]

Isabella loved shopping and regularly combined visits to her relatives with trips to city markets. She made frequent trips to her sister's court in Milan, and to Venice where, in addition to luxury textiles, she also bought glassware and indulged her sweet tooth with marzipan cakes. A regular companion was her sister-in-law Elisabetta Gonzaga, Duchess of Urbino, who was Isabella's closest friend; the pair revelled in travelling incognito, staying in inns like other tourists.[20] Normally, though, these expeditions involved a large entourage of courtiers and servants: on one visit to Lake Garda she took a huge party numbering ninety-three mouths and eighty horses.[21] Above all she made endless trips home to Ferrara. She was very fond of her parents and her siblings – as well as the sweets and biscuits of her childhood – regularly celebrating Carnival at the ducal palace and going on fishing trips with her brothers in the marshes of the Po delta.

As we have seen, Isabella was in Ferrara in February 1502 to welcome Alfonso's bride. His first wife, Anna Sforza, had died in childbirth in November 1497 and Alexander VI's suggestion of his own daughter as a suitable match was intended to provide Cesare with a local alliance to protect his position as Duke of the Romagna. Ercole I had considerable doubts about the match. In some embarrassment, he asked his agents in Rome to investigate the truth of the lurid rumours of lovers, illegitimate children, depravity, even incest, that were already attached to this young girl. Remarkably, she impressed the cautious Ferrarese envoys, who were full of praise: she was 'exceptionally elegant in demeanour and her behaviour is modest, ladylike and polite', they judged, 'and her cheerful manner and gracefulness make her appear even lovelier; I would say we have nothing to fear'.[22] And there was one very important factor in her favour: she had given birth to a son. Moreover, Duke Ercole was able to drive a very hard bargain before accepting Lucrezia as the mother of his descendants: Isabella's dowry had been 25,000 ducats; Lucrezia's was set at 200,000 ducats in cash, as well as jewels worth 100,000 ducats and several more benefits for the duchy.[23]

Court life in Ferrara was very different to Alexander VI's Rome. One wonders what the lively bride made of the classical Greek comedies favoured by Duke Ercole after the bawdy plays that were popular at the Vatican. The duke was famous for his revival of classical theatre and regularly staged these plays, in translations made by his court humanists – it is worth pointing out here that Ercole was the half-brother of Leonello d'Este, famous as one of the pioneers of the revival of the culture of ancient Rome (see Chapter 2). It was evident that the duke enjoyed planning entertainments: 'I am certain,' Beatrice wrote to Isabella, that as the celebrations 'had been conceived and organized by the most illustrious lord our father, there is no doubt that everything will have been perfect.'[24] Among the festivities was a ball in the great hall of the ducal palace followed by a performance of Plautus' *Epidicus*, the first of five comedies staged as part of the wedding celebrations. Later that year the duke started work on a theatre in the palace, the Sala dale Comedie, which would be the first purpose-built theatre of the Renaissance designed according to descriptions by Vitruvius and other classical authors of those of antiquity.[25]

Religious ceremonies too had a more local context. At Epiphany

(6 January) the duke and his courtiers distributed food to the poor in a ceremony in front of the palace. Some of the items came from the ducal larders; the rest was collected from wealthy citizens, and the list of food issued in 1477 gives some idea of how well people ate at this court: suckling pigs, geese, capons, ducks, quails, peacocks, pheasant, partridge, hares, salamis, barrels of olives, salted fish, various sorts of cheeses, pears, oranges, lemons, boxes of sweets, marzipan, spiced breads and wine.[26] On Maundy Thursday Duke Ercole hosted a dinner for poor men, washing their feet in a ceremony deliberately modelled on Christ and the Last Supper, a practice popular at the court in Naples that Eleonora of Aragon had introduced in Ferrara. On St George's Day, the feast of Ferrara's patron saint, the city celebrated with a horse race and other races for men, boys and girls. And there were also summer shopping trips to Venice, where the family could stay in the Este palace on the Grand Canal* to enjoy the fun of Carnival or to see the famous fair held in the city on the Feast of the Ascension.

Lucrezia's new life in Ferrara did not get off to a good start. In June 1502, four months after the wedding, her brother Cesare seized power in Urbino, forcing Duke Guidobaldo and Duchess Elisabetta to flee: Isabella reported the sad arrival of the duke in Mantua 'with only four horses'.[27] Lucrezia was reported to have been appalled by the news, and especially sad as it had been Duchess Elisabetta who had accompanied her on the journey to Ferrara the previous January. And her vivacious personality did not make her popular with Isabella, who was six years her senior. The two women were soon embroiled in a competitive rivalry which they fought out in fashion, hairstyles and display: 'Your ladyship must use your skills to show whose daughter you are,' was the advice given to Isabella by one of her father's courtiers.[28] But, of course, Isabella and Lucrezia had much in common. Both were strong women with a healthy disregard for convention: they each commissioned medals with profile portraits showing the loose, informal hairstyles worn by unmarried girls, not by staid married matrons.[29] They were fiercely competitive patrons of music, each determined to outdo the other, especially in popularizing the *frottola*, a new fashion for songs written by their court poets accompanied by their lutenists and other musicians. When the French ambassador's secretary reported that

---

* Now the Fondaco de' Turchi.

Ferrara, Palazzo del Corte, ceremonial staircase, 1481. A splendid approach to the great hall of the palace, sheltered by a vault supported on one side by an open arcade of fluted Composite columns.

Lucrezia had performed various dances to the accompaniment of her tambourines, Isabella was determined to go one better and allowed herself to be 'persuaded' to entertain the ambassador in person by singing and playing her lute.[30] This performance caused some shock: singing was a pastime usually restricted to the privacy of a lady's own apartments.[31]

Duke Ercole also had concerns about his daughter-in-law, though they were of a more prosaic nature. There were too many Spanish courtiers in her entourage, he considered, and sent many away, but his main concern was her allowance. He had been shocked when she demanded 12,000 ducats a year, and wrote immediately to Isabella asking for details of her budget, sending a courier to bring back her reply as a matter of urgency.[32] Isabella reported that her original allowance had been 6,000 ducats, out of which she had to buy her clothes and pay her servants' salaries, though the cost of their food was borne by her husband. In the end Ercole fixed Lucrezia's allowance at 6,000 ducats – and stubbornly refused to be moved.

The sudden death of Lucrezia's father in August 1503 brought an end to Cesare Borgia's intrigues: Duke Guidobaldo was restored to his duchy of Urbino and Cesare's duchy in the Romagna was quickly dismantled by Julius II. But Alexander VI's death also threatened Lucrezia's own position in Ferrara and Ercole I was advised by Louis XII to annul the marriage now that the political imperatives which had caused it were no longer relevant. Poor Lucrezia – political imperatives had thus far caused her much heartache. She had been obliged to divorce her first husband (Giovanni Sforza, see Chapter 5) on the patently fraudulent grounds that he was impotent so that she could marry Alfonso of Aragon, the illegitimate son of Alfonso II, in order to assist the ambitions of her brother Cesare. Two years later Alfonso had been strangled in his own bed by Cesare's manservant while recovering, under Lucrezia's care, after being viciously stabbed by a group of men on the steps of St Peter's.

Despite the pressure, however, her marriage to Alfonso survived. In September 1502, seven months after the wedding, she gave birth to a premature daughter who died and she herself fell dangerously ill with puerperal fever. Alfonso's affection for Lucrezia was evident – once she had recovered, he travelled to the shrine of the Virgin at Loreto 'in fulfilment of a vow he had made while his wife was ill'.[33] Duke

Ercole, who died on 25 January 1505 at the age of seventy-three, would never know how successful Lucrezia would be in securing the future of the dynasty. Although her second child, a son named Alessandro after his illustrious papal grandfather, lived for less than a month and was followed by a series of miscarriages, in April 1508 Lucrezia finally gave birth to a healthy son, whom they named Ercole after his other grandfather. Ercole was followed by Ippolito (1509); another Alessandro (1514), who died aged two; Leonora (1515); Francesco (1516); and Isabella Maria (1519).

The new duke was a quiet character, eccentric, stubborn like his father and, unlike his sister Isabella, far from ostentatious. He was fascinated by metals and his hobbies included making pottery on his wheel and chess pieces and musical instruments on his lathe. Paolo Giovio thought him 'harsh in features but of a very kindly disposition', and judged him the foremost military commander of the age.[34] Above all, he was a dependable ruler like his father, though he was to face far more challenging situations, including an existential threat to his position. His emblem was a bombshell with the motto *loco et tempore* (time and place), suggesting that he could explode into violence if the time was right.[35]

As duke his first problem was dealing with his three unruly brothers – Ferrante, Cardinal Ippolito and Sigismondo – and their equally difficult half-brother, Giulio. In 1505, Giulio was stabbed in the eyes by servants of Cardinal Ippolito who, in a jealous rage, had ordered the attack because one of Lucrezia's pretty ladies-in-waiting preferred his half-brother to himself. The following year Alfonso discovered that both Ferrante and Giulio were plotting to assassinate him and had them put on trial. They were found guilty and sentenced to death, but the duke reduced the punishment to life imprisonment: Ferrante, who was just twenty-eight, 'was put in a room in the tower with several guards', recorded the chronicler Giovanni Maria Zerbinati, 'and the duke bricked up the windows so that he could not see out'.[36]

Meanwhile in Rome the genial but slippery Borgia pope had been succeeded by Julius II who, as Cardinal Giuliano della Rovere, had a reputation as a notoriously difficult and stubborn man with an iron

constitution to match his iron will. In his favour was the fact that he did not have a dynastic agenda – indeed, this task had already been undertaken by his uncle Sixtus IV, who had given him a red hat over thirty years before, and raised his brother Giovanni della Rovere into the aristocratic elite. Initially, at least, both Ferrara and Mantua had reason to think favourably of the new pope. Although his first priority had been to dismantle Cesare Borgia's duchy in the Romagna, he had not involved Ferrara in the fighting. Nor had Lucrezia been punished, though there had been considerable embarrassment when customs officers in Bologna searched several cartloads of goods bound for Ferrara. When the chests were opened they were astonished to find quantities of priceless jewels, ornaments and other valuables, including a gold cat with two diamonds for eyes, which had been stolen from the papal apartments by one of Cesare Borgia's courtiers as Alexander VI had lain dying the previous summer.[37]

In Mantua, Isabella and Francesco, with the help of Duchess Elisabetta, were making plans for an alliance with Julius II that would benefit both Mantua and Urbino. Duke Guidobaldo and his wife were childless and he wanted to adopt his young nephew Francesco Maria della Rovere as his heir; Isabella and Francesco, for their part, hoped for the marriage of their eldest daughter Eleonora and the future duke. Both steps required papal approval, which Julius II readily gave, with the added bonus of a red hat for Marquis Francesco's brother Sigismondo. Francesco Maria became heir to Urbino in May 1504 and the following spring the betrothal was arranged between the boy, now aged thirteen, and the ten-year-old Eleonora, with a dowry agreed at 30,000 ducats, a sum that was to include clothes and jewels worth 5,000 ducats.[38]

The first signs of trouble with Rome came in 1506 when Julius II decided to restore papal authority in Bologna by forcing out the Bentivoglio family, who were related to both the Este and the Gonzaga by marriage. Marquis Francesco, now acting as commander of the papal army in October in place of Duke Guidobaldo, who was suffering badly from gout, attempted to intervene on behalf of the Bentivoglio but to no avail. In early November the pope, leading his own army into battle (the last pope to do so) with the help of 800 French men-at-arms, 4,000 infantry and fifteen pieces of artillery supplied by Louis XII, forced the Bentivoglio to flee.[39] They sought refuge first in Ferrara,

Dosso Dossi, *Alfonso I d'Este*, c.1530 (Modena, Galleria Estense). The battlefield setting of this portrait commemorated the duke's illustrious career; one contemporary described him as 'the foremost military commander of his age'.

where Alfonso I attempted to deny their presence, but they were soon forced to move to Mantua. Julius II made his triumphal entry into Bologna on 11 November and celebrated his victory with a gigantic bronze statue of himself from Michelangelo, which was erected prominently on the facade of the church of San Petronio in the centre of the city.

Meanwhile, relations between Mantua and Ferrara – between Isabella and Lucrezia – were becoming increasingly icy over an 'affair' between Marquis Francesco and the duchess. In 1505, after the death of her second child and with plague raging in Ferrara, Lucrezia took a trip to Mantua, where she enjoyed a flirtation with Francesco. She did have a penchant for ardent but platonic love affairs: two years earlier she had exchanged passionate love letters and gifts with the Venetian humanist poet Pietro Bembo, who treasured a lock of her golden hair. However, this flirtation was potentially far more damaging. It soon became the topic of fevered court gossip – and an unpleasant shock for Isabella, who was usually tolerant of her husband's affairs, but there is no proof that it was anything more than a platonic friendship.

Francesco was well known for his love of dogs, falcons and horses. The Mantuan stud was famous and both he and Isabella were avid racing fans. Isabella's horse won the annual St George's Day race in Ferrara in 1502, the prize for which was 'gold brocade fringed with fur, and the suckling pig and the cock'.[40] One enterprising author compiled an illustrated manuscript of thirty-five Gonzaga racehorses – starting with the Dinosaur – with a portrait of each one and details of their wins.[41] The marquis also amassed more erudite collections of coins, medals, manuscripts and, very unusually, maps.[42] Politics intervened, even here. In 1506 Isabella wrote to her husband to say that the Venetian authorities had refused to give his painter permission to copy the map of Italy in the Doge's palace because 'they were informed that every day your excellency speaks words that are harmful to the government, not in public where you speak honourably, but in private'.[43]

Francesco continued work on the projects of his father and grandfather, embellishing the family palaces and villas in the countryside around Mantua. He enlarged the villa at Marmirolo – an inventory listed the old and new palaces, a dovecote, an oratory, a mill, fountains, an orchard, garden and hunting park – and he decorated the banqueting hall with life-size portraits of his Arab horses.[44] Several of his residences contained rooms decorated with maps or cityscapes, a fashion deriving from descriptions of ancient Roman villas that had been made popular by Innocent VIII. Among the cities portrayed was Cairo, where his agents regularly shopped for horses.[45] Interestingly, verisimilitude was not important: 'Since you say you have never seen it… we ask you to use your judgement to put in what you like,' the marquis informed Giovanni Bellini, who had previously refused a commission to paint a picture of Paris.[46]

In April 1508 Francesco moved into Palazzo San Sebastiano, a new residence that he had built on the other side of the city to the ducal palace but close to his stud and stables. The ducal palace, which housed the chancery and other court offices, remained the focus of Gonzaga power. Isabella's apartments were also in the ducal palace and, although it was an unusual arrangement, there is no evidence that it was a deliberate move to distance himself from his wife. The couple continued to appear together in public and their correspondence continued its amicable pattern. It is more likely that it was connected to syphilis, a disease he contracted around this time. Isabella's humanist secretary Mario Equicola, reporting the move, wrote: 'Truly he is not well… I don't know exactly what his illness is but I know that he had great pain in his genital member at the beginning of March.'[47]

Sadly little remains of the palace to testify to Francesco's tastes but we know from the archives that it was set in elegant gardens and was a favourite spot for banquets, receptions and theatrical performances. The decoration reflected not only Francesco's military achievements and his hobbies but also his political strategies. The black eagle of Emperor Maximilian on the ceiling of one reception room was balanced with the porcupine of Louis XII in another.[48] In an early example of the ancestor cycles that would become high fashion later in the sixteenth century, Francesco promoted his own military heritage in scenes of Gonzaga triumphs from the expulsion of the Bonacolsi family in 1328, the victory that brought his family to power, down to his own recent victory at Fornovo. The grandest room in the palace was the great hall, a vast room – 105 feet long, 23 feet wide and 22 feet high – designed to display Mantegna's *Triumphs of Caesar*. It is likely that Francesco himself commissioned this famous cycle of nine canvases by the Gonzaga court painter, although some scholars still attribute them to Francesco's grandfather Ludovico. Based on classical descriptions

following pages Andrea Mantegna, *Triumphs of Caesar*, c.1486–1500 (Royal Collection). Four of nine scenes depicting Julius Caesar's return to Rome after defeating the Gauls: the Picture Bearers, the Vase Bearers, the Elephants and the Bearers of Trophies and Bullion. The final scene showed Julius Caesar himself, seated on his chariot at the end of the long procession of booty and prisoners.

of ancient Roman triumphs, the paintings recounted Julius Caesar's return to Rome after his conquest of Gaul, another thinly veiled reference to Francesco's achievement at Fornovo.

Francesco also built an elegant *studiolo* – these rooms were a fashionable addition to the apartments of the nobility for the display of their collections. It was decorated by the Ferrarese painter Lorenzo Costa, who had succeeded Mantegna as court artist after the latter's death in 1506. One of the scenes showed Francesco being led by Hercules along the path of virtue; another showed the Roman goddess Latona turning peasants into frogs, an unusual choice of myth but one that had resonances in marshy Mantua.[49] Rather touchingly, a third showed Isabella and her ladies singing and music-making, a version of the picture that Costa had already painted for Isabella's *studiolo*, and further evidence that Francesco's move to the Palazzo San Sebastiano was not a sign of deteriorating relations between the couple.

Isabella also had her own *studiolo* and an adjoining *grotta* that had been started soon after she arrived in Mantua, but they were far from finished in 1506. Unlike her husband, she concentrated her artistic energies almost exclusively on these two rooms in her private apartments, which was where she, her ladies-in-waiting and friends could meet to eat marzipan cakes, play music and gossip. Both had elaborately carved marble door frames and intarsia panels inlaid with her emblems, notably the so-called 'Pause', which showed stylized musical notes and signs on a stave.[50] The *studiolo* floor was laid with tiles decorated with Gonzaga emblems, such as the sun, the plume, the dog muzzle and the stirrups. This was more a money-saving choice than a deliberate symbol of her loyalty to her husband. The tiles had been left over from a consignment made specially for Francesco in Pesaro to decorate a room at Marmirolo and that Isabella decided would be very useful to seal the floor and stop the mice nesting below from getting into the room.[51]

On the walls of the *studiolo* were five allegorical panels painted by various artists because Isabella, unlike her husband, wanted them to serve as comparisons, or *paragone*. The painters were given very precise instructions based on programmes devised by her humanist advisor Paride da Ceresara, programmes that have proved too abstruse to be fully understood by the modern scholar. The overall image was designed to present Isabella as a virtuous woman of cultured tastes,

Mantua, Palazzo Ducale, Isabella d'Este apartments, *c.*1520. Isabella's love of music is evident in this detail of lutes and other fashionable instruments depicted in the inlaid marquetry decoration of her study.

and an intellectual learned in the classics. Mantegna's *Parnassus* (1497) showed Mars and Venus reigning over the nine Muses dancing below, while Costa's *Allegory of Isabella's Court* (1506) showed her surrounded by musicians.

There were busts of Brutus and Caracalla and an astrolabe on display in the *studiolo*, set on tables made from slabs of classical columns, but most of Isabella's collection of antiquities were kept in the fitted cupboards of the *grotta*.[52] She had what she herself described as 'an insatiable desire for old things'.[53] She certainly inherited her mother's passion for collecting – Eleonora of Aragon owned vases of semi-precious stones, sculpture, paintings, books and 170 pieces of prized Chinese porcelain – but Isabella's collection was on an altogether different scale.[54] An inventory taken after Isabella's death listed over 1,500 items: antique and modern statues in bronze and marble; gold, silver and bronze medals; cameos and vases.[55] She commissioned copies of the Apollo Belvedere and the Laocoon, famous antique statues in Julius II's collection; she bought musical instruments and ceramics; she sourced glassware in Murano and printed editions of classical texts from the famous Aldine press in Venice; she commissioned portraits of herself from Costa, Leonardo and Titian; and she owned several curios, including a huge fish tooth and an item that was believed to be a unicorn horn.[56] It was one of the most important collections of the age and tells us much about Isabella's character: the collection was large by the standards of the period, unprecedentedly so for a woman of the period, and it was especially unusual because collecting antiquities was overwhelmingly a male-gendered hobby in Renaissance Italy.

Meanwhile, politics had begun to intrude not only on the lives of Isabella and Francesco but also of Alfonso and Lucrezia. On 10 December 1508 the two rulers signed the Treaty of Cambrai with Julius II, Emperor Maximilian, Ferdinand II and Louis XII to create a formidable alliance. This was ostensibly for a crusade against the Turks but the subtext was to halt the alarming growth of Venetian power; it envisaged a drastic carving up of the city's 'empire' on the *terraferma*. Louis XII, for example, was to gain Cremona, Brescia, Bergamo and other cities on Milan's eastern borders; Maximilian would take the

previous pages   Pietro Perugino, *Battle between Love and Chastity*, 1505 (Paris, Louvre). Isabella gave Perugino strict instructions detailing the content of this painting, and sent her agents to ensure he complied with her wishes.
Antico, *Hercules and Antaeus*, c.1500 (London, V&A). Nicknamed for his antique style, Pier Jacopo Bonacolsi enjoyed the patronage of the Mantuan court.

cities closest to Venice, including Verona, Vicenza and Padua; while Ravenna and the Romagna territories that Venice had seized in the aftermath of the collapse of Cesare Borgia's duchy were to return to the Papal States; there were also small territorial gains for both Mantua and Ferrara, just enough to tempt them to join the league.

In early April 1509 Julius II appointed Duke Alfonso as captain-general of the church and on 14 May the league's armies inflicted a crushing defeat over Venice at the Battle of Agnadello – but disaster was to follow. Marquis Francesco, a commander in the imperial army, had been suffering from a fever and did not take part in the fighting at Agnadello. He had recovered by August when, as part of the conquest of Venetian territories, he was sent out to take Verona. Unfortunately, while stopping overnight at Isola della Scala on 7 August, the forty-three-year-old veteran was ignominiously surprised in his bed by the Venetians, captured and sent to Venice, where he was imprisoned in the dungeons of the Doge's Palace.

Isabella was left in charge of Mantua – though Julius II decided that she needed male help and gave Cardinal Sigismondo permission to return home. A contemporary described him as 'fat, gouty and partial to oysters', but he was fond enough of Isabella to leave her a bust of Homer in his will.[57] Francesco, by contrast, did not belittle his wife's abilities: 'During our absence we have left the burden and governance of our state to our illustrious consort, knowing that we can rely on her prudence and integrity.'[58] It was not unusual for wives of princes to take over the reins of power in the absence of their husbands, nor for them to take their own decisions – on this occasion Isabella set up licensed brothels for Mantuan prostitutes and banned foreigners from plying the trade.[59] Isabella had been just eight years old when her mother Eleonora of Aragon had taken charge of Ferrara in November 1482, with enemy troops inside the hunting park and her husband lying unconscious in bed. Lucrezia also had experience of government, acting for her father more than once: the papal master of ceremonies recorded a somewhat racy story of how she had asked a cardinal for advice, to be told 'we just need someone to make a note of our conversation'; Lucrezia had replied that she was fully capable of writing, to which the cardinal retorted 'but where is your pen?' – the Italian *penna* meaning 'pen' was also slang for 'penis'.[60]

The marquis was still in prison in December 1509 when Eleonora,

Francesco Francia, *Federigo Gonzaga*, 1510 (New York, Metropolitan Museum of Art). Isabella d'Este commissioned this delightful portrait of her son when the nine-year-old was sent to Rome as a hostage for his father's good behaviour.

now fifteen years old, married Francesco Maria, who had become Duke of Urbino the year before. The bride left Ferrara on 9 December, in thick fog, and Isabella received the information that the couple had consummated their marriage on Christmas night.[61] Isabella was having difficulties in obtaining her husband's release: her first thought had been to exchange him for the Venetian captain-general, Bartolomeo d'Alviano, who had been captured at Agnadello, but Louis XII refused his consent. Fortunately for the Gonzaga, the political situation was about to change, yet again. The victory at Agnadello had left a power vacuum on the Lombard plain and it was being filled by Louis XII. Alarmed by the growing French influence, Julius II turned on his erstwhile ally and signed an alliance with Venice. He also proposed that the imprisoned marquis should take over as commander of the Venetian army – with Francesco's loyalty guaranteed by making his nine-year-old son Federigo a hostage. Francesco was delighted but Isabella was horrified. In the end they compromised: Federigo would be a hostage not in Venice but in Rome, where he could be under the protection of his own family, notably his elder sister Duchess Eleonora and his uncle Cardinal Sigismondo Gonzaga. The marquis was freed in July, Federigo left for Rome and Isabella commissioned a charming portrait of her little boy.

It had been expedient for Isabella and Francesco to become closely tied to Julius II's Venetian alliance but Duke Alfonso, captain-general of the papal army, was in a very different situation. In late November 1509 – before the pope's U-turn – Venice had sent seventeen war galleys up the Po in an attempt to recover territory that had been ceded to the duke after Agnadello. While the soldiers looted and burned villages, Alfonso cleverly hid his artillery to surprise the Venetians and all but destroyed their fleet. And when Julius II changed sides the following February, Alfonso remained loyal to France – he sent the king a pair of his famous cheetahs – and continued to defend Ferrara from Venetian hostility.[62]

War was expensive and Alfonso was obliged to take measures to raise funds. He cut down his household, dismissing several musicians who found employment with Isabella.[63] More controversially, he raised the tolls charged on goods passing through the duchy by one-third: Isabella's agent in Rome reported that Julius II had 'protested forcefully with bitter and ominous words'.[64] But the pope's real fury was directed at Alfonso's refusal to give the pope the loyalty he expected from his captain-general, who instead preferred the protection of a foreign crown. On 9 August Alfonso was excommunicated, deprived of his title and replaced as army commander by his brother-in-law Marquis Francesco – and the marquis made the pope promise that he would have custody of Lucrezia when Ferrara fell.[65]

Julius II lost no time: according to the Venetian ambassador, he was 'burning with impatience to march on Ferrara'.[66] However, Francesco's doctors would not let him fight – was this an excuse to avoid a direct clash with Alfonso? – so the pope replaced him with his nephew Francesco Maria della Rovere, Duke of Urbino. Isabella did what she could to ease the situation for Alfonso I and claimed that it was thanks to her efforts that her son-in-law 'is doing all he can to hold back so that he can avoid the damage that would otherwise be done', while tricking the pope into thinking he was engaged energetically in the war.[67] That August Francesco Maria took Modena and several small towns, but progress was too slow for the impatient pope, who travelled north in September to take charge of the campaign. It must have been a relief to Francesco Maria when his uncle promptly fell ill. It was not until mid-December that he appeared again in public and he surprised everyone by sporting a beard, not a normal fashion for a pope: it was reported that 'he said he would not shave it off until he had driven King Louis of France out of Italy'.[68]

On 2 January Julius II set out from Bologna, carried in a litter, to the small town of Mirandola, which was under attack from Venetian and papal troops. Despite the heavy snow and appalling conditions, Julius II 'lodged in a farm worker's hovel', recorded the historian Guicciardini, 'riding about all the time ordering the positioning of the artillery'.[69] Impatient with what he saw as the incompetence of his commanders, especially Francesco Maria – who evidently was not trying as hard as he could to attack the duchy – he took control but, continued Guicciardini, he 'had no idea of how undignified it was for someone as powerful as the pope to lead his armies in person'. Mirandola surrendered after two days of heavy bombardment and Julius II now set his sights on the city of Ferrara itself.

Alfonso I had had plenty of time to organize his defences. French troops had arrived in November and on 1 December, a Sunday, he published an edict ordering all shops and businesses to close for a week so that everyone could help build fortifications. That Monday morning the whole city was woken early by the blast of the ducal trumpets. Among those assembled for work were the chronicler Giovanni Maria Zerbinati and his sons, friars and monks, and indeed the duke himself: 'Not a single courtier or citizen, young or old, declined to go,' Zerbinati recorded; 'three hundred women moved stones at the Porta di San Benedetto' and 'there were many courtiers and citizens working at the bastion at the Porta di Sotto, some carrying earth, others loading carts or pounding the ground with rammers... and the duke himself was working too, alongside people of every social class.'[70] After Christmas the weather turned unusually cold: the Po froze and the ice had to be broken up to prevent the enemy gaining access to the city. Carnival was cancelled, though Lucrezia ensured that the French captains staying in the palace were entertained with parties.

Fortunately, the enemy never arrived. Despite Julius II's goading, his army moved at a snail's pace. There were difficulties finding supplies so he ordered Cardinal Sigismondo to send bread and seventy pairs of oxen for the artillery carts from Mantua.[71] Alfonso I was proving adept at fending off attacks at his borders, and he was fortunate that the pope was unusually busy on the diplomatic front in April dealing with envoys sent by the emperor to negotiate peace. Ferrara was still free at Easter, 20 April: Lucrezia ordered the Good Friday sermon to be preached in the palace courtyard as the cathedral was forbidden because of the papal indictment. Finally on 22 May news arrived that the Bolognese had defeated Julius II, with the help of the French. Ferrara had been saved: 'The bells rang out, there were fireworks, artillery salvoes and singing, and boys and girls with boughs of blossom in their hands to celebrate the pope's defeat.'[72] Alfonso I celebrated by buying Michelangelo's huge bronze statue of Julius II, which had been toppled from the facade of San Petronio during the riots: he kept the head and melted the rest down to make a cannon, which he named 'La Giulia'.

Although Ferrara was safe for the moment, hostilities between Julius II and Louis XII continued to fester. The king called for a council of the church to depose the pope; Julius retaliated by opening the Fifth Lateran Council to deal with church reform. The stalemate was broken when the pope assembled a formidable coalition against Louis XII: its signatories were Emperor Maximilian, Ferdinand II of Spain, Henry VIII of England, the Swiss and Venice. The two armies met on 11 April

1512 at the Battle of Ravenna, one of the bloodiest battles of the period and a victory for France. Of the 10,000 men killed, the French losses were half those of the allies. Alfonso I's artillery played an important role in the victory: 'It was truly dreadful to see how each cannonball drove a channel through the soldiers, throwing helmets, heads and limbs up into the air; the Spanish were mown down before they could use their weapons,' a witness informed Guicciardini; 'it was ghastly and lasted for four hours.'[73] Unfortunately, one of the dead was Gaston de Foix, commander of Louis XII's army, and his loss badly demoralized the French, who failed to capitalize on their position and fled when the Swiss soldiers finally arrived on Italian soil, allowing Julius II to claim victory instead.

It was a disaster for Duke Alfonso. In June he left for Rome in the hope of negotiating an agreement with Julius II, armed with a safe conduct pass procured for him by Isabella, but it was for his person, not for his duchy.[74] Julius II offered to lift the excommunication and the indictment, but only if Alfonso surrendered the duchy – he was offered the small city of Asti as recompense. The duke refused to be intimidated and travelled home incognito to avoid arrest. His alliance with Louis XII had cost him both Modena and Reggio, which fell to the papal army that month; his title to Ferrara was now under serious threat.

In August 1512 Julius II called a summit of his allies at Mantua in order to carve up the territories they had won at Ravenna. The new Duke of Milan, Isabella was delighted to discover, was to be her nephew Massimiliano, the son of Beatrice and Ludovico il Moro. But there was bad news for Alfonso: the pope intended to destroy Louis XII's Italian allies, the Florentine republic and Ferrara. That autumn the Medici were restored to Florence by force – the Spanish commander Ramón de Cardona brutally sacked the nearby city of Prato to demonstrate what would happen to the Florentines if they persisted with their pro-French politics. Fortunately Ferrara did not suffer the same fate. Apparently the Spaniard fell for Isabella's charms; it seems he enjoyed the banquets hosted by Isabella and Francesco – one of them took place in the great hall of Palazzo San Sebastiano, under Mantegna's canvases of the *Triumphs of Caesar*, which so impressed Cardona that he asked if he could have drawings made of them.[75] Both Isabella and Alfonso must have been relieved the following February when they heard that Julius II had died – but who would be the new pope?

overleaf Giovanni Bellini, *Feast of the Gods*, 1514–29 (Washington, National Gallery). Alfonso I's first painting for his *camerino* depicted the feast hosted by Cybele, goddess of fertility, whose guests fell into a drunken stupor.

In the event it was Giovanni de' Medici, a close ally of Julius II; his election as Leo X in March 1513 brought immediate advantages for both the Gonzaga and Este families. Isabella's son Federigo, now twelve years old, went home after three years as a hostage at the papal court, while Alfonso was much relieved to hear that Leo X intended to restore Modena and Reggio to the duchy. Unfortunately the duke learned just how hollow Leo X's promises were in late 1514 when the cash-strapped pope sold Modena to the Emperor for 40,000 ducats.[76] Moreover, it soon became evident that Leo X's overwhelming priority – indeed, his sole priority – was the enrichment of his family. In March 1516 he confiscated the fief of Urbino, and gave Francesco Maria's title to his nephew, Lorenzo de' Medici (see Chapter 7). There was little Marquis Francesco or Isabella could do except provide shelter for their son-in-law and daughter, and wait for the pope to die.

The succession of Francis I to the French throne on 1 January 1515 was to cause further problems for Mantua, especially after the new king defeated Massimiliano Sforza at the Battle of Marignano in September. The victory marked the start of ten years of French domination in northern Italy: Massimiliano was pensioned off to France, where he died in 1530, and Leo X was quick to change sides to favour the young king, while Francesco, an imperial fiefholder, did what he could to keep on friendly terms with his new neighbour, agreeing to 'lend' (read – pay) the king 12,000 scudi.[77] He also sent his son Federigo to the French court – again, more as a hostage for Mantua's neutrality than an honoured guest – and he was at Milan that December when Leo X and Francis I negotiated the terms of their alliance.

For Alfonso I, the alliance between Leo X and Francis I was good news – though he did install angle bastions to reinforce the circuit of walls around Ferrara.[78] When Lucrezia gave birth to their third son in November the following year, they named him Francesco in honour of the French king, who also stood as the baby's godfather. Duke Alfonso now had more time, and money, to devote to cultural pursuits. He did much to enhance the court's reputation for excellence in music, literature, theatre and the visual arts, established by his parents. Like Isabella, he was an enthusiastic patron of music, employing the Flemish composer Adrian Willaert among his musicians, and collector of antiquities, acquired for him in Rome by the painter Raphael.[79] Guests were entertained with comedies written by his court poet, Ludovico Ariosto. He promoted Alfonso's military talents in *Orlando Furioso*, an epic poem about Charlemagne's defence of Christian Europe that claimed this famous warrior as an ancestor of the Este family. He also extolled the virtues of Lucrezia: 'What can I say of her', he asked; 'she flourishes like a plant in the best soil; she is silver to tin, gold to brass, the garden rose to the field poppy, the luscious bay to the withered willow, a jewel to coloured glass.'[80]

Alfonso spent copiously on embellishing the ducal residences in and around Ferrara. He built the Villa Belvedere on an island in the Po, set in beautiful gardens ornamented with fountains and grottoes. He repaired the ducal palace, which had been damaged by fire in 1509, building new apartments with expensive gilded ceilings, marble floors and glass windows. Like Isabella, he also created his own pair of studies, the so-called *Camerini d'Alabastro* (alabaster rooms) named for the exquisite marble reliefs of mythological scenes by Antonio Lombardo that decorated the smaller chamber.* In the other room were eight panels painted by some of the best artists of the period, notably Giovanni Bellini and Titian, depicting classical texts celebrating love and wine. Unlike Isabella's rooms, the cycle was not based on a formal programme, though Alfonso did ask her humanist Mario Equicola for his advice.[81]

Lucrezia, by contrast, was not a major patron of the arts – perhaps the competitive Este gene was too much for her, though she certainly contributed to the musical development of the court at Ferrara, employing her own singers, lutenists and a ballet teacher as part of her household, as well as her own court poet to write the Petrarchan poetry that her composers set to music.[82] She commissioned several medals embellished with erudite humanist imagery; in the aftermath of the lifting of the siege of Ferrara she was involved with the commission of plaques depicting Alfonso in armour and Lucrezia presenting her eldest son, Ercole, to St Maurelius, patron saint of Ferrara, to thank him for the victory. She is known to have been unusually pious, joining a tertiary order of nuns at the end of her life. Remarkably, she also

---

* The rooms themselves no longer exist and their contents were dispersed at the end of the sixteenth century.

overleaf Titian's *Bacchus and Ariadne*, 1520–23 (London, National Gallery), depicts Bacchus rescuing Ariadne, accompanied by his band of noisy revellers and a pair of the famous Ferrara leopards.

turns out to have been a sharp businesswoman, who invested her spare cash and even her jewellery in land. 'She rises in my esteem every day; she is a very intelligent and astute woman and you need your head straight on to deal with her,' wrote one admirer.[83] Instead of paintings and antiquities, Lucrezia spent her money on marshland, which she then reclaimed to make pasture for her livestock, and fields where she planted crops to sell in the markets and which she could rent out to boost her income even further.[84]

Meanwhile, another powerful ruler had emerged on to the European stage. Charles V, born in 1500, had inherited the duchy of Burgundy from his father at the age of six and become King of Spain in February 1516 after the death of his grandfather, Ferdinand II. Three years later his other grandfather, Emperor Maximilian, died – his election as emperor on 28 June 1519 was unanimous. Ruler of a vast realm that encompassed much of Europe and extended across the Atlantic to the Americas, Charles V was to have a decisive impact on the history of Italy – and on the fortunes of the Renaissance princes.

The spouses of both Isabella and Alfonso died that spring. Francesco died from the syphilis from which he had suffered for ten long years, leaving Isabella and Cardinal Sigismondo as regents for Federigo until the boy reached his twenty-second birthday. Lucrezia tragically died of puerperal fever soon after giving birth to a daughter; she was much mourned by the people of Ferrara, where she had been popular. Isabella celebrated her new position with an altarpiece for the church of San Vincenzo, where her daughter was a nun. It was dedicated to Osanna Andreasi, a woman from a noble Mantua family noted for her religious piety and visions. The focus of a local cult, Osanna had been beatified in 1514 and Isabella had herself portrayed as a pious widow kneeling in prayer.

Alfonso I continued to press Leo X for the return of Modena and Reggio; the pope remained obdurate, though he did do the duke some favours: in April 1519, for example, he agreed to invest Alfonso's nine-year-old son Ippolito as Archbishop of Milan (see Chapter 10). That October there were worrying rumours of a secret agreement between Leo X and Francis I in which the king promised his support if the pope decided to deprive rebellious fief holders of their states – it was unmistakably aimed at Alfonso. Francis I reassured his ally that although he had indeed made that promise, he had no intention of fulfilling it – it is difficult to know whether the duke was reassured or not. Meanwhile, Alfonso continued to annoy Leo X: on one occasion he refused to punish a monk for spreading Protestant ideas; on another he accused the pope of plotting his assassination – while this was probably untrue, it was certain that the pope had drawn up plans to seize Ferrara by force when Alfonso died.[85]

And then in late June 1521 came the shocking news that Leo X had dropped Francis I in favour of an anti-French alliance with Charles V. Isabella could profit from this dramatic announcement: in July Leo appointed Federigo Gonzaga as captain-general of the church and gave the bishopric of Mantua to her second son, Ercole. Her brother, on the other hand, faced the loss of his duchy – once again – as the pope and the emperor made plans to expel the French from Italy. In November they conquered Milan, installing Massimiliano Sforza's younger brother, Francesco Maria, as duke. News of the victory reached Rome on the 24th, while Leo X was at his hunting lodge near Ostia – he returned to the Vatican the next day but fell ill with malaria and died on 2 December. For Alfonso it was an unexpected stroke of good fortune – indeed, he was widely suspected of poisoning the pope – and he celebrated it with a medal, inscribed *De manu leonis* (out of the paw of the lion/Leo).

The new pope, Adrian VI, was Charles V's old tutor and in Spain when the conclave took place – he was, very unusually, elected in his absence on 9 January 1522. 'He could not be more imperial than he is,' Cardinal Sigismondo warned his sister-in-law; 'indeed you could say that the emperor is pope.'[86] Isabella urged Alfonso to moderate his pro-French stance and ally himself more closely with Charles V. The duke sent his heir, Ercole, to Rome where, to his great relief, the pope immediately revoked both Leo X's excommunication and the interdict; he also agreed to restore Modena and Reggio but was prevented from doing so by the College of Cardinals, which voted against the measure. However, Alfonso had heeded Isabella's advice: on 29 November, in a secret agreement with Charles V's envoys, he promised not to sign any alliance hostile to the emperor and to allow free passage through the duchy for the imperial army in return for Charles V restoring the two cities to Este rule

Meanwhile Alfonso I himself, to the disgust of his sons, publicly installed his mistress in a palace in Ferrara. The couple never married

but did have two children, Alfonso (born 1527) and Alfonsino (1530) – as their names suggest, they were ackowledged by the duke. Intriguingly, perhaps to disguise her very modest origins, two surnames were invented for her – it may be that even 'Laura' was not her birth name. In ducal documents of the period she is known as 'Laura Eustochia', the surname deriving from St Eustochium, an early Christian noble Roman virgin who was a devout follower of St Jerome; it is only in later documents that she is also referred to as 'Laura Dianti', the surname of a respectable Ferrarese family.[87] Around 1527 Alfonso commissioned Titian to paint portraits of himself and Laura. The duke was portrayed as a military prince, dressed in his official mantle with a sheathed sword in one hand and the barrel of one of his cannon under the other. The portrait of Laura, by contrast, was far less conventional. She was shown with a fashionable African servant, and her brilliant blue dress and earrings did not belong to the outfit of a respectable aristocratic woman of the period.[88]

Adrian VI's pontificate was brief, and he was followed by Leo X's cousin Giulio de' Medici, who was elected Clement VII on 19 November 1523. Within days of Adrian's death, Alfonso seized the advantage offered by the *sede vacante* to take Reggio; he was about to take Modena when the result of the election was announced and prudently, very prudently in the light of what was to happen, he decided to withdraw

Titian, *Laura Dianti*, c.1525 (Private Collection). One of Titian's great skills was his ability to capture textures: rich blue velvet, crisp white linen and the differing skin tones of the middle-aged mistress and her young slave.

Alfonso I d'Este, copy after Titian, c.1525 (New York, Metropolitan Museum of Art). The original, now lost, was commissioned as a pair with that of Laura.

his troops. A second Medici pope was not good news. Charles V was still hoping to persuade Alfonso to desert Francis I but the duke insisted on his loyalty to France. But the king was playing political games with Alfonso, using him as a pawn in his relations with the pope: the Mantuan ambassador in Rome warned, in code, in November 1524 that 'the king has proposed to give Ferrara to [Clement VII] if he were to ally with France... and the imperialists are very dissatisfied'.[89]

Isabella too tried to persuade her brother to change sides. She had good reason to appreciate the Emperor's growing power in Italy – her nephew Charles of Bourbon, who was one of Francis I's premier nobles and constable of France, had recently defected to join Charles V and had led the imperial army to victory in Provence in the summer of 1524. Clement VII, who had tried in vain to persuade the rival powers to put aside their differences in the interest of church unity, abandoned his policy of neutrality in early 1525 and, with the two armies massing in northern Italy, signed an alliance with Francis I and supported the king's claim to the throne of Naples. When 10,000 French soldiers marched south to claim the kingdom, Bourbon seized the advantage to inflict a crushing defeat on Francis I at the Battle of Pavia on 24 January. In a single day, the decade of French domination of Italian politics was over, Francis I had been taken prisoner, Clement VII's foreign policy was in tatters and Charles V, as Isabella had warned her brother, had begun his inexorable rise to power on the peninsula.

Isabella herself was on the road between Mantua and Pesaro when the battle took place. She was travelling to Rome on pilgrimage for this Holy Year; though she was also keen to get away from her son's intrigues and the highly unsuitable affair he was conducting, which had scandalized the court (see Chapter 7). The position of dowager was not easy, especially for someone as opinionated as Isabella, and now that Federigo had reached his majority, which he did in May 1522, she decided to move to Rome. Travelling with her courtiers, secretary, ladies-in-waiting and her dwarf Morgantino, Isabella spent a few days en route with the Duke and Duchess of Urbino, and with her beloved sister-in-law Elisabetta – sadly, it was to be their last meeting as Elisabetta died early the following year. She arrived in Rome at the beginning of March to a city in uproar, torn by riots between rival French and imperialist factions.

Despite the violence on the streets, the social life of the papal court continued largely uninterrupted. In May Isabella attended a banquet hosted by Clement VII at Villa Madama, the beautiful suburban retreat he had begun building in the hills just outside the walls while a cardinal. She was very envious of his collection and 'the wonderful antiquities which we wished we could own'.[90] She moved into the palace at Santi Apostoli – where Morgantino was apparently very popular with her guests – and spent her time shopping, sightseeing and visiting the cardinals in their palaces, where she could see more 'wonderful antiquities' and enjoy conversations with like-minded collectors.[91] She also had regular audiences with Clement VII, busy lobbying on behalf of her family – one of the hundreds of petitioners and diplomats looking to acquire favours from the beleagured pope, who was 'beset on every side, buffetted like a ship in a storm at sea', as the Mantuan ambassador reported.[92] Foremost on Isabella's agenda was the issue of a cardinal's hat for her nineteen-year-old son Ercole, which the pope had promised over a year earlier but still had not granted – in her impatience, Isabella tended to ignore the pope's more pressing political agenda, and that he had avoided making any cardinals at all, for fear of causing offence to either the French or the imperial factions at court.[93]

Meanwhile the political situation in northern Italy was growing increasingly tense. Francis I, who had been imprisoned in Madrid since his defeat at Pavia, was released after agreeing to renounce his claims to Milan and Naples – however, as soon as he was back on French soil he broke the terms of the agreement and in May 1526 signed the League of Cognac with the pope, Venice, Florence and Milan against Charles V. That July war broke out in earnest in Lombardy when Bourbon seized Milan. And now Duke Alfonso recognized the necessity of changing sides and signed an alliance with Charles V in return for the restoration of Modena.

That autumn imperial troops mustered in huge numbers on the Lombard plain as Bourbon's army was reinforced by troops from Naples and Germany. Unfortunately, by the spring there was no money left to pay the soldiers' wages: the men mutinied and, led by Bourbon, they pillaged their way south, drawn by the legendary wealth of Rome. The situation was serious enough in April for Federigo to order his mother to leave Rome, but his ambassador was unable to get an audience with her as she was preoccupied with her religious observances for Holy Week – when she wrote to her son on 23 April, the Tuesday after

Easter, it was evident that she still had no real concept of the danger than threatened.

Isabella was fortunate to have impressive contacts with the imperial army. Both her nephew Bourbon and her youngest son, Ferrante, aged just twenty and one of Bourbon's commanders, warned her of what was to come and sent advice for ensuring her safety. With the imperial army fast approaching the gates of Rome, Clement VII was so desperate for cash that he announced the sale of red hats at 40,000 ducats each – and Ercole's biretta was delivered to Isabella at the palace at Santi Apostoli on 5 May. The day before, an entry in Isabella's account book recorded that she gave her steward '50 gold scudi to hire fifty soldiers' and another 15 scudi to pay for gunpowder, pikes and other measures to defend the palace, which had also become the refuge for several nobles and their households as well as the ambassadors of Mantua, Venice, Ferrara and Urbino.[94]

The assault on Rome began at dawn on 6 May. Bourbon was killed immediately and no one else had the authority to prevent the catastrophe that followed. It was far, far worse than anyone could have imagined.[95] Many of the soldiers were German Protestants with a well-deserved reputation for brutality; as one eye-witness in Rome shockingly reported:

> It is impossible to describe the sacrileges and violence they have
> committeed; all the innocent orphans at the [Ospedale] Santo Spirito
> are dead and the sick were thrown into the Tiber; the nuns have been
> desecrated and raped; the friars all murdered; the main chapel at St
> Peter's has been torched… and the heads of the Apostles and other
> relics have been stolen.[96]

The mutineers occupied the Vatican palace, using the Sistine Chapel as their stables, incised graffiti into the plaster of newly painted frescoes and ripped out the delicate intarsia wainscotting to use as fuel. Churches were pillaged for their gold vestments, gilded chalices and reliquaries encrusted with jewels; the palaces of the rich were systematically ransacked, stripped of tapestries, hangings, clothes, jewels, furniture, everything of value, and the loot sold on the market stalls in the Campo dei Fiori. Those who could not pay the ransoms demanded were hacked to death, their bodies left to litter the streets. It was carnage on a terrible scale.

Alfonso I's ambassador wrote to him of his horrors of the sack, which had lasted all day and night: 'I am at Santi Apostoli at the house of the illustrious lady,' he wrote on 7 May. 'I have lost everything I had, horses, possessions, everything.'[97] Isabella's guests were incredibly lucky; although they had to pay 60,000 ducats in ransom, Ferrante arranged for armed soldiers to guard the palace and it was one of the very few not to be looted.[98] When the papal army under Francesco Maria della Rovere finally arrived at the gates of Rome on 22 May, they took one look at the chaos and hastily withdrew. Isabella herself had left a week before, fleeing to Civitavecchia with the Venetian ambassador disguised as her porter. She had also hoped to profit from the mayhem, instructing Ferrante to buy the tapestries designed by Raphael for the Sistine Chapel – he managed to find two and they were packed with her belongings for the journey home, but unfortunately they were seized by pirates on the way and sold to a Venetian merchant.[99]

The Sack of Rome was a watershed moment in the history of Italy. Two years later Charles V signed treaties with Francis I and with Clement VII which effectively recognized his position as arbiter of power in Italy. Isabella's sons were prominent among those Italians rewarded for their loyalty: Federigo was made a duke (see Chapter 7), Ercole was appointed cardinal-protector of Spain and legate to the emperor, while Ferrante, who took over as commander of the imperial army in Italy after Bourbon's death, held the key positions of imperial viceroy in Sicily and imperial governor in Milan. Alfonso I, who had earned the implacable enmity of Clement VII by his change of allegiance shortly before the sack, was well rewarded for that decision by Charles V, who overrode papal objections and formally recognized him as ruler of the fiefs of Modena and Reggio. Alfonso was able to balance his new ties to the empire with an alliance to France cemented by the marriage of his heir, Ercole, to Francis I's sister-in-law Renée of France. And, in a curious twist of fate, it was Isabella who again stood at the top of the staircase in the courtyard of the ducal palace on a cold winter's afternoon, this time to welcome her nephew's bride to Ferrara in December 1528 (see Chapter 10).

FRANCESCO MARIA DELLA ROVERE (1490–1538)
Duke of Urbino

FEDERIGO GONZAGA (1500–40)
Marquis of Mantua

Eleonora Gonzaga, *Duchess of Urbino*

Margherita Paleologus, *Duchess of Mantua*

Charles V, *Emperor*

Clement VII, *Pope*

Giulio Romano and Titian, *Artists*

THE NEW
POLITICAL ORDER

Francesco Maria della Rovere

&

Federigo Gonzaga

It was a moment of huge symbolic importance when Charles V stepped on to Italian soil for the first time, on 12 August 1529. He made his grand entry into Genoa late in the afternoon and was rowed ashore from his galley into the harbour on a ceremonial barge, to the thunder of earsplitting salvoes of artillery fired from the port's fortresses. It was a splendid occasion: the emperor was superbly dressed in a coat of cloth-of-gold, and even the slaves rowing his barge were wearing expensive black velvet.[1] The crowds gathered on the quay shouted 'Long live the ruler of all the world!' – and the words were not empty hyperbole.[2] Charles V was the political leader of the Christian world, ruling an empire which stretched across Europe and the Americas. More importantly for the Italians, he was the unchallenged arbiter of political authority on the peninsula.

News of Charles V's forthcoming trip to Italy had been filling the diplomatic pouches since the spring, but it was only after his departure from Barcelona on 26 July that the actual details of the armada became known. Rumours had proliferated about the quantities of soldiers, horses and artillery on the troopships that were sailing across the Mediterranean with the royal galley, and many Italians were apprehensive about the intentions of this all-powerful figure, whose army had brutally sacked Rome just two years previously. Ostensibly the emperor was travelling in peace to Italy, where he hoped to be crowned by the pope – but was this just an excuse to cloak more hostile intentions?

In Venice the news that 14,000 soldiers had disembarked from seventy troopships at Savona, 20 miles to the west of Genoa, and that another 14,000 men, together with heavy artillery, had crossed the Alps and were marching south, was received with consternation.[3] The government ordered the Duke of Urbino, Francesco Maria della Rovere, who was captain-general of the army, to make preparations for the defence of the city and its mainland possessions in case the Emperor's intentions were not as peaceable as had been advertised. Meanwhile the duke's brother-in-law Federigo Gonzaga, Marquis of Mantua, had joined the dignitaries gathering in Genoa to greet the emperor in person. By all accounts their meeting was very cordial: when Federigo bowed to kiss his hand, the emperor forestalled this formality by quickly removing his hat and warmly embracing the marquis, who had earned his gratitude three years earlier for the support he had given to the imperial cause.

The emperor, however, was a realist and recognized the qualities of both men, regardless of their political loyalties. As the Venetian ambassador wrote: 'Naturally his Majesty is very fond of the Marquis of Mantua [but] has a high opinion of the Duke of Urbino, whom he considers very skilled in the arts of war, which he undoubtedly is and I believe he thinks well of him, not ill.'[4] Both princes would need the sanction of Charles V to secure their survival in the new political order that had been established after the Sack of Rome.

Francesco Maria della Rovere was the eldest son of Giovanni della Rovere, who had been a grocer in Savona when his uncle had been elected Sixtus IV, and raised Giovanni not only into the ranks of the minor nobility as Lord of Senigallia but also married him to the daughter of the Duke of Urbino (see Chapter 4). The young prince had spent most of his childhood in Urbino at the court of his uncle Duke Guidobaldo da Montefeltro and Elisabetta Gonzaga, who was aunt not only to Francesco Maria but also to the other protagonist of this chapter, Federigo Gonzaga. Thanks to the popularity of *The Courtier*, written by Duke Guidobaldo's secretary and diplomat Baldassare Castiglione, the ducal court at Urbino has become a byword for Renaissance courtly elegance and learning – and it was here that Francesco Maria acquired the manners and skills of an aristocrat, as well as some of the less attractive traits of the Renaissance prince.

Francesco Maria's career combined the good and the bad, with immense good fortune interspersed with low points that were very low indeed. Having inherited Senigallia after the death of his father in 1501, he lost it a year later when both Urbino and Senigallia were seized by Cesare Borgia to become part of the short-lived Borgia duchy in northern Italy. The twelve-year-old boy was forced to seek refuge with his paternal relations in Savona, in particular his uncle Cardinal Giuliano della Rovere. And then in November 1503 Cardinal Giuliano was elected as Julius II – it was a turning-point in Francesco Maria's career. The new pope promptly reinstated Duke Guidobaldo

and Duchess Elisabetta as rulers of Urbino and Francesco Maria as Lord of Senigallia. More importantly, he also gave his approval for the duke and duchess, who sadly were unable to have children, to adopt Francesco Maria as heir to this papal fief. As nephew of the pope and future Duke of Urbino, the prince's marital prospects dramatically improved: in January 1505, aged fourteen, he was betrothed to the eleven-year-old Eleonora Gonzaga, daughter of Marquis Francesco and Isabella d'Este, and niece to Duchess Elisabetta.

Thanks to Julius II, Francesco Maria was also able to enjoy a prestigious career at the papal court. Appointed Prefect of Rome and given his first military command in 1504, he was made captain-general of the church four years later, formally receiving his baton of command from the papal legate, Cardinal Francesco Alidosi, in a splendid ceremony in San Petronio at Bologna. Unlike other papal nephews, however, Francesco Maria was not totally reliant on his uncle's favour and, interestingly, he identified more with his maternal relatives and his new in-laws than with his irascible uncle and his della Rovere cousins. The humanists at the court of Urbino emphasized his links to the older Montefeltro dynasty rather than the less prestigious papal family and he used his position at the papal court to facilitate favours for the courts of Urbino, Mantua and Ferrara.

Francesco Maria became Duke of Urbino in April 1508, a few weeks after his eighteenth birthday, and his marriage to Eleonora took place at Christmas that year. The new duchess struggled to produce a family for her husband. She gave birth to her first son in 1511, but he died just two months later; and although she bore Francesco Maria another twelve children, tragically only five of them survived into adulthood. Fortunately her second child, a son born in April 1514, was one of the survivors – he was named Guidobaldo after their uncle.

Meanwhile Francesco Maria's career as captain-general of the papal army involved him in Julius II's war against Ferrara, which soon became a very public clash of personalities between the soldier and his uncle. The pope's first move was to undermine his nephew's authority by overruling Francesco Maria's dismissal of Cardinal Alidosi, the papal legate whom he had arrested on charges of financial irregularities. Furious at the lack of progress of the campaign, Julius II had travelled north to take charge in person, and when he demanded an explanation, Francesco Maria replied that he needed more money

Titian, *Francesco Maria I della Rovere*, 1537 (Florence, Uffizi). A martial image for a famous soldier: the duke sent his favourite suit of armour to Venice so that Titian could include it in the portrait.

and more men, and that the weather was appalling – this last excuse was undoubtedly true, as the winter weather was harsh enough to cause the Po to freeze. Julius II, in one of the ungovernable rages for which he was famous, then shouted abuse at his nephew, accusing him of laziness, and suggested that he should return to the brothel where the duke had apparently been spending most of his time gambling with one of his captains, Fabrizio Colonna.[5]

The truth is often elusive on these occasions: the failure of the Ferrara campaign has been blamed on Francesco Maria's lack of military skills, on inadequate munitions and even on the bad weather. We know from his own writings that he was a naturally cautious soldier who placed considerable importance on careful planning: as he explained, for a successful siege, 'you require a well-supplied commissariat, and regular pay, with sufficient artillery and military machines'.[6] But it is also possible that Francesco Maria was deliberately using delaying tactics for political purposes. The Duke of Ferrara, Alfonso I, was the brother of Isabella d'Este, Francesco Maria's redoubtable mother-in-law, and she herself claimed that he was 'doing all he can to hold back so that he can avoid the damage that would otherwise be done' to Ferrara, a tactic that clearly had to be hidden at all costs from Julius II.[7]

Fortunately for Francesco Maria and his various in-laws, Julius's campaign to take Ferrara collapsed in May 1511 when the Bolognese, with the help of the French, successfully rebelled against papal rule. It was widely believed this was the work of traitors in the city and there were credible rumours that it was Cardinal Alidosi himself who had arranged for the gates to be opened under cover of darkness to let in the French. Alidosi escaped in disguise, while Francesco Maria and the army retreated, leaving their artillery behind. Julius II again lost his temper with his nephew and summoned him to Ravenna where he screamed and ranted before dismissing Francesco Maria from his presence. Unfortunately, one of the first people the duke saw on leaving the papal audience chamber was Alidosi – and, unable to restrain his anger, drew his sword and stabbed the cardinal to death.

The duke justified his actions in a letter to his father-in-law Marquis Francesco Gonzaga on grounds of the damage that Alidosi had done to the reputation of both the pope and the church, which had 'been brought to such a pass by his misdeeds that I couldn't stand it any more'.[8] However, it was not the duke's first murder: as a youth of seventeen, he had violently killed his widowed sister's lover, a courtier of his uncle Duke Guidobaldo. It was evident that Francesco Maria was as hot-tempered and irascible as his uncle. However, murder was a crime in Renaissance Italy – and the murder of a cardinal was also an offence against the church. Moreover, with so many witnesses, and with Francesco Maria himself wholly unrepentant, it was inevitable that the case would come to court. Rather surprisingly, in August 1511 the board of six cardinal judges acquitted him after his lawyer justified the assassination on the grounds of Alidosi's treasonable behaviour, and also that the cardinal himself had been guilty of murder and rape while serving as legate to Bologna.

Relations between Francesco Maria and his uncle did not improve. During the trial Julius II had fallen dangerously ill and, although he agreed to absolve his nephew of the sin of murder, the pope refused to receive him at his sickbed – the nature of Julius II's illness is not clear, but he recovered after insisting, against the advice of his doctors, on a diet of plums, strawberries and grapes, washed down with wine.[9] The following spring Francesco Maria taunted his uncle by threatening to join Louis XII, who had openly declared himself as an enemy of the pope by calling for a council to depose Julius II. The pope reacted with characteristic fury, declared his nephew a rebel and exiled him from Rome. One fortunate result of this was that Francesco Maria did not take part in the defeat at the Battle of Ravenna in April 1512 but a month later, when it became clear that the victorious French could not capitalize on their triumph, Julius II forgave his nephew and re-stored his baton of command, giving Francesco Maria the kudos of driving the French out of Italy. He also rewarded his nephew with the fief of Pesaro after Costanzo Sforza died unexpectedly that August. The pope's refusal to recognize Costanzo's uncle as the legal heir was not popular and it was another six months before the cardinals would agree to it, finally ratifying the decision at Julius II's bedside shortly before his death in February 1513 – Francesco Maria later had to buy off Costanzo's uncle for the sum of 20,000 ducats.[10]

Julius II's other legacy to his nephew, more of a poisoned chalice, was his tomb, a grandiose monument begun in 1505 by Michelangelo. Julius II had given the sculptor 1,000 ducats to buy marble in Carrara and had then infuriated him by inexplicably cancelling the project. The pope's executors drew up plans with Michelangelo for a more modest project but work progressed slowly. Vasari, a close friend of the artist, described how Michelangelo was being harassed by Francesco Maria, who claimed that the artist had now received 16,000 ducats and had still not finished.[11] In December 1531 it was the duke himself who was being harassed: 'We have had your letters of the first, second, third, fourth and fifth of December', he wrote to his agent in Rome.[12] Negotiations with the notoriously difficult Michelangelo were complicated by the need to redesign the tomb when it had to be relocated from St Peter's, where Julius II had wished to be buried, to San Pietro in Vincoli, his titular church as cardinal. And it was still unfinished when Francesco Maria died in 1538.

Meanwhile, there was a new pope in the Vatican. Francesco Maria initially found favour with Leo X, who confirmed his position as captain-general of the church; however, as his in-laws had also discovered, family priorities outweighed all other considerations for this Medici pope (see Chapter 6). Francesco Maria was particularly hard hit. In June 1515 Leo X gave the post of captain-general to his own brother, Giuliano de' Medici, and when Giuliano died in February 1516, appointed his nephew Lorenzo de' Medici in Giuliano's place. And worse was to come: Leo X now made plans to confiscate the fief of Urbino from Francesco Maria and give it to Lorenzo instead. Reviving the murder of Cardinal Alidosi as a pretext, the pope accused Francesco Maria of treason and summoned him to Rome but the duke, recognizing the pretext, sent Duchess Eleonora in his place. When 'her ladyship the duchess began to describe how she had gone to Rome to talk to the pope', wrote a Mantuan courtier to Federigo Gonzaga, 'there was no one who did not cry on hearing the dreadful behaviour of the pope', who apparently refused to say a single word in response to her entreaties, but 'just looked at her through his spectacles and shrugged his shoulders'.[13]

Francesco Maria was excommunicated on 27 April 1516 and deprived of his duchy, which was conquered by Lorenzo de' Medici at the head of the papal army: Gubbio fell on 12 May, Pesaro was lost after an eight-day siege and Urbino was taken at the end of the month after Francesco Maria ordered the city to surrender rather than be sacked. He sent his aunt Elisabetta Gonzaga, his wife Eleonora Gonzaga and their son, Guidobaldo, now two years old, to Mantua: on 1 June the Ferrarese chronicler Giovanni Maria Zerbinati noted sadly that 'the duchess his wife and the dowager duchess passed through Ferrara on the Po but they did not disembark because they had been excommunicated'.[14]

Immediately Francesco Maria made plans to reconquer his state. Precious silverware was melted down to raise money: 'The duchess told me yesterday,' wrote a courtier in July 1516, 'that it had been necessary to destroy two basins and ewers which had been designed in the antique manner by Raphael.'[15] Eleonora's jewels were sold and Francesco Maria tried desperately to find allies at the papal court. On 17 January he addressed the College of Cardinals to explain why he was planning action against the pope.[16] He had behaved honourably 'after having lost my fortresses and nearly all my worldly possessions', he said; and he had kept to the promise he had made to Leo X 'not to make any attempt on my state, or disturb his nephew to whom it had been given'. However, despite keeping to his side of the bargain, the pope continued to punish him: 'Harsher interdicts were constantly issued against me, and my distinguished father-in-law has been ordered not to harbour me in his territory; nay, I daily discover plots against my life by poison or dagger,' he added, thinly veiled accusations against the pope himself. And he justified his intention to use force to oust the Medici on the grounds that Leo himself, while still a cardinal, had ordered the brutal sacking of Prato to force the Florentines to accept the Medici back into power in 1512: 'It will be far more justifiable in me,' he added, because 'in the opinion of my own people and of all men except his Holiness, I am the legitimate sovereign.'

Francesco Maria inspired a high degree of loyalty among his men: as he prepared to leave Mantua with his motley army of soldiers, which numbered 8,000 infantry and 1,500 cavalry, they swore an oath 'never to abandon him'.[17] Leo X had complacently dismissed the fiery speech to the cardinals, so neither he nor Lorenzo were prepared for Francesco Maria's sudden assault on Urbino. By the end of February, aided by his loyal subjects, he had reconquered most of the duchy. Unfortunately he was unable to withstand the might of an army three times the size of his own which Lorenzo, with the massive resources of the papacy behind him, had been able to assemble. In true chivalric style, Francesco Maria challenged Lorenzo de' Medici to a fair fight: 'Four thousand men against four thousand... or if [Lord Lorenzo] will fight me alone, so much the better.'[18] Not surprisingly, Lorenzo refused the challenge and continued the war, committing terrible atrocities in the name of the pope – he burned down one town, killing 700 men and fifty old women, while others defended resolutely, the women fighting alongside the men.

Cleverly, Francesco Maria now resorted to guerrilla tactics: he captured a convoy of carts bringing cash from Rome to pay papal troops but in the end the forces – military, political and financial – lined up against him proved insuperable. The penniless ex-duke admitted defeat but he was able to drive a hard bargain as his price for withdrawing: in addition to the immense costs the pope had incurred in the fight to regain the duchy for Lorenzo, he was further beggared by having to pay all Francesco Maria's expenses as well. And Lorenzo's reign was shortlived – he died in April 1519 without an heir and Urbino was absorbed into the Papal States. Francesco Maria had to be patient, waiting for a political solution or for the death of the pope – although, at forty-three years of age, Leo X was still relatively young.

Meanwhile in Mantua that month Francesco Maria's young brother-in-law, Federigo, who was a month short of his nineteenth birthday, became marquis after the death of his father. While under the regency of his mother Isabella d'Este for the next three years, he pursued his military career. Paolo Giovio judged both men to be skilled soldiers and, though he thought that the duke's talents were somewhat superior, neither of them were as talented as Alfonso d'Este, the greatest soldier of the period. 'Next to Duke Alfonso in distinction is Francesco Maria della Rovere, duke of Urbino,' Giovio wrote. 'He is always ruthless' but 'maintains discipline in camp by consistent use of punishments and rewards'; his decisions 'are cautious but enhanced by sound reasoning' and 'in crowded councils of war no man has ever debated more cautiously, prudently and skillfully than he.'[19] He thought Federigo was hampered by political considerations: as marquis of the imperial fief of Mantua, 'he simply could not perform service for the pope... lest he do injury to the emperor' but, he continued, 'wherever action has been required, he has always shown splendid signs of spirited valour'.[20]

Much of Federigo's childhood had been dictated by political considerations. In 1510, at the age of just ten, he had been sent to Rome as hostage for his father's loyalty. He was to spend three years at the court

Titian, *Federigo Gonzaga*, 1528 (Madrid, Prado). Less militaristic than his brother-in-law, Federigo preferred his sumptuous blue velvet doublet to armour, his podgy fingers stroking his little dog.

of Julius II where, surprisingly, he was a great success with the irascible old man. He had apartments in the Vatican and when the pope was seriously ill in 1511, it was little Federigo who persuaded him to sip his broth and he was always welcome in the bedchamber, unlike Francesco Maria.[21] The little boy was thoroughly indulged by Julius II, who gave him a cloth-of-gold coat that had once been worn by Cesare Borgia and took him to see the great cannons in the papal armoury, aptly named 'the Bull', 'the Lion', 'the Wolf' and so on.[22] Among Federigo's other friends was his uncle, Cardinal Sigismondo, who gave him parties with famous entertainers such as the buffoon Fra Mariano, who had once been barber to Leo X's father.[23] His time in the masculine world of Rome gave him experience of a court far grander than that at Mantua.

Although Federigo went back home after the death of Julius II in February 1513, it was not long before he became a hostage for a second time, again as guarantor for his father's good behaviour. The French conquest of Milan in September 1515 altered the political landscape for the pro-imperial marquis, who sent his son to Milan the following month to offer congratulations to Francis I – and to underline his promise that he did not intend to ally against the king. Francis I too took a liking to the young prince, who remained with the royal court when it returned to France the following year. And the king made sure that Mantua's allegiance to France was highly visible: according to the Mantuan ambassador, the king ordered Federigo to cut his hair short 'in the manner that his Majesty had cut', and wear French-style clothes.[24]

In April 1517 Federigo returned to Mantua, where he played an increasingly active role in government due to his father's declining health. During his absence in France, Marquis Francesco had negotiated a bride for his son: Maria Paleologus, the eldest daughter and heir of the ailing Marquis of Monferrat, a small state on the borders of Milan and Savoy. Maria was just eight years old but Federigo was so captivated by her that he decided, very unusually, to marry her there and then, though the consummation of the marriage was to be delayed until her sixteenth birthday in September 1524. It was a decision that would have consequences later, but for the present there was no hurry for Federigo: he was only seventeen himself, and not short of lovers.

Federigo was soon back in France to take part in the royal joust to celebrate the birth of the dauphin on 28 February 1518. It was to be held on 8 May, the feast of St Michael, patron saint of France's chivalric order, and rulers were invited from across Europe. Sadly the marquis was too ill to attend, so Federigo went instead. With the reputation of Mantua at stake, it was critical for the eighteen-year-old to perform well. The marquis, aware of the importance of style and the messages it could convey, bought rolls of expensive Florentine gold cloth for Federigo to take to France where he was to get the royal tailors to make his outfit.[25] The anxious father also instructed Federigo's servant that 'each and every time you give him the lance', the man was to say the words: 'Remember that you are the son of Lord Francesco Gonzaga, Marquis of Mantua.'[26] Federigo had many friends at the French court, where he was a popular figure, and he was a great success at the jousts before unfortunately cutting his leg in one contest; the wound went septic, forcing him to retire from the competition.

By the time Federigo became marquis in April 1519, he had become a devotee of grand display. For his first Carnival in February 1520, he staged his own joust with lavish prizes designed to attract the best knights in Italy. Also in Mantua at this time was Francesco Maria, still stateless, and his family – living on the 6,000 ducats a year which Federigo's father had generously willed to his daughter and son-in-law for as long as they remained in exile.[27] Though there is no evidence of the ex-duke's participation in the joust, we can assume that the exiles took part in the festive celebrations at court, which included banquets and balls, as well as performances of several classical dramas: one of the plays was *La Calandria*, a bawdy comedy based on Plautus' *Menaechmi*, featuring twins and a lot of cross-dressing, which had been written by Cardinal Bernardo Dovizi da Bibbiena and had been first staged at Francesco Maria's court in Urbino in 1513.

That May, Federigo and Francesco Maria travelled to Venice for a brief holiday. The marquis was accompanied 'by his favourite', an unnamed married women who was probably his mistress, Isabella Boschetti – much to the disapproval of his mother, Isabella d'Este, and presumably also of the two 'duchesses' of Urbino, Elisabetta Gonzaga and Eleonora Gonzaga, who were in the party.[28] Their visit coincided with the *Sensa*, the Feast of the Ascension, which was celebrated in Venice in unique style with the annual marriage of the Doge and the sea, a ritual which dated back to the eleventh century and symbolized Venice's domination of the Adriatic. It was the excuse for fifteen days of parties and, typical of this prosperous mercantile republic, an enormous international fair which took place in Piazza San Marco, where hundreds of stalls were set up – Venetian shops had to close – to sell all manner of wares: ribbons and textiles, spices and perfumes, sweetmeats, the glassware for which the city was famous, as well as books and pictures.

Unfortunately, by the end of the year political reality began to intrude on the cordial relations between the two families. On 11 December 1520 Federigo, who relied heavily on his income as a soldier, signed a *condotta* with Leo X for 12,000 ducats a year.[29] The offer was tempting financially, and deliberately so on the part of the pope. Leo X's dislike of Francesco Maria had not abated and he insisted, as a condition of Federigo's employment, that the ex-duke and his family had to leave Mantua – they moved to Venice in early 1521. Another clause, potentially far more lethal, was that Federigo had to be available to fight the emperor if necessary, though this was not a worry as Leo X was currently in an alliance with Charles V.

The following summer Leo X promoted Federigo to captain-general of the church and on 21 November he won a famous victory, his armies ousting the French from Milan. Ten days later, on 1 December 1521, Leo died and the new pope, Adrian VI, who was in Spain when the conclave took place, was elected on 9 January in his absence. Francesco Maria, who had been at Lake Garda when news of the pope's death reached him, immediately dispatched an envoy to Spain from where Adrian VI not only confirmed Federigo's appointment as captain-general but also reinstated a jubilant Francesco Maria as Duke of Urbino. When he went to Rome that September to greet the pope, it was seen that he had adopted two new emblems to celebrate his restoration: one was a palm tree weighted down by a block of marble, with the motto 'though depressed it springs back' to indicate that adversity had not broken him, and he adopted this for his coinage; the other emblem was that of an eagle protecting its young from an attack by another bird of prey.[30]

By the spring of 1523 Francesco Maria and his family were back home, and the duke had started on a massive campaign of building in Pesaro, not only to repair the damage done by the war but also to provide visual evidence of his authority in his new city. There were compelling reasons for this: although he had been closely related to his predecessor as Duke of Urbino, he was the first of a new dynasty to rule in Pesaro and – more importantly – this port on the Adriatic coast, situated on the main route from Rome to Venice, was about to take over from the inaccessible hilltop fortress of Urbino as the prime residence of the ducal court. What was really significant about Francesco Maria's plans to rebuild and renovate Pesaro was his choice of artist. Far from choosing local talent, he instructed his agents in Rome to find an artist who had worked under Raphael and was trained in the *all'antica* style that had become high fashion at the courts of Julius II and Leo X, and introduce it as his own court at Pesaro.

Julius II was one of the greatest patrons of the Italian Renaissance, employing the three leading artists of the period – Raphael, Michelangelo and Bramante – to create projects that in scale and in ambition dwarfed those of his predecessors. Underlining the renewed power of the church, he concentrated his energies on St Peter's, rebuilding the old basilica dedicated to the first pope, and on the Vatican, which he vastly enlarged to create a magnificent space, inspired by the villas of ancient Rome, for papal ceremonial. At the Villa Belvedere behind the palace Bramante designed an ingenious spiral staircase, more a ramp, up which visitors rode through the four orders of classical architecture – Doric, Ionic, Corinthian and Composite – to reach the rooms where the pope displayed his priceless collection of antique sculpture.

Girolamo Genga arrived in Pesaro in August 1522 and was soon busy with the wide range of tasks expected of a Renaissance court artist, which included not only overseeing the design, construction and decoration of the ducal residences, but also more ephemeral decorations required to celebrate state entries, weddings, theatrical performances and other courtly entertainments. Vasari described him as 'painter, sculptor, architect, musician and conversationalist'.[31] Among his responsibilities were buying antiquities and precious stones for Francesco Maria's collection – one of his purchases was, appropriately, a valuable antique cornelian engraved with a portrait of Hannibal, the famous Carthaginian soldier who had once waged war against Rome.[32] Genga also designed a series of outfits for little Guidobaldo – a fisherman, a soldier, a Moor, a gardener and even a nun – so that the boy could dress up in a different one each day during Carnival.[33] Above all, he was responsible for the design, construction and decoration of the new ducal palace in Pesaro. Francesco Maria planned to remodel the old Sforza palace in the centre of the city to create a suitable setting for the display of his authority and, in a striking statement of continuity with the old regime, the duke chose not to alter the facade of this fifteenth-century building. The palace behind, however, was considerably enlarged and lavishly refurbished, and the duke added a hunting park and ornamental gardens that centred on an 'ancient ruin' to create a more fashionable setting for the ducal residence.

Francesco Maria also started work on the defences of Pesaro, incorporating the old Sforza fortress into a new pentagonal circuit of walls fortified with massive angular bastions, designed to strengthen the defences of the port against an attack by armed galleys. He was not wholly convinced of the superiority of artillery. 'I would not say that artillery is no good,' he wrote, 'nor does it always guarantee victory, but I say it is well that it is accompanied by sword, pike and archibusque.'[34] His military opinions, collected in his *Discorsi Militari*, include several anedoctes showing his practical bent: when one engineer brought him a design for fortifying Senigallia, he noticed that the city was not protected from a nearby hill, to which the engineer responded, 'I didn't think much about that; so far as I'm concerned it is enough for the drawing to be beautiful,' to which the duke retorted, 'the drawing itself is beautiful but it won't work well for my Senigallia.'[35]

The duke's military talents were recognized by the Venetians, who appointed him captain-general, an honour celebrated in Venice in June 1524 with a magnificent ceremony in San Marco and ten days of banquets, parties, music, dancing and gondola racing. Moreover, his job soon involved more than mere fighting. Soldiers, he considered, knew far more about defence than architects who, in his own experience, may have been competent draughtsmen but who had little understanding of military matters. The Venetian authorities agreed with him and his role was extended to advising the republic on how best to update the defences of their own territories not only on the mainland but also in their ports on the Adriatic (see Chapter 9).

Meanwhile Marquis Federigo's post as captain-general of the church was confirmed by Clement VII, who had been elected on 19 November 1523 as successor to Adrian VI. However, the new pope was Leo X's cousin – and not only was he as suspicious of Francesco

Maria as Leo himself had been, he also had the Medici family at the top of his agenda. The situation, already fraught with danger, slipped out of control when it became apparent that he was incapable of coping with the perfect storm of political events that overwhelmed him. His treasury was bankrupt; Catholics were leaving the church in droves to join the Protestant rebellion that was spreading rapidly through Germany and other countries north of the Alps; the Turks were advancing unhindered into eastern Europe; Henry VIII was demanding a divorce from Charles V's aunt, Catherine of Aragon; and the armies of Francis I and the emperor were openly fighting for control of Italy and the papacy. Every decision the pope took would anger one side or the other – so he took no decisions, and did everything he could to maintain the Medici as rulers in Florence.

As Clement VII oscillated between support for Francis I or Charles V, Francesco Maria and Federigo found themselves allies one moment, enemies the next. In May 1526 they were on the same side after Clement VII, Francis I and Venice all signed the League of Cognac to counter Charles V's relentless advance across northern Italy. That autumn the emperor responded by sending 12,000 German soldiers across the Alps under the command of Georg von Frundsberg. It was soon evident that neither Francesco Maria nor Federigo was fully committed to the Cognac agreement. The duke failed to act on instructions from Venice to halt Frundsberg, refusing to engage the imperial army in battle because of the appalling November weather and the fact that his army of 9,000 men was powerless against so many Germans.[36] The marquis had more personal reasons: not only was Mantua an imperial fief, but Federigo's brother Ferrante was a commander in the imperial army serving under their cousin Charles of Bourbon. By November it was clear that he had abandoned his position as captain-general of the church after he granted Frundsberg free passage through Mantuan territory, even providing boats to enable the troops to cross the Po – it was this gesture that earned him the gratitude of Charles V and the unusually warm welcome the emperor gave him when they finally met for the first time in Genoa.

Federigo was not the only prince who was now openly supporting the imperial cause: his uncle Alfonso I d'Este, once a staunch ally of France, had also judiciously changed sides. Even Francesco Maria and his Venetian masters, who were nominally allies of the French, understood that the emperor would be the winner in the end, but they understood the diplomatic game well enough to keep their opinions to themselves. It cannot have been much of a surprise when Francesco Maria took to his bed in early January suffering from gout, an opportune attack which kept him out of the fighting until the spring, by which time the imperial army had mutinied and begun its march south towards Rome. The duke was ordered to follow, which he did – slowly – and avoided engaging the enemy who was, after all, marching away from the republic's borders. On 6 May, the day when the imperial troops began their horrendous assault on Rome, he was at Lake Trasimeno, some 125 miles north. It was another two weeks before he reached the edge of the stricken city and, having seen the chaos inside the walls, retreated hastily.

In addition to the papal and Venetian armies, Francesco Maria was also marching with civilian agents of both powers, who had opposing views on what should be done. Francesco Guicciardini, a Medici stalwart and historian who was serving as legate to the papal army, wanted Francesco Maria to launch a bid to rescue Clement VII from the heavily fortified Castel Sant'Angelo, where the pope was hiding with several thousand men, women and children. His Venetian counterpart, by contrast, warned the captain-general to do no such thing and that his government had no intention of risking the lives of their men on such a dangerous enterprise.[37] Unfortunately for Francesco Maria's reputation, the Venetians later issued a government statement denying all knowledge of this 'warning' while Guicciardini accused Francesco Maria of cowardice, and of refusing to rescue the pope in retaliation for Leo X's confiscation of Urbino a decade earlier. What is evident from the documents, however, is that Francesco Maria had put his loyalty to Venice above any allegiance to the republic's allies – and showed this loyalty by following Venetian military policy to the letter, which was to avoid direct confrontation with an enemy army at all costs (see Chapter 9).

In the two years that had elapsed since the Sack of Rome, when Charles V's mutinous army inflicted such unspeakable horrors in the capital of Christendom, the city had slowly begun to recover. Italy too had begun to adjust to the political reality that the peninsula was no longer independent of foreign powers and that the emperor was now the arbiter of power. It was a humiliation that lay just below the surface of the magnificence and splendour of Charles V's reception at Genoa in August 1529. Heads of state and ambassadors from across Italy had gathered in Genoa to greet his arrival with his enormous entourage numbering some 5,000 servants, secretaries and courtiers, as well as thousands of troops. While the size of his entourage did do justice to his great status, the first sight of this mighty ruler did not impress, a fact remarked upon by almost all the eye-witness reports of the event. According to a Mantuan envoy, he was not tall, but 'short like me' as the envoy explained, 'and stoops a little, with a small, long face, pointed beard and his mouth is always open; apart from that he is very well formed, graceful, and good-mannered'.[38] It was true that Charles V did not cut a dashing figure – unlike Francis I, for instance – and had inherited the famous Habsburg lantern jaw; but it was soon evident that the emperor did possess talents more critical to the exercise of power.

The warmth of Charles V's greeting for Marquis Federigo was noted by several observers. The two rulers were the same age, both born in 1500, and spent much of the next few days in each other's company, 'chatting away as if they had been brought up together'. They rode around Genoa 'talking of houses, horses, weapons, war, cities' and, what really impressed the Mantuan envoy, 'whenever his Majesty arrives or leaves he always removes his hat, his face full of pleasure, something he does not do to anyone else'.[39] Charles V left Genoa at the end of August – apparently the air did not agree with him and he had been ill with a fever.[40] Federigo went home, full of optimism for his future, and Francesco Maria continued busily organizing the defences of Venice's borders, until the emperor's intentions became clear.

The coronation of Charles V would mark the end of an era in European history, the last Holy Roman Emperor to be crowned by the pope in a tradition that stretched back over seven centuries to AD 800, when Leo III crowned Charlemagne on Christmas Day in St Peter's. It was also the start of a new political era for Italy. The decision to hold the imperial coronation at Bologna rather than Rome was a political one, dictated in part by Charles V's wish to travel to Germany as soon as possible to support his brother Ferdinand against an invading Turkish army (the Turks took Buda in late August, and laid siege to

Vienna the following month, although they were forced to withdraw in October). And, although Clement VII argued against this break from tradition, he was overruled – it was a small point, but a symbolic one, illustrating just how far the supreme spiritual authority of the pope was now subjugated to secular power.

Clement VII made his formal entry into Bologna on 24 October through a city decked out with draperies, garlands and triumphal arches decorated with biblical and religious imagery underlining the joint responsibilities of pope and emperor in the Christian world. Charles V's entry, which took place on 5 November, was signifcantly more elaborate. The emperor was dressed in armour, his helmet topped by a gilded eagle, and he was accompanied by a huge cavalcade of soldiers and courtiers who rode into the city through streets ornamented with images of ancient Roman emperors and the classical pantheon celebrating his rule over land and sea.

That autumn, as Bologna filled up with dignitaries, Charles V and Clement VII met daily to discuss the political situation. The priority for the pope was financing and supplying the imperial army, which was currently laying siege to Florence to force the city to accept the return of the Medici. One of the more unlikely items to survive in the archives is Charles V's handwritten list of points he wanted to discuss with the pope: the divorce of Catherine of Aragon, 'the queen of England' was top of the list.[41] They were lodged in adjoining apartments in the Palazzo dei Signori, Bologna's medieval town hall on the city's main square. Their rooms were apparently linked by a private door to guarantee some privacy from observation – the arrangement gives a domestic context to the reality of the two most powerful men in Christendom running both the church and the empire from their bedrooms.

The significance of the negotiations was echoed by one chronicler, whose account of the meeting referred to Charles V as Caesar, and Clement VII as Peter.[42] The treaty of Bologna, signed on 29 December and formally proclaimed on 1 January, effectively formalized Charles V's role as supreme authority in Italy, in control of the entire peninsula, with the notable exception of Venice, with whom he had signed an alliance (see Chapter 9). Clement VII was forced to accept the imperial diktat over several issues: the pope objected to Alfonso I d'Este's claim to Modena and Reggio, but these were imperial fiefs and Charles V was within his rights to insist; more contentious was Francesco Maria's rights to Urbino and Pesaro, two papal fiefs in which the pope was obliged to accept Charles V's nominee. Charles V made further signs of favour towards Francesco Maria by the offer of the post of commander of the imperial army in Italy. The duke turned the offer down, saying that he was promised to Venice – and when Charles V asked the Venetian authorities to release the duke, they refused.

For five months Bologna was in effect the capital city of Europe. With both the papal and imperial courts in residence, and Italy's princes and their entourages all attending the event, it must have been one of the most glittering social gatherings of the Renaissance. The saloons and dining halls were thronged with princes, cardinals, ambassadors, prelates, intellectuals, poets and courtiers all vying for advantage, and filled with gossip. Federigo arrived on 20 November, Francesco Maria and Eleonora two days later; Isabella d'Este had been in residence since November, hosting her lavish parties. There were balls, banquets, a tournament in Bologna's main square and hunting expeditions in the foothills of the Apennines. The competitive atmosphere was particularly evident on the dining tables of the rich and powerful, where they showed off the quality and quantity of their silverware, the number of stewards and squires serving the meals, the skills of their carvers and musicians, and the elaboration and cost of the dishes themselves – the second-hand dealers of Bologna had a profitable line hiring out silverware for these banquets.

At the end of January one of Charles V's army commanders gave Federigo Gonzaga an unusual present. 'To demonstrate to the Marquis of Mantua the love he bears him', Anton de Leyva gave him 'a most beautiful' present of ten large artillery pieces, which a Mantuan chronicler considered 'perhaps the most beautiful that have ever been made'.[43] Leyva himself had captured three of them from the Venetians and the other seven from the French during the recent wars – it was a novel choice of gift, a military equivalent as it were, of the hunting dogs and horses that were more common choices in times of peace. Soon afterwards Federigo left Bologna, declining to attend the coronation ceremonies on the grounds that he objected to the Marquis of Monferrato being given precedence over him – as we shall see, the two princes were involved in an unfortunate spat about Federigo's marriage. There is no evidence that he left in a huff; indeed, he might well have gone home to prepare Mantua for the forthcoming visit of Charles V, who intended

overleaf Mantua, Palazzo Te, courtyard, 1525–35. Federigo converted his father's stables to create this splendid suburban villa, designed and decorated by his court artist Giulio Romano as a setting for lavish entertainments.

to break his journey from Bologna to Germany to stay with Federigo for a few days of hunting and feasting.

The imperial coronation involved two rituals. First Clement VII crowned Charles V with the iron crown of Lombardy in a modest ceremony which took place in the chapel of the Palazzo dei Signori on 22 February; this was followed two days later by the much grander ceremony in San Petronio when Clement VII formally crowned him as Holy Roman Emperor. And one of the proud bearers of the imperial insignia in the grand procession into the church was Francesco Maria, who carried the imperial sword. Rather bizarrely, in an attempt to maintain the custom of imperial coronations taking place in St Peter's in Rome, San Petronio had been transformed with temporary decorations to resemble the Constantinian basilica, including three wooden chapels and a porphyry disc placed on the processional route to represent the porphyry slab set in the pavement of St Peter's to mark the spot where Charlemagne himself was crowned over seven centuries before.[44]

Charles V left Bologna in March to travel north to Austria and Germany. On 25 March he arrived in Mantua, where he spent four weeks as the guest of Federigo – Giovio thought him a good host, 'pleasant in disposition, eager, generous, and hospitable'.[45] Above all, the visit was a high honour for the marquis, and one that was appreciably heightened on 8 April when the emperor promoted Mantua to a duchy, giving Federigo the same status as his brother-in-law. The new duke had spent lavishly to ensure that the banquets, balls and other entertainments were of an exceptional quality – the Mantuan chronicler boasted that the tapestries in his guest's apartments, which were woven with gold, silver and silk thread, were worth over 18,000 ducats.[46] Above all, there was a lot of hunting, a pastime of which Charles V, like Federigo, was extremely fond. On one rather overambitious excursion 3,000 beaters, 300 dogs and ten cannon attempted to force the boar out of the forest but the animals refused to run, more petrified by the sound of the 10,000 horses waiting for them.[47] And Mantua too had been transformed for the occasion with temporary architecture that included a copy of Trajan's Column in Rome, 80 feet high and ornamented with scenes which, according to the chronicler 'signified his Imperial Majesty as ruler of the world'.[48] This was just one of several references to Charles V as heir to the emperors of ancient Rome – and there were even more flattering parallels drawn between Charles V and Jupiter, including the scene of Jupiter destroying the rebel giants, an obvious allusion to the emperor's triumph over Italy.

Duke Federigo was exceptionally fortunate in his choice of court artist. Like Francesco Maria, he had been very impressed with the *all'antica* style of Julius II's artists, in particular with Raphael, and he instructed his own agents in Rome to look for a suitable artist for the Gonzaga court. Giulio Romano arrived in Mantua in October 1524, with a judicious present of antique sculpture for his new patron. He soon reorganized the process of artistic production in Mantua by heading a team of craftsmen working in every medium, producing frescoes and panel paintings, sculpture and architecture, but also tapestries, silverware and the stage sets for Federigo's theatrical entertainments – he is even recorded as buying Indian peacocks for his master.[49] It would become one of the greatest patron–artist partnerships of the century: money, taste and creativity combined to produce some of the most impressive works of the sixteenth century, and further enhanced Mantua's already burgeoning reputation as one of the foremost cultural centres in Italy.

Federigo's first project for Giulio Romano was the conversion of his father's stables into a suburban villa, the Palazzo Te. Built on an island in the Mincio ouside the city gates, it had been started in 1525–6 and was largely finished by time of Charles V's visit; by all accounts the emperor was duly struck by what he saw (see Conclusion). One of Giulio Romano's particular skills was his ability to create an impressive effect without unnecessary expense. The villa was built cheaply, not with stone but with brick that was covered with stucco to look like stone. He also had a sense of humour, evidently shared with his patron. The architecture of the Palazzo Te is a humorous take on ancient Rome – less worship, more wit – with 'cracks' in the pediments and sections of the apparently correct *all'antica* frieze that appear, somewhat alarmingly, to be slipping out of place.

Inside, the rooms were frescoed, another cheap and quick medium, with different themes. One devoted to his horses suggests that Federigo had inherited a love of racing from his parents: the horses are each depicted in life-size portraits standing in front of an illusionistic

overleaf Mantua, Palazzo Te, Sala dei Cavalli, 1525–26. The Gonzaga were enthusiastic breeders of racehorses and their stud was famous throughout Italy; this room is devoted to portraits of Federigo's favourite mounts.

screen of *all'antica* piers flanking what appear to be windows through which the visitor could see views of the Mantuan countryside beyond. In another room, the Sala dei Giganti, there was a bravura display of Jupiter hurling thunderbolts at the giants for having the temerity to attack Mount Olympus – with all its overtones of imperial triumph. Strikingly, Giulio Romano's frescoes transformed the entire room into a collapsing palace, with even the 'brickwork' over the doors appearing to disintegrate in the violence of the battle.

Arguably the grandest room in the palace was the banqueting hall, decorated with the legend of Cupid and Psyche that culminated fittingly in their wedding feast. Prominently placed in the wedding scene was a lavishly laden credenza, the sideboard covered with the silver and gilded ewers and dishes that was one of the hallmarks of wealth and prestige at a Renaissance court. The room itself was a hall of veritable Bacchanalian pleasures, 'an image of wit and virility' as one scholar described it.[50] The guests could show off their knowledge of mythology identifying details in the scenes or, more likely, could quaff their wine just as Bacchus and his followers were doing on the walls, which were also covered with eroticized male and female bodies indulging their sensual desires, both suggestively and explicitly.

One of the grandest banquets staged for Charles V's visit took place on 2 April 1530 in this extraordinary room. Federigo certainly understood the value of extravagant dining as one of the ways in which Renaissance princes could demonstrate their magnificence. The inventory of his silver listed 359 individual pieces, weighing a total of some 545 lb, many of which would have been on display that Saturday afternoon.[51] Thanks to the survival of quantities of designs, we know the details of much of Federigo's silver. His serving dishes, bowls, salts, candlesticks, sauce boats, wine coolers, spoons, forks and other tableware were made of gold, silver, rock crystal and other costly materials. They were made to exotic designs by the inventive Giulio Romano, whose surviving drawings include ewers with ducks' heads as spouts and bowls with lizards as handles.

Unfortunately we do not know what Federigo's guests ate at the banquet, which must have been one of the most stunning of the period. However, we know the menu of a much more modest banquet given in Ferrara in January 1529, at which Federigo's mother Isabella d'Este was the guest of honour. This featured ten courses, alternating between

Mantua, Palazzo Te, Sala dei Giganti, 1530–32. Here Giulio Romano depicted the Fall of the Giants; the entire structure appears to be collapsing around the viewer under the onslaught of Jupiter and his thunderbolts.

overleaf Giulio Romano decorated the Sala di Psiche (1527–30) with the story of Cupid and Psyche, creating a sensual backdrop for Federigo's banquets.

hot and cold dishes, with as many as ten different dishes for each course: the fourth course, for example, included roast partridges, rabbits and doves; saffron-flavoured sausages; capons stuffed with salami; pigeons fried with sliced citron; pasta stuffed with bone marrow; freshwater fish roasted with sugar and cinnamon; other fish served in a sweet pinenut sauce; brown trout in broth; roast lampreys; and chestnut pies. Like the other courses, it was followed by an interval during which the diners could recover their appetites and relax as musicians and other performers showed off their talents, in this case an eight-voice choir accompanied by a lute, a viola, a German flute and a trombone.[52] Music was a key component of Renaissance dining and Federigo was a keen patron, employing several musicians who had been part of Leo X's court; he also bought Leo's alabaster organ.[53]

One of the issues discussed during Charles V's stay in Mantua was Federigo's lack of a wife. Although he had married Maria Paleologus in 1517 and his bride had been expected to move to Mantua when she reached the age of sixteen, six years had now passed and she had still not arrived. One of Maria's attractions had been that her father, the Marquis of Monferrat, had named her as heir to the state but unfortunately he had died before this had been officially made legal and her uncle inherited Monferrat. Federigo himself had tired of his child bride and by 1522 had become ambitous for a grander match. A range of alternatives had been suggested, including the daughter of the King of Poland and the sister of the King of Navarre. And there was also his mistress Isabella Boschetti, to whom he appeared as devoted as ever. In 1528 Isabella's husband tried to poison her – we can only guess why – and Federigo, far from using this as an excuse to get rid of the husband, used the crime as a pretext to get rid of Maria by accusing his Paleologus in-laws of attempted murder. He had also successfully petitioned Clement VII that year for a divorce.

Federigo's reluctance to marry had attracted some comment. The Venetian satirist Pietro Aretino, nicknamed the 'scourge of princes' by Clement VII, lampooned Federigo in a play *Il Marescalco*. The central character of the play is a farrier whose duke – a thinly disguised portrait of Federigo – has decided that his servant must take a wife.[54]

previous pages Mantua, Palazzo Te, Sala di Psiche, 1527–30. In addition to his architectural and pictorial projects, Giulio Romano also provided designs for Federigo's silverware, and a marble tomb for the duke's favourite dog.

The farrier, who prefers men, is horrified at the prospect but does his duty out of loyalty to his master and is rewarded by discovering that his 'wife' is in fact a young page, and they all have a good laugh. The homophobic taunt was not aimed at Federigo himself but more as a threat of what would happen if he did not change his behaviour. The punishments for sodomy in Venice were extreme – it was time, as the nurse urged the farrier, for Federigo to 'stop running after youthful pleasures and begin [his] family and household'.

In 1530 he agreed to Charles V's suggestion that he should marry Giulia of Aragon – an unlikely match, his prospective bride being thirty-eight years old and not in the best of health, though Isabella of course was pleased. Meanwhile news arrived that the Marquis of Monferrat had just died and that Maria was now the heir. It is a testament to Federigo's charm that he not only managed to persuade Clement VII to re-endorse his marriage to Maria but he also persuaded the emperor first to agree to the scheme and then, despite the opposition of the Duke of Savoy, agree to invest Federigo as Marquis of Monferrat. And then, on 15 September, while all these negotiations were in full swing, Maria herself suddenly died. A year later Federigo married her younger sister Margherita though he refused to submit to his new mother-in-law's demands that he must end his relationship with Isabella.

Margherita Paleologus arrived in Mantua in October 1531 and Federigo commissioned lavish new apartments for himself and his bride. The duke's rooms in the Palazzo Ducale – now properly the ducal palace – were decorated with more of Federigo's horses and falcons, with one decorated with eleven canvases of Roman emperors painted by the Venetian master Titian (begun 1536).* The focus of his apartments was the Sala di Troia, which was frescoed by Giulio Romano and his team with scenes of the Trojan War (1538).[55] What is striking about the scenes is that they were not taken from Virgil's version of the devious Greeks outwitting the heroic Trojans but from Homer's epic of Greek heroism and Trojan disgrace, an unusual approach which was almost certainly designed to flatter Margherita Paleologus, whose ancestors were the Byzantine Greek emperors of Constantinople.[56] Margherita's own rooms were housed in a separate building, the so-called Palazzina Paleologa, built and decorated by Giulio Romano and connected to

---

*   The canvases were destroyed by fire in 1734.

the Castello San Giorgio by a covered bridge.* It was a big project and only just finished in time to welcome the new duchess who arrived in Mantua on 3 October 1531, a year after the marriage negotiations had been finalized. Over the following eight years Margherita gave birth to seven children, including four sons.

Duke Federigo's activities as a patron were wide-ranging: apart from his work at the Palazzo Ducale and Palazzo Te, he also commissioned costly fortifications for Mantua, new gates and new marketplaces inside the walls. He amassed his own collections of books, medals, coins and curios, large enough to rival those of both his parents. He also owned ancient sculpture, and he was not too fussy about their provenance: shortly after the Sack of Rome, he asked one of his brother's captains to look out for 'pieces of ancient art, heads, legs, busts, or complete statues in bronze or marble'.[57] Federigo's known interest tempted Cardinal Ippolito de' Medici to send him a bust of Emperor Augustus in 1535 which, he claimed, had cost Clement VII over 3,000 ducats, 'the most beautiful thing yet seen' in the hope of political favour.[58] Unusually he also collected foreign art: in 1531 he instructed his agents in Flanders to buy landscapes painted in oil – the agent replied that he had visited all the masters in Antwerp 'and found little that was good and nothing in oil except for some portraits'.[59] When a trader arrived in Mantua in 1535 bringing 300 paintings he had bought in Flanders, he was able to sell the duke 120 landscapes for 400 scudi.[60]

Above all, Duke Federigo was a major patron of Titian, perhaps inspired by his uncle Alfonso I d'Este, who was one of the earliest non-Venetians to collect works by the Venetian master. Federigo owned some thirty paintings by the artist, including religious pictures and portraits as well as the above-mentioned series of Roman emperors. The *Madonna of the Rabbit*, a charming portrait of the Virgin and Child set in a rural landscape, with a shepherd in the background whose features are strongly reminiscent of those of Federigo himself, was sent to Mantua in 1530.[61] His own portrait by Titian, painted in 1528, made no reference at all to Federigo's military achievements,

---

* The Palazzina Paleologa fell into disrepair and was demolished in 1899.

Titian, *Madonna and Child with a Rabbit*, 1530 (Paris, Louvre). A charming domestic portrait of the Virgin Mary and the baby Christ, who is evidently fascinated by the little white rabbit.

nor to his status as a marquis or duke. There are no obvious indicators of military or secular rank – on the contrary, it shows a wealthy
prince, with a taste for luxury, dressed in an expensive dark blue doublet embroidered with gold, a fine linen shirt with its embroidered
cuffs showing at his wrists, two modest rings on his pudgy fingers,
which rest on a delightful lap-dog of a conspicuously non-aggressive
breed, unlike the wolfhounds and other hunting dogs preferred by
other Renaissance princes.

It is very likely that it was Federigo's patronage of Titian that
influenced his brother-in-law Francesco Maria to choose the artist
for a commission for portraits of himself and his duchess, Eleonora
Gonzaga, painted during 1536–7. Unlike Titian's portrait of Federigo,
Francesco Maria had himself portrayed in all his military glory, holding
his baton of command as captain-general of the Venetian troops and
dressed in a magnificent suit of armour which had to be sent to Venice
for Titian to copy. Behind him on a shelf were his batons of service for
Julius II and a branch of oak bearing acorns, a reference to the della
Rovere emblem of an oak tree. Francesco Maria also commissioned
Titian for religious and mythological works as well as portraits of his
ancestors. Vasari recorded that the duke commissioned portraits of his
great-uncle Sixtus IV, his uncles Julius II and Duke Guidobaldo da
Montefeltro and others of famous men of his day, including Charles
V, Francis I, Paul III and Suleiman the Magnificent.[62] Among the
other Titians he owned were a Mary Magdalen and 'a Venus', possibly
Titian's *La Bella*, which the duke bought in 1536.[63]

Duke Francesco Maria's major project was the enlargement of the
Villa Imperiale, which had originally been built by Alessandro Sforza
in the 1450s but was now extended up the hill on which the duke had
won an important victory in 1517 against the armies of Lorenzo de'
Medici and Leo X. The new villa, which cost Francesco Maria over
10,000 scudi, was inspired by the villas of antiquity and, more perti-
nently, by the magnificent suburban villas such as the Villa Madama
or the Villa Farnesina that were under construction in Rome.[64] Set in
elegant gardens and terraces ornamented with fountains, the villa was
designed around a central courtyard that could be used as a theatre,
with a walkway around the roofs of the four sides of the courtyard that
allowed guests to enjoy the spectacular views over the sea on one side
and the Apennines on the other.

Titian, *Eleonora Gonzaga*, 1537 (Florence, Uffizi). Titian has portrayed the
duchess in aristocratic style, dressed in a black velvet dress
and costly jewels, with her little lapdog beside her.

Inside the villa lavish decoration painted by his court artist Girolamo Genga included fictive architecture and landscapes, festoons of greenery and antique busts, with *putti* playing on the curtains, and copious use of the della Rovere emblem of the oak. In pride of place in the ceilings of his main reception rooms were a series of fictive tapestries, held aloft by groups of energetic *putti*, showing scenes of his own achievements. Above all, the scenes emphasized his military prowess, including his appointments as captain-general by Julius II and the Doge of Venice, carrying the imperial sword at Charles V's coronation and leading his troops into battle. His reconquest of Urbino was portrayed in Genga's *Oath at Sermide*, when his troops swore to assist him reconquer Urbino after he had been ousted by Lorenzo de' Medici, a campaign paid for by the sale of Eleonora's jewels.[65]

In her husband's frequent absences, it was Duchess Eleonora who took charge of the supervision of the project, liaising with Genga and organizing the financial affairs. Given her parentage, it is not very surprising to find her closely involved in the process of patronage, construction and decoration. There were frequently problems with funding. On one occasion, Genga informed the duchess, 'I went home to find my house filled with men shouting to the heavens' who threatened to go on strike, refusing to do any more work until they were paid 200 ducats, a proportion of the total owed to them.[66] The duchess managed to raise the money – but she also arranged to take on Genga's son-in-law as an accountant to ensure that in future the book-keeping would be more reliable.

One of the unusual features of the villa is the large number of inscriptions invented by the humanist Pietro Bembo to explain the genesis of the project. One inscription explained the importance of the site as the location of Francesco Maria's victory – and when the duke queried Bembo's use of the adjective 'French' to describe the German *landsknechts* of the papal army, the humanist explained somewhat pedantically that technically they were 'French' because they came from the left bank of the Rhine, which in Roman times had divided Julius Caesar's Gaul from tribal Germania over the river.[67] And Eleonora's role in the building of the villa was also explained at length:

> For Francesco Maria, Duke of the Metaurian States, on his return from
> the wars, his consort Leonora has erected this villa, in token of
> affection and in compensation for sun and dust, for watching and toil,

Pesaro, Villa Imperiale, *c.*1530. Commissioned by Duchess Eleonora, this elegant suburban villa cost over 10,000 scudi and included a walkway around the top of the courtyard walls with a view of the city below.

so that, during an interval of repose, his military genius may here prepare him for still wider renown and richer rewards.[68]

Both Francesco Maria and Federigo had guided their states through the dramatic political changes that transformed the Italian political stage in the early sixteenth century and had culminated in the Sack of Rome and the triumph of Charles V. Francesco Maria continued to act as captain-general of Venice, despite the gout that increasingly plagued him towards the end of his life. Federigo remained loyal to Charles V and was in command of the light cavalry fighting with the imperial army to defend Vienna against the Turks in 1531. Both princes died young, the Duke of Urbino at the age of forty-eight, the Duke of Mantua aged just forty. Francesco Maria died on 22 October 1538, possibly poisoned by his Mantuan barber, though on whose orders it is not known. He was succeeded by his twenty-four-year-old son Guidobaldo II, whose marriage to Giulia Varano, the heiress to the small state of Camerino, would cause severe problems for the new duke with his overlord Paul III. Federigo's heir, Francesco, was still a boy of seven when his father died of syphilis on 28 August 1541 and was buried in the monastery of San Paolo, beside his redoubtable mother, who had died the previous year.

ANDREA GRITTI (1455–1538)
Doge

Zorzi Corner, *Procurator of San Marco*

Antonio Grimani, *Doge*

his son Domenico Grimani, *Cardinal*

his grandson Vettor Grimani, *Procurator of San Marco*

Alvise Pisani, *Procurator of San Marco*

Daniele Barbaro, *Patriarch of Aquileia*

Marcantonio Barbaro, *Procurator of San Marco*

Jacopo Sansovino and Michele Sanmicheli, *Architects*

THE NEW ROME

Doge Andrea Gritti

his cronies

One of the peculiarities noticed by many visitors to Renaissance Venice was the uniformity of dress among the upper echelons of society. Highly stratified, Venetian society was dominated by wealthy merchants who were divided into two distinct status groups: the patricians, who governed the republic, and the so-called *cittadini*, the middle-class citizens who manned its bureaucracy. Although the difference between these two groups was precisely defined in law, this was not so visible on the streets of the city. No Venetian man from either class 'would leave the house by day if he were not dressed in his long coat, which is usually black', reported a Milanese visitor.[1] The ubiquitous full-length black coat – lined with thin silk in summer, thick fur in winter – was standard uniform for patricians and citizens alike. Tradition, however, did dictate more colourful clothes for patricians and citizens holding high office: they were expected to don robes mostly of crimson or scarlet with further subtle distinctions of rank in the shape of their sleeve or stole. The doge himself, as head of state, wore gold for his ceremonial public appearances. More gaudily dressed were patrician youths, too young for government, who were allowed to show off their physique in short doublets and tight multi-coloured hose; while the most flamboyantly dressed women were more likely to be courtesans than the wives and daughters of either patricians or citizens.

The use of conspicuous expenditure to boast wealth and status, the hallmark of the aristocratic elite across Europe, was traditionally discouraged in Venice. The first laws passed by the republic regulating marriage feasts – the dishes that could be served, the number of guests, the presents and so on – dated back to 1299.[2] Later edicts limited expenditure on all manner of extravagance: from dowries, hairstyles, clothes and jewels to the facades of palaces and the decoration of their interiors, and even funerals. The laws were regularly renewed, especially in times of peril for the republic, underlining the belief of many Venetians that deviation from this tradition of austerity incited the wrath of God. This was the morality that had prevailed throughout the fifteenth century, but the city was about to experience a dramatic change in attitudes to wealth and display. The catalyst for this change was the election of Andrea Gritti as doge in 1523.

Titian, *Doge Andrea Gritti*, 1546 (Washington, National Gallery). Energetic and autocratic, Gritti was largely responsible for changing not only the direction of Venetian politics but also the visual appearance of the city itself.

Andrea Gritti was born into privilege and wealth, a member of one of the patrician families that had governed Venice since the thirteenth century. The status of these families – there were around 150 of them – was carefully controlled by custom and law; even more so after 1506 when the birth of every male patrician had to be recorded in an official register, the Golden Book. At the age of twenty-five, like all men of his class, he became eligible to sit on the Great Council. This basic unit of government met every Sunday afternoon to vote on legislation proposed by the more select Senate, the main policy-making body. It also elected the senators and the members of the Council of Ten, which was responsible for state security, as well those patricians nominated to serve on the huge number of magistracies that controlled the lives of ordinary Venetians – the patrician elite accounted for under 5 per cent of the population, the citizens not much more: 80 per cent of Venetians earned their livings as artisans, shopkeepers and labourers.[3]

In this densely populated island city, its streets too narrow for carriages or horses, the patrician elite exercised a level of control of Venetian society that was unparalleled elsewhere in Italy. Patricians sat as judges in Venice's law courts, took charge of the city's defences, controlled the prices of grain, vegetables and meat, and the export of salt. They manned the magistracies that supervised burials, rubbish collection, street cleaning, canal dredging and the upkeep of the rain-water cisterns, which supplied much of the city's fresh water supply; they ensured the streets were patrolled at night to discourage violence, and regulated begging and prostitution – indeed, Venice was famous for its prostitutes, the grandest of whom preferred to be known by the more respectful title of 'courtesan'.

Church appointments in the city were dominated by patricians: the patriarchs of Venice and Aquileia were all patricians, as were the holders of bishoprics and abbacies in Venice's subject towns on the mainland – the abbesses of the city's convents were also chosen exclusively from patrician families. Other members of the elite chose to serve their country abroad as diplomats to foreign courts, from London and across Europe to Constantinople, Alexandria and Isfahan, or as governors in Venice's extensive territories both on the Italian mainland

and down the Adriatic coast. They were also directly involved in military and naval affairs, acting as proveditors in charge of provisioning the troops in time of war; and, although the commander of the army was invariably a professional soldier, usually a foreigner, the admiral of the navy was always a patrician, as were the commanders of the city's fleet of merchant galleys. It was a system like no other but it had proved surprisingly durable: Venice had a reputation for political stability, bolstered by the myth propagated by the regime that the city enjoyed perfect government thanks to the prudent exercise of law and order by a virtuous and self-sacrificing elite who put the interests of the state before their own profit.

Sheltered from the sea by sandbars and from the land by water, the islands of the lagoon were settled in the sixth century by families fleeing the violent upheavals caused by the collapse of the Roman empire. From the start, Venice's cultural and commercial ties were with Constantinople and the empire in the east rather than with Rome. Adopting many of the traditions of the eastern church, some of the city's churches were dedicated to Old Testament prophets, such as Moses (San Moisè) and Samuel (San Samuele); others to the heroes of the eastern church such as John Chrysostom (San Giovanni Crisostomo) or Apollinare (Sant'Aponal). Venice's grandest church, San Marco, was not the cathedral but, following eastern imperial tradition, the doge's private chapel attached to his palace. And its design derived from the churches of the Apostles (Apostoleion) and Hagia Sofia, both in Constantinople. It was lavishly clad, inside and out, with loot pillaged from that city's imperial monuments during the Fourth Crusade (1204) – slabs of coloured marble and elaborately carved capitals, for example, the famous statue of the Tetrarchs and the four bronze horses stolen from the Hippodrome.

Over the centuries Venice had prospered and by 1400 it was one of the largest cities in Europe. During the 1420s the city voted to reverse its tradition of independence from mainland Italy and to expand its authority on to the *terraferma*, where it conquered a number of independent city states including Padua, Treviso, Verona and Bergamo. Rich and powerful, it was a major centre of international trade with its own network of trading posts from Zara, Ragusa (Split) and Corfu on the Adriatic coast to Crete and Cyprus in the eastern Mediterranean and access to the markets of northern Europe through the passes across

the Alps or by sea across the Mediterranean to Spain and France. The range of goods for sale at the Rialto was amazing: vegetables, fruit and meat from the mainland; tapestries and woollen cloth from Flanders; silks and spices from Syria; slaves and salt fish from the Black Sea; gold from Egypt; silver and copper from Germany; wheat from Sicily; sugar and cotton from Cyprus; wine, oil and raisins from Crete. Venice was cosmopolitan: German and Turkish traders each had their own warehouses at the Rialto, and there were thriving communities of Jews, Greeks, Albanians and Slavs living in the city, each with their own places of worship. Some foreigners stayed long enough to qualify for citizen status, which could be granted after twenty-five years' residence but required proof of non-manual occupation and of financial security.

Carpaccio, *Lion of St Mark*, 1516 (Venice, Palazzo Ducale). The image of the Lion of St Mark, symbol of Venice, was prominent on state buildings throughout her possessions down the Adriatic coast and on the Italian mainland.

Venice also had its own industries, of which the most important was the Arsenale, the state shipyard that was probably the largest industrial complex in fifteenth-century Europe. It employed 4,000 men building merchant galleys, men-of-war for fighting at sea and smaller warships designed for action in the rivers and canals of the mainland, as well as factories producing rope, sail, gunpowder and ordnance. The island of Murano, famous then as now as the centre of the city's glass industry, used soda ash imported from Syria to produce high-quality glassware: elaborate gilded and coloured pieces to grace the tables of the rich in Rome, as well as more practical items such as lenses for spectacles, hour glasses, mirrors and window panes, the envy of many visitors. Venice was also a leading centre of printing in Europe. Jacopo de' Barbari's map of Venice (1500) was one of the first large bird's-eye views of any city, while Aldo Manuzio's Aldine press, which employed some thirty humanists and scholars, specialized in publishing the classics of Greek literature and history. By 1550 Venice's publishers produced three times the quantity of books issued in Florence, Rome and Milan combined.

Andrea Gritti followed the traditional path of commerce, going into business as a grain merchant, and married young. His first wife, Benedetta Vendramin, whom he married in 1476 at the age of twenty-one, came from a leading patrician family, though this was not a prerequisite for the Golden Book – it was the father who passed on patrician status to his son and men could choose wives from any background and nationality, so long as there was proof that a legal marriage had taken place. Tragically Benedetta died in childbirth later the same year, though her baby son, Francesco, survived. Andrea's second wife, Maria Donà, also died young, leaving him with two daughters after three years of marriage. He then moved to Constantinople, where he continued to trade as a grain merchant, living with his Greek mistress, who gave him several more sons, though none of them was eligible for the Golden Book.

Arrogant, energetic and sensual, Andrea made a fortune in Constantinople, becoming a leading figure in the Venetian community there and a close friend of the grand vizier. This was a fortunate relationship as it turned out: in 1499, with Venice at war with the Turks, Gritti was accused of spying – he had indeed been gathering information on the enemy fleet, sending his coded reports back home via the Venetian trading post on Corfu – and was imprisoned, but released thanks to the intervention of his powerful friend. In 1503 he returned to Constantinople, this time as ambassador to negotiate the peace treaty ending the war between the two nations. Approaching fifty years of age, Gritti now decided to embark on a career of public service: he served as ambassador to Rome in 1505 and four years later he was elected as a procurator of San Marco. This was a very prestigious appointment and made him one of the key figures in the government. There were just nine procurators and their prime role was to take charge of administering the estates and assets of San Marco and of the upkeep of the basilica itself, together with the clock tower and the procurators' offices that lined its piazza. It was not a particularly lucrative post

– the income was a modest 60 ducats a year, though one of the perks of the job was an apartment in the piazza – but it carried immense influence.[4] Elected for life with an automatic seat in the Senate, the procurators were the most high-ranking patricians in Venice after the doge himself – and, since the fourteenth century, all doges had held this coveted position.

Meanwhile, Venetian expansion on the mainland had begun to cause alarm, and not just to the rulers of Italy. The interests of France were under threat as the city's authority stretched ever closer to the borders of the duchy of Milan, and those of the empire as well after Venice seized Trieste in 1508 along with several other imperial fiefs to the east of the city. That December Maximilian I and Louis XII signed the League of Cambrai, an alliance ostensibly against the growing menace of the Turks but in reality aimed at Venice – and these two powerful monarchs were soon joined by Julius II, Alfonso d'Este, Duke of Ferrara and Francesco Gonzaga, Marquis of Mantua to create a formidable alliance to stem the tide of Venetian expansion on the *terraferma* (see Chapter 6).

On 14 May 1509 the armies of the league inflicted a resounding defeat on Venice at the Battle of Agnadello, forcing the Venetians back to Mestre on the shores of the lagoon. At a stroke, Venice had lost its entire mainland empire – though the immediate terror that the city itself was about to be sacked by foreign troops began to abate over the summer as Maximilian I's troops withdrew. Venice's response was pragmatic: it needed a powerful ally in order to recover its lost towns and cities and the government decided to make peace with Julius II, sending an embassy to Rome to negotiate this peace. With the help of the Venetian Cardinal Domenico Grimani, who had considerable influence at the papal court, they argued that an alliance between Venice and Rome would be the best means of stemming the growth of French influence in northern Italy – and the pope agreed. Most of the lost territories were recovered in the war that followed and Procurator Andrea Gritti played a significant role in the victory.

At the time of the Battle of Agnadello, Gritti was fifty-three years old and serving with a fellow patrician, Zorzi Corner, as proveditor in charge of the Venetian army. Their job, essentially, was to provide the link between the army's military leaders and their political masters in the Doge's Palace. A proveditor's letters of appointment included orders on how he was to take over responsibility from the local governor for everything relating to war.[5] He had to organize supplies of food, weaponry and munitions, and gather intelligence about the enemy; he was also expected to recruit and run spy networks, arrest traitors and arrange for them to be taken back to Venice for interrogation; he also had to locate deserters and have them beheaded immediately to deter others, find funds to pay wages to the troops and arrange what compensation was to be paid when the army left. As proveditor he was also frequently involved in the actual fighting – and he was expected to spend much of his time in the saddle, not a skill that came automatically to a Venetian. The job was dangerous and uncomfortable, and not to everybody's taste. In 1509, at the height of the wars, several patricians refused the appointment: the punishment meted out to one was a large fine of 500 ducats or six months in exile.[6]

By all accounts Gritti excelled as a proveditor: at one stage he asked if he could retire but the Senate refused him permission because 'we have derived so much advantage from the beginning and middle of your service, and expect much more from its end'.[7] He also seems to have relished the fighting, playing an important role in the triumphant reconquest of Padua in July 1509, just two months after Agnadello. A few weeks later he took charge of several prisoners, including some prominent French captains and the commander of the papal army, Francesco Gonzaga, who were to be sent on to Venice for interrogation (see Chapter 6). According to the diarist Marin Sanudo, the loot captured from the enemy also included a much-admired horse, 'worth more than 1,000 ducats'.[8] When Gritti and his party arrived at Padua, the people 'all shouted "Marco! Marco! Victory! Victory!" and all the streets and windows were filled with people'. Sanudo was a little over-optimistic here: the Paduans had been delighted when their city had been liberated from the lion of St Mark and did not relish the ruthless severity with which Gritti now began to reimpose Venetian authority, punishing all who objected to the new regime. Nevertheless, it was an important victory and the event soon took its place in the canon of Venetian triumphs that were depicted on the walls of the Great Council chamber in the Doge's Palace.

In February 1512, during the campaign to retake Venetian territories, Brescia was sacked by the French, leaving 10,000 dead and Gritti a prisoner. It does not seem to have been his fault; the contemporary historian Paolo Giovio thought he deserved better luck, writing that 'surely Fortune has mocked no mortal more intemperately… and cheated no man's abundantly prudent plans more brazenly'.[9] The Venetian government had a strict no-ransom policy, but on this occasion it was agreed to swap Gritti for another prisoner: in proposing this plan to the Great Council the point was made that Gritti 'had exposed his person and life in pursuit of orders from this council' and although 136 voted in favour of the proposed exchange, forty-eight patricians still voted against it.[10] On his return to Venice after a year in France, he was hailed as a hero: 'The palace, the courtyard and the piazza [San Marco] through which he passed on his way to his rooms in the Procuratie were filled with people who all wanted to shake his hand.'[11] His achievements as proveditor were celebrated in a medal with a profile portrait of himself in armour and an inscription recording his position as a Procurator of St Mark on the obverse: on the reverse was an image of a mounted soldier charging to the gates of a city.[12]

The disastrous defeat at Agnadello was to have a profound impact – economic, political and psychological – on Venice. At a financial level, the war to recover the subject towns was a huge drain on the city's resources. These had been significantly depleted by the suspension of income from the *terraferma*, which cut 330,000 ducats from state revenues, some 29 per cent of the total. [13] Putting this into context, the wage bill for the army alone in 1511 came to 538,400 ducats.[14] Worse, with enemy armies patrolling the roads, overland trade routes quickly became inaccessible, closing access to the markets in Italy and across the Alps that were such a key factor in Venice's commercial success – and for a period all trade between the empire and Venice was stopped by imperial decree.

Prices rose steeply; so did taxes and bankruptcies. 'Our state has now come to such a pass,' ran a Senate decree of March 1510, 'that it is necessary to raise a substantial sum of money for its preservation.'[15] In a bid to raise funds, the government announced that it would not pay wages to its employees for six months. Minor government posts such as clerks, brokers, warehousemen and notaries were put up for sale; there was even the opportunity to buy a seat in the Senate for a price of 2,000 ducats, though it came without voting rights.[16] The urgent priority was finding ready cash to pay the army's wages, which had previously been paid out of the coffers of those subject towns where they were garrisoned – Gritti had first-hand experience of the impact that this lack of cash had on the local population, whose animals, crops, possessions and even clothes were forcibly seized by his starving soldiers. He wrote to the government in 1510 asking for more cash: 'God knows,' he explained, it is 'not because I do not appreciate the anxiety or the effort involved but because it seems to me necessary that my soldiers should be paid.'[17] In fact Gritti and his fellow proveditor Zorzi Corner both refused to take their own salaries, though it should be said that, like so many of their class, both men also showed great reluctance to pay their taxes – and, in another measure adopted by the government to raise cash, were on the list of those tax dodgers who were named and shamed in the Great Council.[18]

By early 1511 the situation had become critical and even the wealthy Venetian bankers had begun to feel the strain. It was decided to ask Cardinal Domenico Grimani, who had already proved his worth by negotiating the 1510 peace treaty with Julius II, to procure a loan from the pope's banker Agostino Chigi. The loan was arranged and Venice was saved from bankruptcy, but it was some time before the economy began to recover. In the meantime a series of disasters were blamed on the sinful behaviour of the Venetians. Soon after Agnadello the government attempted to reform the city's convents, passing a series of laws including the order that anyone discovered having sexual relations with nuns was to be exiled for life.[19] In March 1511 there was a violent earthquake forcing senators at a meeting in the Doge's Palace to flee outside in panic; several statues fell off the facade of the palace, including a Justice and some stones ornamented with lilies, though the 'marble St Mark stood firm'.[20] Some hoped that these were portents showing that Venice would survive and that France, whose emblem was a lily, would fall; others urged placating the wrath of God. Another catastrophe added to the city's economic woes when a terrible fire hit the Rialto area in January 1514 and spread rapidly thanks to strong winds, devastating much of the city's commercial district: 'God wants to punish us for our sins,' recorded Sanudo.[21]

The idea that Venice's misfortunes were due to moral corruption provided the context for a revival of the city's sumptuary legislation, forbidding Venetians from unnecessary expenditure on luxuries, notably banquets, clothes and jewels. By this extravagance, ran the decree passed in the Senate in February 1511, 'they show little love for their fatherland since many spend this money without having paid their taxes which are imposed to preserve this state and to secure the existence of us all'.[22] Moreover, it was decided initially that the measures were to be enforced by two officials chosen from among the Procurators of St Mark. A few days later the papal banker Agostino Chigi arrived in Venice to finalize the details of the loan; he was welcomed by Procurator Antonio Grimani, the father of Cardinal Domenico, with a particularly ostentatious banquet. It was an unfortunate but telling coincidence; and it was not the only occasion when the laws were infringed. A law of May 1512 banned all extravagant furnishings such as 'cushions decorated with silk, silver, gold, jewels or pearls' and bedhangings 'made of gold or silver cloth, brocade, velvet, satin, damask'.[23] In 1515 the government set up another more independent body – the *Tre Savi sopra le pompe* (the Three Magistrates for Pomp) – to take over responsibility for policing 'unnecessary expenditure on meals and banquets, on the adornment of women, and on the decoration of houses'.[24] However, a small number of very wealthy patrician families still continued to break the rules: the brides at wedding parties hosted by Procurator Antonio Grimani in 1517 and Procurator Alvise Pisani in 1519, for example, were both dressed in lavish cloth-of-gold and satin dresses 'which are against the laws', as Sanudo recorded, though he did add that Grimani had asked the magistrates for permission.[25]

Many less wealthy patricians were shocked. It appeared to them that these families thought themselves above the law; they certainly thought of themselves as an elite within the patriciate and, indeed, they had become exactly that. In the aftermath of Agnadello, political power had become increasingly concentrated in the hands of this small group of families, whose dominance in the Senate gave them control of the most important offices of state, including the ducal council and the Council of Ten. Many – such as Antonio Grimani and Alvise Pisani, and their close allies, Zorzi Corner and Andrea Gritti – were procurators of St Mark; others were on the lists of those named and shamed in the Great Council for non-payment of their taxes.

Significantly, prominent among this elite were those clans who dominated the church in Venice: the Grimani, Pisani, Corner, Barbaro and Dolfin families. All except one of the patriarchs of Aquileia appointed in the sixteenth century were members of the Grimani or Barbaro families; while, out of the total of nine bishops of Padua appointed over the same period, four were from the Corner family and two from the Pisani. They were also prepared to pay the hefty sums required by Renaissance popes for the purchase of a cardinal's hat: Zorzi Corner's son Marco and Alvise Pisani's son Francesco each paid 20,000 ducats for this privilege.[26] And crucially, it was these men, with their contacts in Rome, who had seized the initiative after Agnadello to negotiate the alliance between Venice and Julius II, and then to arrange the loan from Agostino Chigi, effectively rescuing the republic's economy from the brink of disaster. Above all, this new relationship between Venice and the papacy reflected a significant about-turn from Venice's long-standing tradition of maintaining a healthy distance from Rome.

Moreover, over the past half-century or so subtle changes had begun to take place in the patriciate mentality. Like the war itself, this development had its origins in Venice's decision, taken in the 1420s, to expand the city's influence on to the mainland. Encouraged to buy estates on the *terraferma*, many wealthy patricians began to transfer their fortunes from commerce into land – and their behaviour began to change as they adopted the manners of the local nobility with whom they socialized, jousting and hunting and, significantly, looking down on trade. In the aftermath of Agnadello, with the growing threat to traffic from the Turkish navy in the eastern Mediterranean, the number of Venetian patricians opting to acquire land increased, preferring this safer investment to more risky business ventures. And, of course, although Venetian cardinals may have been patricians at home, they had the status of princes elsewhere in Europe, where they bowed only to popes, kings and emperors.

Although not from one of the families with a tradition of service in the church, Andrea Gritti was a member of this elite within the patrician elite, notably through his friendships with Alvise Pisani and Zorzi Corner. His daughter Benedetta was married to Giovanni Pisani, son of the wealthy banker Alvise. Among Alvise's other children were Francesco, who had been made a cardinal in 1517 at the age of twenty-three; Raffaella, who was the abbess of Sant'Alvise; Elisabetta, the wife of Antonio Grimani; and Andrea, who was married to Zuanne Corner, the son of Zorzi Corner. Zorzi, who had served as proveditor with Gritti during the war after Agnadello, had also been in the same patrician company as Gritti when they were young men.[27] He had unusually compelling aristocratic credentials: his sister Caterina Corner had been Queen of Cyprus, and had given the island to Venice after the death of her husband. Two of his sons were cardinals – Marco (created 1500) and Francesco (created 1528) – and a third was married to Cardinal Francesco Pisani's sister. Two of Cardinal Pisani's nephews who had links to the Grimani family were also members of the group: Daniele Barbaro, Patriarch of Aquileia, and his brother Procurator Marcantonio. The links between the families were intricate and complex, and they illustrate precisely how closely this pro-Roman elite was bound together by common interests that went far deeper than their connections with the church.

At the ducal election following the death of Leonardo Loredan in June 1521, seen by many in this elite as culpable for the defeat at Agnadello, Gritti was one of the leading candidates. This time he lost to Antonio Grimani, whose tenure lasted less than two years, and in May 1523 his name was put forward again. His enemies in the Council inveighed against the election of a man whom they accused of being an authoritarian and arrogant embezzler of state funds, who had 'three bastard sons in Turkey'.[28] But, thanks to Alvise Pisani, wealthy banker and father-in-law of Gritti's daughter, he managed to secure the necessary votes – the minimum required, no more. His election on 20 May 1523 was not greeted with much enthusiasm by the crowds gathered in the piazza in front of San Marco, where few joined in the customary shouting of the new doge's name.[29] Gritti does seem to have attracted respect and odium in equal measures: Sanudo himself rated the new doge as 'the first man of our country and the most worthy', but also recorded that 'everyone deplored his election'. And Gritti must have been aware of his lack of popular appeal: at his coronation ceremony, when it was traditional for the family of the new doge to throw coins to the crowds, he was exceptionally lavish, dispensing coins worth 400 ducats to the crowds, twice the amount usually given.[30]

Sanudo also recorded the completion of the votive portrait that Gritti commissioned from Titian, which by tradition was hung in the palace by every doge. Gritti's portrait showed him being presented to

overleaf *A View of the Doge's Palace and Piazzetta* (Private Collection) by the nineteenth-century artist Carlo Grubacs. The buildings around San Marco and the Doge's Palace were the visual focus of Venetian power and were deliberately designed to display the prestige of the republic.

the Virgin by St Mark, attended by three other saints, Bernardino, Alvise and Marina.* 'It is being said that these three [saints] were responsible for making him doge,' reported Sanudo. St Bernardino because 'he was elected on my day' (20 May); St Marina because 'he recovered Padua on my day' (17 June); and St Alvise because 'I am the name of Sier Alvise Pisani Procurator, his co-father-in-law... and he was responsible for having him elected.'[31]

Designed to ensure a free choice, the system of electing the doge involved the election of a special college of forty-one Great Council members whose names were drawn by lot, while another special committee took charge of the business of government during the interregnum. As with the death of a pope, the doge's gold ring of office was destroyed at his death, along with his official seal, but here the parallels ended: while the power of the Renaissance papacy became increasingly absolute, that of the doge remained resolutely that of first among equals. The doge was not a prince but the chair of a committee consisting of leading patricians chosen from the Council of Ten and other important government bodies. All his decisions had to be taken with the agreement of these councillors, who met daily with the doge to deal with the business of government, receive envoys, read dispatches and digest official reports. The doge also had a quasi-religious role as the ceremonial focus for the annual cycle of feasts and processions that celebrated Venice's unique history, a calendar of Christian rites, many of which derived from the Byzantine east. That the office was far superior to its holder was made conspicuously clear. The doge himself was not glorified as an individual – in the cycles of paintings recording the history of Venice that decorated the interior of the Doge's Palace, it was always Venice who was the monarch, never the doge; and after his death the doge's corpse was returned to his family for private burial in his parish church, like that of any other citizen.

Andrea Gritti's reign of fifteen years was one of the longest in the sixteenth century, second only to Leonardo Loredan (1501–21). He was seventy-eight years old at his election in 1523, slightly older than the

---

* The painting was destroyed in the fire that devastated the interior of the Doge's Palace in 1577.

average age at which doges were elected in the Renaissance – but considerably older than the rulers of other European states, such as Clement VII, who was forty-five years old, Francis I (twenty-nine), or Charles V (twenty-three). By all accounts he was a formidable character, capable of turning on considerable charm when it suited him, but terrifying in his rages. He also had scant respect for convention; he shocked many in the Great Council one autumn day by wearing a new style of mantle, and then by wearing the same item again on Christmas Eve.[32] More seriously, he ignored the rule that forbade the doge from acting without the agreement of his councillors by negotiating in private with foreign envoys, and he had to be reminded more than once of the terms of the oath he had sworn at his election.[33] Charismatic and energetic, Gritti also had a colourful private life: after the unfortunate deaths of his two wives, he had had an array of mistresses – including, it was reported, one nun – and as many as five illegitimate children. Over the years, however, he had replaced the pleasures of the flesh with those of the table. He suffered from gout and was said 'to have told a friend that he was amazed by the deformity of his sore feet, but it was better that these were deformed than his head'.[34] He was also enormously fat. His doctors advised him to avoid the garlic and onions 'which he relished' and his staff were ordered 'not to indulge him even if he asked for them'; after he died on 28 December 1538 it was reported 'that he died of a surfeit of lampreys which had been prepared for Christmas Eve'.[35]

Despite his age Gritti retained the energy to conceive an ambitious vision for the future of his city: to repair the damage that Agnadello had inflicted on the Venetian pysche and to restore its reputation as a major power in Europe. It was a campaign that he conducted on several different fronts: political, military, economic and artistic. His election had come at a tricky moment: with the Habsburg–Valois wars continuing to devastate northern Italy, the borders of Venice's subject towns – those which he himself had fought so hard to recover – were still under threat. One of his first acts was to appoint a military expert, Francesco Maria della Rovere, Duke of Urbino, as captain-general of the Venetian forces (see Chapter 7). According to the terms of the *condotta* when it was renewed in April 1529, the duke was required to fight against anyone except the pope (Urbino was a papal fief) and his soldiers were permitted to keep what they gained, 'except cities'; for its part Venice promised free passage, a house for him and his court, free stabling for Francesco Maria's horses and a *condotta* for his son Guidobaldo.[36] His diplomatic status was also upgraded, much to the annoyance of the Mantuan ambassador, who was furious that he was now outranked by the ambassador of Urbino and refused to attend the important celebrations for the Feast of St Mark in April 1529.[37]

Gritti's success in defending the Venetian mainland empire against both Charles V and Francis I was due in part to the diplomatic skill with which he was able to play off the two sides against each other. He was also adept at exploiting the Turkish threat if necessary: Venetian ambassadors in Constantinople were regularly ordered to encourage the Sultan's campaigns against the empire and thus to curb imperial ambitions in Italy. Venice had an unusually efficient diplomatic network operating throughout Europe – and a network of agents to intercept the correspondence of other rulers. Sanudo's diary entry for 2 September 1529, for example, detailed the contents of nine letters: four were from Venetian governors and proveditors on the *terraferma* but the other five, all intercepts, were between various imperial agents, including one from Charles V himself to the commander of his infantry, Alfonso d'Avalos.[38] However, it was soon evident that Venice could not remain outside the Habsburg–Valois conflict altogether. In 1526, in an attempt to stem Charles V's growing influence on the peninsula, Gritti joined the League of Cognac in an alliance with Francis I and Clement VII against the emperor. As was the custom the Venetians celebrated the event with a formal procession – on this occasion Gritti wore a gold and white cap 'of the sort that symbolizes peace', recorded Sanudo, evidently in an attempt to mollify the audience at home.

In his determination to avoid making the same mistake the Venetians had made when they confronted the enemy head on at Agnadello, and the disasters that ensued, Gritti instructed both Francesco Maria della Rovere and the civilian proveditor appointed to travel with the army to avoid direct contact with the enemy and to make the defence of the Venetian frontiers their sole priority. It was not the behaviour normally expected of a soldier – and it had consequences. One immediate result of the duke's refusal to engage the imperial troops in battle was the Sack of Rome in May 1527 (see Chapter 7). Another was that this policy of evasion earned Gritti the epithet of 'Fabius Maximus', the ancient Roman general who used similar delaying tactics against Hannibal in the Second Punic War.[39] And like Fabius Maximus, both Gritti and

Verona, Porta Nuova, 1533–40. Michele Sanmicheli's design for this imposing city gate exploited the use of rustication and the Doric order to provide an image of strength and impregnability.

his captain-general were widely censured, accused of cowardice, incompetence and even treachery. But, from the Venetian point of view, the policy was highly effective. Venice emerged from the conflict with its independence intact, in contrast to those rulers who had challenged the imperial machine, notably the pope.

In the aftermath of the sack, Gritti continued to protect his borders, seizing Ravenna and Cervia from the Papal States to strengthen them further. When it became clear that Charles V intended to visit Italy in person in 1529 for his coronation, bringing as many as 30,000 soldiers with him, he gave serious consideration to encouraging a French invasion if it turned out that the emperor's intentions were hostile.[40] He ordered the Duke of Urbino to make preparations for war; and raised funds by imposing harsh taxes on river traffic on the *terraferma*, though the fishing boats and barges laden with fresh fish, cabbages, garlic and reeds were exempt.[41] In the event Charles V's army was more a show of strength than an aggressive force and he signed a peace treaty with Clement VII at Bologna on 23 December 1529. To put this 'peace treaty' into context: it established the terms by which Charles V was to extend

his rule, directly or indirectly, to bring Italy under his 'protection'.

Venice, by contrast, was the only one of the major powers that had dominated the peninsula during the fifteenth century to retain its independence – or, in the words of a Roman after the Sack, 'only Venice now upholds the honour of Italy'.[42] When the treaty of Bologna was published in Venice on 1 January 1530, it was evident that Gritti had been able to use Ravenna and Cervia as vital bargaining tools to extract a hefty price for their return to the Papal States, which would be a significant boost to the Venetian economy. The treaty was celebrated with a huge procession in the Piazza San Marco, accompanied by the city's most treasured possessions. There was silverware worth more than 250,000 ducats on display, according to a chronicler: 'The old men said they could not remember ever seeing such joy and pomp as there was for this peace.'[43] It was the end of the era of austerity brought on by the defeat at Agnadello in 1509 and the start of something new.

The economic revival, stimulated by the financial bonus of the settlement with Charles V, was soon underway with measures to encourage the expansion of the woollen, silk and glass industries – the woollen industry in particular benefited from the devastation of Florence during the recent wars, and the Venetian shops had increased their own output tenfold by the middle of the century.[44] But Gritti's ambitions for Venice went far beyond economic and foreign policy: he wanted a radically new image of power for the Venetian state itself. And the pro-Roman policies of Gritti and his allies were eloquently demonstrated in the radical decision to adopt the language of cultural antiquity which defined the other major powers of the peninsula and promote Venice as the new Rome.

Innovation was not a concept that sat easily with the Venetian belief that uniformity and tradition were the pillars that upheld the city's image of political stability. For centuries Venice had asserted its links with Byzantium and the culture of early Christianity. Moreover, Venice had no Roman past – significantly, places like Padua and Verona, which could claim a classical heritage, were subject towns in their *terraferma* empire. Humanists played no part in the Venetian government bureaucracy, as they did in other Italian states – indeed, Venetians who learned Greek invariably did so to enhance their trading prospects in the eastern Mediterranean, not to read Greek literature.

However, the culture of the ancient world that played such a key role at the Renaissance courts of Italy had begun to make an impact in Venice. Classical imagery first appeared in an official context around 1500 with, for example, the figures of Mars and Neptune posing as protectors of Venice that ornamented Jacopo de' Barbari's printed map of the city replacing the more traditional winged lion of St Mark. By 1520 Marin Sanudo could claim that Venice was superior to Rome because it had been founded by nobles rather than by the shepherds Romulus and Remus.[45] There was more evidence of changing attitudes in 1523 after the death of Cardinal Domenico Grimani, who left his collection of art to the state, including twenty-eight chests of antique bronze and marble sculptures, though they were installed in a room in the private apartments of the Doge's Palace rather than put on public display.[46] When Gritti appointed the humanist Pietro Bembo as the city's librarian in 1530, one of his tasks was to compose inscriptions to commemorate the gift.

The first visible signs of change occurred in the late 1520s on the *terraferma*, where the new style was significantly less radical than it would be in Venice. As proveditor of the army, Gritti had been involved in the construction of new defences for Padua and Treviso, and on his retirement in 1517 had written a report arguing for a total renovation of the defences of the subject cities of the *terraferma*, but its conclusions were too radical for the cautious government and it was shelved. As doge, however, he was able to make defence his priority, and take the advice of his captain-general, who had installed innovative angle bastions to resist attacks from increasingly powerful artillery in the fortification of his own cities of Urbino, Pesaro and Senigallia. Around 1526 they first began to appear in the Venetian cities of the *terraferma*, notably in the works of Michele Sanmicheli.[47] Vasari related the possibly apocryphal story of how Sanmicheli, a Veronese military architect employed by Clement VII, had been looking at the fortifications of Verona, Treviso and Padua when the Venetian authorities had become suspicious and arrested him on a charge of spying – after a lengthy interrogation, he had been released, with the promise of employment if he wanted it.[48] By 1529 Sanmicheli was working on the bastions in Verona and in 1535 he was put in charge of all the Venetian defences on the mainland.

overleaf Venice, Library, begun 1537. Jacopo Sansovino's design for the library involved shops on the ground floor, rented out to provide a steady income, and the library itself on the floor above, identified by its use of the Ionic order.

Among his innovative works were two new fortified gates for Verona, the Porta Nuova (begun 1533) and the Porta Palio (begun 1555), in which the strength and power necessary for defence was also given visual expression in the use of rusticated Doric. It is likely that Sanmicheli was aware of the architectural theories of Sebastiano Serlio, who codified rules for each of the orders in Book 4 of his treatise (published in Venice in 1537), assigning different proportions and characteristics to each of them, from the plainest and most solid Tuscan to the most elegant Composite.[49]

It had long been a central tenet of the myth of Venice that the city itself had no need of walls, gates or fortifications – but this was formulated long before the Turks had become a serious threat in the Adriatic. In May 1532 Gritti asked della Rovere to address the government on the subject of the Turkish threat, arguing that there should be a new defence shield not only to protect the city but also its satellite possessions in the Adriatic and the eastern Mediterranean. Sanmicheli was sent to check on the defences down the Dalmatian coast to Corfu and Crete, where the Turks were becoming a serious menace to trade. He also built the Fortezza di Sant'Andrea (begun 1543) on the Lido at the mouth of the lagoon which, like his Verona gates, was similarly massive in size and characterized by solid rusticated Doric columns and a frieze, which was conspicuously carved with the winged lion of St Mark and other symbols of Venetian power.

The radical transformation envisaged by Doge Gritti for Venice itself was directed at San Marco, the political heart of the city. It was here that important visitors disembarked before being received at the Doge's Palace; it was here that the Venetians themselves gathered to celebrate their victories and witness the feasts of the Christian year. The square was surrounded with the images of Venetian authority, the most important of which were the church of San Marco itself and the Doge's Palace. There was also the clock tower, which had been begun in 1496 at an estimated cost of 6,000 ducats, as recorded by the diarist Domenico Malipiero: 'Nevertheless, a start was made to this project so that it shall not seem that this city is completely broke.'[50] The Venetians fully understood the importance of appearance. Lining the main square were the offices of the Procurators of St Mark, the ground floor of which, typical of the Venetian mercantile mentality, was let out as shops.

Venice, Loggetta, 1538–40. Designed by Sansovino to provide a meeting place for patricians, the building was expensively decorated with coloured marble slabs, elegant marble reliefs and bronze statues.

Gritti planned to create a more dignified setting for the display of Venice's renewed authority and his first priority was to tidy up the area. At a practical level, he removed the scruffy wooden stalls where butchers and salami sellers traded their wares, closed the taverns with their unsavoury reputations, and removed the booths of the money-changers clustered around the base of the bell tower.[51] In the new Venice, trade belonged at the Rialto, not in the more noble surroundings of the political focus of the city. There were also attempts to smarten up the festivities that took place in the piazza. In 1525, for example, the government attempted to cancel the traditional highlight of Shrove Tuesday (*Giovedi Grasso*), the beheading of a bull and twelve pigs, a particularly bloodthirsty ritual enacted as a reminder of a twelfth-century rebel bishop and his allies, after which their miniature wooden 'castles' were smashed to pieces by the senators in memory of the crushing defeat inflicted by Venice over the rebels – though the edict seems to have been ignored.[52] Gritti replaced this historical ceremony with a bullfight and more 'noble' entertainments such as dancing masques, pageants and comedies.

The most important building on the piazza, and the focus of state ceremonial, was San Marco. Both the upkeep of the fabric of the building and the administration of its wealth was in the hands of the Procurators of St Mark who, during Gritti's dogeship, included two of his close allies, Antonio Cappello and Vettor Grimani, a nephew of

Cardinal Domenico. Between them they made important changes to the ceremonial setting of ducal power. In 1527, in a move that would change the liturgical aspects of worship at San Marco, they appointed a new *maestro di cappella*, Adrian Willaert, a Flemish composer who specialized in polyphony. His introduction of this innovative style would make Venice the most famous centre of both secular and religious music in Italy.[53] The procurators also commissioned substantial renovations to the choir of the church, where work began in June 1535 under the supervision of Jacopo Sansovino on intarsia panels for the choir stalls, marble singing galleries decorated with bronze reliefs and a new ducal throne ornamented with gilded *all'antica* columns and pediment. The renovations coincided with the move of the traditional seat of the doge from the highly visible position to the right of the entrance to the choir into the newly renovated choir itself, out of sight from the main body of the basilica. Effectively the move transformed the doge from eastern emperor to European prince, though Gritti's explanation for the change was his 'bad legs', or gout.[54]

Sansovino's appointment in 1529 as the *proto* (Greek: first), or chief

Venice, Library, begun 1537. The heavy swags which ornament the frieze of the library exemplify the dramatic visual changes involved in the innovative use of the language of classical antiquity for the display of Venetian power.

supervisor on the procurators' building projects, was a significant moment. At one level, a foreigner was an unusual choice for this prestigious post. Venetian artists were protected by law: in 1505 the German Albrecht Dürer got into trouble on a visit to Venice for contravening the ban on foreign artists from selling their works in the city – they were only allowed to do so during the annual trade fair held for the Feast of the Ascension.[55] More importantly, Sansovino, who was a Florentine by birth, had established his reputation as a sculptor in Rome, where he had worked with artists like Raphael and Michelangelo before fleeing the city during the sack in 1527. One of his clients in Rome had been Cardinal Domenico Grimani – and it is unlikely to be a coincidence that the cardinal's nephew Vettor Grimani was one of the procurators, who now entrusted the sculptor with the design of a radically new state image for Venice.

The most ambitious task undertaken by the procurators and their Roman-trained *proto* was the transformation of the San Marco area, giving visual expression to the power of the patrician government in a radically new style based on the architectural language of ancient Rome. To illustrate just how radical this move was: when the offices on the north side of the piazza were destroyed in a fire in 1512 they had been rebuilt to a design that was broadly similar to the original twelfth-century buildings. Not so this time.

The project involved three new buildings, all designed by Sansovino as a unified scheme: the Mint (begun 1536), facing out on to the lagoon; the Library (begun 1537), opposite the Doge's Palace; and the Loggetta (begun 1538), at the base of the bell tower. The most visible feature of the buildings was their ornamentation with different classical orders chosen to reflect their various functions according to the rules drawn up by Serlio, whose treatise on the orders was published in Venice in 1537. The Mint, which was financed not by the wealth of San Marco but by the freeing of slaves in Cyprus at a price of 50 ducats each, had two storeys (the third was added later), ornamented with Tuscan below and Doric above, both orders rusticated, to reflect the building's function: 'A prison for most precious gold,' as Sansovino's son described it.[56]

The Library was built to house a collection of treasured manuscripts that had been left to the city by Cardinal Bessarion in 1472. Serlio had considered Ionic appropriate for scholars, so that order was an obvious choice for the library itself, which was on the first floor,

overleaf Paolo Veronese, *The Family of Darius before Alexander*, c.1565 (London, National Gallery). Ostensibly on a historical theme, this painting was also a group portrait of members of the Pisani family who commissioned the work.

with a frieze elaborately carved with swags, while the Doric ground floor was occupied by upmarket shops that the procurators rented out to finance the project. The cost of the first sixteen bays came to 28,000 ducats, and they raised more funds by increasing the rents charged to the innkeepers who had been moved out of the piazza into other premises.[57] There were also problems in 1545 when part of the building collapsed: the procurators had Sansovino thrown into prison and temporarily removed from his post, but he was later reinstated and ordered to spend 1,000 ducats doing the rebuilding at his own expense.[58] And in one surprisingly Venetian detail among the classical Roman paraphernalia was a door carved with the date MCXXXIII: not 1133, as you might think, but 1554, counting from the legendary foundation of the republic in AD 421.[59]

The Loggetta, designed as an assembly room for patricians, was, as might be expected, considerably more lavish than the other two buildings, with its elegant Composite columns and opulent marble panels. While the Library and the Mint were both brick structures covered in local Istrian stone, the Loggetta was made of imported marbles and visibly more expensive: the red marble from Verona and the white from Carrara were transported at enormous expense across Italy. The marble panels reflected the antique reliefs on the facade of San Marco, while the colour scheme deliberately reflected the patterning on the facade of the Doge's Palace, the home of patrician government. Also on the facade were four statues of classical figures, Minerva, Apollo, Mercury and Peace, who embodied the characteristics of the ruling class: wisdom, music, eloquence and harmony.

In their private projects, religious and secular, the members of the pro-Romanist faction also went out of their way to display their political affiliation in the adoption of the classical style, though in the highly conservative society of sixteenth-century Venice this process was not quite so straightforward. It was the duty of the rich in Catholic Europe to spend money in a Christian context. In Venice, as elsewhere, wills were filled with charitable donations and invariably provided funds to pay priests to say Masses for their souls, to buy candles for the prayers and often instructions about chapels, altarpieces and tombs. Zorzi

Venice, San Franceso della Vigna, begun 1534. Designed by Jacopo Sansovino, this Franciscan church was Doge Gritti's choice of burial site and he left his ducal robes to the convent to be made into vestments.

Paolo Veronese, *Supper at Emmaus*, 1559 (Paris, Louvre). It was typically Venetian to give a domestic context to Bible stories by including family portraits, such as these two girls cuddling their dog.

Corner's will, for example, left dowries of 25 ducats each to be paid to ten girls for ten years and several tons of flour to be distributed annually to the poor.[60] He also requested to be buried in the lavish marble chapel he had built at Santi Apostoli for the tombs of his parents.

Many of the pro-Romans chose to buy patronage rights to chapels in the Observant Franciscan church of San Francesco della Vigna which the friars were rebuilding to a design by Sansovino (begun 1534) and financing the project by the sale of the chapels. This was Doge Gritti's parish church and it rapidly became the focus for the display of pro-Roman prestige. The list of chapel patrons was headed by Gritti, who left 1,000 ducats in his will for the rights to the main chapel, while the two flanking chapels went to Vettor Grimani's Giustinian in-laws.[61] Vettor himself, who was a key figure in the project, also acquired a chapel with his brother Giovanni, who later acquired the patronage rights to the facade. The rights to the chapel cost them 200 ducats and they spent lavishly on its decoration, which included stuccoes, an altar ornamented with Corinthian columns and a conspicuously Roman *all'antica* coffered vault – it was the grandest chapel in the church.[62]

Traditionally the private palaces of Venetian patricians were remarkably similar, their design and ornamentation visibly derived from the Doge's Palace, windows reflecting the layout of the rooms

inside and the height of each storey conforming to that of their neighbours – indeed one Venetian patrician suggested that this uniformity should be made mandatory.[63] The Venetian instinct for conformity was strong and, interestingly, it took time for this pattern to change. One of Sansovino's first projects in Venice was the design of an ostentatiously grand Roman-style palace (1527–8) on the Grand Canal for Procurator Vettor Grimani. Significantly it was never built, and was almost certainly too ostentatious for the time. Vettor and his brother compromised, keeping the modest and traditional facade of ther family palace at Santa Maria Formosa, but commissioned a grand *all'antica* Doric courtyard and extensive remodelling inside from Sanmicheli (1532–7).[64] In a similar manner, Sansovino's design (*c*.1537) for a palace for Zuanne Dolfin, another member of the pro-Roman elite, was also deliberately unostentatious: while it was ornamented with the classical orders, they were applied to the conventional format for a Venetian palace, and its height was deliberately the same as its neighbours.[65]

Despite their success in restoring Venetian prosperity and reputation, the pro-Romanists remained unpopular at home, especially Doge Gritti. In April 1532, for example, graffiti appeared overnight in the Piazza San Marco urging Venetians 'to wake up' and 'root out the tyrants'.[66] One critic claimed that 'some people also considered that [Gritti] lived too splendidly with too many servants and a display of pomp which overreached the limits of reasonable magnificence'.[67] The criticism embodied exactly how the traditional Venetians viewed the new aristocratic elite. In fact, Gritti's own family palace by San Francesco della Vigna, which he remodelled, was noted for its simplicity. Large but not grand, with traditional plain round-headed windows, it was situated well outside the fashionable city centre, some way from the Grand Canal.

By contrast, the Corner family seems to have been more ostentatious. When he died in 1527 Zorzi Corner left three palaces in Venice to his sons: one at San Polo and two located on the Grand Canal – then, as now, a significantly more expensive location than elsewhere in the city. One of these, at San Cassan, had been left to him by his sister, Queen Caterina; the other, at San Maurizio, he had bought for 20,000 ducats and spent another 10,000 ducats on renovations and decoration.[68] This had been his favourite residence but in August 1532 a fire broke out in the attic in some cases of sugar which had just arrived from Cyprus:

Venice, Palazzo Corner dalla Cà Grande, designed by Sansovino and begun *c*.1545. Unashamedly grand and conspicuously classical, the Palazzo Corner towered over its neighbours in an arrogant manner.

because they were damp they had been taken upstairs to dry out in the summer heat, with a brazier lit that night to speed up the process. Tragically the cargo caught fire, totally destroying the palace and most of its contents. As Sanudo lamented, it was 'the most beautiful palace in Venice and, it could be said, in all Italy, noble, magnificent and luxurious, and burned down to the ground in hours'.[69]

Zorzi's three lay sons successfully petitioned the government to finance part of the rebuilding costs, claiming that the family was still owed Caterina's dowry of 61,000 ducats, but misfortune struck the family again when another fire destroyed their palace at San Polo. A long legal battle then ensued between the brothers over the division of their father's estate, which was not finally settled until 1545: the sole surviving palace at San Cassan went to Girolamo, while Zuanne inherited the remains of the San Polo property and the site at San

The façade of the Villa Barbaro at Maser in the Veneto, 1550s. Palladio's use of a temple façade and flanking porticoes lent a distinctive classical elegance to farm buildings, a style that has proved popular throughout Europe and North America.

Maurizio went to Zorzetto, the son of Zorzi's son Giacomo, who had died while the case was still waiting to be settled.[70] Zuanne and Zorzetto immediately started building on their sites, commissioning ostentatiously Roman designs from Sansovino and Sanmicheli, the architects of the new Roman style. Zorzetto chose Sansovino for his palace at San Maurizio (1545), while Zuanne's palace at San Polo (1545) was by Sanmicheli, who designed an enormous building for his patron on the very cramped site. Sanmicheli then went on to design a Grand Canal palace for Procurator Girolamo Grimani at San Luca (1559). All three were unashamedly classical in their designs, with few gestures to Venetian tradition. The two Corner palaces had rusticated Doric basements with Ionic and Corinthian storeys above, while the Grimani facade did away with the rustication altogether and displayed paired Corinthian columns at all three levels. What is really striking about all three palaces is the way in which they tower over their neighbours – it is easy to see how their patrons developed a reputation for arrogance.

Zorzi Corner had also owned several properties on the *terraferma* – bought as a safe investment to balance more risky commercial ventures – including an estate at Piombino Dese, which had been inherited by his son Girolamo. After Girolamo's death in 1542 it was inherited by his sons: Andrea and Zorzetto, the patron of Sansovino's Palazzo Corner at San Maurizio. The villa went to Andrea with his share of the land, so Zorzetto now commissioned his own villa from a local architect, Andrea Palladio. Palladio had built up a clientele among the rich nobility of Vicenza, for whom he designed villas that were mostly rural retreats. His villas for Venetian clients, however, were usually the centre of an agricultural estate, which needed barns, stables and outbuildings to store equipment and produce. Unlike the villas of wealthy Romans, they were not set in grand gardens – they were surrounded with acres of vines, olives, rice, maize or millet; they had dovecotes and fishponds to supply food in winter. By applying the classical orders to the local vernacular, Palladio developed a distinctive style for these villas, which often included a temple front with columns supporting a pediment, sometimes flanked by colonnades. It was a style designed to add courtly elegance to what were essentially farm buildings, and it appealed to more than the Venetian landowners of the sixteenth century: it would become the hallmark of the landed aristocracy in Britain and the United States.

One of the most delightful, and most Roman, villas was the one Palladio designed for the brothers Daniele and Marcantonio Barbaro, two members of the pro-Roman elite who were related by marriage to both the Pisani and Grimani families. Daniele, who had a chapel in San Francesco della Vigna, was Patriarch of Aquileia and was nominated as a cardinal in 1561, though the title was never published. Marcantonio, who was a Procurator of St Mark, had an illustrious diplomatic career, serving as ambassador to both France and Constantinople. The Ionic temple front of their villa, supporting a pediment elaborately carved with the family coat-of-arms, was flanked by plain arcades cloaking storerooms and barns. After Daniele died in 1570, Marcantonio commissioned Veronese to fresco the interior with scenes depicting classical gods, the seasons and the Muses, and a series of charming *trompe l'oeil* scenes of his family: his wife, their old nurse, their pet

Paolo Veronese, interior frescoes, 1560–61 (Maser, Villa Barbaro).
Veronese's frescoes inside the villa include portraits of Marcantonio
Barbaro's wife and children, their dogs and the old nurse.

lap-dog and parrot and his daughter, a little girl peeking out from behind a 'door'.

In the end, however, it was to prove impossible for the Venetians to resist the relentless, irresistable growth of Turkish power. For Gritti the crunch moment came in 1537 when Francis I signed an alliance with Sultan Suleiman to make a two-pronged assault on the empire, with the French attacking its northern borders in Flanders while the sultan moved against the Balkans in the south. Suleiman sent an envoy to Venice asking Gritti to join the alliance, putting the doge in a quandary. Gritti and his advisors gave a polite response but were careful to commit to nothing. The sultan responded aggressively: he imposed taxes on Venetian merchants trading in his empire and harried Venetian ships in the Mediterranean. The situation began to deteriorate: the Turks seized Corfu in July 1537 and a year later inflicted a decisive defeat on the fleet assembled by Paul III and Charles V at the Battle of Prevesa. The following autumn, in a heated debate in the Senate, Gritti warned of the huge economic costs of going to war against Suleiman, but his opponents won the motion by one vote. By the end of the year Gritti was dead and, as he had predicted, Venice was in the throes of a serious economic crisis, forcing his successor to make peace on very disadvantageous terms.

Titian, *Daniele Barbaro*, c.1545 (Madrid, Prado). Daniele's career of public service included two years in London as Venetian ambassador; he also wrote a commentary on the ancient Roman treatise on architecture by Vitruvius.

The Family of
POPE PAUL III
(r.1534–49)

Pier Luigi Farnese,
Paul's son, Duke of Parma

Vittoria
Paul's granddaughter, Duchess of Urbino

Alessandro
Paul's grandson, Cardinal

Ottavio, *Paul's grandson,*
Duke of Castro

Costanza Farnese
Paul's daughter

Guido Ascanio Sforza
Paul's grandson, Cardinal

DYNASTY

Paul III

&

the Farnese

When Duke Guidobaldo II of Urbino lost his first wife suddenly in February 1547, shortly before her twenty-fourth birthday, Pope Paul III seized the opportunity to recommend his granddaughter Vittoria Farnese as a suitable bride. With no son to inherit his title, the duke was keen to remarry and negotiations were soon underway. Unlike previous attempts to procure a prince for Vittoria, who was now twenty-eight years of age, this one met with success and the couple were married by proxy on 29 June. The dowry was settled at 80,000 scudi in cash and valuables – and, as an additional incentive, the pope offered a red hat to the duke's fourteen-year-old brother Giulio.[1] It was a prestigious match for the Farnese. The della Rovere were one of Italy's leading princely dynasties, while the Farnese had been only minor landowners when Paul III was elected pope in 1534.

The rise of the Farnese from footsoldiers to dukes was a story that would be told and retold on the walls of the family residences, and embellished with its own myths in the process. But the key factor behind this transformation was Paul III himself. He was a very clever politician, expertly steering his ambitions for his children and grandchildren through the twists and turns of the highly complex politics of the period. Above all, he needed to ensure that the Farnese would be powerful enough to survive after his death.

The Farnese came from northern Lazio near Orvieto, little more than yeomen farmers and soldiers in the ranks of the armies fighting the wars that proliferated across Italy in the fourteenth and early fifteenth centuries. It was for loyal service to the papacy during the Schism that a certain Ranuccio Farnese was rewarded with more land in the family's ancestral heartlands; his rising status enabled him to marry his son Pier Luigi into the baronial Caetani family. It was a critical moment in Farnese history: the family was now wealthy enough to look beyond military careers for its sons. So Pier Luigi's second son, Alessandro, was given a humanist education with a view to preparing him for an ecclesiastical career.

Success in the notoriously corrupt society of Renaissance Rome required talent, which Alessandro had, but it also required two factors which were less calculable: luck and the right connections. And here Alessandro was fortunate with his sisters. One, Gerolama, was married to a Florentine, a close associate of the pope's banker Lorenzo de' Medici who sent a letter recommending Alessandro to his contacts at the papal court. The other, Giulia, attracted the attentions of the powerful vice-chancellor Cardinal Rodrigo Borgia and became his mistress. This was more than enough clout to set Alessandro on a church career. Appointed a secretary in the Curia in August 1490, his career really took off two years later when Cardinal Rodrigo was elected as Alexander VI.[2]

The new pope made Alessandro his treasurer and in September 1493 gave him a red hat. From modest beginnings the cardinal now began to use his skills to amass wealth. A tax list dated 1500 gave his annual income as 2,000 ducats, a modest sum; the future Julius II earned ten times that amount.[3] But Cardinal Farnese prospered, not least thanks to two lucky chances: in 1513 his old childhood friend Giovanni de' Medici was elected pope, followed ten years later by Leo X's cousin Clement VII, with whom he took refuge in Castel Sant'Angelo during the Sack of Rome. Alessandro's meteoric rise to power at the papal court was evident in a population census drawn up in 1526–7 showing that his household, with 306 persons, was the largest of all the cardinals in Rome.[4] Moreover, he had developed a reputation for extravagant entertainment, hosting lavish parties for the papal court to enjoy fishing and boar-hunting at his castle at Capodimonte near Lake Bolsena, which he decorated with the first of the many cycles of Farnese history for which the family would become famous.[5] The cardinal had also acquired a mistress, Silvia Ruffini, and several children, who all lived with him in the Palazzo Farnese, at that time a modest residence near the Campo dei Fiori in central Rome, with gardens that reached down to the Tiber.[6]

Wealthy, influential and ambitious, Cardinal Farnese had been a leading candidate in the conclaves of 1521–2 and 1523, but it was not until the next conclave, following the death of Clement VII, that he was elected on 13 October 1534. There were some who thought him too old at sixty-six years of age but he was robust and in good health. Titian's masterly portrait of the pope, painted ten years later, showed him as an old man but one who had retained his faculties and remained an astute politician – indeed, his pontificate would be the longest of the sixteenth century. Nor did his taste for luxuries and pleasure dim much with age. His private account books show payments to goldsmiths, jewellers and cabinet makers, hunstmen and gardeners, tailors and stocking makers, and to suppliers of many pairs of gloves made from the skin of unborn calves.[7] He employed quantities of musicians, including several female singers, and paid his buffoon 36 scudi a year, the same salary as that received by a squire or a chaplain, together with another 11 scudi to buy clothes.[8]

Above all, the church now became the family business which Paul III shared with his son Pier Luigi and several of his grandchildren. He appointed Pier Luigi, a tough mercenary soldier, as captain-general of the papal army, and in 1537 created the duchy of Castro for his son, incorporating the ancestral Farnese fiefs north of Rome into the new state – he was also made Duke of Novara by a reluctant Charles V. A tough mercenary soldier, Pier Luigi was by all accounts an unsavoury character with a reputation for viciousness, though accusations that he raped a bishop who died of shame were certainly slanders invented by his enemies. In December 1534, two months after his election, Paul III shocked the College of Cardinals by giving red hats to his two oldest grandsons: Guido Ascanio, the son of his sister Costanza, had just celebrated his sixteenth birthday but Alessandro, Pier Luigi's eldest boy, was only fourteen years old. The pope also showered them with lucrative benefices. He gave the see of Parma, which had become vacant on his election, to Guido Ascanio, whose father was ruler of the nearby fief of Santa Fiora, while Alessandro acquired the bishoprics of Avignon and Jaén, though Charles V refused to confirm the latter appointment on the grounds that Alessandro was far too young.

Unlike other Renaissance popes, Paul III did not establish an inner circle of advisors – on the contrary, he delegated the running of his administration directly to his immediate family. One wit nicknamed the pope, Pier Luigi and Cardinal Alessandro as 'the Father, the Son and the Holy Ghost'.[9] With Pier Luigi at the head of the papal army, Paul III appointed Cardinal Alessandro to the key post of vice-chancellor and Cardinal Guido Ascanio as the head of the other key curial department, the chamber – and Ranuccio joined his elder brother in the College of Cardinals in 1545, being appointed to head

Titian, *Pope Paul III with his grandsons*, 1545–6 (Naples, Museo di Capodimonte). This revealing image of nepotism shows a cardinal and vice-chancellor of the Church, and a duke married to the emperor's daughter.

the penitentiary, the department dealing with papal dispensations. The key secular appointments also went to family members: the pope's grandson Ottavio became Prefect of Rome in 1538, at the age of fourteen, while the post of castellan of Castel Sant'Angelo went to Matteo Orsini, a relative of Pier Luigi's wife.

That year, 1538, the pope also formalized the position of 'cardinal-nephew' in a papal brief outlining the duties and status of this post. It was to be filled by Cardinal Alessandro, with Guido Ascanio, although two years older, playing the role of understudy to his cousin. His powers were far-reaching: significantly, his signature on diplomatic correspondence and on all letters regarding the government of the Papal States – in other words, the entire secular business of the church – was to carry the same authority as that of the pope. It was a big responsibility for the young man, still only seventeen years old, and the pope ensured he was surrounded with experienced and reliable secretaries. This important move reflected not only Paul III's respect for Alessandro's talents, but also his own realization that he needed to provide a system which would protect his family when he became too old for decision-making.*

The 'family business' faced a daunting agenda at home and abroad. Paul III was the first Roman pope since Martin V over a century earlier, and his election was hugely popular in the city, which had suffered economically during the Medici pontificates. He revived the cycle of feasts and pageants that had been dropped in the impoverished years following the Sack of Rome – the magnificent entries of foreign dignitaries, the raucous celebrations for Carnival, which included the barbaric custom of slaughtering terrified pigs and oxen on Monte Testaccio, and so on. Unfortunately the traditional bullfight on the Capitol for Carnival in 1535 ended in disaster after the bulls escaped, killing eight people and injuring many more – and then one bull blundered its way into the nearby church of Santa Maria in Aracoeli, terrifying the congregation of worshippers.[10]

Paul III did much to revive the Roman economy, fostering growth by encouraging agriculture and trade. His ambitious programme of expenditure on the architectural symbols at the heart of papal authority helped to stimulate the building trades: he injected new life into the

---

*   Remarkably the system of the 'cardinal-nephew' lasted until 1692, when it was officially outlawed by Pope Innocent XII.

reconstruction of St Peter's and added a new ceremonial hall at the Vatican, the Sala Regia, for the official reception accorded to kings and emperors, as well as a new private chapel, the Cappella Paolina, with frescoes by Michelangelo.

Unfortunately for Paul III, the coffers he had inherited from the Medici popes were empty, and his income was less than half that enjoyed by Clement VII.[11] He found some devious ways to raise money: he founded three chivalric orders, charging members for the privilege of the title of knight. But most of his measures were directed at poorer Romans. He cut the interest rates paid on capital invested in the church bank from 10 to 7 per cent and, least popular, imposed swingeing taxes on the stuff of everyday life. His methods could be unscrupulous: in an attempt to halt an uprising against the tax on salt, he cancelled the tax but then, on the same day, imposed the same tax on meat and wine.[12]

The problems outside Rome were a veritable catalogue of disaster. Take the year 1534, for example, the year of Paul III's election: Protestant placards denouncing the Catholic doctrine of the Eucharist appeared on the streets of Paris; the states of Würtemberg, Pomerania, Strasbourg and Münster all became Protestant, and ceased paying funds to Rome, while the Act of Supremacy that established Henry VIII as head of the Church in England drastically reduced the income even further. In what was left of Catholic Europe, the calls for church reform were becoming increasingly urgent. Paul III himself was the subject of many Protestant lampoons and one woodcut took issue with his mistresses and children, portraying him as an old goat playing the bagpipes. In the Mediterranean, Sultan Suleiman's admiral, Khair ad-Din, better known as Barbarossa, continued to harry the Italian coast, and mounted an audacious attempt to kidnap the beautiful wife of Vespasiano Colonna for the sultan's harem; on another occasion the pope gave 6 scudi to two priests who had 'escaped from the hands of Barbarossa'.[13] These problems might have been easier to solve had they not been exacerbated by the continuing The Venetians fully understood the importance of appearance. between Charles V and Francis I.

In 1536 Charles V and Paul III held a summit meeting in Rome to discuss these issues. Preparations for the visit had involved a major programme of urban renewal, costing 50,000 scudi, repairing bridges and roads, demolishing eyesores and clearing away the damage caused by the imperial troops during the Sack.[14] The Emperor's entry on 5

April was a truly magnificent affair, carefully choreographed by Paul III and his humanists to showcase Rome as imperial and Christian capital. The College of Cardinals awaited Charles V's cavalcade on the Via Appia at Domine Quo Vadis, the ninth-century church built to commemorate the precise spot where Christ appeared to St Peter and persuaded him to return to the city and to his martyrdom. And, in a significant change to the normal route across Rome to the Vatican, the emperor was taken through the imperial forum, under the arches of Constantine, Titus and Septimius Severus. But the cavalcade must have unnerved the Romans themselves – it was only nine years since the city had been devastated by mutinous imperial troops – and here they were again, 4,000 soldiers marching in rows of seven, together with 500 cavalrymen and their ruler, Charles V, who, in contrast to everyone else, was simply dressed in a plain purple velvet robe.[15]

Paul III received Charles V from a throne on the steps of St Peter's and escorted his guest into the Vatican. There was an exchange of presents: the pope gave the emperor a missal worth 6,000 scudi that had a gold cover studded with gems and exquisite paintings inside by the famous miniaturist Giulio Clovio.[16] Value was a key component in this ritual – when the two rulers met again in Bologna in 1541, the pope gave the emperor a diamond ring valued at 3,300 scudi.[17] The emperor was on his way north to Germany from Sicily, where he had landed after leading his armada in person to a resounding victory against Barbarossa off Tunis in June 1535; this defeat would, however, prove only temporary and Suleiman's armies were now threatening the southern borders of the empire. In Germany he faced not only the Turkish threat but also the Protestant rebellion, which was causing very real problems for his authority.

Once the ceremony was complete the two rulers got down to business; they had much to discuss. Their first meeting lasted for over six hours and over the next few days they held several more, interspersed with visits to the famous churches and monuments of Rome. Unexpectedly, Charles V prolonged his stay in Rome for the whole of the following week, which was Holy Week, taking part devoutly in the Maundy Thursday and Good Friday rituals, and assisting at Mass on Easter Sunday. A week later he harangued the College of Cardinals in a speech that lasted an hour and a half, blaming all his woes on Francis I and his perfidious behaviour: plotting with troublemakers in the empire, making alliances with the infidel Turks, invading Savoy while his ambassadors assured him that this was not the king's intention, and so on. For Charles V, the French king was the main obstacle to peace. The pro-Habsburg cardinals were enthusiastic but the French cardinals were horrified; the college, like Europe, was sharply divided on the issue of who was to blame. For Paul III it was evident that the king and the emperor needed to meet.

Unlike the Medici popes, Paul III refused to take sides in the Habsburg–Valois conflict – maybe he had learned that lesson from his predecessors – and concentrated, far more actively than they had done, on urging the rivals to make peace. Thanks to his patient diplomacy and his steely refusal to give way to either side, Paul III persuaded the rivals to sign a three-month truce in November 1537 and, when that broke down, to attend his peace conference in Nice the following year in person. The first time that the pope, the emperor and the French king had met for many centuries, the conference at Nice promised to be a unique event. But there were problems from the start: Paul III was unable to enter Nice because the city refused to allow Pier Luigi to garrison his soldiers there; Charles V refused to leave the imperial galley anchored off Villefranche, to the east of Nice; and Francis I arrived late, not to score a point but because he was ill.[18] Paul III held meetings to mediate with representatives of both rulers, sending Cardinal Alessandro and Cardinal Guido Ascanio to talk to both rivals in person, followed by more discussions and visits to each court by diplomats from the other side. Although Charles V and Francis I refused to meet, this was an elite social occasion with both courts taking part in a wide variety of social events, and a ten-year truce was published on 18 June. Remarkably, just as Francis I was about to leave Marseilles, he received a letter from Charles V inviting him to meet face-to-face; Francis I agreed and the two men met at Aigues-Mortes. The meeting was very successful – for the time being at least, the king and the emperor laid their differences aside.

For Paul III the conference had been a triumph; sailing back to Genoa, he tipped the crews of the royal galleys 300 scudi in gratitude for his safe voyage.[19] He had not only achieved a diplomatic coup but he had also secured a huge prize for the Farnese family. Charles V had agreed to the betrothal of his illegitimate daughter Margaret of Austria to the pope's grandson Ottavio; and Francis I had promised to consider the union of his second son, Henri, Duke of Orléans, and Paul III's granddaughter Vittoria. The marriage between Ottavio and Margaret of Austria took place in November 1538, though the plans for the nineteen-year-old Vittoria remained unresolved.

A political tool from an early age, the unfortunate Margaret had already been married at the age of thirteen to Alessandro de' Medici, the illegitimate son of Clement VII and Duke of Florence, who had been assassinated less than a year later. Now, aged fifteen, she was to be married again, this time to a boy two years her junior – as Ottavio's brother Cardinal Alessandro wittily remarked, the emperor 'had given her as a child to a man and as a woman to a child'.[20] Apparently she had objected strongly to the match: apart from the fact that her husband was only thirteen years old, he had no title and his family was of very minor rank, while she was a princess brought up in the luxurious surroundings of the Burgundian court; it was not until 1540 that Paul III invested his son with the duchy of Camerino, a small state in the Apennines east of Perugia. Moreover, Margaret not only refused to say 'I do' at the marriage ceremony that took place in the Sistine Chapel, she also flatly refused to consummate the marriage. Nevertheless the union was celebrated in lavish style in Rome with balls, banquets and fireworks, and the couple moved into the Palazzo Cesi near the Vatican, where the ongoing non-consummation continued to scandalize the Roman court and keep it well supplied with gossip, until it was agreed that Ottavio should join his father-in-law's court in Spain in 1541.

Meanwhile, in another significant shift from the policies of his predecessors, Paul III had firmly grasped the need for church reform. He approved new religious orders founded in response to this urgent issue and gave red hats to prominent theologians and reformers. Soon after his election he had set up a committee manned by reformist cardinals to examine abuses within the church and their report, *De emendenda ecclesia* (1537), was severely critical of the widespread practice of simony at all levels of the church administration, ignorant priests, unworthy appointments and, above all, corruption in Rome. Taking advantage of the uneasy peace that had been established between Charles V and Francis I at Nice, Paul III decided to push the rivals to agree a venue

Titian, *Cardinal Alessandro Farnese*, 1545–6 (Naples, Museo di Capodimonte). Alessandro amassed a splendid collection of antiques, gems and other valuables; his daughter Clelia was said to be the most beautiful woman in Rome.

for the much-needed council to reform the church. In late 1539 he appointed his grandson Alessandro as legate to both rulers, with orders to suggest Vicenza as an appropriate location. It was an important mission for such a young man but Alessandro, now nineteen years old, was turning out to be both intelligent and capable, as well as courteous and kind, though perhaps a little dull.

The cardinal made his entrance into Paris on 31 December; on 1 January he was greeted by Charles V at Nôtre-Dame and together they rode to Francis I's new palace of the Louvre where they were formally welcomed by the king. It was not until after the New Year celebrations were over, and Charles V had left on imperial business, that the detailed negotiations between Francis I and Cardinal Alessandro could begin. Unfortunately they were not very positive: Francis I was evasive, refusing to join either a council or an alliance against the Turks until a permanent peace had been secured with the empire. He was also evasive on the subject of the betrothal of the Duke of Orléans to Alessandro's sister Vittoria.

Cardinal Alessandro now moved on to Ghent for his audience with the emperor; the pope had warned him to ensure that he and his court wore their robes of office at all times, especially in the Netherlands, which was full of Protestants.[21] Charles V's response to the legate was more positive; he promised to continue peace negotiations with Francis I but he demanded that the king must renounce all his claims to territory in Italy, notably to the duchy of Milan, a price Francis I refused to pay. More worryingly, the Turks had responded to Charles V's victory at Tunis by crushing the imperial armada at Prevesa and then marching into Hungary to threaten Budapest. The French, meanwhile, were prepared to making alliances with any enemy of Charles V, including the Turks and the Protestants.

The Protestants had become a very complicated problem. Regardless of his own religious beliefs, Charles V was desperate for a deal which would maintain his authority in the empire, where Protestantism had become the focus of a move for independence from the imperial yoke. Francis I opposed reconciliation in order to break up the empire. In Rome, where the religious context was more pressing, Paul III wanted to negotiate reconciliation between the two theologies but he was facing growing opposition to this approach from the hardline reformers in Rome. They condemned all Protestants as heretics, demanding that those who would not return to the true faith must die, and accused the negotiators of being Lutherans themselves. Under the leadership of Cardinal Gianpietro Carafa, founder of the Theatines, a strict and highly puritanical order of lay clerics, their extremist approach had begun to drown out the voices of moderation at the papal court.

The crunch came in 1541 at the Diet of Regensburg (Ratisbon). There was no question of Paul III sending Cardinal Alessandro as legate to this crucial meeting – what was needed here was theological expertise, and the pope appointed a moderate Venetian Cardinal, Gasparo Contarini, instead. After months of difficult and exhausting discussions, the cardinal managed to negotiate a compromise deal but this was wholly rejected in Rome by Carafa and the extremist reformers who accused the unfortunate Contarini of being a Protestant. Contarini left Rome and died the following summer – a fortunate outcome in view of the fact that a month before his death Paul III set up the Inquisition to root out heresy, and gave the ruthless Cardinal Carafa the top job. The Diet of Regensburg was the last attempt to negotiate a compromise with the Protestants – what had started out as a movement for reform had now split Christian Europe, and even split the Catholic church in Rome.

In a highly symbolic moment, Michelangelo's fresco of the *Last Judgement* in the Sistine Chapel was unveiled in October 1541, revealing the enormity of the gulf between the extremists and the moderates. In literary and artistic circles the fresco was praised as a work of genius – Cardinal Alessandro was one of several patrons who commissioned engravings or small-scale copies.[22] But it was widely condemned in religious terms. Paul III's master of ceremonies thought the nudity disgraceful, while Giovanni Andrea Gilio analysed the fresco according to the biblical text (I Cor. 15) on which it was based: Michelangelo, 'for the sake of his art', Gilio considered, had 'disregarded reverence and even historical truth itself and despised the awe which attaches by right to this stupendous mystery… preferring to place his artistic judgement before religious truth'.[23] By the end of the following year Paul III had demonstrated his recognition of the need to abolish abuses within the church, and the delegates had begun to arrive at Trent for the opening of the council on reform.

Meanwhile, the Farnese had begun to make their presence known in Rome. After Paul III's election Pier Luigi and his children – Vittoria (fifteen), Alessandro (fourteen), Ottavio (ten), Ranuccio (four) and Orazio (three) – had continued to reside at the Palazzo Farnese, where they lived in some style – there is evidence that Pier Luigi's sister Costanza was also living there with her daughter. The ledgers recording Paul III's sundry expenses show that he spent generously on his grand-children over and above the costs of running and feeding the house-hold: the expenses for March 1537 amounted to 268 scudi.[24] Among the items in the accounts was a salary of 15 scudi a month paid to a music teacher for Vittoria; 28 scudi spent on gold thread to embroider her green satin coat; 4 scudi to buy two lutes and strings for Ottavio to learn to play; 12 scudi for an outfit for one of Ranuccio's pages; modest sums to cover his grandsons' gambling debts; and so on.[25] He gave Vittoria 210 scudi 'to go hunting' with Margaret of Austria and paid for twenty-six Farnese coats-of-arms to put on hangings for her apart-ments.[26] After Ottavio's marriage he also paid the not inconsiderable expenses of running the couple's household, which amounted to 23,246 scudi in 1539 and 25,747 scudi in 1540.[27]

The modest palace that Paul III had bought while a cardinal was no longer large enough for Pier Luigi, who decided that the 'first fam-ily' needed a more imposing residence. In March 1541 he drew up a contract with a group of builders and its terms throw an interesting light on the sharp practices of the Roman construction industry. The quality of the building materials, for example, had to be checked by two of the men working on Paul III's own projects; the builders had to use stone from a particular quarry; they were 'not to use any pozzola-na other than that delivered to the wharf'; and the bricks were 'to be well baked and approved by the said [agents]'.[28] Work had started by August that year, when Paul III gave 10 scudi to the works overseer to pay for a meal for the builders and stonecutters.[29]

The Palazzo Farnese was designed to impress. Set on a huge piaz-za, which had required the demolition of several streets and houses, its grandiose entrance boasted Doric columns supporting a splendid barrel vault and its facade was crowned with a massive *all'antica* cor-nice. It was an immensely expensive project – the accounts ledgers for the years 1546–9 record a total of 73,178 scudi spent on the building during that period alone – and there were problems about financing it right from the start.[30] In March 1542, according to the Florentine ambassador, Paul III, Pier Luigi and Cardinal Alessandro had a row about money, with the duke refusing to make a monthly contribution of 400 ducats (4,800 ducats a year) as requested by the pope.[31] It seems that the cardinal also contributed to the building fund, even though it was not his residence, giving his mother Girolama Orsini 250 scudi a month for the works – a shadowy character in Farnese history, Pier Luigi's wife evidently took charge of her husband's project in his absence, like so many other wives of Renaissance rulers.[32]

'In truth the house is full of women', reported a visitor in July 1547, shortly after the betrothal of Vittoria and Guidobaldo della Rovere.[33] Living in the completed apartments on the two upper floors were the ladies of the family: Vittoria's mother, Girolama Orsini; her aunt Costanza Sforza and herself, and their households.[34] The visitor also noted that Vittoria's household included just three ladies-in-waiting, a chaplain, three footmen, three pages and 'six to eight damsels' who included 'one Turk and a baptized Jew whom she brought up and a female dwarf... who has a very ugly face'. Farnese pomp may not have been on show inside the palace but it was very much in evidence when she went out with 'coaches, an infinite number of horses, Farnese footmen dressed in livery... and as many as sixteen pages'.

There was also another focus of family power in Rome: the Palazzo della Cancelleria, which was Cardinal Alessandro's official residence as vice-chancellor, situated not far from the Palazzo Farnese. Built in the late fifteenth century by a previous incumbent of the office, this was the third largest palace in Rome after the Vatican and the Palazzo Farnese, a message that would not have been lost on the observant Romans. Immensely wealthy with an income of over 100,000 scudi, Alessandro was easily the richest cardinal in Rome.[35] He had been a very unwilling cleric – as the eldest son, he could have expected a career in the secular world but his younger brother Ottavio had been only ten years old when Paul III had been elected and it was decided not to risk the pope dying before having the chance to give a red hat to one of the grandsons. Cardinal Alessandro was reportedly furious when Ottavio married Margaret of Austria and he pressed his grandfather, without success, to be allowed to renounce his red hat. He made no effort to remain celibate, however, enjoying the company of plenty of beautiful women and spending lavishly on presents; he gave one courtesan a rosary of valuable gems set in gold.[36] His tastes were luxurious: in her will his sister-in-law Margaret of Austria

overleaf An engraving by Antonio Lafreri of the Palazzo Farnese, Rome, begun 1541. Designed by Antonio da Sangallo and Michelangelo, the Farnese Palace was designed to impress with its grandiose façade and superbly decorated reception rooms.

NBF·

Mo

X L .

48

left him a 'bed cover perfumed with roses and embroidered with gold and silver'.[37] And he presided over an exceptionally cultured court at his palace, famous for its parties, lavish entertainments and theatrical performances. Vasari described evenings there, where he 'often went in the evening to watch the Most Illustrious Cardinal Farnese dine', surrounded by 'many eminent and learned men' talking of art, and how it was the cardinal himself who suggested to Vasari the idea of writing biographies of artists.[38]

Cardinal Alessandro commissioned an erudite cycle of frescoes in honour of his grandfather to decorate the main reception hall in the palace, known as the Sala dei Cento Giorni after the 100 days it reputedly took Vasari to paint it. In the upper register were shields bearing the blue Farnese lilies on their yellow background, flanked by Roman emperors whose achievements matched those of Paul III – such as Emperor Vespasian and his Temple of Peace (*Templum Pacis*) foreshadowing Paul III and St Peter's. Vasari transformed the hall itself into a viewing chamber with complex fictive staircases on each wall leading up to Doric 'rooms' that provided the setting for the paintings. These were not scenes of events in the conventional sense but tableaux filled with allusions to events, recognizable portraits of the men (not women) involved and personifications (usually female) of the virtues that had inspired him.

The tableaux themselves emphasized Paul III's achievements: *Universal Peace*, with portraits of Charles V and Francis I, alluded to the pope's diplomatic triumph at Nice; *Remuneration of Virtue* showed the pope nominating cardinals; *Building St Peter's* depicted Paul III, in the garb of a high priest of the Old Testament, to commemorate his achievements as a patron of the arts; and *Universal Homage* showed him and his grandson accepting gifts of exotic animals from secular rulers, its inscription referring to the golden age under Farnese rule. The historian Paolo Giovio, a humanist attached to Alessandro's court who had been responsible for devising the decorative programme for the room, also took charge of its execution while Alessandro was away, keeping his patron informed of its progress by letter. 'Your lordship will salivate when you see what has been done in the great hall for some 300 portraits at this price,' he wrote; Vasari claims he was paid 1,000 ducats for the project.[39] And Giovio was particularly thrilled to see that his own portrait was included in the *Remuneration of Virtue* scene.

Paul III Distributes Benefices, 1546 (Rome, Palazzo della Cancelleria).
Vasari's fresco included portraits of many of Cardinal Alessandro's circle, notably Pietro Bembo, Giacomo Sadoleto and Reginald Pole, who all received red hats from Paul III.

Meanwhile, in the real world, where there was little universal homage and no peace, Paul III and Cardinal Alessandro were facing a political situation that had begun to spiral out of control. The Council of Trent had opened amid much anticipation in early 1543 but the hostility between Charles V and Francis I showed no signs of abating. The king continued to sow dissent in the empire by offering support to Germany's Protestant princes, while Charles V responded by signing an alliance with Henry VIII and declaring war on the French. In Rome there were worries that the emperor was losing patience with Paul III's refusal to take sides in the Habsburg–Valois struggle. And then in late June there was real panic in the city when Barbarossa's fleet anchored at the mouth of the Tiber. The French ambassador was forced to admit in public that the Turks were not about to attack Rome but that Barbarossa was en route to raid the coast of Spain, which unfortunately denied the pirate the element of surprise – in revenge, on his return a year later he looted the islands of Procida and Ischia, taking thousands of prisoners to serve as slaves on the sultan's galleys.[40] With war dividing northern Europe and the Turkish threat growing by the day, the Council of Trent was suspended in July and that November Paul III again appointed Cardinal Alessandro as legate to France and the empire to act as mediator.

Unfortunately relations had begun to deteriorate on all sides. Neither Francis I nor Charles V trusted each other and both were suspicious of Paul III's motives. The emperor, in particular, worried that Cardinal Alessandro was in France to finalize arrangements for the marriage of his sister Vittoria and the king's son. When Alessandro arrived in Worms, Charles V accused him and his grandfather of pro-French sympathies, and when the cardinal tried to justify Paul III's position, the emperor brusquely interrupted:

> Monsignor, thanks to us you are Archbishop of Monreale, your father is Duke of Novara, Ottavio Farnese received the hand of our daughter with an income of 20,000 ducats... and now the Vicar of Christ, who has received so many benefits from us, is ready to join forces with the King of France or rather, we should say, with the Turks.[41]

Cardinal Alessandro kept his temper but the mission had been a complete failure.

In the end it was not Farnese diplomacy but a chronic lack of funds that brought Charles V and Francis I to the negotiating table in 1544. That September they signed the Peace of Crépy, agreeing on their separate spheres of influence in Europe; Francis I finally gave up his claim to Milan, leaving Paul III's policy options even more dependent on imperial sanction than before. Initially this was not a problem. Paul III was able to reopen the Council of Trent in March 1545, though it soon ran into difficulties, this time because of the opposition of the German Protestant princes. In April Cardinal Alessandro left Rome as legate to Charles V once again, this time at the express request of the emperor, who was attending the Diet of Worms. Cardinal Alessandro travelled quickly, covering the 375 miles from Rome to Trent in just eight days.[42] He had stopped off in Mantua to discuss the pope's failing health with Cardinal Ercole Gonzaga and, after three days of discussions with the legates in Trent, he crossed the Alps into Germany.

The journey now became considerably more dangerous for a Catholic cardinal. Although he was not wearing his official robes, nor travelling with his usual imposingly large entourage, nevertheless there was always the threat of anti-Catholic violence. He had already been advised to avoid Augsburg before receiving a letter from Cardinal Truchsess begging him not to travel through Württemberg, because of the danger posed by the Protestant duke and his subjects. The twenty-four-year-old Alessandro, better known for his cultured conversation than intrepid deeds, apparently considered travelling through the duchy in disguise so that they could ride on the direct route to Worms but was persuaded to take a 'safer' detour instead. He still had to travel through the Protestant city of Ulm, where he was shocked by the bareness of the medieval cathedral, shorn of all its paintings, ornaments and costly embroidered altarcloths.[43] After arriving in Worms he went into a bookshop, where he was surprised to find only Protestant texts, and remonstrated with the bookseller, himself a Protestant, urging him to recant: his courtiers were horrified at Alessandro's lack of caution, although fortunately he was still not wearing his cardinal's robes.

Cardinal Alessandro was given a warm welcome by Charles V, which must have come as a relief after his last rather disagreeable encounter with the emperor. Paul III had entrusted his legate with two main tasks: to get Charles to agree to support a crusade against the Turks, and to order his bishops to attend the Council of Trent. Charles agreed to both, with some reluctance over the last issue, but his decision was eased by Cardinal Alessandro's promise that there would be papal assistance – money and men – for the emperor's forthcoming war against the Protestant League of Schmalkalden. Politics and religion apart, there was another reason for the improved relations between the empire and Rome – after finally submitting to her husband, Margaret of Austria was now pregnant, with the baby expected in late summer.

Unfortunately the reconciliation between Paul III and Charles V was to be of very brief duration. The pope took immediate advantage of the emperor's show of goodwill at Worms to create a Farnese duchy out of the papal fiefs of Parma and Piacenza, two wealthy cities on the Lombard plain between Bologna and Milan. This move had been carefully planned: the pope had been bishop of Parma and had used his position to build up a network of support with the leading noble families in the area, using the cement of marital alliances starting with that of his daughter Costanza to the Count of Santa Fiora. The move was not popular with the new duke's neighbours in Mantua and Ferrara: 'To us, whose states were won by our ancestors with much adversity and hard work,' Cardinal Ercole Gonzaga informed his cousin, Duke Ercole d'Este, 'it is a strange thing to see a duke of two similar cities created overnight, like a mushroom.'[44] Nor was Charles V very happy with Paul III's decision to appoint Pier Luigi as the first duke: the emperor insisted that he would only agree to the plan if the title went directly to his own son-in-law Ottavio. However, Pier Luigi was equally adamant and the pope, refusing to be overruled, issued the official bull on 26 August giving the duchy of Parma and Piacenza to his son, whose old title of Duke of Castro now passed down to Ottavio.

The next day, 27 August, the new Duchess of Castro gave birth to twin boys, who were named Alessandro and Carlo after their illustrious great-grandfather and grandfather. Sadly Carlo only lived a month, but Alessandro thrived. Margaret's initial refusal to consummate the marriage had worried Charles V, who gently remonstrated with his daughter for failing to do her duty which he thought was 'unworthy of a Christian and especially of you who is my daughter'.[45] When Ottavio returned to Italy in May 1543 after an absence of over a year in Spain, the rumour mill reported enthusiastically that he had finally been allowed into the marital bed. Paul III was thrilled. His private account books record several presents to the pregnant Margaret: a gold chain at New Year costing 47 scudi, as well as 'gold items made in France' worth 133 scudi.[46] Anticipating the imminent arrival of his great-grandchildren, the ledger recorded a final payment for the 2,000 scudi which he had spent on embroidered hangings 'to congratulate her on her happy birth'.[47] A few days after the arrival of the twins, the pope tipped Margaret's musicians 4 scudi and gave the wet nurse a present of 200 scudi (100 for each baby).[48]

On visiting the new mother for the first time on 5 September, Paul III reportedly told Margaret that he had always known her 'to be good and sensible and in this she had been most prudent as, fearing that his Holiness and his Imperial Majesty would fall out, she has given birth not only to one son but to two, so that they can have one each'.[49] He also gave her a particularly valuable 'gold basin and ewer, a goblet and a wonderful salt in pure gold and in the goblet there were many coins... which they say were from those found in St Peter's tomb'.

By all accounts Margaret of Austria was a very pious woman, who must have appreciated the gift from the pope, but she was also a very wealthy one. Charles V had given her several properties in the kingdom of Naples for her dowry but she had also inherited much from her first husband, Alessandro de' Medici. Clement VII had died in 1534 leaving his Florentine property to his illegitimate son and his Roman property to his nephew, Cardinal Ippolito de' Medici. The cardinal had died very suddenly of malaria in the summer of 1535, and all his possessions were inherited by Alessandro. And then Alessandro himself died in January 1537, assassinated by a distant cousin, leaving all his non-Florentine possessions to his widow. Margaret inherited the Medici palaces in Rome: the Palazzo Madama,* begun by Leo X, and the exquisite Villa Madama, built by Clement VII. She also inherited a priceless collection of valuables, including stunning classical statuary and 'an agate dish, cameos and diamonds... worth over 90,000 scudi'.[50] There was a long dispute between the Medici and the Farnese, and much bad blood, over the ownership of the estate, which was finally settled in 1587, much in Margaret's favour. In the mean time she moved into the Palazzo Madama in central Rome, where her twins were born and which she

---

* The Palazzo Madama is now the official seat of the Italian Senate.

embellished with a *studiolo* decorated with stuccoes and eight scenes of events in her father's life by Daniele da Volterra.[51]

The Farnese themselves were able to delve into the papal coffers to acquire the trappings of aristocratic power, a parallel to their political campaign to establish themselves in Italy's ruling elite. Both Pier Luigi and Cardinal Alessandro began to amass a variety of conspicuously expensive artworks. Among Pier Luigi's commissions was a set of tapestries depicting scenes from the life of Alexander the Great, an obvious allusion to his father.[52] Cardinal Alessandro spent lavishly on the *Farnese Hours* (1538–46), illustrated with gilded miniatures set in borders filled with Farnese portraits and *all'antica* detail by Giulio Clovio – it took the artist nine years to complete. Both father and son commissioned ostentatiously expensive caskets: Pier Luigi's has not survived but Alessandro's *Cassetta Farnese* (begun *c.*1543) is a sumptuous gilded silver affair, decorated with statues of classical gods and mythological scenes engraved on rock crystal panels by the goldsmith Giovanni Bernardi.[53]

Above all, the Farnese were patrons of Titian – imitating not only Federigo Gonzaga and Francesco Maria della Rovere (see Chapter 7), but also Charles V, who had by this time also recognized the painter's talents (see Conclusion). Titian's first Farnese portrait was not for the family itself but for the Venetian patrician Andrea Corner, who commissioned a portrait of Cardinal Alessandro's brother Ranuccio Farnese (1542) as a present for his mother, Girolama Orsini. This charming picture of the twelve-year-old boy showed him in the uniform of the Knights of Malta – three years later the boy would be given a cardinal's hat by his grandfather. When offered the commission to paint a portrait of the pope, the Farnese agent in Venice reported to Cardinal Alessandro that Titian was 'ready to portray the whole of the most illustrious house of your lordship, even the cats'.[54] And indeed there are portraits of all the family (though not the pets): two of the shrewd, wily pope; the hard, fierce Pier Luigi; the somewhat gauche Cardinal Alessandro; and the obsequious Ottavio. There are none of the wives, though Cardinal Alessandro did have his mistress portrayed in the guise of Danaë, rather aptly receiving Jupiter in her lap in the form of a shower of gold.

The portrait of Paul III, Alessandro and Ottavio, which Titian began in late 1545, was deliberately designed to publicize Paul's ambitions for his family: Alessandro as heir to his own papal throne and Ottavio as heir to the Farnese's secular state, Parma and Piacenza. Paul III must have hoped that, with the support of Charles V, both ambitions were strong possibilities – in the end, however, it did not turn out as the pope had planned. Over the next two years relations between the Farnese and the emperor deteriorated to such an extent that Paul III was obliged to rethink his political priorities, and the portrait was never properly finished.[55]

Paul III's quarrel with Charles V centred on the Protestant revolt. In Rome where the voices of moderation and reconciliation had been drowned out by hardline reformers, compromise on matters of faith had become impossible. But for Charles, himself a devout Catholic, the issue was not spiritual faith but worldly authority. To hold the empire together he needed to find a way to reconcile Protestants and Catholics. And this position became even more entrenched in 1547 when he won a resounding victory over the Protestants at the Battle of Mühlberg, at the head of a coalition with several Protestant princes to whom he had

Farnese Casket, 1543–61 (Naples, Museo di Capodimonte). Giovanni Berardi's silver gilt casket was ornamented with scenes from classical mythology.
overleaf Titian, *Danae*, 1546 (Naples, Museo di Capodimonte). A portrait of Cardinal Alessandro's mistress, a courtesan of exceptional beauty, appropriately receiving her lover disguised as Jupiter in a shower of gold.

promised religious toleration as the price of their support. There was no way Paul III could support Charles V, especially after the emperor passed the edict *Interim* (1548) giving freedom of worship to his subjects of both faiths.

But the catalyst that broke the long association between the emperor and the pope was the murder of Pier Luigi, who was violently assassinated at his castle in Piacenza on 10 September 1547 by men employed by Ferrante Gonzaga, Charles V's governor of Milan. Gonzaga seized Piacenza – though he failed to take Parma, thanks to a spirited defence by the new duke, Ottavio. Gonzaga had been suspicious of the political and military ambitions of his dangerous new neighbour, and had been itching to get rid of Pier Luigi since Paul III created the duchy in 1545. Charles V, equally suspicious but less rash, initially counselled patience – Paul was almost eighty years old, he could not live much longer – but did give his consent to Gonzaga's plan to oust Pier Luigi, though he insisted that there must be no violence. Gonzaga ignored the caveat and, having thrown the duke's bleeding corpse out of the window, sacked the palace and occupied Piacenza. Virtually none of the lavish furnishings that ornamented Pier Luigi's apartment were ever returned, though contemporary accounts estimated that the silver, tapestries and other valuables removed that day came to over 50,000 ducats.[56]

Although the emperor denied any involvement, and sent an envoy to Italy to offer his condolences to the Farnese, the family itself did not doubt that the murder had been done on his orders. It was to have repercussions at many levels, not least Paul III's abrupt scrapping of his policy of neutrality, a policy he had stubbornly and successfully maintained for thirteen years, to side with France, where Henri II had recently succeeded to the throne after the death of his father Francis I, against the emperor. The alliance was cemented by the betrothal of his youngest grandson Orazio, aged sixteen, and the king's illegitimate nine-year-old daughter Diane of France. The marriage of Paul's granddaughter Vittoria and Duke Guidobaldo della Rovere, who had been betrothed in June, was now delayed. Indeed, there were some doubts in Urbino about the wisdom of this union, but it finally went ahead in January, with the new duchess making colourful entries into her husband's subject territories before arriving at Urbino on 2 February 1548.

Titian, *Pier Luigi Farnese*, 1546 (Naples, Museo di Capodimonte). Paul III appointed his aggressive and violent son as captain-general of the papal army, but chose to entrust more delicate diplomatic business to his grandsons.

Vittoria's younger brother Ottavio was now Duke of Parma and Piacenza, thrust unexpectedly into the spotlight at the age of just twenty-three. Luckily he had been in Parma when his father had been murdered and had been able to safeguard that city from Ferrante Gonzaga's assault, but Charles V refused to recognize his title to either city. He also refused Paul III's request to return the papal fief and demanded Parma as well, offering Ottavio a title in the kingdom of Naples in recompense. Paul III then suggested that Parma and Piacenza should be returned to the Papal States and Ottavio made Duke of Camerino, a plan which Cardinal Alessandro told the pope would not be acceptable to his brother. Paul III ignored his grandson's advice and sent an agent to take charge of Parma on his behalf. Now Ottavio rebelled: he rode to Parma, where the papal agent refused to allow him to enter, and he ignored Paul III's orders for him to return to Rome. Deeply upset by this quarrel with a favourite grandson, the pope lost his temper, caught a chill and died five days later – though not before Cardinal Alessandro had made him sign an official document ordering the restoration of both Parma and Piacenza to Ottavio.

The conclave that followed Paul III's death was long and arduous for those involved. Conditions were unpleasant in the extreme in the Vatican: 'There is so much smoke from the candles and torches that are lit there, and so much dirt, and such a terrible stench from the lavatories' that many cardinals worried about falling ill, warned the Mantuan ambassador on 31 December 1549.[57] But the conclave was to last another six weeks before Giovanni Maria del Monte was elected Julius III on 8 February, after promising to restore Ottavio as Duke of Parma and Piacenza. Unfortunately for the Farnese, the new pope's true colours were soon revealed: far from supporting them, Julius III made an alliance with Charles V. Having deprived Ottavio of the duchy, he exiled the Farnese from Rome. Ottavio now looked to his grandfather's ally Henri II for help in restoring his authority in his duchy and the Habsburg–Valois struggle turned violent yet again. The marriage between his younger brother Orazio and Henri's illegitimate daughter Diane took place in February 1552; Orazio was sadly to die fighting for France at the Battle of Hesdin a year later. In April 1552,

Antonis Mor, *Duke Alessandro Farnese*, 1557 (Parma, Galleria Nazionale).
Ottavio Farnese's son was a bold soldier and astute politician. His uncle
Philip II appointed him governor of the Netherlands, where he restored
Spanish authority over Protestant rebels.

when Charles V was obliged to recall his troops from northern Italy to quell a rebellion against his authority in the empire, Julius III was forced to sign a truce with the French and restore the duchy to the Farnese. The dynasty had survived the first test of its power.

During Pier Luigi's tenure as Duke of Parma and Piacenza he had built visible evidence of his authority in aggressively defensive walls and bastions in both cities, though he made Piacenza his official residence. Designed to protect the Farnese from both external attack and internal rebellion, these projects involved the destruction of many churches and convents, and did much to fuel his unpopularity among his subjects. To separate himself from his father's legacy, Ottavio established his capital in Parma, living first in the episcopal palace which had belonged to his grandfather and then, because this was not grand enough, in another palace he built in the city. The Palazzo del Giardino, as the second palace was known, was set in magnificent gardens with fountains, grottoes, a labyrinth and 'groves of orange trees, oaks, pines and plane trees', a visitor recorded; the woods were 'stocked with wild game for hunting; ponds full of fish; dens of untamed animals', including two lions and a leopard.[58] He also built two villas in the hills outside the city to escape the summer heat; they too were set in superb gardens.

With Ottavio resident in Parma, Margaret of Austria began work on a large palace in Piacenza, a massive five-storey block set in gardens which was never finished. Although the couple famously disliked each other – they did not have any more children after the twins born in 1545 – the decision to have two separate residences almost certainly had more to do with the need to provide evidence of ducal authority in both cities. They made much of the dynastic angle, commissioning portraits of their heir, Alessandro (the surviving twin): as a young man dressed in the height of fashion by Antonis Mor; and in *Parma embracing Alessandro Farnese*, an allegory depicting the ten-year-old heir already in battle armour.

Cardinals Alessandro and Ranuccio were back in Rome in 1552, and Ranuccio celebrated the family's survival by decorating a room in the Palazzo Farnese with a cycle of scenes of family history, which were begun by Francesco Salviati that year. Four of the eight scenes commemorated the achievements of Paul III but the other four depicted the military exploits of four ancestors – three of whom were named Ranuccio, and some more mythical than others. Fact and fiction combined to create a legend for the Farnese, giving them the same sort of roster of heroic ancestors performing acts of military glory as that possessed by older aristocratic dynasties. Cardinal Alessandro had a more detailed version of the legend in fourteen scenes painted on the walls and ceilings of one of the reception rooms at his villa at Caprarola. The six early scenes, with learned inscriptions written in proper antique style, provided visual proof of such fictitious events as the founding of Orbetello in 1100 or Guido Farnese becoming Prince of Orbetello in 1313. And the eight events dating from after 1534 included scenes of Alessandro's own achievements, notably his visits as legate to Paris and Worms, as well as the family's most recent victory over Parma.

Cardinal Alessandro was one of the greatest patrons of the period. His major architectural project was the construction of the villa at Caprarola in the Farnese estates north of Rome. Begun in 1559, it was built on the foundations of a pentagonal fortress started by Paul III and set in superb gardens ornamented with grottoes and fountains. In Rome, in addition to his main residence, the Palazzo della Cancelleria, he also inherited the magnificent Palazzo Farnese after Cardinal Ranuccio died in 1565, and finished the decoration of the palace, where he displayed his impressive collection of antique sculpture. He bought villas and gardens in Rome, including the elegant Villa Farnesina with its lovely frescoes by Raphael painted around 1518 for the papal banker Agostino Chigi.

According to one recent study, Cardinal Alessandro spent 60 per cent of his income on the expenses of his large household, which numbered some 270 people; and 60 per cent of that sum – just over a third of his income – went on food.[59] Evidently one ate well at this cardinal's table. The average consumption of meat in his palace came to 887 grams, while the average daily amount of wine drunk was 1.62 litres – compared with 573 grams of meat and 0.85 litres of wine at the table of a less wealthy cardinal; or 75 grams of meat and 0.25 litres of wine that were the diet of ordinary citizens in Valladolid.[60]

In a career of almost fifty-five years, Alessandro had seen eight popes and witnessed the transformation from the worldly Renaissance to the authoritarian years of the Counter-Reformation. Indeed, his own pattern of patronage altered after the reforms initiated after the completion of the Council of Trent in December 1563. The following

year he took priestly orders – previously cardinals from princely families were excused this irrevocable step on the grounds that they might be needed to perform dynastic duties for their families. He also became cardinal-protector of several of the confraternities that were proliferating in post-Tridentine Rome. He restored and renovated churches of his benefices, and spent lavishly on religious projects: for example, he gave a cross and two candlesticks costing 18,000 scudi to St Peter's.[61] In 1568 he built the Gesù for the Jesuits, the mother church of their order in Rome, and in the last three years of his life he spent 450,000 scudi, which amounted to a third of his income, on good works.[62] It was said that he owned the three most beautiful things in Rome: Palazzo Farnese, the Gesù, and his daughter Clelia. After his death in 1589 he was buried amid much pomp in his tomb at the Gesù: the Venetian ambassador lamented that Rome had lost a cardinal unequalled for his experience, taste, generosity and charity to the poor.[63]

The Farnese had been very successful in their bid for dynastic power: they had had their fair share of luck but, above all, they had been fortunate in Paul III, an astute politician who had lived long enough to give them a chance to secure their position. When Ottavio died in 1586 the duchy of Parma and Piacenza was inherited by his son Alessandro, who had moved from Italy to the Netherlands with his mother Margaret of Austria when she was appointed Governor of the Netherlands by her half-brother Philip II, who had become King of Spain in 1559 after the death of his father, Charles V. Royal connections led to a royal marriage when Alessandro married Maria of Braganza in 1565; he went on to have a stellar career, in charge of Philip II's army restoring royal authority in the Spanish Netherlands. Although Castro was razed to the ground by a papal army in 1649, the family retained the duchy of Parma and Piacenza for another century.

Rome, Gesù, begun 1568. In his forties, Cardinal Alessandro took priestly orders. His new piety was evident in his conspicuous patronage of the Jesuits, including a costly new church for the order.

ERCOLE II D'ESTE (1508–59)
Duke of Ferrara

IPPOLITO D'ESTE (1509–72)
Cardinal, his brother

Renée of France, *his wife*

Alfonso II, *Duke of Ferrara, his son*

COSIMO DE' MEDICI (1519–74)
Duke of Florence

Giovanni de' Medici, *Cardinal, his son*

Lucrezia, *Duchess of Ferrara, his daughter*

Catherine de' Medici, *Queen of France*

Paul IV (r.1555–59), Pius IV (r.1559–65) and Pius V (r.1566–72), *Popes*

PRECEDENCE AND REFORM

The Este

&

Cosimo de' Medici

I n 1562 an anonymous document appeared in Florence claiming the superiority of the Duke of Florence over the Duke of Ferrara. The claim was robustly repudiated in Ferrara: 'The duke of Ferrara has so many noble subjects that he does not need to show that he precedes the Duke of Florence'; he has 'the authority of the blood of true nobility', the author boasted, and rules over 'counts, barons and marquises... not mere citizens and merchants', this last a jibe at Florence's republican origins.[1] The Este were old nobility: they could trace their lineage back to the twelfth century. In 1242, when Azzo d'Este became Lord of Ferrara, the Medici were mere jobbing moneylenders to the aristocracy. By 1500 the Este were Dukes of Modena (1452) and of Ferrara (1471), while the Medici were still commoners and, in fact, had been exiled by those 'citizens and merchants' who governed Florence. Latecomers to the dynastic stage, they only acquired the status of a ruling house in 1532 after the republic was forced to surrender to the Medici pope Clement VII, who installed his illegitimate son Alessandro as the first duke – when he was assassinated in 1537, the title passed to his cousin Cosimo I.

The rivalry between the two houses dated back to September 1541 when Cosimo I took offence at being placed on Charles V's left-hand side during the emperor's entry into Lucca for a conference with Paul III, while Ercole II d'Este was given the position of honour on the right. Cosimo was gauche – he was just twenty-two years old and had only been duke for four years – and it was presumptuous of him to claim, in the face of all the rules governing precedence, that his parvenu dynasty was superior. Nevertheless, he doggedly continued to assert his claim. By Christmas the rivalry was being fought out by proxy at the papal court; in 1545 Cosimo abruptly recalled his ambassador at the French court after an incident of precedence being given to the Ferrarese envoy.[2] The quarrel quickly descended to a more petty level that year when Cosimo poached two of Ercole II's Flemish weavers so that he too could have the tapestries for which Ferrara was famous.[3] Evidently it was the kudos of having his own workshop that mattered to Cosimo – it would have been cheaper to buy the hangings in Flanders and ship them home.[4]

Cosimo I's ultimate ambition was not merely to be given precedence

Agnolo Bronzino, *Cosimo I de' Medici*, 1545–6 (Florence, Uffizi).
One of hundreds of portraits commissioned by
Cosimo I to give visual expression to his right to rule.

COS
MEDIC

over the Este: he wanted the parvenu house of Medici to be recognized as the premier dynasty in Italy, with the title of King of Tuscany – it is worth pointing out here that in 1545 he still had to conquer much of Tuscany, let alone to persuade Paul III to grant him a royal title that would outrank the pope's own Farnese family. This is the story of the battle between the Este and Medici princes, fought not by armies but just as viciously in politics, diplomacy, culture and, above all, in the five papal conclaves that took place between 1549 and 1566.

Cosimo I spent prodigal sums on creating an appropriate setting in Florence for the display of his new rank. He was hard-working and conscientious, with a high opinion of himself, traits all nurtured by his doting mother, Maria Salviati, who had devoted herself to his upbringing after she was widowed. He commissioned hundreds of portraits of himself – life-size statues, medals, cameos, images painted on canvas and tin, in fresco cycles – in modern armour, in classical armour, as Emperor Augustus, even an Apotheosis. The success of his economic policy provided limitless funds with which to buy the trappings of ducal prestige: one of his agents was instructed to look for 'a pearl the size of a pear'; another spent 600 scudi on nine antique busts for the ducal collection, 'most beautiful and very rare', but had difficulty finding the 'fifty rubies' that the duke also wanted.[5] Cosimo amassed notable collections of valuable gems, antique statues, maps, books, curiosities and, of course, the costly tapestries that decorated his palaces and villas, as well as a rare collection of Etruscan antiquities, to provide visual evidence of his claim to be ruler of all Tuscany.[6] His marriage to Eleonora of Toledo, the daughter of Charles V's viceroy in Naples, cemented Cosimo I's alliance with Charles V; and Eleonora secured the future of the dynasty in practical terms by bearing him eleven children. Above all, he was a snob and anxious to eradicate any association with his family's mercantile origins. Reinventing Medici tradition, he promoted his ancestors not as bankers but as international statesmen and patrons of the arts. And, like other new dynasties of the sixteenth century, he provided visual proof of his lineage in ancestor cycles commissioned to decorate his palaces, though he had to invent several military heroes to bolster the theme of glory on the battlefield.

The Este, by contrast, had no need for ancestor cycles to prove their lineage, which was impeccable if a little exotic. Court humanists boasted of the family's ancestors not just as brave soldiers but as royalty: Ludovico Ariosto's epic *Orlando Furioso* traced their descent from King Priam of Troy and Charlemagne, a line they shared with Charles V. Ercole II's grandfathers were Duke Ercole I of Ferrara and Alexander VI, the infamous Borgia pope; his grandmothers were Eleonora of Aragon, daughter of King Alfonso I of Naples, and Vanozza de' Cataneis, landlady of several taverns in Rome. The trappings of aristocratic prestige at the Este court had been acquired over several generations, not bought new. And the city enjoyed the reputation of being one of the leading courts of Renaissance Italy.

Traditionally Ferrara was an ally of France and, although this policy had come under considerable pressure during the Habsburg–Valois wars (see Chapter 7), Alfonso I had ensured that his eldest sons had close ties with the French court. His heir, Ercole, married Renée of France: she was the daughter of Louis XII and her elder sister, Claude, who died in 1524, had been Francis I's first queen. Ercole was staid, cautious and unimaginative, but proved a good ruler. His brother Ippolito, destined for the church and appointed Archbishop of Milan at the age of nine, had joined the French court in 1536, becoming a favourite with Francis I – the two men shared many interests, not least hunting, gambling and women. Moreover, with no chance of a Frenchman being elected as pope, the king groomed Ippolito as his preferred candidate for the papal tiara, showering him with lucrative French benefices and persuading Paul III to grant him a red hat (1538).

Ippolito was one of the few of Francis I's favourites to survive the palace coup after the king's death in 1547. Henri II too showed special favour to the Italian prince: they hunted together, played energetic games of tennis and gambled; Ippolito was regularly invited to sit with the king in the royal chapel and, an even more conspicuous honour, to dine at the royal table.[7] In 1549 Henri appointed Ippolito to the prestigious position of cardinal-protector in Rome to represent the interests of the French crown in consistory meetings between the pope and his cardinals. 'All Rome assembled at the windows and along the streets through which I passed', he boasted, in French, to Henri II, describing his formal entry into the city that July.[8] Ippolito was now the senior 'French' cardinal at the papal court, holding seven French sees, including the prestigious archbishopric of Lyon, and nineteen abbeys, among which were Chaalis, set amid the royal hunting park just north of Paris and the Norman abbey of Jumièges.[9] With an annual income of 80,000 scudi, over half of it from France, he was one of the richest cardinals in Rome.[10] And he went out of his way to display his political allegiance: many of his musicians were French, as were his coachman and his tailor; he wore French-style clothes, drank French wines and employed French cooks in his kitchen.[11]

Cosimo I's ambassador was impressed: 'The Cardinal of Ferrara is the most splendid and most noble lord, and there is hardly another cardinal in the College who can equal his birth, wealth and followers though there are those who think he is too fond of showing off in an overly ostentatious manner.'[12] Ippolito was a Renaissance cardinal *par excellence*: his luxurious tastes were evident in his jewels, silver and clothes; he had mistresses and children; his coach horses were named Sweetheart, Beauty, Damsel and Pet; he perfumed his beard with jasmine oil and his gloves with ambergris and musk; and he much preferred the tight-fitting doublets and hose of the secular world to the shapeless garments of the church.[13]

The ambitions of these two princes – Ippolito for the papal tiara, Cosimo for the royal crown of Tuscany – were about to clash. The conclave after Paul III's death in November 1549 would be the first of five held between 1549 and 1566 in which the rivalry between the urbane cardinal and the prickly duke directly affected the result. Of course

anon, *Cardinal Ippolito d'Este*, 1537 (Liverpool, Walker Art Gallery). Son of a duke and grandson of a pope, Ippolito was able to buy himself a Church career though he failed in his ambition to be chosen for the papal tiara.

Cosimo himself could not take part, but he exercised his influence by inserting his own agent among the courtiers and other conclavists with the cardinals in the Vatican – a practice that was, strictly speaking, forbidden, but Europe's secular rulers mostly ignored the rule. The conclave opened on 29 November and, thanks to unprecedented levels of interference from outside, it was to be one of the longest of the century. Cosimo I's own choice was Giovanni Maria del Monte, a president of the Council of Trent, though in public he backed Charles V's candidate, Cardinal Juan Alvarez de Toledo, who was his wife's uncle. Ippolito, who was the French candidate, made astute use of delaying tactics to ensure that the conclave was still in action when the French cardinals finally arrived in late December but, with both sides able to block the election of rival candidates while lacking the ability to acquire the necessary two-thirds majority to elect their own, it became deadlocked. It took another month of futile intrigues, in halls where the stench of disease was becoming unbearable, before Cosimo's choice, Cardinal del Monte, was elected as Julius III on 8 February. Ippolito, who had played a key role in negotiating the compromise, was rewarded with the governorship of Tivoli.

Cosimo's manner may not have endeared him to his contemporaries but his devious political skills were earning respect. Two years later the Sienese asked Henri II for help to expel the imperial garrison stationed in the city. Cosimo offered no resistance as troops led by Henri II's commander Pietro Strozzi marched across his border; he had no intention, he assured the new governor of Siena – none other than Cardinal Ippolito – of fighting the French. Behind the scenes, however, that is exactly what he was planning. Siena and its territories would give his claim to be ruler of all Tuscany considerably more credibility; it was also a chance to destroy the Florentine exiles with Strozzi, whose father had been executed by Cosimo for treason.

Cosimo I's true intentions became known in May 1553 when details of the plot he was planning were leaked to Ippolito. The Sienese involved were executed but it left the cardinal with the impossible task of trying to maintain the authority of the French crown while army commander Strozzi urged him to force regime change in Florence. But the quarrel gave Cosimo I time to make plans. First he appointed one of Charles V's generals, Giangiacomo Medici, Marquis of Marignano, to command his army – no relation to Cosimo but from a Milanese patrician family of the same name. Then he provoked the Sienese into declaring war on Florence, giving him the pretext he needed to attack the French. Ippolito finally left in May 1554 to resume his duties as cardinal-protector of France – despite his failure in Siena, he had not fallen out of favour with Henri II. And back in Rome he was to come into conflict with Cosimo again rather sooner than he might have expected. Julius III died on 23 March 1555, just as the Florentine army was coming to the end of the long, weary siege of Siena – the following month the duke would emerge victorious from both the siege and the conclave.

The conclave opened on 5 April, split as usual between imperial and French factions; but this time there was a third group, who wanted a pope more committed to reform. Ippolito was a front runner and raised money from Ercole II and Henri II to bribe the conclave.[14] He asked his brother 'as urgently as possible if you could send a remittance of 25,000 scudi which I can then offer to the College'; the king promised benefices worth a similar amount to secure votes for his protégé.[15] Cosimo, of course, was determined to avoid Ippolito's election: he had been on the verge of victory when a letter arrived at the conclave, intercepted, or so Cosimo claimed, by his agents, containing the alarming news that Strozzi's troops were marching on Rome to force the election of a French cardinal.[16] Ippolito dismissed the letter as a forgery, which it undoubtedly was, but Cosimo's intervention had destroyed his chances. The cardinals regrouped in favour of the pious Marcello Cervini, who was elected as Marcellus II on 9 April. Ippolito informed his brother that 'tonight a pope has been elected whom I could not more dislike', and he must have been relieved when Marcellus II died, amid inevitable rumours of poison, after just three weeks in office.[17]

On 15 May the cardinals found themselves back in their cramped cubicles in the Vatican, as divided as before: Cosimo aligned with the emperor against Ippolito and the French, and the reformers with their own spiritual agenda. This time Cosimo had inserted an agent among the conclavists of Innocenzo del Monte, a boy Julius III had picked up on the streets of Parma and persuaded his brother to adopt, scandalizing all Italy by giving this fifteen-year-old 'nephew' a red hat. Ippolito, the agent reported, had 'captivated the young cardinals', including del Monte, by his 'promises and great offers'.[18] This time the French faction, led by Ippolito, joined forces with the reformers and outwitted the imperialists to elect the hardliner Gianpietro Carafa as

Paul IV. The new pope, a month short of his seventy-ninth birthday, was in excellent health and loved a glass of strong red wine with his dinner, possibly his only moderate trait. Appointed inquisitor-general by Paul III, he was a zealot in the cause of church reform. His piety was extreme; he was dictatorial and stubborn, hated being contradicted and was prone to terrifying rages. He knew he was widely disliked – indeed, he saw his election as evidence that God personally had entrusted him with the task of rooting out Protestant heresy, a task that for him was almost an addiction.

Ippolito was an early victim of the new regime – if he had expected a reward for his support during the conclave, he was sadly mistaken. He was exactly the type of cardinal detested by the reformers. Within weeks he was charged with simony, buying votes in the recent election, summarily deprived of the posts of cardinal-protector, governor of Tivoli and Archbishop of Milan, and exiled to Ferrara. He left Rome in August 1555, returning home to lick his wounds. And the future must have looked increasingly bleak that November when his beloved daughter Renea died from a septic throat abscess. He remained in the political wilderness for four frustrating years. Exile in provincial Ferrara had its advantages – an enviable life of ease in his palaces and villas, with plenty of time for hunting with his peregrines, fishing expeditions in the marshes of the Po delta, and lively games of tennis – yet the quantities of payments for letters to the papal court, and for the replies delivered in person by Ferrara's postmaster, show just how much he yearned to be back at the centre of power.

In truth, Ippolito was fortunate to avoid the reign of terror unfolding in Rome under Paul IV and his cardinal-nephew, the unprincipled Carlo Carafa, a soldier by trade with a reputation for debauchery. Neapolitan aristocrats by birth, they loathed the Spanish who had annexed their city – Paul IV insultingly described them as the 'sperm of Jews and Arabs'.[19] The pope refused to recognize Charles V's decision to abdicate in 1555, worn out by years of hard work, and nor would he recognize the emperor's heirs: his brother Ferdinand of Habsburg as emperor and his son Philip as King of Spain and ruler of Charles's extensive possessions in Flanders and the Americas. Cardinal

Carlo then 'discovered' a Spanish plot to assassinate the pope, who was persuaded to declare war on Charles V – a fiasco, which saw the Spanish viceroy in Naples, the Duke of Alba, march his troops unhindered to the gates of Rome.

Conditions in the city steadily worsened. The price of food rocketed thanks to the war, as did the taxes imposed to pay for it. The grim pope banned the ribald fun of the Carnival; he cleared beggars from the streets and forced Jews to wear yellow hats and move into the ghetto that he built down by the Tiber. The Inquisition, under its new general Michele Ghislieri, tortured, imprisoned or executed hundreds of Romans on the merest whiff of Protestant sympathies, and anyone else who failed to conform to Paul IV's strict moral code: rapists, blasphemers, homosexuals, actors, even those who failed to observe the Friday ban on meat. The pope himself attended trials in person every Thursday. One Roman noble was arrested for having a Jewish mistress; a bishop was sent to prison for having relations with a courtesan; while a painter was condemned as a heretic for not painting a crucifix in the proper manner.[20] Ippolito was shocked as news of his colleagues reached Ferrara. Cardinal Guido Ascanio Sforza, arrested because his brother was fighting with the Spanish army, had to pay the huge sum of 200,000 scudi to secure his release from Castel Sant'Angelo.[21] Cardinal Giovanni Morone, a devout Christian of high moral character but detested by Paul IV, had also been imprisoned, charged with heresy by the Inquisition. Although a tribunal found him entirely innocent of the charges, the pope refused to release the unfortunate man.

Outside Rome Paul IV gave the Inquisition responsibility for church reform and closed the Council of Trent. Ghislieri's heretic hunters kept an unusually close watch on the Este court in Ferrara, where Duchess Renée was open about her Protestant sympathies. In 1554 Ercole II had been obliged to order her to go to confession and Mass at Easter; that autumn she had been formally charged with heresy and forced to repudiate her beliefs. The duke also expelled some of her household – who turned out to be convicted heretics living under assumed names – and, worried about the influence she had over their daughters, who had already been attending Protestant services in the ducal palace, sent the two girls to the care of their aunt, the abbess of Corpus Domini.[22]

Under Ghislieri the Inquisition also drew up its notorious *Index of Forbidden Books* (1559), listing works deemed to be heretical that were ceremonially destroyed in bonfires in cities across Italy. Ippolito's own library of some 200 books, left in Rome when he went into exile, was ransacked by the officials of the Inquisition, who seized works by Machiavelli, a large Bible and the highly controversial translation and commentary on the New Testament by the Dutch humanist Erasmus, its seven volumes lavishly bound in gold-tooled leather.[23]

In Florence, Cosimo I was feeling the heat. On 12 August 1558 the diarist Agostino Lapini recorded that the duke issued an edict ordering all unfrocked priests and others 'who have left their convents without legitimate reasons, to return', an order that had to be reissued a month later ordering them to obey 'within three days' or they would be arrested.[24] In 1552 he had bowed to pressure from the Inquisition and Eleonora's uncle, Cardinal Juan de Toledo, to hold an auto-da-fé in Florence, in the hopes that this public burning of those found guilty by the Inquisition would result in favours from Julius III. But he could expect little from the anti-Spanish Paul IV – certainly not his coveted royal title – and had nothing to gain from currying favour in Rome. Evidence of his piety, however, was visible in projects such as the fresco cycle in the choir of San Lorenzo; it was unveiled in July 1558, recorded Lapini, 'with the Flood and the Resurrection of the Dead painted by master Jacopo Pontormo which some liked and some did not'.*[25] The duke also did what he could to protect his subjects from the Inquisition, using delaying tactics to avoid sending suspected heretics to Rome, but he was quick to adopt the *Index of Forbidden Books*, ordering the public burning of banned texts on 18 March when Lapini reported the lighting of bonfires in the piazzas at the Baptistery, the Duomo and Santa Croce, though the duke reportedly ordered his agents to 'make more show than effect'.[26]

Dislike of Paul IV altered traditional loyalties across Italy: even the enmity between the Medici and the Este began to thaw when they realized that an alliance could benefit both sides. Its value to Cosimo I was reflected in the huge dowry of 200,000 scudi he shelled out for a union between the families.[27] Ercole II pointed out its political benefits, 'not only for the increased importance of our houses but also maybe… for the calming of poor Italy'.[28] Plans for a marriage between Ercole's heir Alfonso and Cosimo I's eldest daughter Maria had been finalized when the seventeen-year-old bride died from a violent fever

---

* The frescoes in the choir were destroyed in 1738.

in November 1557. Although it was widely rumoured in Florence that Cosimo I himself had murdered his eldest child, having discovered that she was having an affair with one of his own pages, this is unlikely.[29] Cosimo's courtiers reported the distraught father weeping inconsolably, and Duke Ercole agreed to continue with the project, replacing Maria with her younger sister. The marriage of Alfonso and Lucrezia, aged twenty-four and thirteen respectively, was celebrated in Florence four months later although, with the bride too young to consummate the union, she remained at home while her husband left for the French court.

That summer marked the end of an era in European politics. In September Charles V died at the age of only fifty-eight and, with both Spain and France bankrupt, Philip II and Henri II signed the treaty of Cateau-Cambrésis on 25 April 1559, bringing to an end decades of warfare. The peace was to be guaranteed by two Habsburg–Valois marriages but tragically, during a tournament held in Paris to celebrate this double betrothal, Henri II was pierced in the eye by a shattered lance, dying in terrible pain ten days later on 10 July. He was only forty years old; he left his throne to his sickly fifteen-year-old son, Francis II, with his widow, Catherine de' Medici, as regent. In Ferrara Ippolito dressed his household in black. 'The death of the king is truly terrible, an appalling loss to everyone,' he wrote to his nephew Alfonso, who was still in France. Henri II had been a close friend, and 'for my part I can say I have never felt such grief, but this is God's will and we must accept it'.[30]

The news that Paul IV had died on 18 August must have been received with delight in both Ferrara and Florence, though it was not a surprise: his health had been on the decline since January, when he had been forced to sack Carlo Carafa. He had been able to overlook his scandalous abuse of his position as cardinal-nephew, but the discovery that he 'sins so abominably, making no distinction between men or women', according to the Cardinal of Lorraine, had appalled this abstemious, pious old man.[31] In Rome the news had been greeted by an orgy of violence, as the mob set fire to the palace of the Inquisition and

Alessandro Allori, *Lucrezia de' Medici*, c.1560 (Raleigh, North Carolina Museum of Art). Despite her robust appearance in this portrait, Lucrezia was frail and sickly, and died of tuberculosis at the age of fifteen.

destroyed the statue of Paul IV on the Capital, 'kicking its head through the streets of Rome like a football', as the Ferrarese envoy reported.[32] Then came news that Cardinal Carlo had ordered the murder of his own sister-in-law for adultery – Carlo's brother Giovanni killed the unfortunate lover himself – and there were well-founded rumours that Giovanni's son, Cardinal Antonio, had stolen a casket of valuables from Paul IV's bedroom. Even Philip II's influential voice joined the widespread demands that the Carafa family must be deprived of their titles and estates, an issue which was to play an important role in the forthcoming conclave.

Plans for the election were well underway. Following her dead husband's wishes, Catherine de' Medici named Ippolito as her candidate, and asked Cosimo I to use 'the considerable influence that I know you have with many of the cardinals in the College... to do all you can to have my cousin the Cardinal of Ferrara elected pope'.[33] Cosimo may have shared her surname but the Este were closer. Thanks to the family's preference for French marriages, Ippolito had close marital ties to the dowager queen: his niece Anna was aunt to Catherine's daughter-in-law, Mary Queen of Scots; and his sister-in-law Renée had been aunt to Catherine's husband, Henri II Catherine was also keen on 'having a man of such birth and standing on the holy throne', but Cosimo refused his support. Indeed it was evident that he preferred men of less exalted backgrounds: recently he had been grooming Cardinal Giovanni Medici, younger brother of Marquis Giangiacomo, his able army commander, for the papal tiara.

The conclave opened on 5 September divided into three equal groups: the Spanish, the French and the cardinals who had been created by the dead pope, who were led, by tradition, by the ex-cardinal-nephew. This last group, which was composed largely of zealous reformists under the leadership of the dissolute Carlo Carafa, was to have an unprecedented say in this election. With the French cardinals still en route for Rome, Ippolito kept the conclave open with similar delaying tactics to those he had used in 1549: as many as twenty names were read out from the voting slips at each session, 'making it possible to drag out these negotiations for as long as is wanted before coming to agreement on the creation of a pope', he explained to his brother Ercole; 'and now it is a question of prolonging the conclave until Guise arrives'.[34] The imperial ambassador judged Ippolito to be 'one of the deftest diplomats France ever had'.[35] The French duly arrived and the election was effectively deadlocked.

Then, on 4 October, Ippolito learned that Duke Ercole had died the previous day from a sudden fever, aged just fifty-one. Ippolito wrote to the new duke: 'You can imagine how much his unexpected death has distressed me,' he grieved, 'it happened so suddenly; one day I had news that he was ill and the next that he was dead.'[36] Losing his beloved brother, with whom he had played and squabbled over the years, was a shock but there were more urgent matters to deal with: 'I am so very sorry that I am locked up in a place where I can do so little to help you.' Alfonso was still in France, leaving a potentially dangerous power vacuum in Ferrara and, with Ippolito unable to leave Rome, it was Alfonso's mother, Duchess Renée, who had to maintain authority in Ferrara. His father-in-law Cosimo I seized the opportunity to send troops to Ferrara, ostensibly to ensure the smooth transition of power – but who knew what his real motives might have been. It was a foretaste of the new regime: Cosimo would expect Alfonso to prioritize his links with his father-in-law rather than the traditional ties between Ferrara and France. And the new dynamic was soon evident inside the conclave.

Meanwhile, the conclave went on and on, tempers fraying as the cardinals almost, but never quite, reached the necessary two-thirds majority. After three months the stench was so bad that the Sistine Chapel, where nineteen cardinals had their cubicles, had to be fumigated. The harassed master of ceremonies lost control: illegal visitors came in most nights, notably Philip II's ambassador – one evening he got into a fistfight with Cardinal Louis of Guise.[37] Cosimo I's candidate, Giovanni Medici, was outed as a liberal who favoured a pragmatic solution to the Protestant issue, anathema to the zealots who wanted zero-toleration. The duke was not dismayed. Not only did he continue to work against Ippolito, he also bullied Alfonso, taking advantage of his naïvety. When Alfonso arrived back in Italy, Cosimo met him at Livorno:

> I explained to his Highness that his uncle is deluding himself because he has been excluded by King Philip; Farnese thinks little of him; Carpi's friends are his enemies; and Carafa makes a fool of him... and I have told [Ippolito] to stop wasting time and to vote for Medici.[38]

Harsh words and only partly true – it was not so clear cut as Cosimo assumed.

Cosimo was unaware that Catherine de' Medici was still scheming on Ippolito's behalf and had offered buy Carafa's support with a title and a large sum of money. Carafa's agenda was not a religious one: as his brother Giovanni had urged, 'it really does not matter who is elected, all that is important is that the new pope understands that he owes his election to the Carafa family'.[39] Unfortunately for Ippolito, in late November he lost two vital votes: one cardinal died in his cell and another was so ill that he had to leave the Vatican. With his own chances over, he now agreed to campaign for Medici. But Carafa had raised his price: he demanded Medici's personal assurance that, if elected, he would guarantee all the Carafa titles and estates. Ippolito knew Medici was too principled to agree to this so he asked Cosimo I to write a letter making these promises on behalf of Medici – but certainly without the cardinal's permission. Finally, after much arm-twisting and a twelve-hour Mass to celebrate Christmas Day, the cardinals elected Medici as their new pope, Pius IV.

It was soon evident that Pius IV would be a very different ruler to his predecessor. Within six months of the election he had arrested Carlo and Giovanni Carafa, who were put on trial, judged guilty of murder and treason, and condemned to death. The new pope's own choice of cardinal-nephew, Carlo Borromeo, was a more fitting appointment: Borromeo, who was only twenty-one when he received his red hat a month after the election, would play a significant role in the Counter-Reformation – and prove that not all nepotist appointments, nor all young ones, were necessarily bad.* Pius IV also reopened the Council of Trent, with Cardinal Morone as president – proof, if any were needed, that he believed Morone to be innocent of the heresy for which he had been imprisoned by Paul IV. And, while he confirmed Cardinal Ghislieri as head of the Inquisition, he severely limited the scope of its powers.

There was also public recognition for the roles played by Ippolito and Cosimo in the Vatican. Two days after the election Ippolito had an audience with the pope: 'Yesterday the Cardinal of Guise and I visited his Holiness who showed much gratitude for the favour he has

---

* Carlo Borromeo was canonized in 1610, just twenty-five years after his death.

Tivoli, Villa d'Este, loggia, begun 1563, designed by Pirro Ligorio.
overleaf Tivoli, Villa d'Este, Fountain of the Cascade and Water Organ, 1566–72. The organ, admired and imitated across Europe, used water to force air into pipes and thereby play musical notes.

received from our hands and we are extremely satisfied,' he reported jubilantly to his nephew.[40] Pius IV had promised significant favours both to France and to Ferrara, including a red hat for Alfonso II's dissolute brother, Luigi. Ippolito had been restored to his posts as cardinal-protector of France and governor of Tivoli and, above all, rehabilitated at the papal court, where he would play a leading role during Pius IV's pontificate. For Cosimo there was the signal honour of a red hat for his fifteen-year-old son, Giovanni, who was made a cardinal at the end of January along with Borromeo.

Giovanni de' Medici arrived in Rome in March 1560 for the arcane ceremonies that would invest him as a cardinal. In another mark of favour to the duke, Pius IV gave the boy the title of Santa Maria in Domnica, which had belonged to the first Medici cardinal (later Leo X), moving the current incumbent to a new church – and, after Giovanni's tragic death from malaria in November 1562, Pius IV gave a red hat and the same title to Giovanni's younger brother, Ferdinando. The cardinals competed for the favour of this new member of the college. Alessandro Farnese, one of Ippolito's great rivals, hosted a banquet in his honour at the Villa Madama; another rival, Cardinal Rodolfo Pio da Carpi, gave him a large porphyry table, causing problems for Giovanni's majordomo, who had to arrange transport of this weighty but valuable object back to Florence.[41] Not to be outdone, Ippolito entertained the young man and gave him several presents, including eleven medals from his own collection and an expensive coach, a novelty in Rome, which cost Ippolito some 700 scudi and had an interior lavishly furnished with purple velvet.[42]

Ippolito, delighted to be back at the papal court after his years of exile, lived in conspicuously magnificent and ostentatious style. His main residence was the Palazzo Monte Giordano (now Palazzo Taverna) in the centre of town; and he also had a villa on the Quirinal, the Palazzo Monte Cavallo.* Here he could escape the oppressive heat of the narrow streets below to enjoy panoramic views across Rome or a game of tennis in his new tennis court; he could walk around the superb gardens, where he showed off his collection of classical sculptures

---

* The Quirinal was known as Monte Cavallo in the Renaissance after the two colossal statues of the horse-tamers which crowned the hill (later identified as Castor and Pollux, the Dioscuri); the palace is now the site of the Palazzo del Quirinale, the official residence of the President of Italy.

Castello, Villa Medici, Grotto of the Animals, c.1565. Ambitious for power, Cosimo I copied the Roman emperor Augustus by adopting the goat Amalthea, who suckled Jupiter in classical mythology, as his personal emblem.

amid groves of aromatic trees and plants. Early in 1566 Pius IV had given him an adjoining plot of land – another favour from the grateful pope – which the cardinal seems to have planted as a vegetable garden that spring with spinach, chives, artichokes, cabbages, garlic and broad beans.[43] He also built a magnificent villa at Tivoli in the hills north-east of Rome, which he had started in 1550 when Julius III had appointed him as governor – this was where he spent July and August, leaving a skeleton staff in Rome, including a footman whose job it was to water the plants at Monte Cavallo.[44]

Villas were high fashion in mid-sixteenth-century Rome. Inspired by descriptions of the luxurious palaces of rich patricians set in ornamental gardens that had once covered the hills of the city, they provided elegant sites for the display of collections of antique sculpture, often incorporated into sumptuous fountains. Many cardinals employed antiquarian experts to supervise these collections, which were proudly recommended to visitors in contemporary guide books. The Quirinal boasted not only Ippolito's villa but also that of his rival, Cardinal Carpi – though Ippolito could claim that his had been built on the site of 'the residence of Roman courtesans'.[45] And his villa at Tivoli, set in gardens designed by his own antiquarian, Pirro Ligorio, was close to the remains of a villa built by Emperor Hadrian, where Ligorio unearthed several more statues for the cardinal's collection.

Cosimo I too built spectacular *all'antica* villas for the display of his own impressive collections. At his family's estate at Castello he laid out gardens filled with fountains, grottoes and statues, ancient and modern, including the famous Grotto of the Animals with its ubiquitous goats. Cosimo's use of the goat, or the zodiac sign of Capricorn, was a deliberate attempt to promote himself as a second Augustus, having come to power like the emperor in January after the assassination of a relation. The French essayist Michel de Montaigne, who was in Italy in 1580–1, visited Castello, where he was amused by the jets of water which caught the visitors unawares, soaking their clothes 'in imitation of the trickle of fine rain'.[46] What really impressed him, though, was the use of water at 'the famous palace and garden of the cardinal of Ferrara' at Tivoli, where it was used to power an organ that played music, and made all sorts of other sounds including cannon fire and birdsong, and also produced beautiful rainbows when the sun shone through great torrents.[47]

Niccolò Tribolo, *Hercules and Antaeus*, c.1543 (Castello, Villa Medici).
The image of Hercules, which was an ancient symbol of the Florentine republic, was adopted by Cosimo I to reinforce his right to rule over the city.

Meanwhile Cosimo I's hopes that Pius IV would grant him a royal title were boosted when the pope invited him to make a state visit to Rome, with the offer of guest apartments in the Vatican palace.[48] As one of the leading cardinals at court, Ippolito was closely involved with the Medici visit: he was given the honour of meeting the duke and duchess at the Porta del Popolo in early November and hosted several events for the couple. In early December they were the guests of honour at a banquet at Montecavallo – and it was probably this occasion that prompted him to consign thirty-six silver plates and other items to a goldsmith with instructions to use them to create an exceptionally grand candelabrum. The pope, too, made all possible show of favouring the duke. He presented Cosimo with lavish presents including antique statues and a colossal granite column which had recently been found in the ruins of the Baths of Caracalla. And Pius IV also agreed to grant the title of Duke of Bracciano to Cosimo's son-in-law Paolo Giordano Orsini, so that his daughter Isabella had the same status as her sister, Lucrezia, Duchess of Ferrara. However, to his frustration, the pope remained equivocal on the issue of the royal title that Cosimo wanted so badly.

In April 1561 Cosimo's daughter Lucrezia died from tuberculosis in Ferrara at the tragically young age of fifteen, destroying the alliance that had kept the squabble about precedence at bay. And it was not long before the issue erupted again with the publication of the document mentioned at the beginning of this chapter that outlined the reasons why Cosimo I, Duke of Florence, claimed supremacy over his erstwhile son-in-law, Alfonso II, Duke of Ferrara. The reasoning was quite complex. Some of the arguments were spurious, such as the claim that the duchy of Florence, created in 1532, was older than that of Ferrara because the Este had quarrelled with Paul III in 1539. Other arguments used by Cosimo were more compelling, such as the fact that the republic of Florence had enjoyed precedence over the Este marquisate prior to the creation of the duchy; moreover, Florence covered a much larger territory than Ferrara.[49] Ultimately, his argument rested on the fact that the dukes of Florence were independent lords, while those of Ferrara were vassals of the pope – and this was to prove a prescient reminder of what was to happen.[50] But, for the time being, the Este claim to precedence as the much older dynasty held sway.

Meanwhile, in 1561 Ippolito was appointed legate to the Colloquy of Poissy, Catherine de' Medici's first attempt to heal the breach between the Catholics and Protestants in France, where antagonism between the faiths had split the French court, with political rivals lining up on either side of the religious divide – the Bourbons with the Protestants, the Guise family with the Catholics. It was a mark of Pius IV's deep understanding of the issues at stake that he agreed to support the dowager queen's desire for reconciliation, a policy that had been decisively rejected by the zealous Catholics in Rome. They were so appalled when it was announced that Ippolito was to be legate that the pope agreed to send Diego Laynez, the general of the Jesuits, as part of the legate's entourage. It is difficult to imagine a greater contrast than that between Ippolito, the urbane politician, sleek and well-fed, and the Spaniard Laynez, austere, black-robed and aggressively anti-Protestant. The colloquy was not a success and soon degenerated into a bitter row over the nature of the Eucharist, the key article of faith dividing the two sides. Laynez reduced Catherine de' Medici to tears by insisting that she must expel all Protestants from France, a move which she knew would destroy the kingdom. But Ippolito went out of his way to support the queen by attending a Protestant sermon at her request. Laynez was profoundly shocked at this unprecedented move and it created a major scandal in Rome. Pius IV rebuked Ippolito for not keeping his attendance more secret; Ippolito himself justified his decision on the grounds that he wanted to 'try to understand the reasons that move men'.[51]

Back in Italy Cosimo I had taken another step in his campaign against the Este: in 1564, on hearing that his ex-son-in-law Alfonso II was planning a second marriage to one of the daughters of Ferdinand I, he promptly followed suit, opening his own negotiations with the emperor for a second imperial princess as a bride for his heir, Francesco. Ferdinand I died in July 1564, to be succeeded by his son Maximilian II, who was keen to get his sisters off his hands, but equally determined to make Cosimo pay for the privilege. After lengthy diplomatic bargaining it was decided that Barbara, the older of the two eligible daughters, would become Duchess of Ferrara while the younger, Joanna, would be betrothed to Francesco. As part of the deal Cosimo I had to loan 300,000 florins to Maximilian to fund the war against the Turks in Hungary – by contrast, Alfonso II fought in the war in person.[52] Alfonso and Barbara were married on 5 December 1565, Francesco and

overleaf Agnolo Bronzino, *Allegory of Venus, Cupid and Time*, c.1542–5 (London, National Gallery). This picture's theme is love: it has been suggested that the screaming man on Cupid's left is suffering from syphilis, one of love's torments.

Joanna eleven days later. Cosimo had been determined to make the Florentine celebration especially grandiose, and decided to redecorate the main reception hall of the Palazzo Ducale with a spectacular cycle, painted by Vasari and his assistants, covering the history of Florence. As the project evolved it became increasingly obvious that the focus of the cycle was the Medici dynasty. The scenes involving the trade guilds, which had played such a key role in the early life of the republic, were replaced by battles starring the Medici in prominent, though often fictional, roles.[53] And the central tondo on the ceiling, which was to have been *Florence in Glory*, was replaced by the *Apotheosis of Cosimo I*.

Pius IV died from the complications of gout a week before the wedding feast. His great achievement had been to complete the pressing issue of church reform through the Council of Trent. On 13 November 1564 he issued the bull *Professio fide*, which defined the basic tenets of the Catholic faith: papal infallibility, transubstantiation, the intercession of saints and the other beliefs repudiated by the Protestants. For Ippolito the most immediate result was that he had to be ordained, along with several of his colleagues from princely houses including his cousin Ercole Gonzaga and Alessandro Farnese.[54] Pius IV had also made radical reforms to conclave procedure to avoid the chaos of his own election. The Sistine Chapel, for example, was no longer to be converted into a dormitory: instead – a more fitting use for the pope's own chapel – it was to become the place where the voting would now take place; other regulations included more stringent searches of goods going into and out of the Vatican. The security measures seem to have worked: we have only one letter from Ippolito from this conclave, in contrast to the hundreds that have survived from the other conclaves he attended. From Ippolito's point of view, the most unwelcome change was the order that the conclave was to open exactly ten days after the death of the pope, a regulation that would have a very negative impact on his ability to keep the election open until his colleagues could arrive from France – and on this occasion in particular as travel across the snow-bound Alps in mid-winter would be a challenge.

Pius IV had also made plans for this conclave with his cardinal-nephew Carlo Borromeo: he had created forty-six red hats, flooding the college with his appointees to give Borromeo a controlling interest in the election, which opened on 19 December. In fact the cardinals divided into four distinct factions: Ippolito's French party; the Spanish, led by Alessandro Farnese; Pius IV's cardinals, led by Borromeo; and the hardline reformers, whose leader was Michele Ghislieri, the grim inquisitor-general, with his coarse black Dominican habit under his cardinalatial robes. The plan hatched by Pius IV and Borromeo was to make a surprise bid to elect Giovanni Morone, a pragmatic reformer and obvious successor to Pius IV, when the cardinals assembled for morning prayers on the first day before voting started. Unfortunately for them, during the night Ghislieri had discovered the plan and had visited Ippolito's cubicle to ask for his help – it is difficult to imagine two less likely allies, but Ippolito sought the help of Farnese and together they forestalled Borromeo's efforts: Morone failed by just two votes.

With the French cardinals still to arrive, there was little Ippolito could do for his own party, except to attempt the same delaying tactics he had used on earlier occasions. But these were not so successful as they had been in the past and he had to watch as the vote count of Cosimo's candidate, Giovanni Ricci, slowly but surely advanced. A Tuscan from the small city of Montepulciano, which had become part of Cosimo's realm after his conquest of Siena, Ricci was from a modest background – once again, the parvenu duke was favouring a candidate without noble status. He had made his way up the church hierarchy by hard work and luck, but above all a sharp eye for business, which had earned him a cardinal's hat. By 2 January his share of the votes was approaching the magic two-thirds majority and Borromeo countered his bid by reminding the cardinals of Ricci's far from blameless private life: he lived in style in Rome with a villa on the Pincian Hill, a Portuguese mistress, several illegitimate children and a priceless collection of Chinese porcelain which he had amassed, along with his mistress, while serving as papal legate in Lisbon. And then rumours started to circulate that Philip II objected to this man of the world, and had nominated the zealous reformer Ghislieri as his candidate instead. The Spanish ambassador accused Ippolito of starting this rumour to damage the Dominican's chances; then the imperial ambassador accused Cosimo I of intercepting letters from Emperor Maximilian, which was true, though the information they contained was nothing new. And then suddenly, on 7 January, it was announced that a new pope had

overleaf Florence, Santa Croce, nave remodelled 1565–71. Vasari's renovations, commissioned by Cosimo I to conform to the reforms governing Counter-Reformation church design, replaced the jumble of medieval chapels and altars with uniform niches along the side aisles.

been elected – Inquisitor Ghislieri. The French cardinals, who arrived that evening, were too late to prevent this significant victory for the extremists over the moderates in the college, like Ippolito.

Ghislieri chose the name Pius V in memory of Pius IV but, in truth, his aims as pope could hardly have been more different from his benign predecessor. An inflexible disciplinarian, he had been appointed to head the Inquisition and had been responsible for the reign of terror in Rome under Paul IV. One of his first acts was to rehabilitate Paul IV's family, who had been disgraced by Pius IV, and he condemned to death the judge who had found the Carafa brothers guilty.[55] A devotee of evangelical poverty, he was parsimonious and ascetic: his lunch consisted of bread, soup and two eggs, while his evening meal was a light vegetable soup with salad and shellfish – he ate meat just twice a week, and threatened his cook with excommunication if he included any forbidden ingredient in his dishes.[56]

Pius V's moves to abolish taxes on wine and flour, to make usury illegal and to encourage agriculture were popular in Rome. His commitment to reforming abuses in the church was unwavering; he pursued heresy with relentless zeal and reformed the religious orders in line with the decrees of the Council of Trent.* His efforts to reform the morals of ordinary people, however, were greeted with horror, especially after he rebuilt the palace of the hated Inquisition and used it to stamp out blasphemy and public immorality. Though he managed to expel the Jews from the Papal States, he did fail to expel all prostitutes from Rome and make adultery subject to the death penalty. One observer recorded that there were more executions in one month than in the four years of Pius IV's pontificate; another thought that he was turning Rome into a monastery.[57]

Ippolito's relations with the new pope were not particularly cordial. The cardinal spent as little time as he could at the papal court, where his influence had begun to wane. He was also increasingly ill with gout, and indeed died of its complications six months after Pius V. While the pope accused him of simony, he did not go as far as Paul IV and charge him with the crime, though he did consider Ippolito's behaviour at the Colloquy of Poissy to be the reason for the recent escalation of religious violence in France – especially the Protestant victories. But their relations were mainly soured by an ongoing dispute

---

* His commitment to reform was recognized in 1712, when he was canonized.

between Rome and Ferrara over the export of salt from the Este works at Comacchio. Ippolito was regularly called to the Vatican to explain Alfonso II's actions, especially his nephew's continued defiance of a ban on the trade that the pope had instituted to protect the papal salt works at Cervia.[58]

Then, in 1567, there was a bombshell for the Este dynasty. On 23 May Pius V issued the bull *Prohibitio alenandi feudi* banning papal fiefs from being inherited by illegitimate heirs. This was a radical move: indeed, it is salutary to consider how many of the great princely patrons of the Renaissance had in fact been illegitimate. And the bull seems to have been directed precisely at the Este themselves: Alfonso II and his first wife, Lucrezia de' Medici, had not had children, but that could be readily explained as she suffered from tuberculosis; a second wife with no offspring was harder to explain. Still without an heir after two years of marriage, rumours had begun to circulate that he was unable to sire children and, according to his doctor, the reason was a congenital defect.[59] Alfonso's designated heir was his illegitimate cousin Cesare – but Pius V's bull had made this illegal. Increasingly alarmed that the Este really were about to lose the duchy of Ferrara, as visible proof of his family's rights to the state, in 1577 he decorated the courtyard of the ducal palace in the city with some 200 portraits of every conceivable Este ancestor to demonstrate the legitimacy of his authority.

Cosimo I, by contrast, went out of his way to curry favour with Pius V. According to the diarist Agostino Lapini, whose detailed account of the doings of the ducal court tells us much about Florence at this period, the duke had already begun to institute the reforms of the Council of Trent regarding the design of churches. At Santa Croce and Santa Maria Novella, the major Franciscan and Dominican foundations respectively in Florence, he had removed the elaborate rood screens that were typical of medieval churches across Europe and separated the choir from the main body of the church. The Council of Trent had recommended removing the screens and moving the choir to a new position behind the altar, to allow the congregation an uninterrupted view of the miracle of the Eucharist that took place at the altar during Mass. In March 1565 Lapini recorded the building of a new altar at Santa Maria Novella, some 12 feet in front of the old one, and the destruction of the choir 'which had been there for many many years, that ruined all [the church's] beauty'.[60]

One sign that Cosimo I might have begun to submit to papal pressure came on 15 May 1567 when the duke and his sons attended Mass in the Duomo – along with 25,000 other Florentines – to welcome the new archbishop to Florence.[61] Lapini recorded the entry of Archbishop Antonio Altoviti into his diocese: 'He has been archbishop of Florence for nineteen years but this is the first time he has been here in the flesh.' Altoviti was the son of a prominent opponent of the Medici, who would fight with the French under Pietro Strozzi in the 1550s and whose possessions had been confiscated by the duke. Altoviti's appointment as archbishop in May 1548 had not been welcomed by Cosimo, and up to this point he had refused permission for Altoviti to enter the city.

Altoviti's arrival in Florence acted as a stimulus on the religious life in the city. In May 1567 Lapini reported that 'the Jews here in Florence start to wear a yellow O on their caps' and the following year the diarist recorded that Cosimo I began a new convent in memory of his wife, Eleonora of Toledo, who had died of tuberculosis in 1562, and embellished the Duomo with an elaborate new choir made of costly coloured marbles.[62] The first celebration of the new Tridentine Mass in the city took place on 28 November 1568, the first Sunday in Advent.[63] The following Easter, Archbishop Altoviti instituted a new ritual for washing the feet of poor men on Maundy Thursday. This ceremony was not new, Lapini explained, 'but this year the archbishop decided to do this new ritual at his own expense', which included giving the men bread and coins 'and a white cloth cap each with a garland of olives on their heads above the said cap'.[64]

There was also pressure on Cosimo I from Rome regarding the case of Pietro Carnesecchi, a loyal Medici supporter whose career had flourished at the court of Clement VII. He was suspected of heresy but had so far had managed to survive attempts to interrogate him by calling on his friends in high places. He was first called to the Inquisition under Paul III, who cleared him all charges; he was able to call on the Venetian authorities to protect him in 1557 when he was condemned by Paul IV, even after his effigy was burned in Rome.[65] Unfortunately Cosimo I refused to protect him in 1566 when, six months after Pius V's election, he was charged again. Cosimo I agreed to hand him over to the Inquisition – and, having endured an auto-da-fé in the presence of the College of Cardinals in September 1567, he was executed ten days later.

Finally Cosimo I's efforts to ingratiate himself with the grim Pius V bore fruit. On 13 December 1569 'a most solemn Mass of the Holy Ghost... was sung by Archbishop Altoviti as a sign of the great happiness of our duke who has been given a royal crown above his coat-of-arms by Pope Pius V', recorded Lapini, for his services to the church.[66] On 4 March 1570 in Rome, the fourth Sunday in Lent, Pius V conferred on Cosimo I the Golden Rose for outstanding services to the church and crowned him as grand duke. He had achieved his dream, although Maximilian II refused to recognize the title. Cosimo was now to be addressed as 'Serene Highness' with the status of royalty – and convincingly outranked the Este and indeed all the other Italian princes as well.

Cardinal Ippolito died in 1572 and Grand Duke Cosimo two years later. Thanks to Pius V the Medici had become grand dukes, and the Este had lost their contest with the upstart regime in Florence. When Alfonso II died in 1597, still without a legitimate heir, Pope Clement VIII invoked Pius V's bull and dispossessed his illegitimate cousin, Cesare, who was obliged to leave Ferrara, though he retained the duchies of Reggio and Modena, where the dynasty now took up residence. The great works of Renaissance art commissioned by the Este family over the past two centuries now belonged to the pope and his family – though fortunately for us the family papers were removed to Modena, where they are a treasure trove for historians. And in the long run the Este survived: Cosimo's descendants died out in 1737 while Cesare's successors ruled Modena until 1796, when the city was conquered by Napoleon's armies.

FRANCIS I (1494–1547)
King of France

CHARLES V (1500–58)
Emperor

Philip II
Son of Charles V, King of Spain

Ferdinand I
Brother of Charles V, Emperor

Mary of Hungary
Sister of Charles V, governor of the Netherlands

Henri II
Son of Francis I, King of France

CONCLUSION

CONQUERORS

R arely were imperial elections contested so viciously as the one following the death of Maximilian I on 12 January 1519. Charles V, King of Spain and grandson of the dead emperor, a month short of his nineteenth birthday, was the obvious dynastic candidate but this immensely powerful position was not hereditary. Francis I of France, with the backing of the pope, decided to enter the competition; there was even talk of Henry VIII of England becoming a third candidate. In the end it was Charles V who was elected but the election had cost both rulers substantial sums, as much as 500,000 ducats each, in bribes. More important, however, was the barrage of propaganda with which each tried to sway public opinion in the empire, where the Germans were encouraged to hate everything French, while the French extolled the virtues of their monarchy; who would make the better emperor and what were the relative merits of their two cultural traditions.

One unfortunate result of this contest was to underline the intensity of the rivalry between the two rulers, which went far deeper than their own political differences. Daubed on the walls of Rome when Charles V made his state entry there in 1536 was a piece of graffiti showing the emperor riding on a shrimp: as one of his allies remarked, it must have been 'done by Frenchmen and if not, then by their allies'.[1]

The rivalry between Francis I and Charles V ripped Europe apart, and its after-effects were to endure well beyond their lifetimes. We have seen how king and emperor vied for political control in Italy, their armies fighting over Milan and Naples, and their diplomats in Rome using less violent means to urge the pope to side with one rather than the other, with varying degrees of success. But they also fought bloody battles over Flanders, Burgundy, Navarre and other lands on their shared borders. They drew Henry VIII into their quarrel: his daughter Princess Mary was betrothed first to Francis I's son, then to Charles V himself, before she finally married the emperor's son the year after she became queen. Although he bore the title of Most Christian King, Francis I compromised his faith by making alliances with the pagan sultan and the heretic Protestants. Charles V, the Holy Roman emperor, made himself master of Italy, having instructed his commander to capture and imprison the pope, and making no attempt to stop his army from indulging in a brutal sack of the capital of Christendom.[2]

Amid all this animosity it is often forgotten that the two men became brothers-in-law in 1530 after Francis I married the emperor's sister Eleanor as part of the Treaty of Madrid – the rivals signed many peace treaties over the years, and broke most of them. In fact they had much in common, not least a love of hunting and of women. Above all, they both had compelling motives for demonstrating the nature of their power and, moreover, they had access to resources that far outstripped those of the Italian princes. They both amassed huge collections of valuable tapestries, jewels, artworks and other Italian artefacts, some acquired as presents or the spoils of war.

Monarchs no less than princes understood the importance of the display of magnificence and also its competitive nature, so it should come as no surprise to find that both monarchs were patrons on a superb scale. What is more surprising is the readiness with which they adopted the language of the princes of Renaissance Italy, who were in effect their subjugated foes. But, of course, both rulers could claim to be the heirs to the emperors of ancient Rome – and, indeed, both were the heirs of Charlemagne, the first Holy Roman Emperor. They also drew parallels between the quality of their own artistic patronage and that of Alexander the Great, famous not only for his military brilliance but also for his patronage of the legendary painter, Apelles. As heirs to imperial glory, they used the language of antiquity to create their own images for the display of power and prestige. The results were far from uniform: each adapted the image of ancient Rome to suit his particular circumstances. And the art-historical tradition that the culture of medieval Europe vanished beneath the onslaught of the superior classical, Italian style is to miss the essential role played in their projects by context and locus.

Francis I was handsome and jovial, a well-built man who enjoyed energetic sports, in particular hunting and real tennis. He ate well, held dances most evenings at court and could be seen taking part in the mock battles staged for the celebration of royal marriages and other events. By all accounts he was good company, intelligent and

well educated with little time for the customary formalities of courtly etiquette. Above all he was a survivor. His emblem was a salamander in flames, inspired by the ancient belief that this lizard-like monster could endure fire: it first appeared on a medal of the young ten-year-old prince with the words *Nutrisco et extinguo*, a shortened form of the motto 'I feed upon the good (fire) and put out the evil one'.[3] He had been just twenty years old when he inherited the throne of France from his cousin Louis XII on New Year's Day 1515. Later that year he won his first major victory in Italy when he conquered the duchy of Milan and for a decade France was the dominant power in northern Italy. And though the king's dream of an Italian empire was crushed at the Battle of Pavia in February 1525, when he was taken prisoner by Charles V, it was many years before the king himself acknowledged this fact.

Francis I was not the first French king to have dreams of an Italian empire – nor the first to delight in the culture of the peninsula. When Charles VIII conquered Naples in 1495, he and his troops ransacked the royal castles there, seizing quantities of artefacts – 'the grandest furnishings of wealth' – including silver platters, a 'table made of gold and silver', bedroom chests, carpets, tapestries and precious books, but they had to leave their booty behind on the battlefield near Parma on the way home.[4] His successor, Louis XII, acquired a collection of Italian paintings and both kings returned from Italy with Italian craftsmen in their trains who were subsequently employed on the royal châteaux at Amboise and Blois, though little of their work has survived the later renovations. And Italian art evidently made an impression on Louis XII's governor in Milan, Cardinal Georges d'Amboise, who amassed a large collection of Italian art and whose château at Gaillon (1502) can be seen as the first Renaissance building in France.

Early in Francis I's reign he began the remodelling of several of the royal châteaux in the Loire valley, one of his favourite hunting grounds. At Blois he added a new wing and an elaborate staircase (1515–24), which showed obvious signs of Italian influence, as did the new château he built at Chambord (begun 1519). After his defeat at Pavia and his return from imprisonment in Madrid he concentrated on asserting his authority with drastic reforms to the government of his kingdom, establishing a centralized administration in Paris. In order to provide visible evidence of these reforms he turned his attention from the Loire valley to his capital, where he began to spend

Jean Clouet, *Francis I*, c.1530 (Paris, Louvre). Tall, attractive and self-confident, Francis I devoted himself to hunting, gambling and women.

overleaf Fontainebleau, Galerie François Ier, begun c.1533. The gallery made effective use of the king's favourite emblems, notably the cock, the salamander and the lion.

lavishly on royal residences in and around the city. He renovated the medieval palace at Saint-Germain-en-Laye and updated the shabby royal fortress of the Louvre in the centre of Paris, adding the square court (begun 1546). He built the Château of Madrid (1528) just outside the walls in the Bois de Boulogne.* Designed as a retreat from the cares of government, where he could 'find his pleasure and relaxation in hunting', this palace was apparently inspired by a hunting lodge he had seen outside Madrid while a prisoner of Charles V.[5]

Easily his most important project, however, was the remodelling of Fontainebleau, another old hunting lodge some 40 miles south of Paris. Transformed into a superb setting for the display of his royal prestige, and imperial ambitions, this soon became his primary residence. Among his additions were the Porte Dorée, a splendid three-storey *all'antica* entrance, as well as a ceremonial staircase and the famous *Galerie François Ier*. The king's salamander was conspicuously evident on fireplaces and other details throughout the palace, while the decoration of the gallery, with its painted panels and stucco sculpture, was based on the exploits of classical gods and goddesses. According to Vasari the paintings also included twenty-four scenes of the life of Alexander the Great and thirteen allegorical scenes of the achievements of Francis I himself.[6]

The new additions were Italianate in style and strikingly innovative in France, and it is no coincidence that the two artists responsible for their design were both Italian: Giovanni Battista Rosso and Francesco Primaticcio. Their employment at the French court had a marked impact on more than just Francis I's building projects: they also revolutionized the design of masques and other court entertainments, as well as the elaborate ephemeral decorations erected for formal entries, notably that of Charles V into Paris in 1540. Rosso, a Florentine by birth but trained in Rome, arrived in France around 1530 and was appointed to take overall charge of the decoration of the *Galerie François Ier*. It is evident that it was Francis I himself who was the prime force behind this dramatic change of style: he asked Federigo Gonzaga, whom he knew well (see Chapters 6 and 7), to recommend a stucco expert, and the marquis sent him Primaticcio, one of his own men who had been trained under his own court artist Giulio Romano. Primaticcio was

---

* The Château of Madrid was largely demolished in the 1790s.

first mentioned in the royal expense accounts in 1533 when he was paid for stuccoes and paintings in one of the rooms at Fontainebleau.[7]

Francis I attracted several other artists to France, most famously Leonardo da Vinci. Vasari recounted how the king, visiting Milan for the first time after his conquest of the city 1515, had been so impressed with the artist's *Last Supper* that he was determined to transport it back to France but that his craftsmen had been unable to devise a method of removing the fresco without damaging it.[8] Leonardo moved to France in 1516 at the invitation of the king and, though he does not seem to have taken up any artistic role at the French court, he spent the last three years of his life in a house provided by Francis I near the royal château at Amboise. The Florentine goldsmith Benvenuto Cellini moved to the French court in 1540, creating two of his most famous works for the king: his exquisite gilded and jewelled salt cellar designed in the form of a ship and his celebrated relief of a nymph that was intended to ornament the Porte Dorée at Fontainebleau. The king was less successful in his attempts to lure Michelangelo, who turned down the offer made by Francis I's ambassador in Venice of a house and a handsome salary awaiting the sculptor at the French court.[9]

Significantly, however, Francis I preferred local painters for his official portraits, notably the Fleming Joos van Cleve and the

Frenchmen Jean Clouet and his son François who succeeded his father as the king's court painter in 1540. Particularly interesting for us are the 200 or so chalk drawings by the Clouets as studies for portraits of members of the royal family and courtiers. The portrait of Francis I (1538) by Titian, which was taken from a medal of the king rather than in the flesh, was a present from Pietro Aretino, perhaps part of a campaign to promote his friend's artistic talents in the wider European arena. Francis I seems to have recognized Titian's undoubted talent and offered him employment at the French court but the painter turned down the invitation – as we shall see, he was busy elsewhere.

Francis I amassed an enormous collection of Italian art, becoming a connoisseur and a collector in a way that Charles V never would. Vasari refers to hundreds of examples of Italian paintings and sculpture belonging to the king. He seems to have shown a precocious interest in the subject, almost certainly inspired by his mother, Louise of Savoy. When he was just ten years old his secretary wrote to Marquis Francesco Gonzaga, Federigo's father, asking for 'some pictures by those excellent Italian masters, as they give him so much pleasure'.[10] He commissioned copies of the tapestries designed by Raphael for the Sistine Chapel and those of the history of Scipio Africanus designed by Giulio Romano, which cost over 20,000 ducats.[11] Many of the works in his collection were diplomatic presents, such as Raphael's *St Michael* (1517) and the *Holy Family* (1518) given to him by Leo X. He also had a taste for more erotic imagery. In 1518, in response to hearing that the king wanted pictures by Italian artists, in particular female nudes, Marquis Francesco sent him one by Lorenzo Costa. Cosimo I later curried favour with the king with a present of Bronzino's *Allegory of Venus, Cupid and Time* (c.1542–5), described by Vasari as a painting of 'Cupid kissing a nude Venus with Pleasure with Gaming and other pastimes on one side, and Fraud and Jealousy with the other passions of Love on the other'.[12]

Francis also amassed a substantial collection of antiquities – not so many original works, as the authorities banned the removal of these from Rome, but copies. When Cardinal Bibbiena was in France as papal legate in 1515 he noticed that Francis's collection lacked sculpture and, seizing the chance of doing a favour for the king, promised to ask Leo X to send him some 'beautiful works'.[13] In 1540, more in the spirit of friendship than diplomacy, Cardinal Ippolito d'Este gave the king a bronze copy of the famous antique statue of the thorn-puller known as the Spinario.[14] That year, in a move that suggested that the king was developing a more archeological interest in the remains of antiquity, Francis I sent Primaticcio to Rome to buy ancient sculpture. Most importantly the artist was to take moulds of the famous antique statues in the city, including the *Laocoön*, *Venus Felix* and the *Apollo Belvedere* from the Vatican collection, as well as sections of the reliefs on Trajan's Column and the great horse from the statue of Marcus Aurelius on the Capitol.[15]

Vasari claimed that Primaticcio bought 125 pieces, though he does not specifiy what they were; they were shipped back to France with the moulds, which were cast in bronze to provide statuary for the gallery and gardens at Fontainebleau.[16] The procedure of casting from moulds taken from original sculptures was a skill which had been known in antiquity and had been revived on a small scale in late fifteenth-century Italy. However, it was a very complicated technique and the scale of Francis I's project was not only unprecedented but also conspicuously expensive – though they did not cast the mould of the great horse, which was put in one of the courtyards at Fountainebleau, renamed the Cour de Cheval Blanc.[17]

One of Francis I's most active agents was the Florentine Battista della Palla, who 'commissioned all the sculptures and pictures that he could in order to send them to King Francis in France and he was also buying antiques of all sorts... so long as they were by the hands of good masters, and every day he was packing them into crates to send to France'.[18] According to Battista himself, he had been given instructions by the king and his family 'to provide them with a large quantity of excellent antiquities of whatever sort, marbles, bronzes, medals, or pictures by painters worthy of his Majesty, which he has taken great pleasure in all his life'.[19] He did not have much luck in Rome, where no one was prepared to sell him anything of value, so he went to Florence in early 1529 to see what his contacts there could do. Unfortunately the government had more pressing business – not least, trying to negotiate a peace treaty with Charles V – and were unwilling to get involved in acquiring works for Francis I's art collection. So Battista went out on to the streets of the city to try the personal approach. When he called at the house of Pierfrancesco Borgherini he was received not by the merchant but by his wife, who angrily refused to part with the

paintings he wanted to buy, which were several scenes from the life of Joseph from her bedroom. She was furious, and roundly abused him: 'This bed which you want to take for your own purposes and for greed... this is my marriage bed, given to me by my husband's father,' she screamed and, calling him 'a vile dealer in second-hand goods', ordered him out of her house.[20] In the end he did find enough works to ship back to Marseilles, including works by Michelangelo and Pontormo. One of the few items still to be found in France was a statue of *Nature* (1528–9) by Niccolò Tribolo, which showed the goddess nursing various living creatures: 'The first row of breasts being adorned with putti... in various beautiful poses, holding swags in their hands, while the next tier of breasts is covered with quadrupeds, and at her feet are many different kinds of fish,' Vasari described, and 'it is held very dear by the king'.[21]

Francis I's successors adapted the language of classical antiquity to display the power and prestige of their crown in ways that were increasingly French: Philibert de l'Orme's treatise on architecture, for example, might have been inspired by that of Vitruvius but it contained designs for a French order of columns. The distinctively national styles that emerged in painting, sculpture and architecture reinforced a sense of national identity at a time when the authority of the French crown was increasingly under threat during the Wars of Religion (1562–98). And, thanks to ill luck and ill health, the royal house of Valois did not survive the wars. Francis I's son Henri II was killed in an accident during a tournament in 1559, to be succeeded by his three sons in turn: Francis II, who died of an ulcer in 1560; Charles IX, who succumbed to tuberculosis in 1574; and Henri III, who was assassinated in 1589. The throne was inherited by their Protestant brother-in-law Henri of Navarre, who finally won his capital by converting to Catholicism with the famous, if apocryphal, phrase 'Paris is worth a Mass'.

Nevertheless, the fame of Francis I's palace of Fontainebleau spread quickly across Europe and soon became the standard for the display of royal prestige. His ambitious reinvention of the French royal image was hugely influential in England, where Henry VIII attempted to outdo his rival. The costly ephemeral decorations erected by both

Niccolò Tribolo, *Nature*, c.1529 (Fontainebleau, Musée Nationale). Statues of multi-breasted goddesses were popular items in Italian garden fountains where their nipples were often used as spouts.

kings for their summit meeting on the Field of the Cloth of Gold near Calais in 1520 have become a byword for opulence and extravagance, and impressed even the Italians who were present. At Henry VIII's death the royal tapestry collection listed over 2,000 pieces; Francis I's collection numbered less than a quarter of that total.[22] The English king was interested enough in the culture of antiquity – or perhaps simply in outshining his rival – for Francis I to promise him copies from the moulds Primaticcio had brought over from Rome, but politics intervened and this favour never materialized. And, like Francis I, Henry VIII also favoured northern European painters for his portraits, notably Hans Holbein, whose work also included chalk sketches of courtiers, and the Flemish miniaturists Gerard and Lucas Horenbout.

Henry VIII was a lavish patron of the arts, all the more so with the enormous increase in his wealth after the Dissolution of the Monasteries (1536–9). The king's decision to split from Rome was provoked more by political than religious considerations: the result of his fury that the pope would not grant him a divorce from Catherine of Aragon. Other rulers had been granted the same favour, not least Louis XII of France, but Catherine was Charles V's aunt and the pope had bowed to imperial pressure. Girolamo da Treviso's *Four Evangelists Stoning the Pope*, showing the pope trampled on the ground with Avarice and Hypocrisy, was an eloquent statement of his attitude to this papal decision.

The sole survivor of Henry VIII's major projects is Hampton Court Palace, which he received as a gift from Cardinal Wolsey and converted into a royal palace with the addition of apartments, a great hall and a tennis court. Sadly little remains of the other two grand palaces he built, both designed as rivals to Francis I's Fontainebleau: Whitehall (1530–6) and Nonsuch (begun 1538). Like the French king, Henry VIII employed Italian craftsmen, though on a far smaller scale. Nicholas Bellin from Modena, who had worked with Primaticcio at Fontainebleau, used his skills in the decoration of Nonsuch. He also employed Girolamo da Treviso, an Italian painter who had worked at the Palazzo Te in Mantua. According to Vasari, he was also an expert on fortifications and died fighting with the English army at the siege of Boulogne in 1544.[23] Henry VIII also commissioned an Italian artist for a tomb for his father Henry VII. The design by Florentine sculptor Pietro Torrigiani included a sarcophagus which was conspicuously ornamented with *all'antica* detail; and Torrigiani also designed the tombs of Henry's mother Elizabeth of York and his grandmother Margaret Beaufort, which were all placed in Henry VII's chapel in Westminster Abbey.

Henry VIII was succeeded by his son and two daughters – Edward VI (1547–53) took his father's break with Rome a step further by imposing Protestantism on England; Mary I (1553–8), the daughter of Catherine of Aragon, reversed her half-brother's acts by reinstating Catholic worship and obedience to the pope in Rome, making martyrs of many Protestants in the process; and Elizabeth I (1558–1603) reinstated Protestantism as the official religion of the country, though she tolerated Catholics until she discovered that they were plotting to assassinate her and return the Church of England once again to Rome. Strikingly, Elizabeth I made her dislike of French and Spanish interference in her affairs abundantly evident in the image she adopted for the display of her own power and prestige, which was conspicuous for its lack of interest in the culture of classical antiquity. The second half of the sixteenth century saw England, like France, torn apart by decades of religious conflict which played its part in the demise of Henry's Tudor dynasty.

Charles V's Habsburg dynasty, by contrast, was destined to survive for many more centuries. Born at Ghent in 1500, the son of Philip, Duke of Burgundy and Joanna of Spain, Charles was destined to be the most powerful ruler of his age. Brought up first by his great-grandmother Margaret of York (the aunt of Henry VIII's mother Elizabeth of York), and then by his aunt, Margaret of Austria (not to be confused with his illegitimate daughter), he spent his childhood in Flanders. At the age of six he became Duke of Burgundy, ruler of the Low Countries; he was fifteen when he was appointed as regent of Castile for his insane mother and the following year became King of Spain after the death of his maternal grandfather Ferdinand of Aragon, also inheriting the Spanish possessions in the Americas. Three years later his other grandfather died, leaving him master of Austria and the Habsburg lands; later that year, he was elected emperor.

As ruler he faced daunting problems. Protestantism, which had started out as a call for church reform, rapidly developed into a full-scale rebellion against the Catholic church in the empire, where two-thirds of his cities adopted the new religion – and it even penetrated his own family when his nephew, the son of his brother Ferdinand, became a Protestant. Moreover, the issue of faith soon acquired a more dangerous political context when Protestantism became the focus for a full-scale rebellion against his authority not only in the empire but also in the Low Countries. The empire faced a second challenge on its southern borders, where the expansionist policies of Sultan Suleiman saw Ottoman authority extend up the Balkans to the walls of Vienna. He faced rebellions in Peru and Spain; and continual challenges to his authority in Italy. War was expensive and the demands made on his treasury brought it to the verge of bankruptcy.

All Renaissance courts were peripatetic, though none moved around on the same scale of that of Charles V. At the age of seventeen he sailed from Flushing to Spain, arriving there just a month before Luther published his Ninety-five Theses, the event that would spark the beginning of the Reformation, which would have such a profound impact on his rule. From then on for the rest of his life Charles travelled ceaselessly around his huge realm – though he did not undertake the perilous voyage to his possessions across the Atlantic. Easily the most-travelled head of state of the period, he sailed across the notoriously rough Bay of Biscay four times in all, across the Mediterranean six times, and through the Alps four times, though never during the winter months. He retired in October 1556 at the age of fifty-six, moving to the monastery of Yuste, some 150 miles west of Madrid, where he died two years later, exhausted.

Charles V appointed governors to rule in his various territories and wherever possible these were family members, often female. In Spain his wife, Isabella of Portugal, took charge of the government during his many absences until she died in childbirth in 1539, when she was re-placed by their son Prince Philip. His brother Ferdinand of Austria act-ed as his representative in the empire; and his aunt Margaret of Austria was succeeded as Governor of the Netherlands by his sister Mary of Hungary. By contrast, his representatives in his Italian possessions – his governor in Milan and his viceroy in Naples – were courtiers, Spanish or Italian, and often men who had served in the imperial army.

Hard-working, introverted and pious, Charles V took his respon-sibilities as monarch seriously. He was a very different character to the

Titian, *Charles V with dog*, 1533 (Madrid, Prado). The Emperor
had been so impressed with Titian's portrait of Federigo Gonzaga
that he appointed the artist as his official portraitist.

jovial Francis I. Although shy, his manner was gentle and courteous, and he was a healthy youth: according to the Venetian ambassador he ate mostly roast meat, taking 'no soup, and no sweetmeats', and he was to suffer painfully from gout in old age.[24] He was short in stature, with a long pale face and a pronounced lantern jaw, inherited from his interbred Habsburg ancestors, which he tried to disguise with a skimpy beard. He may not have cut the same martial figure as the French king, but he was equally competitive in his enjoyment of his favourite leisure pursuit, hunting.

His emblem, which he adopted as a youth, was a pair of columns with the motto *Plus Oultre* (Further Still). Associated with the Burgundian Order of the Golden Fleece, the most prestigious chivalric order in Renaissance Europe, the columns referred to the legendary Pillars of Hercules at the Straits of Gibraltar. It was intended to symbolize Charles V's desire to outdo the achievements of the classical hero Hercules, but of course it was also an eminently appropriate device for an emperor whose realm extended across the Atlantic.

Charles V saw himself as successor to Charlemagne, the secular ruler of a Christian Europe whose responsibility was to defend his religion. His propagandists, however, were more enthusiastic in their efforts to promote him as the wise and just heir to Julius Caesar, Augustus, Marcus Aurelius and the other emperors of ancient Rome. When he first visited Rome in 1536, the ephemeral decorations erected to welcome him included countless references to his Roman heritage – and the official cavalcade that escorted him along the city streets and through the ruins of the capital included members of Rome's best families dressed up as ancient Roman senators to act as his tour guides and answer his queries.[25] In a similar fashion, when Charles V and his son Philip travelled through the Low Countries in 1548–9 in order for the emperor's subjects to swear an oath of allegiance and give formal recognition to the prince as his father's heir, the decorations put up by the various cities hailed Charles V as heir to his ancient predecessors. In Ghent, for example, the five triumphal arches erected for the occasion each displayed a different classical order, from Tuscan to Composite. In Antwerp, the commercial and financial centre of northern Europe, they were hailed as heirs to Abraham and Isaac, David and Solomon, and several famous fathers and sons of antiquity, notably Philip of Macedon and Alexander the Great, Vespasian and Titus, and Trajan

Leone Leoni, *Charles V and Philip II*, 1550 (New York, Metropolitan Museum of Art). This double portrait of the Emperor and his son was carved by Leoni in sardonyx, imitating antique Roman imperial cameos.

and Hadrian.[26]

It is not easy to define Charles V's oeuvre as a patron. Much of the expenditure on imperial projects in his realm was commissioned by those who held the positions of power on his behalf, government committees or individual rulers. In Naples, for example, it was his viceroys who commissioned the extensive work on fortifications around the coastline of southern Italy to defend the kingdom from Turkish attack. In the Low Countries it was Mary of Hungary, as we shall see, who was responsible for Charles V's projects. As governor of the Netherlands, her principal residence was the medieval Coudenberg palace in Brussels,* decorated with *all'antica* details including a triumphal arch with Charles V seated on an eagle, the imperial emblem, with an inscription referring to him as the Roman Emperor. In Prague and Innsbruck it was the emperor's brother Ferdinand of Austria who commissioned and employed the Milanese sculptor and architect Paolo Stella to design the palaces and churches that gave visible expression to imperial authority in the Habsburg lands.

One of the few major projects with which Charles V was directly connected was the royal palace at Granada, which he began in 1527. A massive square block surrounding a central courtyard, it was a conspicuously expensive project on which apparently Charles V expected to spend 48,000 ducats for its construction. Unmistakably classical in style, its facade had a heavily rusticated ground floor and entrance portals ornamented with paired Doric, Ionic and Corinthian columns, while the huge circular courtyard inside was also supported on Doric and Ionic columns. The design has some stylistic links to Federigo Gonzaga's Palazzo Te and art historians have also drawn parallels between the palace and Clement VII's Villa Madama outside Rome. But it was not quite so simple. Charles V's use of the architectural language of ancient Rome certainly had imperial overtones but there were other resonances. The palace is situated inside the walls of the medieval Moorish palace of the Alhambra, and in this context its classical style with its Roman overtones was intended to convey the Christian victory over the Moors won by Charles V's grandfather Ferdinand of Aragon in 1492.

In a much less imperial, more domestic, setting, Charles V also built a modest set of rooms for himself to use in his retirement at the

---

* The medieval Coudenberg Palace was destroyed by fire in 1731.

Granada, Palace of Charles V, begun 1527. The introduction of the classical language of architecture had extra resonance in Spain where it gave visible expression to the Christian conquest of the Moors in 1492.

monastery at Yuste. Built along the nave wall of the monastery church, with a hatch through which he could follow the services taking place in there, the house had kitchens and storerooms as well as a courtyard and loggias looking out on to the gardens. He furnished the rooms with portraits of his favourite members of his family – his wife, his son Philip and Philip's wife Mary I of England.[27] He also took several sets of tapestries, including a cycle of the life of the Virgin, which had belonged to his mother, Joanna of Castile, sumptuously expensive and glittering with gold and silver thread.[28]

Charles V's sister, Mary of Hungary, who acted as his governor in the Netherlands from 1531 to his abdication in October 1555, proved an efficient administrator and astute politician. She was also a prolific patron of the arts – though it has to be said that much of the time she was acting as agent for the emperor. The prime focus of her authority in the Low Countries was her palace at Binche, outside Brussels, a medieval castle which the emperor gave her in 1545. She commissioned the Flemish architect Jacques de Broeucq, who spent several years in Rome as part of his training, to rebuild the castle, which in both scale and ornamentation was intended to rival Fontainebleau – ironically, it was burned down just nine years later by the armies of Henri II in reprisal for an assault by imperial troops on French royal property. According to the English ambassador at the time, the palace had been 'buylded altogether *à l'antiqua* without any kynde of such defenses as are requisyte for the wars of nowe a dayes'.[29] During its brief life, Mary of Hungary's palace was famous for the unusually imaginative nature of the tournaments, feasts, mock battles and masques with which she entertained her guests. The chivalric masque she put on in August 1549 for her brother Charles V, her nephew Philip and her sister Eleanor, widow of Francis I, was particularly extravagant. The guests were treated to the sight of wild men breaking in to the palace – the 'wild men' were dressed in green and yellow cloth-of-gold with elaborate feathered headdresses – and kidnapping court ladies who were enjoying themselves at a ball; the damsels were then taken to a nearby castle from where a troupe of knights rescued them the following day.[30]

Although we know little about the exterior appearance of Binche

previous pages   Granada, Palace of Charles V, begun 1527. The design of this imperial residence is thought to derive from Clement VII's Villa Madama in Rome, which was inspired by literary descriptions of the villas of antiquity.

we are better informed about the interior, thanks to a drawing of the 'wild men' masque which took place in the great hall. The room was distinctly classical with a great barrel vault supported by pilasters topped with human busts (herms), with a fireplace decorated with medals of Roman emperors including Julius Caesar and Hadrian. But the rest of the decoration, far from glorifying imperial grandeur and supremacy, warned of the dangers of abusing such great power. On the walls between the herms were tapestries depicting the Seven Deadly Sins – and it was Pride that hung behind the throne.[31] There were also enormous paintings, 8 feet high, of the so-called *Condemned*, rulers of classical mythology who were all condemned to eternal torture as a punishment for their sins. It was the punishments that were portrayed, in gruesome detail – Sisyphus forever pushing his boulder up the hill only for it to roll down, forcing him to start again; Tityus having his liver pecked out by a vulture, and so on.

Alongside these somewhat puritanical images of power were more conventional pieces that were deliberately resonant of Fontainebleau: a set of copies of the famous classical statues from the Vatican collection which Francis I had commissioned in 1540. In 1549 Mary of Hungary sent the sculptor Leone Leoni to Paris to buy the moulds which Primaticcio had taken in Rome and which were, he had heard, up for sale. 'This will please the emperor, who allowed me four days leave for the project,' he wrote to Ferrante Gonzaga, Charles V's governor in Milan, where Leoni worked as Master of the Mint, with a salary of 150 ducats a year and a house.[32] Evidently both the emperor and his sister were involved in this project. Leoni duly bought Primaticcio's moulds and arranged for them to be transported to his house in Milan where he cast the bronzes for Binche – and afterwards, as he had shrewdly anticipated, was able to set up a lucrative business making copies for other wealthy patrons.[33]

Charles V fully understood the value of propaganda and, in a campaign to assert his authority in Europe, celebrated his achievements in a very public manner. Taking advantage of the new and inexpensive medium of printing, which was rapidly becoming a powerful propaganda tool for the Protestant cause, he ensured that news of his own triumphs was widely disseminated. There were accounts of his coronation ceremony in Bologna in 1530, illustrated with woodcuts; genealogies of the Habsburg ancestry; prints designed by the court artist Pieter Coecke van Aelst charting the royal progress made by the emperor and his son through the Low Countries in 1548–9; and an elaborate illustrated account of the unprecedentedly splendid funeral obsequies held by Philip II for his father in 1558.

One of the most famous accounts was devoted to Charles V's victory over the Turks at Tunis (1535), which was woven into a series of very expensive tapestries, and also published as a series of prints to enable the story of the campaign reach a wider public. As if anticipating his victory, Charles V took two poets, two historians and a painter on the voyage across the Mediterranean – and it was the painter, Jan Cornelisz Vermeyen, who designed the tapestries, and included himself sketching in the scenes. Verisimilitude was evidently important for Charles V. The *Conquest of Tunis* cycle, which consisted of twelve tapestries, measuring over 15 feet high and 8–12 feet wide, was commissioned by Mary of Hungary on her brother's behalf. The contract with Vermeyen for cartoons was signed in June 1546, with the painter forbidden from taking on any other commissions.[34] Nine months later a contract was signed with the weaver, specifying the exact amount of gold and silver to be used; unfortunately the manufacture of the tapestries took much longer than expected, and an imperial edict had to be issued to allow the weaver to breach guild regulations and take on extra staff.[35]

Another cycle of twelve engravings, which appeared in 1556, the year after his abdication, celebrated the major achievements of Charles V's reign with the victories over his foes: the Turks, the French, the Protestants, the pope, and America. Eleven of the prints depicted individual victories: over Francis I at the Battle of Pavia; over the pope in the Sack of Rome and Clement VII imprisoned in Castel Sant'Angelo where he was forced to sign a treaty of submission; over the Turks at Tunis and again at Vienna, a scene which included both Charles V and his brother Ferdinand, though neither of the two Habsburg princes was actually present at this battle; and Charles V's defeat of the Protestants at the Battle of Mühlberg. His victory over the native populations of America showed them as cannibals roasting joints of imperial soldiers on their fires, in need of the civilizing influence of the Spanish. Most significantly, the first scene showed Charles V surrounded by all his defeated opponents who, with the exception of the sultan, were all shown attached to the emperor by ropes of bondage. It was a highly eloquent statement of the enormous scale of Charles V's domination in Europe.

Charles V also boasted of the magnitude of Habsburg power in Europe – and the Christian nature of that power – in a series of stained glass windows in the cathedral at Brussels. The windows showed the emperor himself and his five living siblings, each with their spouse, in the act of pious devotion: Charles himself with Isabella of Portugal; Catherine and John III of Portugal (brother of Isabella); Mary and Louis II of Hungary; Ferdinand of Austria and Anne of Hungary (the sister of Louis); and Eleanor and Francis I of France. His dead sister Isabella had been married to the King of Denmark, Norway and Sweden. Even the crown of England would be inside the Habsburg dynastic grasp after Philip's marriage to Mary I in July 1554.

The power of the Habsburg dynasty was an important theme of Charles V's projects but he flaunted his heritage in ancestor cycles of a kind largely unknown in Italy. They were not painted on walls but cast in life-size bronze statues – appropriately, an infinitely more costly undertaking and visible evidence of imperial superiority. Maximilian I had planned twenty-eight large bronze statues of Habsburg men and women for his tomb, an ambitious project that was completed by Charles V's brother Ferdinand of Austria, and later installed in the Hofkirche at Innsbruck. The cycle traced the Habsburg dynasty back to King Arthur, Clovis, the first Christian King of the Franks, and Theodoric, King of the Ostrogoths, though most of the statues were of more recent family members. Charles V himself commissioned a series of bronze statues of his family from Leoni, which were on display at Mary of Hungary's palace at Binche and later installed by Philip II in his royal mausoleum at the Escorial, outside Madrid.

Perhaps surprisingly, unlike his rival Francis I, Charles V showed little interest in collecting works by the masters of the Italian Renaissance, or in employing Italian artists. His own tastes were for the art of northern Europe, though he made two important exceptions – Leoni, as we have seen, and Titian, both of whom were talented portraitists. It was not that he was ignorant of Italian art: it is worth remembering that Charles V spent far more time in Italy than Francis I, and travelled far more widely across the peninsula. We know he was interested in what he saw: on his arrival in Genoa, his first visit to Italy, observers noted that he spent some time inspecting the scenes painted on the triumphal arches for his entry into the city; and other chroniclers describing other entries reported the same behaviour.[36] And when he visited Mantua after his coronation at Bologna in 1530, and was taken round the Palazzo Te, he was full of praise for the work that Federigo Gonzaga had commissioned at this suburban villa: 'I saw that his Majesty was completely amazed by what he saw in the large hall and he stood there for half an hour looking at [the frescoes] praising everything to the skies.'[37] Though perhaps it tells us more about the emperor that after the meal 'his Majesty said he wanted to go and play tennis on the marquis's court which was most beautifully laid out... and they played tennis for perhaps four hours... betting 20 gold scudi on each match and at the end his Majesty had lost 60 scudi'.[38]

Above all, Mantua was where Charles V saw Titian's work for the first time, in particular his portrait of Marquis Federigo. Titian's career in Italy is instructive. Appointed official state painter in Venice in 1516, his early patrons had all been local and by 1530 he had made enough money to buy himself a house with a garden in the city.[39] Portraits were an important part of his official role, and he was paid 25 ducats for a single figure.[40] During the 1530s he started to take on commissions for patrons on the mainland, where he could charge more than in Venice – among this new class of patron were Italy's leading princely courts, notably Alfonso I d'Este, Duke of Ferrara; Federigo Gonzaga, Marquis of Mantua; Francesco Maria della Rovere, Duke of Urbino; and in the 1540s he was also employed by the Farnese.

It was Federigo Gonzaga who engineered the first meeting between Titian and Charles V in 1529, shortly before the emperor's coronation at Bologna in February 1530. Unfortunately the painter was dismissed with the insulting offer of 'just one ducat' for a portrait, half the amount he paid a courtesan for a night of pleasure.[41] But that was before Charles V visited Mantua en route from Bologna to Germany, and saw the artist's work. When the emperor returned to Italy in October 1532, the marquis made sure that Charles V sat for his portrait. Unfortunately this first painting has been lost, though it is known through several copies, including one by Rubens (1603). It showed a three-quarter-length figure of the emperor dressed in expensively gilded armour with an unsheathed sword in his right hand. Usually a

Titian, *Charles V on Horseback*, 1548 (Madrid, Prado), a sympathetic portrait of a man whose life was devoted to duty.
overleaf Titian, *Venus and Adonis*, 1554 (Madrid, Prado), the first of a series of scenes of classical mythology painted by Titian for Philip II based on stories from Ovid's *Metamorphoses*.

symbol of conquest, the drawn sword was not a standard format for imperial portraits – nor was it a common genre in Italy – but it does seem to have been a motif associated with earlier portraits of Charles V, his own personal hallmark.[42]

The emperor was so pleased with the result that he rewarded Titian with 500 ducats, more than he could have earned for a large altarpiece filled with figures, and made him a knight of the Golden Spur.[43] In the official document appointing him a knight, Charles V drew the parallel between Alexander the Great and Apelles, the only artist who had the right to portray his patron. Titian was to paint at least five more portraits of Charles V. From this point onwards, he was effectively court painter to the emperor and most of his works were destined for Habsburg courts, above all for Binche and Madrid.

In 1548 Charles V invited Titian to Augsburg, where the artist spent nine months and painted over twelve portraits of the emperor and his family, who were in residence in the city for the Diet.[44] Intended for a gallery of family portraits that Charles V and Mary of Hungary were planning at Binche, they included portraits of Mary of Hungary, Ferdinand of Austria and three of the emperor, one showing him seated at a table with Empress Isabella. Unfortunately they have all been lost, with the exception of the famous portrait of *Charles V on Horseback* which commemorated the imperial victory over the Protestants at the Battle of Mühlberg the previous year.

Over the following seven years Titian, with the help of his workshop assistants, painted at least seventy pictures for the imperial family and court, and a third of these were for Mary of Hungary, including nineteen portraits and two of the canvases for the *Condemned* cycle in the great hall at Binche.[45] Charles V also commissioned Titian to paint the *Trinity* (1554) for the monastery at Yuste. The altarpiece showed Charles in a white linen shift being presented to God moments after his death, aided by the prayers of his wife, his son and his two favourite sisters, Eleanor of France and Mary of Hungary – it meant so much to him that he specified in his will that he wanted a copy of the painting to be carved in relief on his tomb.[46] In 1550–1 Titian was back in Augsburg, this time at the invitation of Charles V's son Philip, to paint more dynastic images, one of which showed Philip's increasingly frail, elderly father. The prince also commissioned Titian to paint ten large pictures on religious and mythological subjects in return for a

Titian, *Tarquin and Lucrezia*, 1569–71 (Cambridge, Fitzwilliam Museum). Another mythological scene for Philip II but this is a brutal depiction of rape, the reluctant Lucrezia screaming in terror as Tarquin threatens her with a dagger.

Titian, *Philip II in armour*, 1550 (Madrid, Prado). Titian first met Philip in
1548 when he probably sat for this portrait, a masterly depiction of the gauche
twenty-one-year-old prince dressed in his parade armour.

large pension. This commission resulted in the first of a series of the so-called poesie, based on stories from Ovid's *Metamorphoses*, and invariably featuring one or more nude women: such as *Danae* (1554), *Venus and Adonis* (1554) and *Diana and Calisto* (1559).

Charles V died in 1558, dividing his great realm between his brother and his son. Ferdinand I became emperor and ruler of the ancestral Habsburg lands in Austria, while his possessions in Spain, the Low Countries, Italy and the Americas went to Philip, who became King of Spain. He staged what was arguably the most ostentatious show of imperial grandeur since antiquity in Brussels for his father's funeral obsequies – its centrepiece was a huge triumphal ship drawn by sea monsters and manned by Faith, Hope and Charity. He continued his father's patronage of Titian, who produced a huge number of works, religious and secular, for the new king. And he exploited the classical language of architecture for royal projects in both Spain and the Low Countries.

The impact of the rivalry between Charles V and Francis I on the politics of sixteenth-century Europe was immense. And if Charles V won the power struggle then it is France who won the victor's laurels in the cultural evolution of Europe.

Veronese, *Venus and Adonis*, c.1580
(Madrid, Prado), a painting bought c.1650
by the Spanish court artist Diego Velázquez
for the royal collection.

Dates in Family trees are birth and death
Papal dates are regnal

ABBREVIATIONS USED IN THE FAMILY TREES
Names of rulers are <u>underlined</u>
* indicates a person also entered in a second family tree
† illegitimate children in italic

APPENDICES

Family Trees

&

List of Popes

Table 1

The Aragon Kings of Naples

Ferdinand I of Aragon
1380–1416
m Eleanor of Albuquerque

Alfonso I 1395–1458
King of Aragon (Alfonso V) 1416
King of Naples 1435
m Maria of Castile

† Ferrante I 1425–94
m Isabella
di Chiaramonte

† Maria d 1449
*m *Leonello d'Este,*
Marquis of Ferrara

† Eleonora d after 1475
m Marino Marzano,
Prince of Rossano

Alfonso II 1448–95
*m *Ippolita Sforza*

Eleonora
1450–93
*m *Ercole d'Este,*
Duke of Ferrara

Federigo
1452–1504
m Anne of Savoy

Ferrante II
1469–96

Isabella
1470–1524
*m *Giangaleazzo*
Sforza, Duke of Milan

† Sancia
1478–1506
m Jofrè Borgia,
Prince of Squillace

456

Juan II 1398–1479
King of Aragon 1458

Ferdinand II of Aragon
1452–1516
m Isabella of Castile

see Table 9

Giovanni	Beatrice	† Maria d 1470?
1452–1504	1457–1508	*m Antonio Piccolomini,*
Cardinal	*m Matthias Corvinus,*	*Duke of Amalfi*
	King of Hungary	

*and many more
illegitimate
children*

† Alfonso
1481–1500
*m *Lucrezia Borgia*

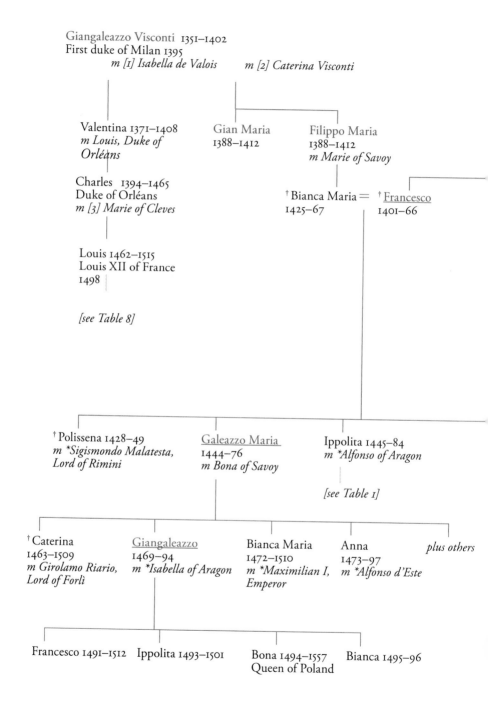

Giangaleazzo Visconti 1351–1402
First duke of Milan 1395
　　　m [1] Isabella de Valois　　　　m [2] Caterina Visconti

Valentina 1371–1408
m Louis, Duke of
Orléans

Gian Maria
1388–1412

Filippo Maria
1388–1412
m Marie of Savoy

Charles 1394–1465
Duke of Orléans
m [3] Marie of Cleves

†Bianca Maria = †Francesco
1425–67　　　1401–66

Louis 1462–1515
Louis XII of France
1498

[see Table 8]

†Polissena 1428–49
m *Sigismondo Malatesta,
Lord of Rimini

Galeazzo Maria
1444–76
m Bona of Savoy

Ippolita 1445–84
m *Alfonso of Aragon

[see Table 1]

†Caterina
1463–1509
m Girolamo Riario,
Lord of Forlì

Giangaleazzo
1469–94
m *Isabella of Aragon

Bianca Maria
1472–1510
m *Maximilian I,
Emperor

Anna
1473–97
m *Alfonso d'Este

plus others

Francesco 1491–1512　　Ippolita 1493–1501　　Bona 1494–1557
Queen of Poland

Bianca 1495–96

Table 2

The Visconti & Sforza rulers of Milan

† Muzio Attendolo
called 'Sforza' 1396–1424

† Alessandro 1409–73
Lord of Pesaro 1444
    m [1] Costanza Varano   *m [2] *Sveva da Montefeltro*

Battista 1446–72
*m *Federigo da Montefeltro,
Duke of Urbino*

[see Table 6]

Costanzo 1447–83
m Camilla of Aragon

† Giovanni 1466–1510
Lord of Pesaro
*m [1] *Maddadela Gonzaga*
*m [2] *Lucrezia Borgia*
m [3] Ginevra Tiepolo

Sforza 1451–79
m. Lipetto di Rossi

Ludovico 1452–1508
*m *Beatrice d'Este*

Ascanio 1455–1505
Cardinal 1484

*plus others
including at
least 17 illegitimate
children*

† Cesare b 1491

Ercole (Massimiliano)
1493–1530
Duke 1512–15

Francesco
1495–1535
Duke 1521–35

Table 3

The Este of Ferrara & Modena

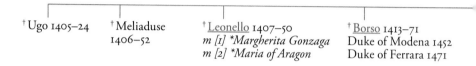

| † Ugo 1405–24 | † Meliaduse 1406–52 | † <u>Leonello</u> 1407–50
m [1] *Margherita Gonzaga
m [2] *Maria of Aragon | † <u>Borso</u> 1413–71
Duke of Modena 1452
Duke of Ferrara 1471 |

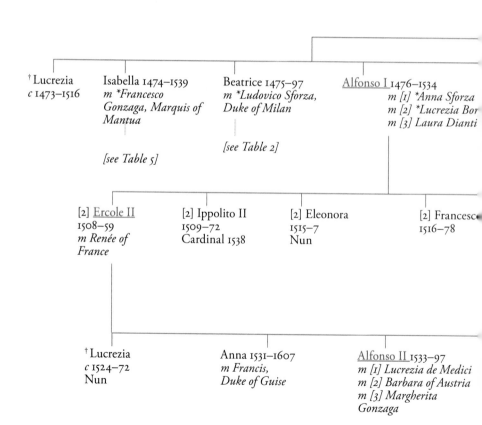

| † Lucrezia
c 1473–1516 | Isabella 1474–1539
m *Francesco
Gonzaga, Marquis of
Mantua

[see Table 5] | Beatrice 1475–97
m *Ludovico Sforza,
Duke of Milan

[see Table 2] | <u>Alfonso I</u> 1476–1534
m [1] *Anna Sforza
m [2] *Lucrezia Bor
m [3] Laura Dianti |

| [2] <u>Ercole II</u>
1508–59
m Renée of
France | [2] Ippolito II
1509–72
Cardinal 1538 | [2] Eleonora
1515–7
Nun | [2] Francesc
1516–78 |

| † Lucrezia
c 1524–72
Nun | Anna 1531–1607
m Francis,
Duke of Guise | <u>Alfonso II</u> 1533–97
m [1] Lucrezia de Medici
m [2] Barbara of Austria
m [3] Margherita
Gonzaga |

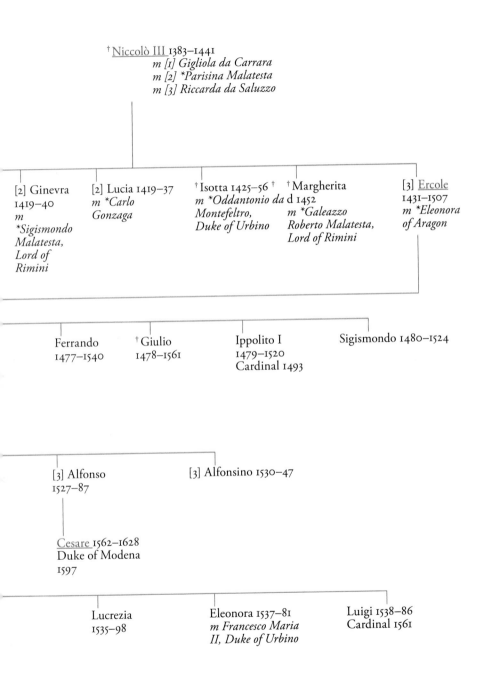

† Niccolò III 1383–1441
    m [1] Gigliola da Carrara
    *m [2] *Parisina Malatesta*
    m [3] Riccarda da Saluzzo

[2] Ginevra
1419–40
m
*Sigismondo
Malatesta,
Lord of
Rimini*

[2] Lucia 1419–37
*m *Carlo
Gonzaga*

† Isotta 1425–56 †
*m *Oddantonio da
Montefeltro,
Duke of Urbino*

† Margherita d 1452
*m *Galeazzo
Roberto Malatesta,
Lord of Rimini*

[3] Ercole
1431–1507
*m *Eleonora
of Aragon*

Ferrando
1477–1540

† Giulio
1478–1561

Ippolito I
1479–1520
Cardinal 1493

Sigismondo 1480–1524

[3] Alfonso
1527–87

[3] Alfonsino 1530–47

Cesare 1562–1628
Duke of Modena
1597

Lucrezia
1535–98

Eleonora 1537–81
*m Francesco Maria
II, Duke of Urbino*

Luigi 1538–86
Cardinal 1561

461

Table 4

The Malatesta of Rimini

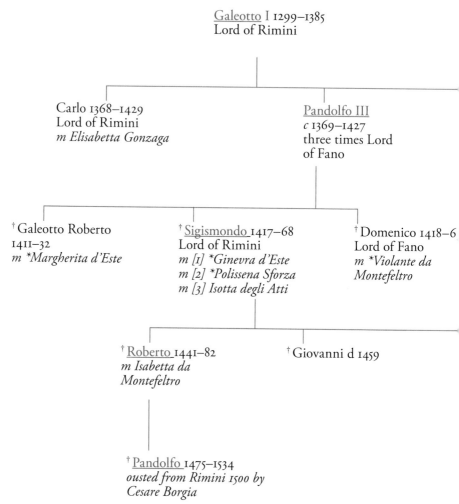

Galeotto I 1299–1385
Lord of Rimini

Carlo 1368–1429
Lord of Rimini
m Elisabetta Gonzaga

Pandolfo III
c 1369–1427
three times Lord
of Fano

† Galeotto Roberto
1411–32
*m *Margherita d'Este*

† Sigismondo 1417–68
Lord of Rimini
*m [1] *Ginevra d'Este*
*m [2] *Polissena Sforza*
m [3] Isotta degli Atti

† Domenico 1418–6
Lord of Fano
*m *Violante da
Montefeltro*

† Roberto 1441–82
*m Isabetta da
Montefeltro*

† Giovanni d 1459

† Pandolfo 1475–1534
*ousted from Rimini 1500 by
Cesare Borgia*

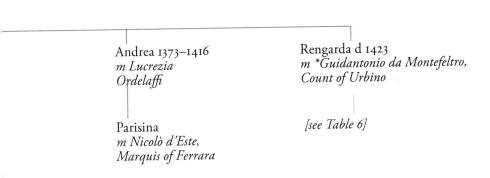

Andrea 1373–1416
m Lucrezia
Ordelaffi

Parisina
m Nicolò d'Este,
Marquis of Ferrara

Rengarda d 1423
*m *Guidantonio da Montefeltro,*
Count of Urbino

[see Table 6]

† Sallustio
1450–70

† Valerio
d 1471

plus at least
eight more
illegitimate
children

Table 5

The Gonzaga of Mantua

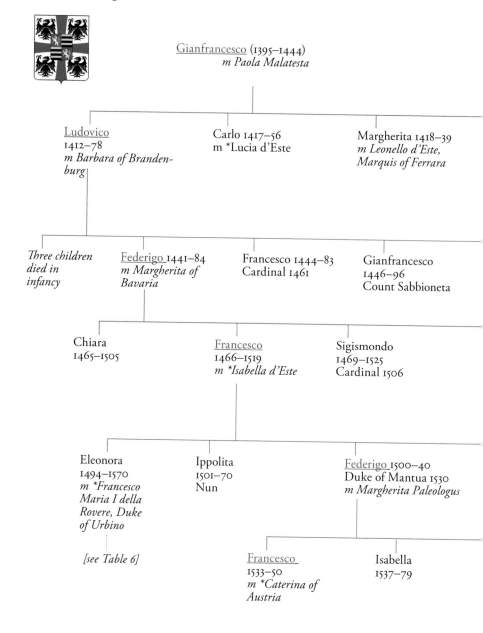

Gianfrancesco (1395–1444)
m Paola Malatesta

Ludovico
1412–78
*m Barbara of Branden-
burg*

Carlo 1417–56
*m *Lucia d'Este*

Margherita 1418–39
*m Leonello d'Este,
Marquis of Ferrara*

Three children
died in
infancy

Federigo 1441–84
*m Margherita of
Bavaria*

Francesco 1444–83
Cardinal 1461

Gianfrancesco
1446–96
Count Sabbioneta

Chiara
1465–1505

Francesco
1466–1519
*m *Isabella d'Este*

Sigismondo
1469–1525
Cardinal 1506

Eleonora
1494–1570
*m *Francesco
Maria I della
Rovere, Duke
of Urbino*

[see Table 6]

Ippolita
1501–70
Nun

Federigo 1500–40
Duke of Mantua 1530
m Margherita Paleologus

Francesco
1533–50
*m *Caterina of
Austria*

Isabella
1537–79

464

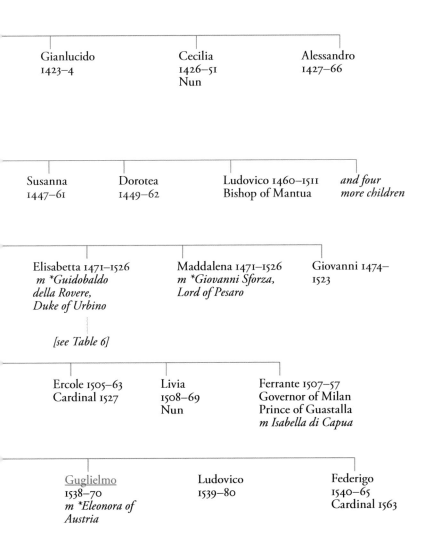

Gianlucido
1423–4

Cecilia
1426–51
Nun

Alessandro
1427–66

Susanna
1447–61

Dorotea
1449–62

Ludovico 1460–1511
Bishop of Mantua

*and four
more children*

Elisabetta 1471–1526
*m *Guidobaldo
della Rovere,
Duke of Urbino*

[see Table 6]

Maddalena 1471–1526
*m *Giovanni Sforza,
Lord of Pesaro*

Giovanni 1474–
1523

Ercole 1505–63
Cardinal 1527

Livia
1508–69
Nun

Ferrante 1507–57
Governor of Milan
Prince of Guastalla
m Isabella di Capua

Guglielmo
1538–70
*m *Eleonora of
Austria*

Ludovico
1539–80

Federigo
1540–65
Cardinal 1563

Table 6

The Montefeltro & Della Rovere in Urbino & Pesaro

(2) Oddantonio	(2) Violante	(2) Sveva 1434–78
1427–44	1430– after 1482	*m *Alessandro*
Duke of Urbino 1444	*m *Domenico Malatesta*	*Sforza, Lord of*
*m *Isotta d'Este*		*Cesena*

	four	(2) Isabetta 1461–1521
	illegitimate	*m *Roberto Malatesta,*
	sons	*Lord of Rimini*

Guidobaldo II
1514–74
  m [1] Giulia Varano
  *m [2] *Vittoria Farnese*

Francesco Maria II
1549–1631
Urbino reverted to the
Papal States after his death

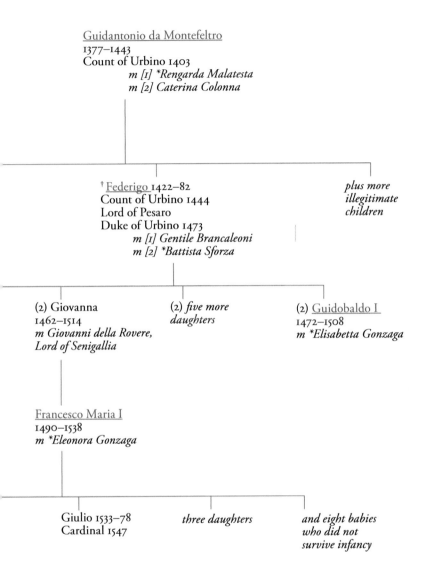

Guidantonio da Montefeltro
1377–1443
Count of Urbino 1403
    *m [1] *Rengarda Malatesta*
    m [2] Caterina Colonna

† Federigo 1422–82
Count of Urbino 1444
Lord of Pesaro
Duke of Urbino 1473
    m [1] Gentile Brancaleoni
    *m [2] *Battista Sforza*

*plus more
illegitimate
children*

(2) Giovanna
1462–1514
*m Giovanni della Rovere,
Lord of Senigallia*

(2) *five more
daughters*

(2) Guidobaldo I
1472–1508
*m *Elisabetta Gonzaga*

Francesco Maria I
1490–1538
*m *Eleonora Gonzaga*

Giulio 1533–78
Cardinal 1547

three daughters

*and eight babies
who did not
survive infancy*

Table 7

The Farnese

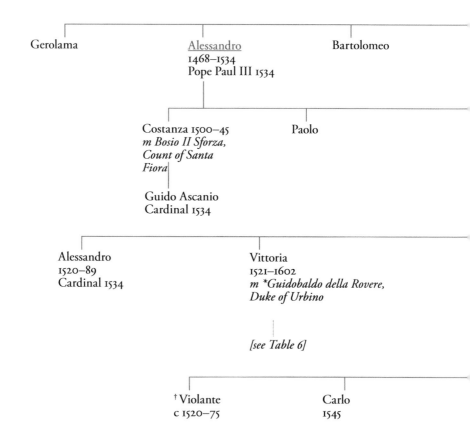

Gerolama

Alessandro
1468–1534
Pope Paul III 1534

Bartolomeo

Costanza 1500–45
m Bosio II Sforza,
Count of Santa
Fiora

Paolo

Guido Ascanio
Cardinal 1534

Alessandro
1520–89
Cardinal 1534

Vittoria
1521–1602
*m *Guidobaldo della Rovere,*
Duke of Urbino

[see Table 6]

† Violante
c 1520–75

Carlo
1545

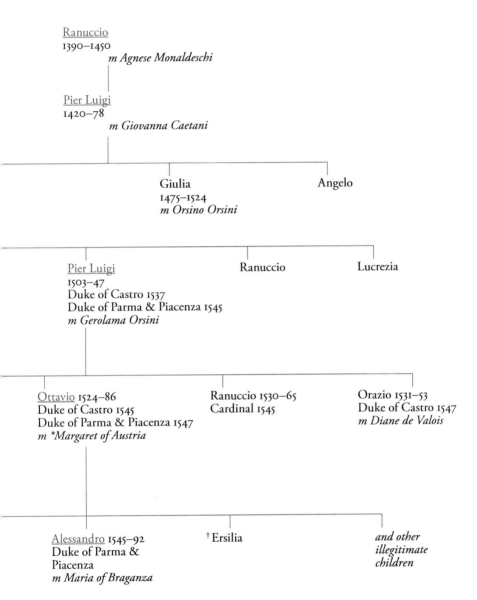

Ranuccio
1390–1450
   m Agnese Monaldeschi

Pier Luigi
1420–78
   m Giovanna Caetani

Giulia
1475–1524
m Orsino Orsini

Angelo

Pier Luigi
1503–47
Duke of Castro 1537
Duke of Parma & Piacenza 1545
m Gerolama Orsini

Ranuccio

Lucrezia

Ottavio 1524–86
Duke of Castro 1545
Duke of Parma & Piacenza 1547
*m *Margaret of Austria*

Ranuccio 1530–65
Cardinal 1545

Orazio 1531–53
Duke of Castro 1547
m Diane de Valois

Alessandro 1545–92
Duke of Parma &
Piacenza
m Maria of Braganza

† Ersilia

*and other
illegitimate
children*

Table 8

The Valois Kings of France

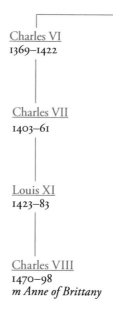

Charles VI
1369–1422

Charles VII
1403–61

Louis XI
1423–83

Charles VIII
1470–98
m Anne of Brittany

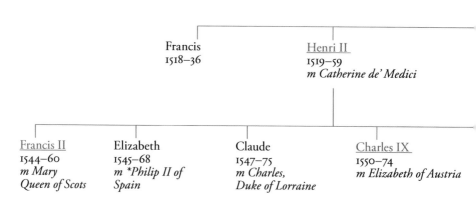

Francis
1518–36

Henri II
1519–59
m Catherine de' Medici

Francis II
1544–60
*m Mary
Queen of Scots*

Elizabeth
1545–68
*m *Philip II of
Spain*

Claude
1547–75
*m Charles,
Duke of Lorraine*

Charles IX
1550–74
m Elizabeth of Austria

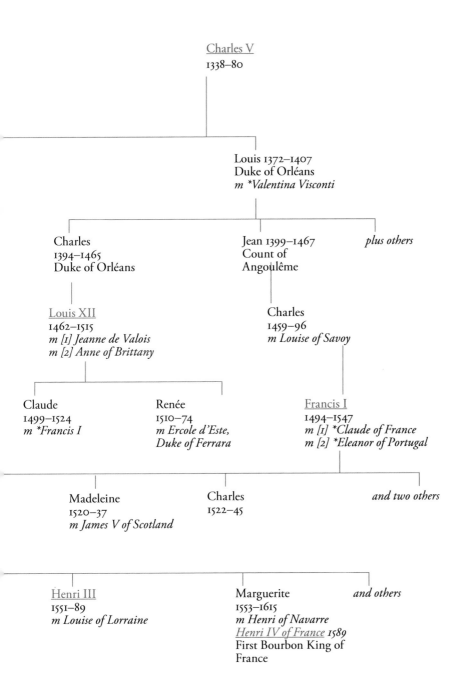

Charles V
1338–80

Louis 1372–1407
Duke of Orléans
m *Valentina Visconti

Charles
1394–1465
Duke of Orléans

Jean 1399–1467
Count of
Angoulême

plus others

Louis XII
1462–1515
m [1] Jeanne de Valois
m [2] Anne of Brittany

Charles
1459–96
m Louise of Savoy

Claude
1499–1524
m *Francis I

Renée
1510–74
m Ercole d'Este,
Duke of Ferrara

Francis I
1494–1547
m [1] *Claude of France
m [2] *Eleanor of Portugal

Madeleine
1520–37
m James V of Scotland

Charles
1522–45

and two others

Henri III
1551–89
m Louise of Lorraine

Marguerite
1553–1615
m Henri of Navarre
Henri IV of France 1589
First Bourbon King of
France

and others

Table 9

The Habsburg rulers of the Empire & Spain

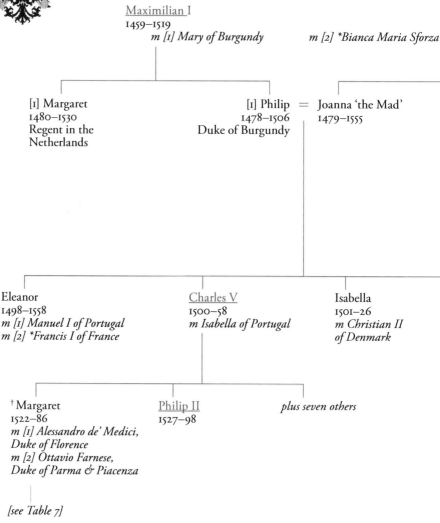

Maximilian I
1459–1519
  m [1] Mary of Burgundy   *m [2] *Bianca Maria Sforza*

[1] Margaret
1480–1530
Regent in the
Netherlands

[1] Philip = Joanna 'the Mad'
1478–1506   1479–1555
Duke of Burgundy

Eleanor
1498–1558
m [1] Manuel I of Portugal
*m [2] *Francis I of France*

Charles V
1500–58
m Isabella of Portugal

Isabella
1501–26
*m Christian II
of Denmark*

†Margaret
1522–86
*m [1] Alessandro de' Medici,
Duke of Florence*
*m [2] Ottavio Farnese,
Duke of Parma & Piacenza*

Philip II
1527–98

plus seven others

[see Table 7]

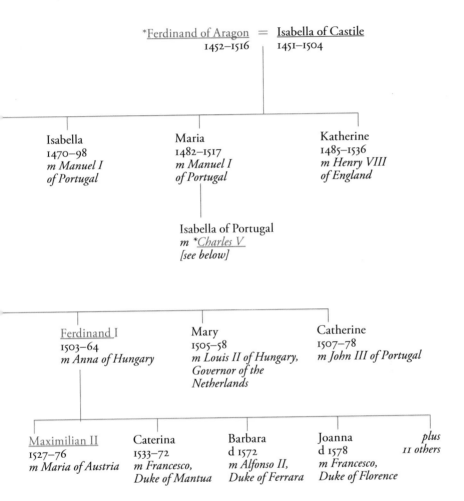

*Ferdinand of Aragon = Isabella of Castile
1452–1516   1451–1504

Isabella
1470–98
m Manuel I
of Portugal

Maria
1482–1517
m Manuel I
of Portugal

Katherine
1485–1536
m Henry VIII
of England

Isabella of Portugal
m *Charles V
[see below]

Ferdinand I
1503–64
m Anna of Hungary

Mary
1505–58
m Louis II of Hungary,
Governor of the
Netherlands

Catherine
1507–78
m John III of Portugal

Maximilian II
1527–76
m Maria of Austria

Caterina
1533–72
m Francesco,
Duke of Mantua

Barbara
d 1572
m Alfonso II,
Duke of Ferrara

Joanna
d 1578
m Francesco,
Duke of Florence

plus
11 others

Table 10

The Popes

1417–1431	Martin V	*Oddo Colonna*
1431–1447	Eugene IV	*Gabriele Condulmer*
1447–1455	Nicholas V	*Tommaso Parentucelli*
1455–1458	Calixtus III	*Alonso Borja*
1458–1464	Pius II	*Enea Silvio Piccolomini*
1464–1471	Paul II	*Pietro Barbo*
1471–1484	Sixtus IV	*Francesco della Rovere*
1484–1492	Innocent VIII	*Giovanni Battista Cibò*
1492–1503	Alexander VI	*Rodrigo Borgia*
1503	Pius III	*Francesco Todeschini–Piccolomini*
1503–1513	Julius II	*Giuliano della Rovere*
1513–1521	Leo X	*Giovanni de' Medici*
1522–1523	Adrian VI	*Adrian Florenz Dedal of Utrecht*
1523–1534	Clement VII	*Giuliano de' Medici*
1534–1549	Paul III	*Alessandro Farnese*
1550–1555	Julius III	*Giovanni Maria del Monte*
1555	Marcellus II	*Marcello Cervini*
1555–1559	Paul IV	*Gianpietro Carafa*
1559–1565	Pius IV	*Giovanni Angelo Medici*
1566–1572	Pius V	*Michele Ghislieri*
1572–1585	Gregory XIII	*Ugo Boncompagni*
1585–1590	Sixtus V	*Felice Peretti*
1590	Urban VII	*Gianbattista Castagna*
1590–1591	Gregory XIV	*Niccolò Sfondrati*
1591	Innocent IX	*Giovanni Antonio Fachinetti*
1591–1605	Clement VIII	*Ippolito Aldobrandini*

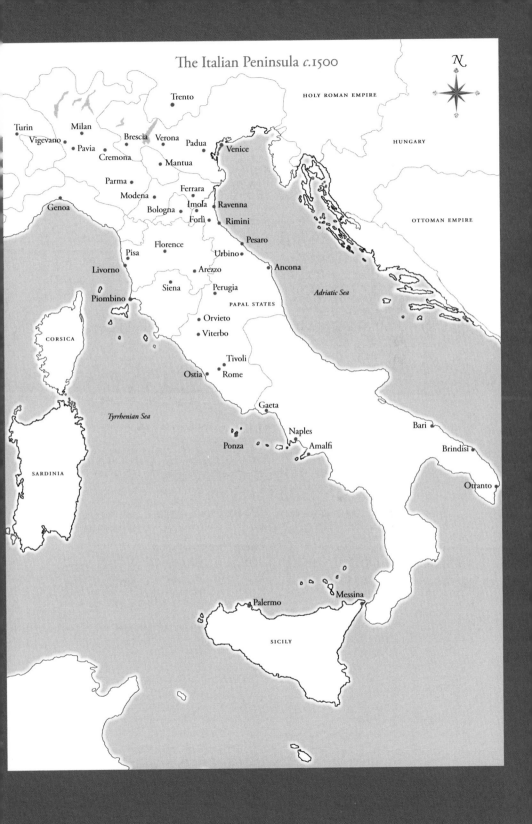

The Italian Peninsula *c.*1500

N

HOLY ROMAN EMPIRE

HUNGARY

OTTOMAN EMPIRE

Turin
Milan
Vigevano
Pavia
Brescia
Verona
Padua
Venice
Cremona
Mantua
Trento
Parma
Modena
Ferrara
Genoa
Bologna
Imola
Ravenna
Forlì
Rimini
Florence
Pesaro
Pisa
Urbino
Livorno
Arezzo
Ancona
Piombino
Siena
Perugia

Adriatic Sea

PAPAL STATES

CORSICA

Orvieto
Viterbo

Tivoli
Ostia
Rome

Tyrrhenian Sea

Gaeta

Bari

SARDINIA

Ponza
Naples
Amalfi

Brindisi

Otranto

Palermo
Messina

SICILY

Adams, Nicholas, 'Censored anecdotes from Francesco Maria I della Rovere's *Discorsi Militari*', *Renaissance Studies*, 13 (1999), 55–62.

Adelson, Candace, 'Cosimo I de' Medici and the foundation of tapestry production in Florence', in Giancarlo Garfagnini (ed.), *Firenze e la Toscana dei Medici nell'Europa del '500* (Florence, 1983), pp. 899–924.

Ady, Cecilia M., *A History of Milan under the Sforza* (London, 1907).

———— 'Morals and manners of the Quattrocento', in George Holmes (ed.), *Art and Politics in Renaissance Italy* (Oxford, 1993), pp. 1–18.

Ariosto, Ludovico, *Orlando Furioso* (Harmondsworth, 1975).

Atlas, Allan W., *Music at the Aragonese Court of Naples* (Cambridge, 1985).

Barocchi, Paola and Giovanna Gaeta Bertelà, *Collezionism mediceo. Cosimo I, Francesco I e il Cardinale Ferdinando* (Modena, 1993).

Baxandall, Michael, 'A dialogue on art from the court of Leonello d'Este', *Journal of the Warburg and Courtauld Institutes*, 26 (1963), 304–26.

———— 'Guarino, Pisanello and Manuel Chrysoloras', *Journal of the Warburg and Courtauld Institutes*, 28 (1965), 183–204.

Benedetti, Alessandro, *Diario de bello Carolino*, ed. and trans. Dorothy M. Schullian (New York, 1967).

Bentley, Jerry H., *Politics and Culture in Renaissance Naples* (Princeton, 1987).

Bertini, Giuseppe, 'Center and periphery: Art patronage in Renaissance Piacenza and Parma', in Charles M. Rosenberg (ed.), *The Court Cities of Northern Europe* (Cambridge, 2010), pp. 71–137.

Bertolotti, A., 'Spese segrete e pubbliche di Paolo III', *Atti e Memorie delle RR. Deputazioni di storia patria per le provincie dell'Emilia*, 3 (1878), 169–212.

Bestor, Jane Fair, 'Titian's portrait of Laura Eustochia: The decorum of female beauty and the motif of the black page', *Renaissance Studies*, 17 (2003), 628–73.

Black, Christopher F., *The Italian Inquisition* (New Haven and London, 2009).

Blastenbrei, Peter, 'The soldier and his cardinal: Francesco Sforza and Nicolò Acciapacci, 1438–1444', *Renaissance Studies*, 3 (1989), 290–302.

Bornstein, Daniel, 'The wedding feast of Roberto Malatesta and Isabetta Montefeltro: Ceremony and power', *Renaissance & Reformation*, 24 (1988), 101–17.

Borsi, Franco, *Leon Battista Alberti* (Milan, 1973).

Botley, Paul, 'Giannozzo Manetti, Alfonso of Aragon and Pompey the Great: A crusading document of 1455', *Journal of the Warburg and Courtauld Institutes*, 67 (2004), 129–56.

Boucher, Bruce, 'Leone Leoni and Primaticcio's moulds of antique sculpture', *Burlington Magazine*, 123 (1981), 23–6.

Bourne, Molly, 'Towards the study of the Renaissance courts of the Gonzaga', *Quaderni di Palazzo Te*, 3 (1996), 80–1.

———— 'Renaissance husbands and wives as patrons of art: The *Camerini* of Isabella d'Este and Francesco II Gonzaga', in Sheryl E. Reiss and David G. Wilkins (eds), *Beyond Isabella. Secular Women Patrons in Renaissance Italy* (Kirksville, 2001), pp. 93–123.

———— *Francesco II Gonzaga. The Soldier-Prince as Patron* (Rome, 2008).

———— 'The art of diplomacy: Mantua and the Gonzaga, 1328–1630', in Charles M. Rosenberg (ed.), *The Court Cities of Northern Italy* (Cambridge, 2010), pp. 138–95.

Brown, B. L., 'The patronage and building history of the tribune of SS. Annunziata in Florence', *Mitteilungen des Kunsthistorisches Institutes in Florenz*, 25 (1981), 59–146.

Brown, C. M., '"Lo insaciabile desiderio nostro de cose antique": New documents on Isabella d'Este's collection of antiquities', in Cecil H. Clough (ed.), *Cultural Aspects of the Italian Renaissance: Essays in Honour of Paul Oskar Kristeller* (Manchester and New York, 1976), pp. 324–53.

———— 'Documents regarding Duke Federico II Gonzaga's interest in Flemish art', *Source: Notes in the History of Art*, 11 (1992), 17–20.

Brown, Patricia Fortini, *Private Lives in Renaissance Venice* (New Haven, 2004).

Bryce, Judith, '"Fa finire uno bello studio et dice volere studiare": Ippolita Sforza and her books', *Bibliothèque d'Humanisme et Renaissance*, 64 (2002), 55–69.

Buchanan, Iain, 'Designers, weavers and entrepreneurs: Sixteenth-century Flemish tapestries in the Patrimonio Nacional', *Burlington Magazine*, 134 (1992), 380–4.

Bueno de Mesquita, Daniel M., 'The privy council in the government of the Dukes of Milan', in *Florence and Milan: Comparisons and Relations* (Florence, 1989), 1:135–56.

———— 'The Conscience of the Prince', in George Holmes (ed.), *Art and Politics in Renaissance Italy* (Oxford, 1993), pp. 159–83.

Burchard, Johannes, *Liber Notarum*, abridged in *Dans le Secret des Borgia* (Paris, 2003).

Burns, Howard, 'The Gonzaga and Renaissance Architecture', in David Chambers and Jane Martineau (eds), *Splendours of the Gonzaga* (London, 1981), pp. 27–38.

Butters, Humfrey, 'Florence, Milan and the Barons' War', in Gian Carlo Garfagnini (ed.), *Lorenzo de' Medici Studi* (Florence, 1992), pp. 281–308.

Cashman, Anthony B. III, 'The problem of audience in Mantua: Understanding ritual efficacy in an Italian Renaissance princely state', *Renaissance Studies*, 16 (2002), 355–65.

———— 'Performance anxiety: Federico Gonzaga at the court of Francis I and the uncertainty of ritual action', *The Sixteenth-Century Journal*, 33 (2002), 333–52.

Casola, Pietro, *Canon Pietro Casola's Pilgrimage to Jerusalem in the Year 1494*, ed. M. Margaret Newett (Manchester, 1907).

Cevizli, Antonia Gatward, 'Mehmed II, Malatesta and Matteo de' Pasti: A match of mutual benefit between the "Terrible Turk" and a "Citizen of Hell"', *Renaissance Studies*, 31 (2017), 43–65.

Chambers, David S., *The Imperial Age of Venice 1380–1580* (London, 1970).

———— 'The housing problems of Cardinal Francesco Gonzaga', *Journal of the Warburg and Courtauld Institutes*, 39 (1976), 21–58.

———— 'Sant'Andrea at Mantua and Gonzaga Patronage 1460–72', *Journal of the Warburg and Courtauld Institutes*, 40 (1977), 99–127.

———— 'Cardinal Francesco Gonzaga in Florence', in Peter Denley and Caroline Elam (eds), *Florence and Italy* (London, 1988), pp. 241–61.

———— 'Virtù militare del Cardinale Francesco Gonzaga', in Carlo Marco Belfanti et al. (eds), *Guerri, stati e città: Mantova e l'Italia Padana dal secolo XIII al XIX* (Mantua, 1988), pp. 215–29.

———— 'An unknown letter by Vittorino da Feltre', *Journal of the Warburg and Courtauld Institutes*, 52 (1989), 219–21.

———— 'Bartolomeo Marasca, master of Cardinal Gonzaga's household (1462–1469)', *Aevum*, 63 (1989), 265–83.

———— *A Renaissance Cardinal and his Worldly Goods* (London, 1992).

———— 'The Enigmatic eminence of Cardinal Sigismondo Gonzaga', *Renaissance Studies*, 16 (2002), 330–54.

———— *Popes, Cardinals and War. The Military Church in Renaissance and Early Modern Europe* (London and New York, 2006).

———— 'A Condottiere and his books: Gianfrancesco Gonzaga (1446–96)', *Journal of the Warburg and Courtauld Institutes*, 70 (2007), 33–97.

Chambers, D. S. and Jane Martineau, *Splendours of the Gonzaga* (London, 1981).

Chambers, David S. and Brian Pullan, *Venice. A Documentary History 1450–1630* (Oxford, 1992).

Chastel, André, *The Sack of Rome, 1527* (Princeton, 1983).

Chatenet, Monique, 'Hippolyte II d'Este à la cour de France à travers la correspondance des ambassadeurs de Ferrare et de Mantoue', in Marina Cogotti and Francesco Paolo Fiore (eds), *Ippolito II d'Este. Cardinale, principe, mecenate* (Rome, 2013), pp. 67–72.

Cheles, Luciano, *The Studiolo of Urbino: An Iconographic Investigation* (Wiesbaden, 1986).

Clark, Leah R., 'The peregrinations of porcelain. The collections of Duchess Eleonora d'Aragona of Ferrara', *Journal of the History of Collections* ** (2019), **

Clough, Cecil H., 'The library of the Dukes of Urbino', *Librarium*, 9 (1966), 101–5.

———— 'Federigo da Montefeltro's Artistic Patronage', *Journal of the Royal Society of Arts*, 126 (1978), 718–34.

———— 'Federigo da Montefeltro: The good Christian prince', *Bulletin of the John Rylands University Library of Manchester*, 67 (1984), 293–348.

———— 'Federico da Montefeltro and the Kings of Naples: A study in fifteenth-century survival', *Renaissance Studies*, 6 (1992), 113–72.

Cockram, Sarah, 'Interspecies understanding: Exotic animals and their handlers at the Italian Renaissance court', *Renaissance Studies*, 31 (2017), 277–96.

Coffin, David R., *The Villa in the Life of Renaissance Rome* (Princeton, 1979).

Commines, Philippe de, *Mémoires de Commines* (Paris, 1843).

Corradini, Elena, 'Medallic portraits of the Este: Effigies *ad vivum expressae*', in Nicholas Mann and Luke Syson (eds), *The Image of the Individual* (London, 1998), pp. 22–39.

Corvisieri, C., 'Il trionfo romano di Eleonora d'Aragona nel Giugno del 1473', *Archivio della Società Romana per la Storia Patria*, 1 (1878), 475–91 (part 1); 10 (1887), 639–87 (part 2).

DBI, *Dizionario Bibliografico degli Italiani* (www.treccani.it/biografie).

Delle Donne, Fulvio, 'Il trionfo, l'incoronazione mancata, la celebrazione letteraria: I paradigmi della propaganda di Alfonso il Magnanimo', *Archivio Storico Italiano*, 169 (2011), 447–76.

Dennistoun, James, *Memoirs of the Dukes of Urbino* (London, 1851).

Dorez, L., *La Cour du Pape Paul III d'après les régistres de la Trésorie Secrète*, 2 vols (Paris, 1932).

Duni, Matteo, 'Impotence, witchcraft and politics: A Renaissance case', in Sara F. Matthews-Grieco (ed.), *Cuckoldry, Impotence and Adultery in Europe (15th-17th Century)* (Farnham, 2014), pp. 85–101.

Duruy, George, *Le Cardinal Carlo Carafa (1519-1651)* (Paris, 1882).

Eiche, Sabine, 'July 1547 in Palazzo Farnese', *Mitteilungen des Kunsthistorischen Institutes in Florenz*, 33 (1989), 395–401.

Eiche, Sabine (ed.), *Ordine et officii de casa de lo illustrissimo Signor Duca de Urbino* (Urbino, 1999).

Eisenbichler, Konrad, 'Charles V in Bologna: The self-fashioning of a man and a city', *Renaissance Studies*, 13 (1999), 430–9.

Eisler, Colin, 'A portrait of L. B. Alberti', *Burlington Magazine*, 116 (1974), 529–30.

Elam, Caroline, 'Art in the service of liberty. Battista della Palla, art agent for Francis I', *I Tatti Studies*, 5 (1993), 33–109.

Erlanger, Rachel, *Lucrezia Borgia* (London, 1978).

Ettlinger, Helen S., 'Visibilis et invisibilis: The mistress in Italian Renaissance court society', *Renaissance Quarterly*, 47 (1994), 770–92.

Fabriczy, C. von, 'Toscanische und oberitalienische Künstler in Diensten der Aragonese zu Neapel', *Repertorium für Kunstwissenschaft*, 20 (1897), 85–120.

Fenlon, Iain, *The Ceremonial City. History, Memory and Myth in Renaissance Venice* (New Haven, 2007).

Ferrière, Hector de la, *Lettres de Catherine de Médicis*, 8 vols (Paris, 1880).

Filangieri, R., 'Rassegna critica delle fonti per la storia di Castel Nuovo', *Archivio Storico per le Provincie Napoletane*, 62 (1937), 5–71 (parts 1–2); 63 (1938), 3–87 (parts 3–4).

Finlay, Robert, 'Fabius Maximus in Venice: Doge Andrea Gritti, the war of Cambrai, and the rise of Habsburg Hegemony, 1509–1530', *Renaissance Quarterly*, 53 (2000), 988–1031.

Forti Grazzini, Nello, 'Gli arazzi di Ferrara nei secoli XV e XVI', in Jadranka Bentini (ed.), *Este a Ferrara. Una corte nel Rinascimentale* (Milan, 2004), pp. 197–201.

Franceschini, Chiara, 'La corte di Renata di Francia (1528–1560)', in Alessandra Chiappini et al. (eds), *Storia di Ferrara vol. VI: Il Rinascimento. Situazioni e personaggi* (Ferrara, 2000), pp. 186–214.

Francesco di Giorgio, *Trattati*, ed. C. Maltese, 2 vols (Milan, 1967).

Frommel, Christoph Luitpold, *Der Römische Palastbau der Hochrenaissance*, 3 vols (Rome, 1973).

Fubini, Riccardo, 'Federico da Montefeltro e la congiura dei Pazzi: politica e propaganda alla luce di nuovi documenti', in Giorgio Cerboni Baiardi, Giorgio Chittolini and Piero Floriani (eds), *Federico di Montefeltro. Lo stato. Le arti. La cultura*, 3 vols (Rome, 1986), 1:355–470.

Gáldy, Andrea, 'The Scrittoio della Calliope in the Palazzo Vecchio', *Renaissance Studies*, 19 (2005), 699–709.

——— 'Lost in antiquities: Cardinal Giovanni de' Medici (1543–1562)', in Mary Hollingsworth and Carol M. Richardson (eds), *The Possessions of a Cardinal: Politics, Piety, and Art 1450–1700* (University Park, 2010), 153–65.

Gamrath, Helge, *Farnese. Pomp, Power and Politics in Renaissance Italy* (Rome, 2007).

Ghirardo, Diane Yvonne, 'Lucrezia Borgia as entrepreneur', *Renaissance Quarterly*, 61 (2008), 53–91.

Gilbert, Creighton E., *Italian Art 1400–1500. Sources and Documents* (Eaglewood Cliffs, 1980).

Gilbert, Felix, 'Venice in the crisis of the League of Cambrai', in J. R. Hale (ed.), *Renaissance Venice* (Totowa, 1973), pp. 274–92.

——— *The Pope, His Banker, and Venice* (Cambridge, MA, 1980).

Giovio, Paolo, *Notable Men and Women of our Time*, trans. Kenneth Gouwens (Cambridge, MA, 2013).

Gnoli, D., 'Un censimento della popolazione di Roma avanti il sacco borbonico', *Archivio della Reale Società di Roma di Storia Patria*, 17 (1894), 375–507.

Goldthwaite, Richard A., *The Building of Renaissance Florence* (Baltimore and London, 1980).

Gombrich, E. H., '"That rare Italian Master…": Giulio Romano, court architect, painter and impresario', in David Chambers and Jane Martineau (eds), *Splendours of the Gonzaga* (London, 1981), pp. 77–85.

Gonzaga, Luigi, *Cronaca del soggiorno di Carlo V in Italia (dal 26 luglio 1529 al 25 aprile 1530)*, ed. Giacinto Romano (Milan, 1892).

Goodgal, Dana, 'The Camerino of Alfonso I d'Este', *Art History*, 1 (1978), 162–90.

Gronau, Georg, 'Die Kunstbestrebungen der Herzöge von Urbino', *Jahrbuch der preussischen Kunstsammlungen*, 27 (1906), Beiheft, 1–44.

Guicciardini, Francesco, *Storia d'Italia*, 6 vols (Rome, 1967).

——— *Storie Fiorentine* (Milan, 1998).

Gundersheimer, Werner L., *Ferrara. The Style of a Renaissance Despotism* (Princeton, 1973).

Hale, J. R., 'War and public opinion in Renaissance Italy', in E. F. Jacob (ed.), *Italian Renaissance Studies* (London, 1960), pp. 94–122.

———— 'The early development of the bastion: An Italian chronology c.1450 – c.1534', in J. R. Hale, J. R. L. Highfield and B. Smalley (eds), *Europe in the Late Middle Ages* (London, 1965), pp. 466–94.

——'Renaissance armies and political control: The Venetian proveditorial system 1509–1529', *The Journal of Italian History*, 2 (1979), 11–31.

Haskell, Francis and Nicholas Penny, *Taste and the Antique* (New Haven and London, 1981).

Herrero Carretero, C., 'Les tapisseries', in *Charles Quint, Tapisseries et armures des collections royales d'Espagne* (Brussels, 1994), pp. 43–113.

Hersey, George L., *Alfonso II and the Artistic Renewal of Naples 1485–95* (New Haven and London, 1969).
———— *The Aragonese Arch at Naples 1443–1475* (New Haven and London, 1973).

Hollingsworth, Mary, *Patronage in Renaissance Italy* (London, 1994).
———— 'Alberti: A courtier and his patrons', in Cesare Mozzarelli, Robert Oresko and Leandro Venturi (eds) *La Corte di Mantova nell'età di Andrea Mantegna* (Rome, 1997), pp. 217–24.
———— 'Ippolito d'Este: A cardinal and his household in Rome and Ferrara in 1566', *The Court Historian*, 5 (2000), 105–26.
———— *The Cardinal's Hat. Money, Ambition and Housekeeping in a Renaissance Court* (London, 2004).
———— 'Coins, cloaks and candlesticks: The economics of extravagance', in Michelle O'Malley and Evelyn Welch (eds), *The Material Renaissance* (Manchester, 2007), pp. 260–87.
———— 'A cardinal in Rome: Ippolito d'Este in 1560', in Jill Burke and Michael Bury (eds), *Art and Identity in Early Modern Rome* (Aldershot, 2008), pp. 81–94.
———— *Conclave 1559* (London, 2013).
———— *The Medici* (London, 2017).

Hope, Charles, 'Titian's role as official portrait painter to the Venetian republic', in *Tiziano e Venezia* (Vicenza, 1980), pp. 301–5.
———— 'Artists, patrons, and advisors in the Italian Renaissance', in G. F. Lytle and S. Orgel (eds), *Patronage in the Renaissance* (Princeton, 1981), pp. 293–343.
———— 'La produzione pittorica di Tiziano per gli Asburgo', in *Venezia e la Spagna* (Milan, 1988), pp. 49–72.
———— 'Tiziano e la committenza', in *Tiziano* (Venice, 1990), 77–84.
———— 'The early history of the Tempio Malatestiano', *Journal of the Warburg and Courtauld Institutes*, 55 (1992), 51–154.
———— 'Titian's life and times', in *Titian* (London, 2003), pp. 9–28.
———— 'Cacce e baccanali nei Camerini d'Este', in Jadranka Bentini (ed.), *Una corte nel Rinascimento* (Milan, 2004), pp. 169–72.

———— 'Titian's Life and Times', in *Titian* (London: 2003), 9–28.

———— 'Tiziano e la committenza', in *Tiziano* (Venice: 1990), 77–84.

Hopkins, Andrew, 'Architecture and *Infirmitas*. Doge Andrea Gritti and the cChancel of San Marco', *Journal of the Society of Architectural Historians*, 57 (1998), 182–97.

Horn, Hendrik J., *Jan Cornelisz Vermeyen, Painter of Charles V and his Conquest of Tunis: Paintings, Etchings, Drawings, Cartoons, Tapestries* (Doornspijk, 1989).

Howard, Deborah, *Jacopo Sansovino. Architecture and Patronage in Renaissance Venice* (New Haven and London, 1987).

Hurtubise, Pierre, 'Une vie de palais: la cour du cardinal Alexandre Farnèse vers 1563', *Renaissance and Reformation*, 16 (1992), 37–54.

Ianziti, Gary, 'A humanist historian and his documents: Giovanni Simonetta, secretary to the Sforzas', *Renaissance Quarterly*, 34 (1981), 491–516.
———— 'The rise of Sforza historiography', in *Florence and Milan: Comparisons and Relations* (Florence, 1989), 1:79–94.

Ilardi, Vincent, 'The banker-statesman and the condottiere prince: Cosimo de' Medici and Francesco Sforza (1450–1464)', in *Florence and Milan: Comparisons and Relations* (Florence, 1989), 1:217–39.

James, Carolyn, 'Marriage by correspondence: Politics and domesticity in the letters of Isabella d'Este and Francesco Gonzaga, 1490–1519', *Renaissance Quarterly*, 65 (2012), 321–52.

Jones, Philip J., 'The end of Malatesta rule in Rimini', in E. F. Jacob (ed.), *Italian Renaissance Studies* (London, 1960), pp. 217–55.

Kent, F. W., *Lorenzo de' Medici and the Art of Magnificence* (Baltimore and London, 2004).

Kliemann, Julian, *Gesta Dipinte: la grande decorazione nelle dimore italiane dal Quattrocento al Seicento* (Milan, 1993).

Knecht, Robert J., *Renaissance Warrior and Patron: The Reign of Francis I* (Cambridge, 1994).

Lane, Frederic C., *Venice. A Maritime Republic* (Baltimore, 1973).

Langdon, Gabrielle, *Medici Women: Portraits of Power, Love, and Betrayal* (Toronto, 2006).

Lapini, Agostino, *Diario Fiorentino* (Florence, 1900).

Lee, Egmont, *Sixtus IV and Men of Letters* (Rome, 1978).

Lefevre, Renato, *Madama Margherita d'Austria (1522–1586)* (Rome, 1986).

Lettenhove, H. Kervyn de, *La Toison d'Or* (Brussels, 1907).

Lewis, Douglas, 'Patterns of preference: Patronage of sixteenth-century architects by the Venetian patriciate', in G. F. Lytle and S. Orgel (eds), *Patronage in the Renaissance* (Princeton, 1981), pp. 354–80.

Lippincott, Kristen, 'The neo-Latin historical epics of the north Italian courts: An examination of "courtly culture" in the fifteenth century', *Renaissance Studies*, 3 (1989), 415–28.

Lockwood, Lewis, *Music in Renaissance Ferrara 1400–1505* (Oxford, 1984).

Luzio, A., *Isabella d'Este e il Sacco di Roma* (Milan, 1908).

Luzio, A. and R. Renier, 'Delle relazioni di Isabella d'Este Gonzaga con Ludovico e Beatrice Sforza', *Archivio Storico Lombardo*, 17 (1890), 74–119, 346–99, 619–74.
———— *Mantova e Urbino, Isabella d'Este ed Elisabetta Gonzaga nelle relazione famigliare, e nelle vicende politiche* (Turin, 1893).

Machiavelli, Niccolò, *Tutti l'opere di Niccolò Machiavelli*, 3 vols (London, 1772).

Mack Smith, Denis, *A History of Sicily. Medieval Sicily 800–1713* (London, 1969).

Madariaga, Salvador de, *Carlo Quinto* (Novara, 1973).

Mallett, Michael, *Mercenaries and their Masters* (London, 1974).
———— 'Diplomacy and war in later fifteenth-century Italy', in Gian Carlo Garfagnini (ed.), *Lorenzo de' Medici. Studi* (Florence, 1992), pp. 233–56.

Mallett, Michael and Christine Shaw, *The Italian Wars 1494–1559* (Oxford, 2012).

Marinesco, Constantin, 'Les affaires commerciales en Flandre d'Alphonse V d'Aragon, roi de Naples (1416–1458)', *Revue historique*, 221 (1959), 33–48.

Martines, Lauro, *Power and Imagination* (London, 1979).
———— *April Blood* (London, 2003).

Maurer, Maria F., 'A love that burns: Eroticism, torment and identity at the Palazzo Te', *Renaissance Studies*, 30 (2016), 370–88.

Mazzi, Maria Serena, 'La fame e la paura della fame', in Jadranka Bentini et al. (eds), *A tavola con il principe* (Ferrara, 1988), pp. 153–69.

McGrath, Elizabeth, 'Ludovico il Moro and his Moors', *Journal of the Warburg and Courtauld Institutes*, 65 (2002), 67–94.

Messisbugo, Cristoforo di, *Banchetti Composizioni di vivande e aparecchio generale* (Venice, 1960).

Millon, Henry A. and Vittorio Magnago Lampugnani (eds.), *The Renaissance from Brunelleschi to Michelangelo. The Representation of Architecture* (London, 1994).

Miranda, Salvador, *The Cardinals of the Holy Roman Church* (1998–2015) http://ww2.fiu.edu/~mirandas/cardinals/cardinals.htm

Mitchell, Bonner, *The Majesty of State: Triumphal Progresses of Foreign Sovereigns in Renaissance Italy (1494–1600)* (Florence, 1986).

Montaigne, Michel de, *The Complete Works. Essays, Travel Journal and Letters* (London, 2003).

Muir, Edward, 'The doge as *Primus Inter Pares*: Interregnum rites in early sixteenth-century Venice', in S. Bertelli and G. Ramakus (eds), *Essays Presented to Myron P. Gilmore* (Florence, 1978), 1:145–60.

Müller, Theodor, *Das Konklave Pius' IV. 1559* (Gotha, 1889).

Müntz, Eugène, 'Un Mécène italien au Xve siècle: Les Lettres, les arts à la cour de Rome pendant le règne de Sixte IV', *Revue des deux mondes*, 51 (1881), 154–92.

Murry, Gregory, *The Medicean Succession. Monarchy and Sacral Politics in Duke Cosimo dei Medici's Florence* (Cambridge, MA, 2014).

Musacchio, Jacqueline Marie, *The Art and Ritual of Childbirth in Renaissance Italy* (New Haven and London, 1999).
———— 'Weasels and pregnancy in Renaissance Italy', *Renaissance Studies*, 15 (2001), 172–87.

Newton, Stella Mary, *The Dress of the Venetians 1495–1525* (Aldershot, 1988).

Occhipinti, Carmelo, *Carteggio d'arte degli ambasciatori estensi in Francia (1536–1553)* (Pisa, 2001).

Onians, John, *Bearers of Meaning* (Princeton, 1988).

Pacifici, Vincenzo, *Ippolito d'Este, Cardinale di Ferrara* (Tivoli, 1920).

Pade, Marianne, 'Guarino and Caesar at the court of the Este', in Marianne Pade, Lene Waage Petersen and Daniela Quarta (eds), *La corte di Ferrara e il suo mecenatismo 1441–1598* (Copenhagen, 1990), pp. 71–91.

Parker, Geoffrey, *Emperor. A New Life of Charles V* (New Haven and London, 2019).

Partner, Peter, *The Pope's Men. The Papal Civil Service in the Renaissance* (Oxford, 1990).

Pastor, Ludwig von, *The History of the Popes from the Close of the Middle Ages*, 29 vols (London, 1894–1951).

Pederson, Jill, 'Henrico Boscano's *Isola beata*: New evidence for the Academia Leonardi Vinci in Renaissance Milan', *Renaissance Studies*, 22 (2008), 450–75.

Pellegrini, Marco, *Ascanio Maria Sforza: La parabola politica di un cardinale-principe del Rinascimento* (Rome, 2002).
———— 'A turning-point in the history of the factional system in the Sacred College: The power of the pope and cardinals in the age of Alexander VI',

in Gianvittorio Signorotto and Maria Antonietta Visceglia (eds), *Court and Politics in Papal Rome 1492–1700* (Cambridge, 2002), pp. 8–30.

Pernis, Maria Grazia and Laurie Schneider Adams, *Federico da Montefeltro and Sigismondo Malatesta* (New York and Washington DC, 1996).

Perry, Marilyn, 'The statuario pubblico of the Venetian Republic', *Saggi e memorie di storia dell'arte*, 8 (1972), 75–253.

Petrucelli della Gattina, Ferdinando, *Histoire Diplomatique des Conclaves*, 2 vols (Paris, 1864).

Piccolomini, Aeneas Silvius, *Secret Memoirs of a Renaissance Pope*, ed. F. A. Gragg and L. C. Gabel (London, 1988).

Pinelli, Antonio and Orietta Rossi, *Genga architetto. aspetti della cultura urbinate del primo 500* (Rome, 1971).

Piseri, Federico, '*Filius et servitor*. Evolution of dynastic consciousness in the titles and subscriptions of the Sforza princes' familiar letters', *The Court Historian*, 22 (2017), 168–88.

Podestà, B., 'Carlo V a Roma', *Atti della Società Romana per Storia Patria*, 1 (1878), 303–34.

Pontano, Giovanni, 'Ioannis Ioviani Pontani to Charitéo: On splendour', *Journal of Design History*, 15 (2002), 222–7.

Prizer, William F., 'Isabella d'Este and Lucrezia Borgia as patrons of music: The frottola at Mantua and Ferrara', *Journal of the American Musicological Society*, 38 (1985), 1–33.
———— 'North Italian Courts, 1460–1540', in Iain Fenlon (ed.), *Man and Music: The Renaissance* (London, 1989), pp. 133–55.

Quint, David, 'Political allegory in the *Gerusalemme Liberata*', *Renaissance Quarterly*, 43 (1990), 1–29.

Ray, Meredith K., 'Impotence and corruption: Sexual function and dysfunction in Early Modern books of secrets', in Sara F. Matthews-Grieco (ed.), *Cuckoldry, Impotence and Adultery in Europe (15th–17th Century)* (Farnham, 2014), pp. 125–46.

Rebecchini, Guido, 'Exchanges of works of art at the court of Federico II Gonzaga with an appendix on Flemish art', *Renaissance Studies*, 16 (2002), 381–91.
———— 'After the Medici. The New Rome of Pope Paul III Farnese', *I Tatti Studies*, 11 (2007), 147–200.

Ribier, Guillaume, *Lettres et Mémoires d'Estat, des Roys, Princes, Ambassadeurs, et autres Ministres, sous les règnes de François premier, Henri II et François II*, 2 vols (Blois, 1667).

Richardson, Carol M., 'Francesco Todeschini Piccolomini (1439–1503), Sant'Eustachio and the Consorteria Piccolomini', in Mary Hollingsworth and Carol M. Richardson (eds), *The Possessions of the Cardinal. Politics, Piety and Art 1450–1700* (University Park, 2010), pp. 46–60.

Richardson, Glenn, *Renaissance Monarchy* (London, 2002).

Robertson, Clare, *Il Gran Cardinale. Alessandro Farnese, Patron of the Arts* (New Haven, 1992).

Robin, Diana, *Filelfo in Milan* (Princeton, 1991).

Romano, Serena, 'Patrons and painting from the Angevins to the Spanish Habsburgs', in Marcia B. Hall and Thomas Willette (eds.), *Naples* (Cambridge, 2017), pp. 171–232.

Ronchini, A., 'Giorgio Vasari alla corte del Cardinale Farnese', *Atti e Memorie delle R. Deputazioni di Storia Patria per le provincie modenesi et parmensi*, 2 (1864), 121–8.

Roover, Raymond de, *The Rise and Decline of the Medici Bank 1397–1494* (Washington DC, 1999).

Rosenberg, Charles M., 'The double portrait of Federigo and Guidobaldo da Montefeltro: Power, wisdom and justice', in Giorgio Cerboni Baiardi, Giorgio Chittolini, and Piero Floriani (eds.), *Federigo di Montefeltro: Le Arti* (Rome, 1986), pp. 213–22.
———— *The Este Monuments and Urban Development in Renaissance Ferrara* (Cambridge, 1997).

Ross, Janet, *Lives of the Early Medici as Told in Their Correspondence* (London, 1910).

Rotondi, P., *The Ducal Palace at Urbino*, 2 vols (London, 1950).

Ryder, A. F. C., 'La politica italiana di Alfonso d'Aragona (1442–1458),' *Archivio Storico per le Provincie Napoletane*, 38 (1958), 43–106.
———— 'The evolution of imperial government in Naples under Alfonso V of Aragon', in J. Hale, R. Highfield and B. Smalley (eds.), *Europe in the Late Middle Ages* (London, 1965), pp. 332–57.
———— 'Antonio Beccadelli: A humanist in government', in Cecil H. Clough (ed.), *Cultural Aspects of the Italian Renaissance. Essays in Honour of Paul Oskar Kristeller* (Manchester and New York, 1976), pp. 123–40.
———— *The Kingdom of Naples under Alfonso the Magnanimous* (Oxford, 1976).
———— *Alfonso the Magnanimous, King of Aragon, Naples and Sicily, 1396–1458* (Oxford, 1990).
———— 'Ferdinando I d'Aragona, re di Napoli', *Dizionario Biografico degli Italiani*, 46 (1996), xx.

Rzepińska, Maria, 'The peculiar greyhounds of Sigismondo Malatesta. An attempt to interpret the fresco of Piero della Francesca in Rimini', *L'Arte*, 13 (1971), 45–65.

Salvini, Roberto, 'The Sistine Chapel: Ideology and architecture', *Art History*, 3 (1980), 144–57.

Santuosso, Antonio, 'An account of the election of Paul IV to the pontificate', *Renaissance Quarterly*, 31 (1978), 486–98.

Sanudo, Marin, *Diarii*, ed. R. Fulin et al. (Venice, 1879–1903).

Schofield, Richard, 'Ludovico il Moro and Vigevano', *Arte Lombarda*, 62 (1986), 93–140.
———— 'A humanist description of the architecture for the wedding of Hian Galeazzo Sforza and Isabella d'Aragona (1489)', *Papers of the British School in Rome*, 56 (1988), 213–40.
———— 'Florentine and Roman elements in Bramante's Milanese architecture', in *Florence and Milan: Comparisons and Relations* (Florence, 1989), 1:201–22.
———— 'Leonardo's Milanese architecture: Career, sources and graphic techniques', *Achademia Leonardi Vinci*, 4 (1991), 111–56.

Shaw, Christine, *Julius II. The Warrior Pope* (Oxford, 1996).

Shearman, John, 'The chapel of Sixtus IV', in M. Giacometti (ed.), *The Sistine Chapel: Michelangelo Rediscovered* (New York, 1986), pp. 22–91.

Shemek, Deanna, 'Aretino's "Marescalco": Marriage woes and the duke of Mantua', *Renaissance Quarterly*, 16 (2002), 366–80.

Shephard, Tim, 'Constructing Isabella d'Este's musical decorum in the visual sphere', *Renaissance Studies*, 25 (2011), 684–706.

Signorini, Rodolfo, 'A dog named Rubino', *Journal of the Warburg and Courtauld Institutes*, 41 (1978), 317–20.
———— 'Acquisitions for Ludovico II Gonzaga's library', *Journal of the Warburg and Courtauld Institutes*, 44 (1981), 180–3.

Simonetta, Marcello, 'Federico da Montefeltro contro Firenze: Retroscena inediti della congiura dei Pazzi', *Archivio Storico Italiano*, 161 (2003), 261–84.

Spencer, J. R., *Filarete's Treatise on Architecture* (New Haven and London, 1965).

Steinitz, Kate Trauman, 'The voyage of Isabella of Aragon: from Naples to Milan, January 1489', *Bibliothèque d'Humanisme et Renaissance*, 23 (1961), 17–33.

Stenhouse, William, 'Visitors, display and reception in the antiquity collections of late- Renaissance Rome', *Renaissance Quarterly*, 58 (2005), 397–434.

Strong, Roy, *Art and Power. Renaissance Festivals 1450–1650* (Woodbridge, 1984).

Swain, Elisabeth Ward, 'The wages of peace: The *condotte* of Ludovico Gonzaga, 1436–1478', *Renaissance Studies*, 3 (1989), 442–52.

Syson, Luke and Dillian Gordon, *Pisanello. Painter to the Renaissance Court* (London, 2001).

Tafuri, Manfredo, *Venice and the Renaissance* (Cambridge, MA and London, 1989).
———— *Ricerca del Rinascimento. Principi, città, architetti* (Turin, 1992).

Talvacchia, Bette L., 'Homer, Greek heroes and Hellenism in Giulio Romano's *Hall of Troy*', *Journal of the Warburg and Courtauld Institutes*, 51 (1988), 235–42.

Taylor, Valerie, 'Banquet plate and Renaissance culture: A day in the life', *Renaissance Studies*, 19 (2005), 621–33.

Torello-Hill, Giulia, 'The exegesis of Vitruvius and the creation of theatrical spaces in Renaissance Ferrara', *Renaissance Studies*, 29 (2014), 227–46.

Tristano, Richard M., 'The precedence controversy and the devolution of Ferrara: A shift in Renaissance politics', *Sixteenth-Century Journal*, 48 (2017), 681–709.

Tuohy, Thomas, *Herculean Ferrara: Ercole d'Este (1471–1505)* (Cambridge, 1996).

Van de Put, Albert, 'Two Drawings of the Fêtes at Binche for Charles V and Philip (II) 1549', *Journal of the Warburg and Courtauld Institutes*, 3 (1939–40), 49–57.

Vasari, Giorgio, *Le vite de' più eccelenti pittori, scultori, et architettori*, ed. Gaetano Milanese, 9 vols (Florence, 1906).

Vasić Vatovec, Corinna, *Luca Fancelli architetto: epistolario gonzaghesco* (Florence, 1979).

Vasseur, Jean-Marc, '1536–1550. L'irrésistable ascension d'Hippolyte le "Magnifique"', in Marina Cogotti and Francesco Paolo Fiore (eds.), *Ippolito II d'Este. Cardinale, principe, mecenate* (Rome, 2013), pp. 115–37.

Vespasiano da Bisticci, *The Vespasiano Memoirs: Lives of Illustrious Men of the XVth Century*, trans. William George and Emily Waters (London, 1926).

Virgil (Loeb edition), 2 vols (London and New York, 1920).

Visceglia, Maria Antonietta, 'Il ceremoniale come linguaggio politico', in Maria Antonietta Visceglia and Catherine Brice (ed.), *Cérémonial et Rituel à Rome (XVIe-XIXe siècles)* (Rome, 1997), pp. 117–76.

Welch, Evelyn Samuels, 'Galeazzo Maria Sforza and the Castello di Pavia, 1469', *Art Bulletin*, 71 (1989), 352–75.
———— 'The process of Sforza patronage', *Renaissance Studies*, 3 (1989), 370–86.

———— *Art and Authority in Renaissance Milan* (New Haven and London, 1995).

———— 'Women as patrons and clients on the courts of Quattrocento Italy', in Letizia Panizza (ed.), *Women in Italian Renaissance Culture and Society* (Oxford, 2000), 18–34.

———— *Shopping in the Renaissance* (New Haven and London, 2005).

———— 'Art on the edge: Hair and hands in Renaissance Italy', *Renaissance Studies*, 23 (2009), 241–68.

Weller, A. S., *Francesco di Giorgio 1439–1501* (Chicago, 1943).

Westfall, C. W., 'Chivalric declaration: The Palazzo Ducale in Urbino as a political statement', in H. Millon and L. Nochlin (eds), *Art and Architecture in the Service of Politics* (Cambridge, MA, 1978), pp. 20–45.

Williams, Robert, 'The Sala Grande in the Palazzo Vecchio and the precedence controversy between Florence and Ferrara', in Philip Jacks (ed.), *Vasari's Florence. Artists and Literati at the Medicean Court* (Cambridge, 1998), pp. 163–81.

Woods-Marsden, Joanna, 'How quattrocento princes used art: Sigismondo Pandolfo Malatesta of Rimini and *cose militare*', *Renaissance Studies*, 3 (1989), 387–414.

———— 'Images of castles in the Renaissance: Symbols of "signoria", symbols of tyranny', *Art Journal*, 48 (1989), 130–7.

———— 'Art and political identity in fifteenth-century Naples: Pisanello, Cristoforo di Geremia, and King Alfonso's imperial fantasies', in Charles M. Rosenberg (ed.), *Art and Politics in Late Medieval and Early Renaissance Italy, 1250–1500* (Notre Dame and London, 1990), pp. 11–37.

———— 'The sword in Titian's portraits of Emperor Charles V', *Artibus et Historiae*, 34 (2013), 201–18.

Wright, Alison, 'The myth of Hercules', in Gian Carlo Garfagnini (ed.), *Lorenzo il Magnifico e il suo mondo* (Florence, 1994), 323–39.

Yriarte, Charles, *Un Condottiere au XVe siècle. Rimini: Études sur les lettres et les arts à la cour des Malatesta* (Paris, 1882).

Zambotti, Bernardino, *Diario ferrarese dal anno 1476 sino al 1504*, in *Rerum Italicarum Scriptores*, new series, vol. 24 pt. 7 (Bologna, 1928).

Zancani, Diego, 'Writing for women rulers in Quattrocento Italy: Antonio Cornazzano', in Letizia Panizza (ed.), *Women in Italian Renaissance Culture and Society* (Oxford, 2000), pp. 57–74.

Zapperi, Roberto, 'Alessandro Farnese, Giovanni della Casa and Titian's Danae in Naples', *Journal of the Warburg and Courtauld Institutes*, 54 (1991), 159–71.

Zerbinati, Giovanni Maria, *Croniche di Ferrara* (Ferrara, 1989).

Zimmerman, T. C. Price, *Paolo Giovio. The Historian and the Crisis of Sixteenth-Century Italy* (Princeton, 1995).

*ss*condottieridiventura.it
Dizionario biografico degli Italiani

Notes

INTRODUCTION

1   Thomas Tuohy, *Herculean Ferrara: Ercole d'Este (1471–1505)* (Cambridge, 1996), pp.157–60.

2   Ibid., p.237.

3   Ibid., p.220.

I   USURPERS

1   A. F. C. Ryder, *Alfonso the Magnanimous, King of Aragon, Naples and Sicily, 1396–1458* (Oxford, 1990), p.203; A. F. C. Ryder, *The Kingdom of Naples under Alfonso the Magnanimous* (Oxford, 1976), p.301.

2   Ryder, *Alfonso the Magnanimous*, p.204.

3   Ryder, *Kingdom of Naples*, p.29 n.13.

4   Aeneas Silvius Piccolomini, *Secret Memoirs of a Renaissance Pope*, ed. F. A. Gragg and L. C. Gabel (London, 1988), pp.123–4.

5   Jerry H. Bentley, *Politics and Culture in Renaissance Naples* (Princeton, 1987), p.51; Vespasiano da Bisticci, *The Vespasiano Memoirs: Lives of Illustrious Men of the XVth Century*, trans. William George and Emily Waters (London, 1926), pp.60–1.

6   Ryder, *Kingdom of Naples*, p.76.

7   Vespasiano, *Memoirs*, pp.69–70.

8   Quoted in Ryder, *Kingdom of Naples*, p.25.

9   Ryder, *Kingdom of Naples*, pp.27–28 n.5; Ryder, *Alfonso the Magnanimous*, p.114.

10 Elisabeth Ward Swain, 'The wages of peace: The *condotte* of Ludovico Gonzaga, 1436–1478', *Renaissance Studies*, 3 (1989), 445 n.7.

11 Ryder, *Alfonso the Magnanimous*, p.208.

12 Ibid., pp.207–8.

13 condottieridiventura.it (Francesco Sforza).

14 Raymond de Roover, *The Rise and Decline of the Medici Bank 1397–1494* (Washington DC, 1999), pp.56, 59.

15 A. F. C. Ryder, 'The evolution of imperial government in Naples under Alfonso V of Aragon', in J. Hale, R. Highfield and B. Smalley (eds.), *Europe in the Late Middle Ages* (London, 1965), pp.351–2.

16 Denis Mack Smith, *A History of Sicily. Medieval Sicily 800–1713* (London, 1969), p.96; Luke Syson and Dillian Gordon, *Pisanello. Painter to the Renaissance Court* (London, 2001), p.241 n.74.

17 Ryder, *Kingdom of Naples*, p.275.

18 Ibid., p.47.

19 On Sforza's campaign, see Peter Blastenbrei, 'The soldier and his cardinal: Francesco Sforza and Nicolò Acciapacci, 1438–1444', *Renaissance Studies*, 3 (1989), pp.291–3.

20 Bentley, *Politics and Culture*, pp.13, 141–2.

21 Ryder, *Kingdom of Naples*, pp.284–5.

22 George L. Hersey, *The Aragonese Arch at Naples 1443–1475* (New Haven and London, 1973), pp.63–4.

23 Fulvio delle Donne, 'Il trionfo, l'incoronazione mancata, la celebrazione letteraria: I paradigmi della propaganda di Alfonso il Magnanimo', *Archivio Storico Italiano*, 169 (2011), pp.462–70.

24 Ryder, *Kingdom of Naples*, pp.359–61; *Dizionario Biografico degli Italiani* [DBI], 'Alfonso V d'Aragona, re di Napoli'.

25 Francesco di Giorgio, *Trattati*, ed. C. Maltese, 2 vols (Milan, 1967), 1:3.

26 Joanna Woods-Marsden, 'Images of castles in the Renaissance: Symbols of "signoria", symbols of tyranny', *Art Journal*, 48 (1989), p.133; R. Filangieri, 'Rassegna critica delle fonti per la storia di Castel Nuovo', *Archivio Storico per le Provincie Napoletane*, 62 (1937), pp.23–4.

27 On the arch, see Hersey, *The Aragonese Arch*, passim.

28 Filangieri, 'Rassegna critica', 4:83 doc.7.

29 Ibid., 4:22–30; Ryder, *Alfonso the Magnanimous*, p.344 and n.191.

30 Filangieri, 'Rassegna critica', 1:10.

31 Ibid., 1:10–11.

32 Ibid., 4:83 doc.7.

33 Ibid., 1:18–20

34 Allan W. Atlas, *Music at the Aragonese Court of Naples* (Cambridge, 1985), p.101.

35 Filangieri, 'Rassegna critica', 4:77–8.

36 Ibid., 4:43.

37 Ryder, *Kingdom of Naples*, p.76 nn. 145, 188; Constantin Marinesco, 'Les affaires commerciales en Flandre d'Alphonse V d'Aragon, roi de Naples (1416–1458)', *Revue historique*, 221 (1959), p.37.

38 H. Kervyn de Lettenhove, *La Toison d'Or* (Brussels, 1907), p.103.

39 Marinesco, 'Les affaires commerciales', pp.38, 45–7.

40 Ryder, *Kingdom of Naples*, p.70, nn. 97–100; Ryder, *Alfonso the Magnanimous*, 347.

41 Bentley, *Politics and Culture*, pp.56–9; Ryder, *Kingdom of Naples*, p.78.

42 Serena Romano, 'Patrons and painting from the Angevins to the Spanish Habsburgs', in Marcia B. Hall and Thomas Willette (eds.), *Naples* (Cambridge, 2017), p.194.

43 Woods-Marsden, 'Art and political identity in fifteenth-century Naples: Pisanello, Cristoforo di Geremia, and King Alfonso's imperial fantasies', in Charles M. Rosenberg (ed.), *Art and Politics in Late Medieval and Early Renaissance Italy, 1250–1500* (Notre Dame and London, 1990), p.13.

44 Syson and Gordon, *Pisanello*, p.38.

45 Woods-Marsden, 'Art and political identity', passim; Syson and Gordon, *Pisanello*, pp.123–30.

46 Ryder, *Kingdom of Naples*, pp.55–7.

47 Ibid., pp.73–4.

48 Ibid., p.190.

49 Atlas, *Music at the Aragonese Court*, pp.32–3.

50 Ryder, *Kingdom of Naples*, pp.57–8.

51 Ibid., p.52 n.100.

52 Bentley, *Politics and Culture*, p.10.

53 Ibid., pp.52, 89.

54 Ibid., p.47.

55 Paul Botley, 'Giannozzo Manetti, Alfonso of Aragon and Pompey the Great: A crusading document of 1455', *Journal of the Warburg and Courtauld Institutes*, 67 (2004), pp.136–7.

56 Bentley, *Politics and Culture*, pp.56–9.

57 A. F. C. Ryder, 'Antonio Beccadelli: A humanist in government', in Cecil H. Clough (ed.), *Cultural Aspects of the Italian Renaissance. Essays in Honour of Paul Oskar Kristeller* (Manchester and New York, 1976), passim; Bentley, *Politics and Culture*, pp.84–95.

58 Bentley, *Politics and Culture*, pp.224–8.

59 Ibid., p.60; Ryder, *Kingdom of Naples*, p.81.

60 Bentley, *Politics and Culture*, pp.108–22.

61 Ibid., pp.228–32.

62 Ibid., pp.113–20.

63 A. F. C. Ryder, 'La politica italiana di Alfonso d'Aragona (1442–1458),' *Archivio Storico per le Provincie Napoletane*, 38 (1958), pp.52–3.

64 Quoted in Ryder, *Kingdom of Naples*, pp.28–9.

65 Ryder, 'La politica italiana', p.56.

66 David S. Chambers, *Popes, Cardinals and War. The Military Church in Renaissance and Early Modern Europe* (London and New York, 2006), pp.45–6.

67 On the campaign, see Ryder, 'La politica italiana', pp.58–61.

68 Vespasiano, *Memoirs*, p.70.

69 Ryder, 'La politica italiana', pp.59–60; Michael Mallett, *Mercenaries and their Masters* (London, 1974), pp.204, 272.

70 Ryder, *Kingdom of Naples*, p.174.

71 Ryder, 'La politica italiana', p.62.

72 Ibid., pp.70–1.

73 Piccolomini, *Secret Memoirs*, p.45.

74 Lauro Martines, *Power and Imagination* (London, 1979), pp.190–201.

75 Evelyn Samuels Welch, 'Women as patrons and clients on the courts of Quattrocento Italy', in Letizia Panizza (ed.), *Women in Italian Renaissance Culture and Society* (Oxford, 2000), p.25.

76 Diana Robin, *Filelfo in Milan* (Princeton, 1991), p.65 n.43.

77 Machiavelli, *Tutti l'opere di Niccolò Machiavelli*, 3 vols (London, 1772), 1:217.

78 Robin, *Filelfo in Milan*, p.87 n.26.

79 Daniel M. Bueno de Mesquita, 'The privy council in the government of the Dukes of Milan', in *Florence and Milan: Comparisons and Relations* (Florence, 1989), p.139.

80 Federico Piseri, '*Filius et servitor*. Evolution of dynastic consciousness in the titles and subscriptions of the Sforza princes' familiar letters', *The Court Historian*, 22 (2017), pp.173–6.

81 Evelyn Samuels Welch, 'Galeazzo Maria Sforza and the Castello di Pavia, 1469', *Art Bulletin*, 71 (1989), p.362.

82 Vincent Ilardi, 'The banker-statesman and the condottiere prince: Cosimo de' Medici and Francesco Sforza (1450–1464)', in *Florence and Milan: Comparisons and Relations* (Florence, 1989), p.229.

83 Piccolomini, *Secret Memoirs*, p.110.

84 Ilardi, 'The banker-statesman', p.229.

85 Gary, Ianziti, 'A humanist historian and his documents: Giovanni Simonetta, secretary to the Sforzas', *Renaissance Quarterly*, 34 (1981), pp.493–7.

86 Mallett, *Mercenaries and their Masters*, pp.91, 124–5; Evelyn Samuels Welch, 'The process of Sforza patronage', *Renaissance Studies*, 3 (1989), p.371.

87 Robin, *Filelfo in Milan*, p.57 n.6.

88 Gary Ianziti, 'The rise of Sforza historiography', in *Florence and Milan: Comparisons and Relations* (Florence, 1989), p.85.

89 Robin, *Filelfo in Milan*, p.62.

90 Ianziti, 'The rise of Sforza historiography', pp.89–92.

91 Robin, *Filelfo in Milan*, pp.78–9.

92 Ibid., p.46.

93 Ibid., p.11 n.4.

94 Marinesco, 'Les affaires commerciales', p.37.

95 Ludwig von Pastor, *The History of the Popes from the Close of the Middle Ages*, 29 vols (London, 1894–1951), 2:143–4.

96 Ryder, *Kingdom of Naples*, p.300.

97 Ibid., p.70; Atlas, *Music at the Aragonese Court*, pp.102–3.

98 Ryder, *Alfonso the Magnanimous*, pp.348–57.

99 Ibid., pp.397–8.

100 Ibid., p.397; Piccolomini, *Secret Memoirs*, pp.69–70.

101 Swain, 'The wages of peace', p.446.

102 Welch, 'Women as patrons', p.25; Robin, *Filelfo in Milan*, p.56.

103 Pastor, *History of the Popes*, 2:291.

104 Piccolomini, *Secret Memoirs*, p.72.

105 Pastor, *History of the Popes*, 2:552–53 doc.46.

106 Piccolomini, *Secret Memoirs*, p.89.

107 Piseri, *'Filius et servitor'* pp.176–8.

108 J. R. Spencer, *Filarete's Treatise on Architecture* (New Haven and London, 1965), ff. 7v–8r.

109 John Onians, *Bearers of Meaning* (Princeton, 1988), pp.165–70.

110 Ilardi, 'The banker-statesman', pp.231, 238 n.88.

111 Ibid., p.229.

2 KNIGHTS AND HUMANISTS

1 Tuohy, *Herculean Ferrara*, p.4.

2 Werner L. Gundersheimer, *Ferrara. The Style of a Renaissance Despotism* (Princeton, 1973), p.77 n.17; Helen S. Ettlinger, 'Visibilis et invisibilis: The mistress in Italian Renaissance court society', *Renaissance Quarterly*, 47 (1994), pp.786–7.

3 Philippe de Commines, *Mémoires de Commines* (Paris, 1843), 7:2.

4 Gundersheimer, *Ferrara*, p.79.

5 Ibid., p.86.

6 Charles M. Rosenberg, *The Este Monuments and Urban Development in Renaissance Ferrara* (Cambridge, 1997), p.52.

7 Elena Corradini, 'Medallic portraits of the Este: Effigies *ad vivum expressae*', in Nicholas Mann and Luke Syson (eds), *The Image of the Individual* (London, 1998), pp.27, 195 n.40.

8 Gundersheimer, *Ferrara*, p.95.

9 Marianne Pade, 'Guarino and Caesar at the court of the Este', in Marianne Pade, Lene Waage Petersen and Daniela Quarta (eds), *La corte di Ferrara e il suo mecenatismo 1441–1598* (Copenhagen, 1990), pp.75, 77–8.

10 Gundersheimer, *Ferrara*, p.81.

11 Ryder, 'La politica italiana', p.55.

12 Gundersheimer, *Ferrara*, p.121.

13 Ibid., p.121 n.50.

14 Corradini, 'Medallic portraits of the Este', p.25; Syson and Gordon, *Pisanello*, p.87.

15 Corradini, 'Medallic portraits of the Este', pp.23, 193 n.7.

16 Ibid., p.25.

17 Syson and Gordon, *Pisanello*, p.123.

18 Lewis Lockwood, *Music in Renaissance Ferrara 1400–1505* (Oxford, 1984), pp.44–5.

19 Gundersheimer, *Ferrara*, p.102.

20 Ibid., p.106.

21 Ibid., p.95.

22 Tuohy, *Herculean Ferrara*, p.7.

23 Michael Baxandall, 'A dialogue on art from the court of Leonello d'Este', *Journal of the Warburg and Courtauld Institutes*, 26 (1963), pp.304–26, 304.

24 Baxandall, 'A dialogue on art', p.316.

25 Nello Forti Grazziani, 'Gli arazzi di Ferrara nei secoli XV e XVI', in Jadranka Bentini (ed.), *Este a Ferrara. Una corte nel Rinascimentale* (Milan, 2004), pp.197–8.

26 Tuohy, *Herculean Ferrara*, pp.312, 363.

27 Michael Baxandall, 'Guarino, Pisanello and Manuel Chrysoloras', *Journal of the Warburg and Courtauld Institutes*, 28 (1965), pp.186–7.

28 Baxandall, 'A dialogue on art', p.309.

29 Franco Borsi, *Leon Battista Alberti* (Milan, 1973), p.20.

30 Syson and Gordon, *Pisanello*, p.112.

31 Colin Eisler, 'A portrait of L. B. Alberti', *Burlington Magazine*, 116 (1974), p.530.

32 Rosenberg, *The Este Monuments*, p.208 n.28.

33 James Dennistoun, *Memoirs of the Dukes of Urbino* (London, 1851), 1:85.

34 Maria Grazia Pernis and Laurie Schneider Adams, *Federico da Montefeltro and Sigismondo Malatesta* (New York and Washington DC, 1996), p.28.

35 Pernis and Schneider, *Federico da Montefeltro*, p.29.

36 Dennistoun, *Memoirs of the Dukes of Urbino*, 1:78–9.

37 Philip J. Jones, 'The end of Malatesta rule in Rimini', in E. F. Jacob (ed.), *Italian Renaissance Studies* (London, 1960), p.231.

38 Cecil H. Clough, 'Federico da Montefeltro and the Kings of Naples: A study in fifteenth-century survival', *Renaissance Studies*, 6 (1992), p.116.

39 Ryder, *Kingdom of Naples*, p.262.

40 Ibid., pp.269, 276, 279.

41 Mallett, *Mercenaries and their Masters*, p.196.

42 Ettlinger, 'Visibilis et invisibilis', pp.773–4 and passim.

43 Pernis and Schneider, *Federico da Montefeltro*, p.13.

44 Joanna Woods-Marsden, 'How quattrocento princes used art: Sigismondo Pandolfo Malatesta of Rimini and *cose militare*', *Renaissance Studies*, 3 (1989), pp.389, 390 n.12.

45 Woods-Marsden, 'Images of castles', p.131.

46 Woods-Marsden, 'How quattrocento princes used art', p.395.

47 Syson and Gordon, *Pisanello*, p.224.

48 Ibid., pp.35, 64.

49 Cecil H. Clough, 'Federigo da Montefeltro's Artistic Patronage', *Journal of the Royal Society of Arts*, 126 (1978), pp.721–2.

50 Woods-Marsden, 'How quattrocento princes used art', pp.400–1.

51 Pernis and Schneider, *Federico da Montefeltro*, p.163; Piccolomini, *Secret Memoirs*, p.104.

52 Woods-Marsden, 'Images of castles', pp.132–3.

53 Kristen Lippincott, 'The neo-Latin historical epics of the north Italian courts: An examination of "courtly culture" in the fifteenth century', *Renaissance Studies*, 3 (1989), p.419.

54 Charles Hope, 'The early history of the Tempio Malatestiano', *Journal of the Warburg and Courtauld Institutes*, 55 (1992), pp.58–9.

55 Maria Rzepińska, 'The peculiar greyhounds of Sigismondo Malatesta. An attempt to interpret the fresco of Piero della Francesca in Rimini', *L'Arte*, 13 (1971).

56 Hope, 'The early history of the Tempio Malatestiano', p.66.

57 Henry A. Millon and Vittorio Magnago Lampugnani (eds.), *The Renaissance from Brunelleschi to Michelangelo. The Representation of Architecture* (London, 1994), p.485 cat. 98.

58 Piccolomini, *Secret Memoirs*, p.104.

59 Hope, 'The early history of the Tempio Malatestiano', p.52 n.5.

60 Onians, *Bearers of Meaning*, p.127.

61 Hope, 'The early history of the Tempio Malatestiano', p.86.

62 Woods-Marsden, 'Images of castles', pp.132, 136 n.27.

63 Piccolomini, *Secret Memoirs*, p.104.

64 Ettlinger, 'Visibilis et invisibilis', p.777.

65 Piccolomini, *Secret Memoirs*, p.178.

66 Pastor, *History of the Popes*, 3:117.

67 David S. Chambers, 'The housing problems of Cardinal Francesco Gonzaga', *Journal of the Warburg and Courtauld Institutes*, 39 (1976), p.44 doc.5.

68 Pastor, *History of the Popes*, 3:125.

69 Ibid., 3:120, 126.

70 Antonia Gatward Cevizli, 'Mehmed II, Malatesta and Matteo de' Pasti: A match of mutual benefit between the "Terrible Turk" and a "Citizen of Hell"', *Renaissance Studies*, 31 (2017).

71 Mallett, *Mercenaries and their Masters*, p.89.

72 Gundersheimer, *Ferrara*, p.126.

3   A FAMILY MAN

1   Piccolomini, *Secret Memoirs*, p.110.

2   Virgil, *Georgics*, III.12.

3   Anthony B. Cashman III, 'The problem of audience in Mantua: Understanding ritual efficacy in an Italian Renaissance princely state', *Renaissance Studies*, 16 (2002), pp.359, 361–2.

4   Molly Bourne, 'The art of diplomacy: Mantua and the Gonzaga, 1328–1630', in Charles M. Rosenberg (ed.), *The Court Cities of Northern Italy* (Cambridge, 2010), p.150.

5   D. S. Chambers and Jane Martineau, *Splendours of the Gonzaga* (London, 1981), p.110 cat. 16.

6   Pernis and Schneider, *Federico da Montefeltro*, p.123 n.75.

7   David S. Chambers, 'An unknown letter by Vittorino da Feltre', *Journal of the Warburg and Courtauld Institutes*, 52 (1989), p.220.

8   Welch, 'Women as patrons', p.21.

9   Swain, 'The wages of peace', p.445.

10 B. L. Brown, 'The patronage and building history of the tribune of SS. Annunziata in Florence', *Mitteilungen des Kunsthistorisches Institutes in Florenz*, 25 (1981).

11 Swain, 'The wages of peace' , p.452 n.27.

12 Ibid., p.443.

13 Ibid., p.442.

14 DBI, 'Ludovico III Gonzaga, marchese di Mantova'.

15 Swain, 'The wages of peace', pp.445, 451.

16 Ibid., pp.447–8.

17 Piccolomini, *Secret Memoirs*, p.115.

18 Ibid., p.29.

19 Ibid., pp.114–15.

20 Borsi, *Leon Battista Alberti*, p.142.

21 Pastor, *History of the Popes*, 3:62 n.

22 Piccolomini, *Secret Memoirs*, p.126.

23 Pastor, *History of the Popes*, 3:75 n.

24 Piccolomini, *Secret Memoirs*, p.117.

25 Corinna Vasić Vatovec, *Luca Fancelli architetto: epistolario gonzaghesco* (Florence, 1979), pp.87–8.

26 David S. Chambers, 'Cardinal Francesco Gonzaga in Florence', in Peter Denley and Caroline Elam (eds), *Florence and Italy* (London, 1988), p.242.

27 David S. Chambers, *A Renaissance Cardinal and his Worldly Goods* (London, 1992), p.50 and n.3.

28 David S. Chambers, 'Virtù militare del Cardinale Francesco Gonzaga', in Carlo Marco Belfanti et al. (eds), *Guerri, stati e città: Mantova e l'Italia Padana dal secolo XIII al XIX* (Mantua, 1988), p.215 and n.2.

29 Chambers, 'Cardinal Francesco Gonzaga in Florence', pp.253–58 doc.7.

30 Howard Burns, 'The Gonzaga and Renaissance Architecture', in David Chambers and Jane Martineau (eds), *Splendours of the Gonzaga* (London, 1981), p.28.

31 Mary Hollingsworth, 'Alberti: A courtier and his patrons', in Cesare Mozzarelli, Robert Oresko and Leandro Venturi (eds), *La Corte di Mantova nell'età di Andrea Mantegna* (Rome, 1997), passim.

32 Borsi, *Leon Battista Alberti*, p.142.

33 Vasić Vatovec, *Luca Fancelli architetto*, p.86 (27 February 1460); on the Virgilio, see Burns, 'The Gonzaga and Renaissance Architecture', p.29 and n.17.

34 David S. Chambers, 'Sant'Andrea at Mantua and Gonzaga Patronage 1460–72', *Journal of the Warburg and Courtauld Institutes*, 40 (1977), p.103.

35 Chambers, 'Sant'Andrea at Mantua', pp.100–9.

36 Borsi, *Leon Battista Alberti*, p.154.

37 Ibid., p.149.

38 Vasić Vatovec, *Luca Fancelli architetto*, p.91 (27 December 1463).

39 Ibid., p.135 (2 August 1475).

40 Borsi, *Leon Battista Alberti*, p.163.

41 Ibid., p.163.

42 Vasić Vatovec, *Luca Fancelli architetto*, p.97.

43 Bourne, 'The art of diplomacy', p.152; Syson and Gordon, *Pisanello*, pp.116–17.

44 Rodolfo Signorini, 'Acquisitions for Ludovico II Gonzaga's library', *Journal of the Warburg and Courtauld Institutes*, 44 (1981), p.181.

45 Vasić Vatovec, *Luca Fancelli architetto*, p.181.

46 Ibid., p.180.

47 Bourne, 'The art of diplomacy', p.158; Chambers, 'Sant'Andrea at Mantua', p.101 n.13.

48 Rodolfo Signorini, 'A dog named Rubino', *Journal of the Warburg and Courtauld Institutes*, 41 (1978), passim.

49 Chambers and Martineau, *Splendours of the Gonzaga*, pp.118–21 cat. 29.

50 Swain, 'The wages of peace', pp.448–9.

51 Ibid., pp.449–50.

52 Chambers, *Renaissance Cardinal*, p.23 n.156.

53 David S. Chambers, 'A Condottiere and his books: Gianfrancesco Gonzaga (1446–96)', *Journal of the Warburg and Courtauld Institutes*, 70 (2007), p.37 n.24.

54 Molly Bourne, *Francesco II Gonzaga. The Soldier-Prince as Patron* (Rome, 2008), p.30 n.2.

55 Chambers, *Renaissance Cardinal*, p.20 n.133.

56 Chambers, 'The housing problems of Cardinal Francesco Gonzaga', pp.22–3.

57 Chambers, *Renaissance Cardinal*, p.14.

58 David S. Chambers, 'Bartolomeo Marasca, master of Cardinal Gonzaga's household (1462–1469)', *Aevum*, 63 (1989), pp.275–6.

59 Chambers, *Renaissance Cardinal*, p.6.

60 Chambers, 'Virtù militare del Cardinale Francesco Gonzaga', p.215.

61 Chambers, *Renaissance Cardinal*, pp.7, 9.

62 Chambers, 'Sant'Andrea at Mantua', pp.110, 124–5 doc.18.

63 Ibid., p.111.

64 Vasić Vatovec, *Luca Fancelli architetto*, pp.119–20.

65 Ibid., p.120.

66 Chambers, *Renaissance Cardinal*, p.76 n.211.

67 Chambers, 'Sant'Andrea at Mantua', pp.111, 126 doc.21.

68 Chambers, 'Cardinal Francesco Gonzaga in Florence', p.23.

69 Chambers, 'Sant'Andrea at Mantua', pp.113–14 and doc.23.

70 Chambers, *Renaissance Cardinal*, p.24.

71 Ibid., pp.105–10.

72 Ibid., pp.60–4.

73 Ibid., pp.37 n.7, 78 n.221.

74 Ibid., p.78 n.223.

75 Ibid., pp.115–16.

4   CONSPIRACY AND GREED

1 Janet Ross, *Lives of the Early Medici as Told in Their Correspondence* (London, 1910), pp.205–7.

2 Cecil H. Clough, 'Federigo da Montefeltro: The good Christian prince', *Bulletin of the John Rylands University Library of Manchester*, 67 (1984), p.327; Dennistoun, *Memoirs of the Dukes of Urbino*, 1:51.

3 Clough, 'Federico da Montefeltro and the Kings of Naples', p.162.

4 Pernis and Schneider, *Federico da Montefeltro*, pp.14–15; C. W. Westfall, 'Chivalric declaration: The Palazzo Ducale in Urbino as a political statement', in H. Millon and L. Nochlin (eds), *Art and Architecture in the Service of Politics* (Cambridge, MA, 1978), p.22.

5 Pernis and Schneider, *Federico da Montefeltro*, p.29.

6 Clough, 'Federico da Montefeltro and the Kings of Naples', pp.158–9.

7 Ibid., p.119.

8 Ibid., p.118 n.27.

9 condottieridiventura.it (Federigo da Montefeltro).

10 Ryder, *Kingdom of Naples*, p.265.

11 Clough, 'Federico da Montefeltro and the Kings of Naples', pp.122–3.

12 DBI, 'Ferdinando I d'Aragona, re di Napoli'.

13 Carol M. Richardson, 'Francesco Todeschini Piccolomini (1439–1503), Sant'Eustachio and the Consorteria Piccolomini', in Mary Hollingsworth and Carol M. Richardson (eds.), *The Possessions of the Cardinal. Politics, Piety and Art 1450–1700* (University Park, 2010), p.46.

14 Pastor, *History of the Popes*, 3:104–05.

15 Ibid., 3:149–50.

16 Clough, 'Federico da Montefeltro and the Kings of Naples', p.132 n.81.

17 Ibid., p.129.

18 DBI, 'Ferdinando I d'Aragona, re di Napoli'.

19 Pastor, *History of the Popes*, 3:338.

20 Filangieri, 'Rassegna critica', 4:30–1.

21 Ibid., 2:68–9; Hersey, *The Aragonese Arch*, p.77.

22 Hersey, *The Aragonese Arch*, pp.42–4.

23 Ibid., p.41.

24 Bentley, *Politics and Culture*, pp.62–3.

25 Atlas, *Music at the Aragonese Court*, p.73.

26 Ibid., p.52.

27 Bentley, *Politics and Culture*, p.77.

28 Ibid., p.99.

29 Ibid., pp.127–30.

30 Giovanni Pontano, 'Ioannis Ioviani Pontani to Chariteo: On splendour', *Journal of Design History*, 15 (2002), p.227.

31 Clough, 'Federico da Montefeltro and the Kings of Naples', p.116.

32 Vespasiano, *Memoirs*, pp.108–9.

33 Ryder, *Kingdom of Naples*, pp.73–74 and n.122.

34 Michael Mallett, 'Diplomacy and war in later fifteenth-century Italy', in Gian Carlo Garfagnini (ed.), *Lorenzo de' Medici. Studi* (Florence, 1992), p.249.

35 Sabine Eiche (ed.), *Ordine et officii de casa de lo illustrissimo Signor Duca de Urbino* (Urbino, 1999), pp.98–101.

36 Luciano Cheles, *The Studiolo of Urbino: An Iconographic Investigation* (Wiesbaden, 1986), p.10.

37 Dennistoun, *Memoirs of the Dukes of Urbino*, 1:131.

38 Ibid., 1:132–3.

39 Clough, 'Federico da Montefeltro and the Kings of Naples', p.148.

40 P. Rotondi, *The Ducal Palace at Urbino*, 2 vols (London, 1950), 1:109; Martines, *Power and Imagination*, p.310.

41 Martines, *Power and Imagination*, p.310.

42 Clough, 'Federigo da Montefeltro's Artistic Patronage', pp.8–10.

43 Cecil H. Clough, 'The library of the Dukes of Urbino', *Librarium*, 9 (1966), p.102; Vespasiano, *Memoirs*, pp.102–4.

44 Pastor, *History of the Popes*, 4:214 n.

45 C. Corvisieri, 'Il trionfo romano di Eleonora d'Aragona nel Giugno del 1473', *Archivio della Società Romana per la Storia Patria*, 1 (1878), 2:653.

46 Corvisieri, 'Il trionfo romano di Eleonora d'Aragona', 2:648–52.

47 Welch, 'Women as patrons', p.20.

48 Pastor, *History of the Popes*, 4:254.

49 Ibid., 4:247–48 n.

50 Egmont Lee, *Sixtus IV and Men of Letters* (Rome, 1978), pp.32–3 n.90, 147–8 n.108.

51 Jacqueline Marie Musacchio, *The Art and Ritual of Childbirth in Renaissance Italy* (New Haven and London, 1999), p.21.

52 Clough, 'The library of the Dukes of Urbino', p.102.

53 Alison Wright, 'The myth of Hercules', in Gian Carlo Garfagnini (ed.), *Lorenzo il Magnifico e il suo mondo* (Florence, 1994), p.332; F. W. Kent, *Lorenzo de' Medici and the Art of Magnificence* (Baltimore and London, 2004), pp.50–1.

54 Pastor, *History of the Popes*, 4:249–50.

55 Ibid., 4:261.

56 Charles M.Rosenberg, 'The double portrait of Federigo and Guidobaldo da Montefeltro: Power, wisdom and dynasty', in Giorgio Cerboni Baiardi, Giorgio Chittolini, and Piero Floriani (eds.), *Federigo di Montefeltro: Le Arti* (Rome, 1986), passim.

57 Lauro Martines, *April Blood* (London, 2003), p.103.

58 Ibid., p.104.

59 Pastor, *History of the Popes*, 4:279.

60 Martines, *April Blood*, p.100.

61 Pastor, *History of the Popes*, 4:290.

62 Martines, *April Blood*, p.152.

63 Ibid., p.153.

64 Ibid., p.155.

65 Riccardo Fubini, 'Federico da Montefeltro e la congiura dei Pazzi: politica e propaganda alla luce di nuovi documenti', in Giorgio Cerboni Baiardi, Giorgio Chittolini and Piero Floriani (eds), *Federico di Montefeltro. Lo stato. Le arti. La cultura* (Rome, 1986), pp.462–6 doc.5.

66 Marcello Simonetta, 'Federico da Montefeltro contro Firenze: Retroscena inediti della congiura dei Pazzi', *Archivio Storico Italiano*, 161 (2003), p.270 n.22.

67 Ibid., p.265 n.9.

68 Ibid., pp.264–7.

69 Ibid., p.266.

70 Ibid., p.270 n.22.

71 Dennistoun, *Memoirs of the Dukes of Urbino*, 1:236.

72 A. S. Weller, *Francesco di Giorgio 1439–1501* (Chicago, 1943), p.347 doc.23; George L. Hersey, *Alfonso II and the Artistic Renewal of Naples 1485–95* (New Haven and London, 1969), p.73.

73 Pastor, *History of the Popes*, 4:334; Bentley, *Politics and Culture*, p.29.

74 Bentley, *Politics and Culture*, p.66.

75 Pastor, *History of the Popes*, 4:335.

76 Chambers, *Popes, Cardinals and War*, p.78.

77 Martines, *April Blood*, p.7.

78 Mallett, 'Diplomacy and war in later fifteenth-century Italy', p.247.

79 Ibid., p.248.

80 Clough, 'Federigo da Montefeltro: The good Christian prince', pp.294–300.

81 On the commission for the church and altarpiece, see Clough, 'Federigo da Montefeltro: The good Christian prince', pp.317–22.

82 Clough, 'Federico da Montefeltro and the Kings of Naples', p.160.

83 Bentley, *Politics and Culture*, pp.32–3; Hersey, *Alfonso II and the Artistic Renewal of Naples*, p.4.

84 Hersey, *Alfonso II and the Artistic Renewal of Naples*, p.23 n.22.

85 Hersey, *Alfonso II and the Artistic Renewal of Naples*, pp.71–2.

86 Ibid., p.77.

87 Johannes Burchard, *Liber Notarum*, abridged in *Dans le Secret des Borgia* (Paris, 2003), p.99.

88 Bernardino Zambotti, *Diario ferrarese dal anno 1476 sino al 1504*, in *Rerum Italicarum Scriptores*, new series, vol.24 pt. 7 (Bologna, 1928), p.231.

89 Alessandro Benedetti, *Diario de bello Carolino*, ed. and trans. Dorothy M. Schullian (New York, 1967), p.67.

5 NEST OF VIPERS

1 Cecilia M. Ady, *A History of Milan under the Sforza* (London, 1907), p.114.

2 Ibid., p.121.

3 Ibid., p.124.

4 Burchard, *Liber Notarum*, p.48.

5 Elizabeth McGrath, 'Ludovico il Moro and his Moors', *Journal of the Warburg and Courtauld Institutes*, 65 (2002), passim.

6 Paolo Giovio, *Notable Men and Women of our Time*, trans. Kenneth Gouwens (Cambridge, MA, 2013), p.141.

7 DBI, 'Ascanio Maria Sforza'.

8 Marco Pellegrini, *Ascanio Maria Sforza: La parabola politica di un cardinale-principe del Rinascimento* (Rome, 2002), p.137.

9 Jill Pederson, 'Henrico Boscano's *Isola beata*: New evidence for the Academia Leonardi Vinci in Renaissance Milan', *Renaissance Studies*, 22 (2008).

10 Ianziti, 'The rise of Sforza historiography', p.80; McGrath, 'Ludovico il Moro and his Moors', p.75.

11 Richard Schofield, 'Leonardo's Milanese architecture: Career, sources and graphic techniques', *Achademia Leonardi Vinci*, 4 (1991), p.114.

12 Ibid., pp.113–16.

13 Evelyn Samuels Welch, *Art and Authority in Renaissance Milan* (New Haven and London, 1995), p.177.

14 Richard Schofield, 'Ludovico il Moro and Vigevano', *Arte Lombarda*, 62 (1986), pp.116–17.

15 Richard Schofield, 'Florentine and Roman elements in Bramante's Milanese architecture', in *Florence and Milan: Comparisons and Relations* (Florence, 1989), p.213.

16 Schofield, 'Ludovico il Moro', p.103.

17 Ibid., pp.96–7.

18 Ibid., p.118.

19 Richard Schofield, 'A humanist description of the architecture for the wedding of Hian Galeazzo Sforza and Isabella d'Aragona (1489)', *Papers of the British School in Rome*, 56 (1988), pp.217–18.

20 Julian Kliemann, *Gesta Dipinte: la grande decorazione nelle dimore italiane dal Quattrocento al Seicento* (Milan, 1993), p.13.

21 McGrath, 'Ludovico il Moro and his Moors', p.71 n.15.

22 Schofield, 'A humanist description', pp.215, 230.

23 Matteo Duni, 'Impotence, witchcraft and politics: A Renaissance case', in Sara F. Matthews-Grieco (ed.), *Cuckoldry, Impotence and Adultery in Europe (15th-17th Century)* (Farnham, 2014), p.85; on the dowry, see DBI, 'Isabella d'Aragona, duchessa di Milano'.

24 Kate Trauman Steinitz, 'The voyage of Isabella of Aragon: from Naples to Milan, January 1489', *Bibliothèque d'Humanisme et Renaissance*, 23 (1961), p.22.

25 Duni, 'Impotence, witchcraft and politics', p.86.

26 Ibid., pp.85–6.

27 Meredith K. Ray, 'Impotence and corruption: Sexual function and dysfunction in Early Modern books of secrets', in Sara F. Matthews-Grieco (ed.), *Cuckoldry, Impotence and Adultery in Europe (15th- 17th Century)* (Farnham, 2014), pp.129–31.

28 Duni, 'Impotence, witchcraft and politics', p.86.

29 Ibid., p.92.

30 Ibid., pp.92–3.

31 Welch, 'Women as patrons', pp.22, 31 n.16.

32 McGrath, 'Ludovico il Moro and his Moors', p.72.

33 Welch, *Art and Authority in Renaissance Milan*, pp.223–35.

34 Jacqueline Marie Musacchio, 'Weasels and pregnancy in Renaissance Italy', *Renaissance Studies*, 15 (2001), pp.173–5.

35 Pellegrini, *Ascanio Maria Sforza*, p.403; Martines, *Power and Imagination*, p.310.

36 Pellegrini, *Ascanio Maria Sforza*, p.39.

37 Pastor, *History of the Popes*, 5:285 n.

38 Francesco Guicciardini, *Storia d'Italia*, 6 vols (Rome, 1967), 1:2.

39 Pastor, *History of the Popes*, 5:532–33 doc.8.

40 Ibid., 5:380.

41 Burchard, *Liber Notarum*, pp.42–3.

42 Ibid., p.55.

43 Welch, *Art and Authority in Renaissance Milan*, pp.225–7.

44 Cecilia M. Ady, 'Morals and manners of the Quattrocento', in George Holmes (ed.), *Art and Politics in Renaissance Italy* (Oxford, 1993), pp.5–6.

45 Rachel Erlanger, *Lucrezia Borgia* (London, 1978), p.36.

46 Burchard, *Liber Notarum*, p.96.

47 Ady, *A History of Milan under the Sforza*, p.145.

48 Francesco Guicciardini, *Storie Fiorentine* (Milan, 1998), pp.189–90.

49 Pastor, *History of the Popes*, 5:409–10.

50 Ibid., 5:415 n.

51 A. Luzio and R. Renier, 'Delle relazioni di Isabella d'Este Gonzaga con Ludovico e Beatrice Sforza', *Archivio Storico Lombardo*, 17 (1890).

52 Martines, *Power and Imagination*, p.312.

53 Ady, *A History of Milan under the Sforza*, p.149.

54 DBI, 'Ascanio Maria Sforza'.

55 Burchard, *Liber Notarum*, p.106.

56 Pastor, *History of the Popes*, 5:424.

57 Pellegrini, *Ascanio Maria Sforza*, p.532.

58 Ibid., p.532.

59 Giovio, *Notable Men and Women of our Time*, p.55.

60 Commines, *Mémoires*, 7:6.

61 Duni, 'Impotence, witchcraft and politics', p.95.

62 Benedetti, *Diario de bello Carolino*, p.206 n.31.

63 Burchard, *Liber Notarum*, p.136.

64 Pastor, *History of the Popes*, 5:450.

65 Benedetti, *Diario de bello Carolino*, p.67.

66 Pastor, *History of the Popes*, 5:479–80.

67 Guicciardini, *Storia d'Italia*, 1:11.

68 Michael Mallett and Christine Shaw, *The Italian Wars 1494–1559* (Oxford, 2012), p.182.

69 J. R. Hale, 'War and public opinion in Renaissance Italy', in E. F. Jacob (ed.), *Italian Renaissance Studies* (London, 1960), p.95.

70 Guicciardini, *Storia d'Italia*, 2:13.

71 Burchard, *Liber Notarum*, pp.243, 284, 304.

72 Ibid., p.227.

73 Luzio and Renier, 'Delle relazioni di Isabella d'Este Gonzaga'.

74 Daniel M. Bueno de Mesquita, 'The Conscience of the Prince', in George Holmes (ed.), *Art and Politics in Renaissance Italy* (Oxford, 1993), p.164.

75 Welch, *Art and Authority in Renaissance Milan*, p.222.

76 Pastor, *History of the Popes*, 5:501.

77 Ibid., 5:498–9.

78 Marco Pellegrini, 'A turning-point in the history of the factional system in the Sacred College: The power of the pope and cardinals in the age of Alexander VI', in Gianvittorio Signorotto and Maria Antonietta Visceglia (eds), *Court and Politics in Papal Rome 1492–1700* (Cambridge, 2002), p.22.

79 Burchard, *Liber Notarum*, p.240.

80 Pastor, *History of the Popes*, 5:520.

81 Welch, *Art and Authority in Renaissance Milan*, p.222.

82 Pastor, *History of the Popes*, 6:63.

83 Sarah Cockram, 'Interspecies understanding: Exotic animals and their handlers at the Italian Renaissance court', *Renaissance Studies*, 31 (2017), p.284.

84 Burchard, *Liber Notarum*, p.338.

85 Ibid., p.441.

---

6   SURVIVORS

1 Zambotti, *Diario ferrarese*, p.314.

2 Tuohy, *Herculean Ferrara*, pp.243, 245.

3 Bourne, *Francesco II Gonzaga*, p.34; Evelyn Samuels Welch, *Shopping in the Renaissance* (New Haven and London, 2005), pp.253–4.

4 A. Luzio and R. Renier, *Mantova e Urbino, Isabella d'Este ed Elisabetta Gonzaga nelle relazione famigliare, e nelle vicende politiche* (Turin, 1893), p.70 n.1.

5 Carolyn James, 'Marriage by correspondence: Politics and domesticity in the letters of Isabella d'Este and Francesco Gonzaga, 1490–1519', *Renaissance Quarterly*, 65 (2012), p.332 n.35.

6 Molly Bourne, 'Renaissance husbands and wives as patrons of art: The *Camerini* of Isabella d'Este and Francesco II Gonzaga', in

Sheryl E. Reiss and David G. Wilkins (eds), *Beyond Isabella. Secular Women Patrons in Renaissance Italy* (Kirksville, 2001), p.94.

7 Zambotti, *Diario ferrarese*, pp.252–3.

8 Benedetti, *Diario de bello Carolino*, p.101.

9 Ibid., pp.85, 89; Zambotti, *Diario ferrarese*, p.253.

10 Benedetti, *Diario de bello Carolino*, p.107.

11 DBI, 'Francesco II Gonzaga, marchese di Mantova'.

12 DBI, 'Isabella d'Este, marchesa di Mantova'.

13 Creighton E.Gilbert, *Italian Art 1400–1500. Sources and Documents* (Eaglewood Cliffs, 1980), pp.135–6.

14 Welch, *Shopping in the Renaissance*, pp.256–7.

15 Tuohy, *Herculean Ferrara*, p.84; Cockram, 'Interspecies understanding', pp.282–4.

16 Musacchio, *The Art and Ritual of Childbirth*, p.39.

17 Clark.

18 Welch, *Shopping in the Renaissance*, p.250.

19 Ibid., p.251.

20 Ibid., p.260.

21 Ibid., p.247.

22 Pastor, *History of the Popes*, 6:109.

23 Diane Yvonne Ghirardo, 'Lucrezia Borgia as entrepreneur', *Renaissance Quarterly*, 61 (2008), p.59.

24 Tuohy, *Herculean Ferrara*, p.277.

25 Giulia Torello-Hill, 'The exegesis of Vitruvius and the creation of theatrical spaces in Renaissance Ferrara', *Renaissance Studies*, 29 (2014), p.230; Tuohy, *Herculean Ferrara*, pp.117–19.

26 Maria Serena Mazzi, 'La fame e la paura della fame', in Jadranka Bentini et al. (eds), *A tavola con il principe* (Ferrara, 1988), p.165.

27 Luzio and Renier, *Mantova e Urbino*, p.125.

28 William F.Prizer, 'Isabella d'Este and Lucrezia Borgia as patrons of music: The frottola at Mantua and Ferrara', *Journal of the American Musicological Society*, 38 (1985), p.5 n.14.

29 Evelyn Samuels Welch, 'Art on the edge: Hair and hands in Renaissance Italy', *Renaissance Studies*, 23 (2009), pp. 245–7.

30 Zambotti, *Diario ferrarese*, p.324; Prizer, 'Isabella d'Este and Lucrezia Borgia', pp.5–7.

31 Shephard, Tim, 'Constructing Isabella d'Este's musical decorum in the visual sphere', *Renaissance Studies*, 25 (2011), pp.691–3.

32 Prizer, 'Isabella d'Este and Lucrezia Borgia', pp.11–14; see Welch, *Shopping in the Renaissance*, p.255 for a different interpretation.

33 Zambotti, *Diario ferrarese*, p.342.

34 Giovio, *Notable Men and Women of our Time*, pp.131–3.

35 Hale, 'War and public opinion in Renaissance Italy', p.98.

36 Giovanni Maria Zerbinati, *Croniche di Ferrara* (Ferrara, 1989), p.62.

37 Zambotti, *Diario ferrarese*, p.356 n.5.

38 Luzio and Renier, *Mantova e Urbino*, p.157.

39 Mallett and Shaw, *The Italian Wars*, p.82.

40 Zambotti, *Diario ferrarese*, p.287.

41 Chambers and Martineau, *Splendours of the Gonzaga*, p.147 cat. 75.

42 Bourne, 'The art of diplomacy', p.162.

43 David S. Chambers and Brian Pullan, *Venice. A Documentary History 1450–1630* (Oxford, 1992), pp.405–6.

44 Bourne, Molly, 'Towards the study of the Renaissance courts of the Gonzaga', *Quaderni di Palazzo Te*, 3 (1996), pp.80–1.

45 Bourne, 'Renaissance husbands and wives', p.108.

46 Gilbert, *Italian Art 1400–1500*, pp.140–1.

47 Bourne, 'Renaissance husbands and wives', pp.99, 116 n.26.

48 Ibid., p.103.

49 Ibid., p.108.

50 Shephard, 'Constructing Isabella d'Este's musical decorum', pp.699–701.

51 Bourne, 'Renaissance husbands and wives', pp.96–7.

52 C. M. Brown, '"Lo insaciabile desiderio nostro de cose antique": New documents on Isabella d'Este's collection of antiquities', in Cecil H. Clough (ed.), *Cultural Aspects of the Italian Renaissance: Essays in Honour of Paul Oskar Kristeller* (Manchester and New York, 1976), p.328.

53 Ibid., p.324.

54 Clark.

55 Brown, 'Lo insaciabile desiderio', passim.

56 Bourne, 'The art of diplomacy', pp.166–7.

57 David S. Chambers, 'The enigmatic eminence of Cardinal Sigismondo Gonzaga', Renaissance Studies, 16 (2002), pp.330, 333.

58 James, 'Marriage by correspondence', p.334.

59 Cashman, 'The problem of audience in Mantua', p.362.

60 Burchard, *Liber Notarum*, p.374.

61 Luzio and Renier, *Mantova e Urbino*, pp.193–5.

62 Cockram, 'Interspecies understanding', p.290.

63 Prizer, 'Isabella d'Este and Lucrezia Borgia', p.8.

64 Christine Shaw, *Julius II. The Warrior Pope* (Oxford, 1996), pp.258–9.

65 Ady, 'Morals and manners of the Quattrocento', p.13.

66 Pastor, *History of the Popes*, 6:342.

67 Luzio and Renier, *Mantova e Urbino*, p.206.

68 Pastor, *History of the Popes*, 6:339 n.

69 Guicciardini, *Storia d'Italia*, 2:9.

70 Zerbinati, *Croniche di Ferrara*, pp.104–5.

71 Chambers, 'The enigmatic eminence of Cardinal Sigismondo Gonzaga', pp.343–4 & n.100.

72 Zerbinati, *Croniche di Ferrara*, p.116.

73 Pastor, *History of the Popes*, 6:400.

74 Ibid., 6:420 n.

75 Bourne, 'Renaissance husbands and wives', p.107.

76 Pastor, *History of the Popes*, 7:103.

77 Anthony B. Cashman III, 'Performance anxiety: Federico Gonzaga at the court of Francis I and the uncertainty of ritual action', *The Sixteenth-Century Journal*, 33 (2002), p.336.

78 J. R. Hale, 'The early development of the bastion: An Italian chronology c.1450 – c.1534', in J. R. Hale, J. R. L. Highfield and B. Smalley (eds), *Europe in the Late Middle Ages* (London, 1965), p.490.

79 Dana Goodgal, 'The Camerino of Alfonso I d'Este', *Art History*, 1 (1978), p.175.

80 Ludovico Ariosto, *Orlando Furioso* (Harmondsworth, 1975), 13:69–70.

81 Charles Hope, 'Artists, patrons, and advisors in the Italian Renaissance', in G. F. Lytle and S. Orgel (eds), *Patronage in the Renaissance* (Princeton, 1981), p.315 and n.41; Charles Hope, 'Cacce e baccanali nei Camerini d'Este', in Jadranka Bentini (ed.), *Una corte nel Rinascimento* (Milan, 2004), p.170.

82 Prizer, 'Isabella d'Este and Lucrezia Borgia', p.3.

83 Ghirardo, 'Lucrezia Borgia as entrepreneur', p.56.

84 Ibid., pp.60–5 and passim.

85 Pastor, *History of the Popes*, 8:41 n.

86 Ibid., 9:26 n.

87 Bestor, Jane Fair, 'Titian's portrait of Laura Eustochia: The decorum of female beauty and the motif of the black page', *Renaissance Studies*, 17 (2003), pp.637–8.

88 Ibid., p.644.

89 Pastor, *History of the Popes*, 9:495 doc.34.

90 A. Luzio, *Isabella d'Este e il Sacco di Roma* (Milan, 1908), p.15.

91 Ibid., p.13.

92 Pastor, *History of the Popes*, 9:502 doc.44.

93 Ibid., 9:384 n.4.

94 Luzio, *Isabella d'Este e il Sacco di Roma*, p.77.

95 For details of the sack, see André Chastel, *The Sack of Rome, 1527* (Princeton, 1983).

96 Pastor, *History of the Popes*, 9:506 doc.49.

97 Ibid., 9: 504–5 doc.48.

98 Ibid., 9:411.

99 Chastel, *The Sack of Rome*, p.97.

7 A NEW POLITICAL ORDER

1 Marin Sanudo, *Diarii*, ed. R. Fulin et al. (Venice, 1879–1903), 51:398–99; Bonner Mitchell, *The Majesty of State: Triumphal Progresses of Foreign Sovereigns in Renaissance Italy (1494–1600)* (Florence, 1986), p.136.

2 Pastor, *History of the Popes*, 10:68.

3 Sanudo, *Diarii*, 51:399–403.

4 Salvador de Madariaga, *Carlo Quinto* (Novara, 1973), pp.296–7.

5 Chambers, *Popes, Cardinals and War*, p.121; Shaw, *Julius II*, p.269.

6 Dennistoun, *Memoirs of the Dukes of Urbino*, 3:52.

7 Luzio and Renier, *Mantova e Urbino*, p.206.

8 Shaw, *Julius II*, p.278.

9 Ibid., pp.286–7.

10 Antonio Pinelli and Orietta Rossi, *Genga architetto. aspetti della cultura urbinate del primo 500* (Rome, 1971), p.186 n.33.

11 Giorgio Vasari, *Le vite de' più eccelenti pittori, sculturi, et architettori*, ed. Gaetano Milanese, 9 vols (Florence, 1906), 7:192.

12 Georg Gronau, 'Die Kunstbestrebungen der Herzöge von Urbino', *Jahrbuch der*

preussischen Kunstsammlungen, 27 (1906), p.5 doc.3.

13 Luzio and Renier, *Mantova e Urbino*, pp.228–9.

14 Zerbinati, *Croniche di Ferrara*, p.140.

15 Luzio and Renier, *Mantova e Urbino*, p.230.

16 Dennistoun, *Memoirs of the Dukes of Urbino*, 2:358–60.

17 Ibid., 2:361–2.

18 Ibid., 2:366.

19 Giovio, *Notable Men and Women of our Time*, p.133.

20 Ibid., pp.135–7.

21 Shaw, *Julius II*, p.286.

22 Chambers, *Popes, Cardinals and War*, p.129.

23 Chambers, 'The enigmatic eminence of Cardinal Sigismondo Gonzaga', pp.352–3.

24 Welch, 'Art on the edge', p.254.

25 Cashman, 'Performance anxiety', p.342.

26 Ibid., p.343.

27 Luzio and Renier, *Mantova e Urbino*, p.241 n.5.

28 Ibid., p.243 n.1.

29 DBI, 'Federigo II Gonzaga, marchese di Mantova'.

30 Dennistoun, *Memoirs of the Dukes of Urbino*, 2:405.

31 Vasari, *Le vite de' più eccelenti pittori*, 6:322.

32 Ibid., 6:413–14.

33 Pinelli and Rossi, *Genga architetto*, p.115.

34 Nicholas Adams, 'Censored anecdotes from Francesco Maria I della Rovere's *Discorsi Militari*', *Renaissance Studies*, 13 (1999), p.56.

35 Ibid., p.56.

36 Dennistoun, *Memoirs of the Dukes of Urbino*, 2:426–7.

37 J. R. Hale, 'Renaissance armies and political control: The Venetian proveditorial system 1509–1529', *The Journal of Italian History*, 2 (1979), p.30.

38 Sanudo, *Diarii*, 51:369–72.

39 Ibid., 51: 432–33.

40 Ibid., 51:428.

41 Geoffrey Parker, *Emperor. A New Life of Charles V* (New Haven and London, 2019), p.191 and pl.13.

42 Konrad Eisenbichler, 'Charles V in Bologna: The self-fashioning of a man and a city', *Renaissance Studies*, 13 (1999), p.436.

43 Luigi Gonzaga, *Cronaca del soggiorno di Carlo V in Italia (dal 26 luglio 1529 al 25 aprile 1530)*, ed. Giacinto Romano (Milan, 1892), p.190.

44 Eisenbichler, 'Charles V in Bologna', p.435.

45 Giovio, *Notable Men and Women of our Time*, p.137.

46 Gonzaga, *Cronaca del soggiorno di Carlo V in Italia*, p.244.

47 Ibid., p.257.

48 Ibid., p.243.

49 E. H. Gombrich, '"That rare Italian Master…": Giulio Romano, court architect, painter and impresario', in David Chambers and Jane Martineau (eds), *Splendours of the Gonzaga* (London, 1981)', p.81.

50 Maria F. Maurer, 'A love that burns: Eroticism, torment and identity at the Palazzo Te', *Renaissance Studies*, 30 (2016), p.375.

51 Valerie Taylor, 'Banquet plate and Renaissance culture: A day in the life', *Renaissance Studies*, 19 (2005), p.622.

52 Cristoforo di Messisbugo, *Banchetti Composizioni di vivande e aparecchio generale* (Venice, 1960), p.48.

53 William F. Prizer, 'North Italian Courts, 1460–1540', in Iain Fenlon (ed.), *Man and Music: The Renaissance* (London, 1989), p.150.

54 Deanna Shemek, 'Aretino's "Marescalco": Marriage woes and the duke of Mantua', *Renaissance Quarterly*, 16 (2002), passim.

55 Bourne, 'The art of diplomacy', pp.170–2.

56 Bette L. Talvacchia, , 'Homer, Greek heroes and Hellenism in Giulio Romano's *Hall of Troy*', *Journal of the Warburg and Courtauld Institutes*, 51 (1988), pp.235–6.

57 Chastel, *The Sack of Rome*, pp.98–9.

58 Guido Rebecchini, 'Exchanges of works of art at the court of Federico II Gonzaga with an appendix on Flemish art', *Renaissance Studies*, 16 (2002), p.383.

59 C. M. Brown, 'Documents regarding Duke Federico II Gonzaga's interest in Flemish art', *Source: Notes in the History of Art*, 11 (1992), p.18.

60 Rebecchini, 'Exchanges of works of art', p.385.

61 Charles Hope, 'Titian's life and times', in *Titian* (London, 2003), p.19.

62 Vasari, *Le vite de' più eccelenti pittori*, 7:444.

63 Charles Hope, 'Tiziano e la committenza', in *Tiziano* (Venice, 1990), p.81.

64 Pinelli and Rossi, *Genga architetto*, pp.185–6 n.32.

65 Kliemann, *Gesta Dipinte*, pp.21–8.

66 Pinelli and Rossi, *Genga architetto*, pp.315–17.

67 Ibid., p.319 (22 August 1533).

68 Dennistoun, *Memoirs of the Dukes of Urbino*, 3:46.

---

8   THE NEW ROME

1   Pietro Casola, *Canon Pietro Casola's Pilgrimage to Jerusalem in the Year 1494*, ed. M. Margaret Newett (Manchester, 1907), p.143.

2   Patricia Fortini Brown, *Private Lives in Renaissance Venice* (New Haven, 2004), p.150.

3   Chambers and Pullan, *Venice*, p.241.

4   Deborah Howard, *Jacopo Sansovino. Architecture and Patronage in Renaissance Venice* (New Haven and London, 1987), p.9.

5   Hale, 'Renaissance armies and political control', pp.15–16.

6   Ibid., p.23.

7   Ibid., p.19.

8   Sanudo, *Diarii*, 9:72–3.

9   Giovio, *Notable Men and Women of our Time*, p.99.

10   Hale, 'Renaissance armies and political control', p.22.

11   Robert Finlay, 'Fabius Maximus in Venice: Doge Andrea Gritti, the war of Cambrai, and the rise of Habsburg Hegemony, 1509–1530', *Renaissance Quarterly*, 53 (2000), p.1002 n.68.

12   Iain Fenlon, *The Ceremonial City. History, Memory and Myth in Renaissance Venice* (New Haven, 2007), p.80.

13   Frederic C. Lane, *Venice. A Maritime Republic* (Baltimore, 1973), p.237.

14   Felix Gilbert, *The Pope, His Banker, and Venice* (Cambridge, MA, 1980), pp.127–8 n.40.

15   Chambers and Pullan, *Venice*, p.143.

16   Gilbert, *The Pope, His Banker, and Venice*, p.30.

17   Ibid., p.31.

18   Felix Gilbert, 'Venice in the crisis of the League of Cambrai', in J. R. Hale (ed.), *Renaissance Venice* (Totowa, 1973), pp.287, 288.

19   Ibid., p.278.

20   Chambers and Pullan, *Venice*, pp.188–9.

21   Sanudo, *Diarii*, 17:506.

22   Gilbert, *The Pope, His Banker, and Venice*, p.25.

23   Manfredo Tafuri, *Venice and the Renaissance* (Cambridge, MA and London, 1989), p.201 n.24.

24   Chambers and Pullan, *Venice*, p.178.

25   Tafuri, *Venice and the Renaissance*, p.7; Sanudo, *Diarii*, 24:341, 28:71.

26   Burchard, *Liber Notarum*, p.353; Salvador Miranda, *The Cardinals of the Holy Roman Church (1998-2015)*, (Francesco Pisani).

27   Chambers and Pullan, *Venice*, p.251 (31 July 1527).

28   DBI, 'Andrea Gritti'.

29   Sanudo, *Diarii*, 34:159.

30   Edward Muir, 'The doge as *Primus Inter Pares*: Interregnum rites in early sixteenth-century Venice', in S. Bertelli and G. Ramakus (eds), *Essays Presented to Myron P. Gilmore* (Florence, 1978), p.154.

31   Sanudo, *Diarii*, 55:19.

32   Stella Mary Newton, *The Dress of the Venetians 1495–1525* (Aldershot, 1988), p.27.

33   Finlay, 'Fabius Maximus in Venice', p.989.

34   Andrew Hopkins, 'Architecture and *Infirmitas*. Doge Andrea Gritti and the chancel of San Marco', *Journal of the Society of Architectural Historians*, 57 (1998), p.187.

35   Ibid., p.194.

36   Sanudo, *Diarii*, 50:151–2.

37   Ibid., 50:211.

38   Ibid., 51:461–74.

39   Finlay, 'Fabius Maximus in Venice', passim.

40   Sanudo, *Diarii*, 50:59, 62.

41   Ibid., 51:466.

42   David S.Chambers, *The Imperial Age of Venice 1380–1580* (London, 1970), p.30.

43   Gonzaga, *Cronaca del soggiorno di Carlo V in Italia*, pp.168–9.

44   Lane, *Venice. A Maritime Republic*, p.309.

45   Chambers, *The Imperial Age of Venice*, pp.25–6.

46   Marilyn Perry, 'The statuario pubblico of the Venetian Republic', *Saggi e memorie di storia dell'arte*, 8 (1972), p.219 and passim.

47   Hale, 'The early development of the bastion', p.490.

48   Vasari, *Le vite de' più eccelenti pittori*, 6:343.

49   Onians, *Bearers of Meaning*, pp.271–7.

50   Chambers and Pullan, *Venice*, p.394.

51   Howard, *Jacopo Sansovino*, p.11.

52 Fenlon, *The Ceremonial City*, p.111.

53 Ibid., pp.69–70.

54 Hopkins, 'Architecture and *Infirmitas*', p.187.

55 Chambers and Pullan, *Venice*, p.409 n.52.

56 Howard, *Jacopo Sansovino*, pp.39, 41; Onians, *Bearers of Meaning*, p.288.

57 Howard, *Jacopo Sansovino*, pp.31, 165 n.76.

58 Ibid., pp.20–1.

59 Ibid., p.165 n.83.

60 Chambers and Pullan, *Venice*, p.252.

61 Douglas Lewis, 'Patterns of preference: Patronage of sixteenth-century architects by the Venetian patriciate', in G. F. Lytle and S. Orgel (eds), *Patronage in the Renaissance* (Princeton, 1981), p.368.

62 Howard, *Jacopo Sansovino*, p.159; Vasari, *Le vite de' più eccelenti pittori*, 7:95–6.

63 Tafuri, *Venice and the Renaissance*, p.3.

64 Lewis, 'Patterns of preference', p.367.

65 Howard, *Jacopo Sansovino*, pp.126–32; Manfredo Tafuri, *Ricerca del Rinascimento. Principi, città, architetti* (Turin, 1992), pp.317–27.

66 Sanudo, *Diarii*, 56:76.

67 Hopkins, 'Architecture and *Infirmitas*', p.194.

68 Sanudo, *Diarii*, 56:751–4.

69 Ibid., 56: 751–4.

70 Howard, *Jacopo Sansovino*, pp.137–8.

9   DYNASTY

1 DBI, 'Guidubaldo II Della Rovere, duca d'Urbino'.

2 Peter Partner, *The Pope's Men. The Papal Civil Service in the Renaissance* (Oxford, 1990), p.231.

3 Pastor, *History of the Popes*, 6:91–2.

4 D. Gnoli, 'Un censimento della popolazione di Roma avanti il sacco borbonico', *Archivio della Reale Società di Roma di Storia Patria*, 17 (1894), pp.387, 471.

5 Kliemann, *Gesta Dipinte*, p.37.

6 Christoph Luitpold Frommel, *Der Römische Palastbau der Hochrenaissance*, 3 vols (Rome, 1973), 2:103.

7 A. Bertolotti, '"Spese segrete e pubbliche di Paolo III', *Atti e Memorie delle RR. Deputazioni di storia patria per le provincie dell'Emilia*, 3 (1878), passim.

8 Pastor, *History of the Popes*, 11:357; Bertolotti, ''Spese segrete e pubbliche di Paolo III', p.183; Mary Hollingsworth, 'Ippolito d'Este: A cardinal and his household in Rome and Ferrara in 1566', *The Court Historian*, 5 (2000), pp.112–13.

9 Clare Robertson, *Il Gran Cardinale. Alessandro Farnese, Patron of the Arts* (New Haven, 1992), p.210.

10 Guido Rebecchini, 'After the Medici. The New Rome of Pope Paul III Farnese', *I Tatti Studies*, 11 (2007), p.163.

11 Pastor, *History of the Popes*, 11:301–2.

12 Rebecchini, 'After the Medici', p.167.

13 Bertolotti, ''Spese segrete e pubbliche di Paolo III', p.103.

14 B. Podestà, 'Carlo V a Roma', *Atti della Società Romana per Storia Patria*, 1 (1878), p.316.

15 Pastor, *History of the Popes*, 11:243–5.

16 Podestà, 'Carlo V a Roma', p.342 n.2.

17 Bertolotti, ''Spese segrete e pubbliche di Paolo III', p.186.

18 Mary Hollingsworth, *The Cardinal's Hat. Money, Ambition and Housekeeping in a Renaissance Court* (London, 2004), p.206.

19 L. Dorez, *La Cour du Pape Paul III d'après les régistres de la Trésorie Secrète*, 2 vols (Paris, 1932), 2:228.

20 Rebecchini, 'After the Medici', p.167.

21 Pastor, *History of the Popes*, 11:366.

22 Robertson, *Il Gran Cardinale*, p.158.

23 Pastor, *History of the Popes*, 12:611, 619.

24 Dorez, *La Cour du Pape Paul III*, 2:29–36.

25 Ibid., 2:10, 12, 46, 68, 108 and passim.

26 Bertolotti, ''Spese segrete e pubbliche di Paolo III', p.183.

27 Helge Gamrath, *Farnese. Pomp, Power and Politics in Renaissance Italy* (Rome, 2007), Appendix 2.

28 Frommel, *Der Römische Palastbau der Hochrenaissance*, 2:107–8 doc.43.

29 Ibid., 2:108–9 doc.46.

30 Pastor, *History of the Popes*, 12:580 n.1.

31 Frommel, *Der Römische Palastbau der Hochrenaissance*, 2:109 doc.47.

32 Sabine Eiche, 'July 1547 in Palazzo Farnese', *Mitteilungen des Kunsthistorischen Institutes in Florenz*, 33 (1989), p.400 doc.1.

33 Ibid., pp.400–1 doc.2.

34 Ibid., p.396.

35 Robertson, *Il Gran Cardinale*, p.11.

36 Roberto Zapperi, 'Alessandro Farnese, Giovanni della Casa and Titian's Danae in Naples', *Journal of the Warburg and Courtauld Institutes*, 54 (1991), pp.161–2.

37 Renato Lefevre, *Madama Margherita d'Austria (1522–1586)* (Rome, 1986), p.245.

38 Vasari, *Le vite de' più eccelenti pittori*, 7:681–2.

39 A. Ronchini, 'Giorgio Vasari alla corte del Cardinale Farnese', *Atti e Memorie delle R. Deputazioni di Storia Patria per le provincie modenesi et parmensi*, 2 (1864), pp.126–7; Vasari, *Le vite de' più eccelenti pittori*, 6:447.

40 T. C. Price Zimmerman, *Paolo Giovio. The Historian and the Crisis of Sixteenth-Century Italy* (Princeton, 1995), p.194.

41 Pastor, *History of the Popes*, 12:188.

42 Ibid., 12:218–19.

43 Ibid., 12:221.

44 Ibid., 12:675–76 doc.29.

45 Lefevre, *Madama Margherita d'Austria*, p.136.

46 Bertolotti, ''Spese segrete e pubbliche di Paolo III', p.192.

47 Ibid., p.195.

48 Ibid., pp.195–6.

49 Lefevre, *Madama Margherita d'Austria*, p.169.

50 Ibid., pp.151–2.

51 Vasari, *Le vite de' più eccelenti pittori*, 3:682, 7:56–7.

52 Robertson, *Il Gran Cardinale*, p.25.

53 Ibid., pp.38–48.

54 Ibid., p.70.

55 Ibid., p.72.

56 Giuseppe Bertini, 'Center and periphery: Art patronage in Renaissance Piacenza and Parma', in Charles M. Rosenberg (ed.), *The Court Cities of Northern Europe* (Cambridge, 2010), p.109.

57 Pastor, *History of the Popes*, 13:29 n.4.

58 Bertini, 'Center and periphery', p.110.

59 Pierre Hurtubise, 'Une vie de palais: la cour du cardinal Alexandre Farnèse vers 1563', *Renaissance and Reformation*, 16 (1992), p.39.

60 Ibid., p.42.

61 Pastor, *History of the Popes*, 20:574 n.2.

62 Ibid., 21:242.

63 Ibid., 21:242.

10 PRECEDENCE AND REFORM

1 Richard M. Tristano, 'The precedence controversy and the devolution of Ferrara: A shift in Renaissance politics', *Sixteenth-Century Journal*, 48 (2017), pp.688–90.

2 Maria Antonietta Visceglia, 'Il ceremoniale come linguaggio politico', in Maria Antonietta Visceglia and Catherine Brice (ed.), *Cérémonial et Rituel à Rome (XVIe-XIXe siècles)* (Rome, 1997), pp.126, 163 n.164.

3 Forti Grazzini, 'Gli arazzi di Ferrara', pp.198–9.

4 Candace Adelson, 'Cosimo I de' Medici and the foundation of tapestry production in Florence', in Giancarlo Garfagnini (ed.), *Firenze e la Toscana dei Medici nell'Europa del '500* (Florence, 1983), p.915.

5 Paola Barocchi and Giovanna Gaeta Bertelà, *Collezionismo mediceo. Cosimo I, Francesco I e il Cardinale Ferdinando* (Modena, 1993), pp.3 doc.1, 7–8 doc.5.

6 Andrea Gáldy, 'The Scrittoio della Calliope in the Palazzo Vecchio', *Renaissance Studies*, 19 (2005).

7 Monique Chatenet, 'Hippolyte II d'Este à la cour de France à travers la correspondance des ambassadeurs de Ferrare et de Mantoue', in Marina Cogotti and Francesco Paolo Fiore (eds), *Ippolito II d'Este. Cardinale, principe, mecenate* (Rome, 2013), p.72.

8 Guillaume Ribier, *Lettres et Mémoires d'Estat, des Roys, Princes, Ambassadeurs, et autres Ministres, sous les règnes de François premier, Henri II et François II*, 2 vols (Blois, 1667), 2:220.

9 Jean-Marc Vasseur, '1536–1550. L'irrésistable ascension d'Hippolyte le "Magnifique"', in Marina Cogotti and Francesco Paolo Fiore (eds), *Ippolito II d'Este. Cardinale, principe, mecenate* (Rome, 2013), p.117.

10 Mary Hollingsworth, 'A cardinal in Rome: Ippolito d'Este in 1560', in Jill Burke and Michael Bury (eds), *Art and Identity in Early Modern Rome* (Aldershot, 2008), pp.82–3.

11 Mary Hollingsworth, *Conclave 1559* (London, 2013), p.26.

12 Vincenzo Pacifici, *Ippolito d'Este, Cardinale di Ferrara* (Tivoli, 1920), pp.120–1 n.4.

13 Hollingsworth, *The Cardinal's Hat*, pp.176–82.

14 Hollingsworth, *Conclave 1559*, pp.31–2.

15 Hollingsworth, 'A cardinal in Rome', p.81.

16 Pacifici, *Ippolito d'Este*, p.262 n.2.

17 Hollingsworth, *Conclave 1559*, p.31.

18 Antonio Santuosso, 'An account of the election of Paul IV to the pontificate', *Renaissance Quarterly*, 31 (1978), p.490.

19 Ferdinando Petrucelli della Gattina, *Histoire Diplomatique des Conclaves*, 2 vols (Paris, 1864), 2:111.

20 Pastor, *History of the Popes*, 14:265–8.

21 Ibid., 14:99, 102.

22 Chiara Franceschini, 'La corte di Renata di Francia (1528–1560)', in Alessandra Chiappini et al. (eds), *Storia di Ferrara vol. VI: Il Rinascimento. Situazioni e personaggi* (Ferrara, 2000), pp.196–8.

23 Carmelo Occhipinti, *Carteggio d'arte degli ambasciatori estensi in Francia (1536–1553)* (Pisa, 2001), pp.327–31.

24 Agostino Lapini, *Diario Fiorentino* (Florence, 1900), pp.122, 124.

25 Ibid., pp.121–2.

26 Ibid., p.124; Gregory Murry, *The Medicean Succession. Monarchy and Sacral Politics in Duke Cosimo dei Medici's Florence* (Cambridge, MA, 2014), p.159.

27 Gabrielle Langdon, *Medici Women: Portraits of Power, Love, and Betrayal* (Toronto, 2006), p.140.

28 Ibid., p.140.

29 Ibid., p.115.

30 Hollingsworth, *Conclave 1559*, p.19.

31 George Duruy, *Le Cardinal Carlo Carafa (1519–1651)* (Paris, 1882), pp.296–97 n.4; Pastor, *History of the Popes*, 14:228–9.

32 Petrucelli della Gattina, *Histoire Diplomatique des Conclaves*, 2:118.

33 Hector de la Ferrière, *Lettres de Catherine de Médicis*, 8 vols (Paris, 1880), 1:123–4.

34 Hollingsworth, *Conclave 1559*, p.94.

35 Theodor Müller, *Das Konklave Pius' IV. 1559* (Gotha, 1889), p.33

36 Hollingsworth, *Conclave 1559*, p.125.

37 Ibid., p.204.

38 Petrucelli della Gattina, *Histoire Diplomatique des Conclaves*, 2:150.

39 Pastor, *History of the Popes*, 15:15.

40 Hollingsworth, *Conclave 1559*, pp.223–4.

41 David R. Coffin, *The Villa in the Life of Renaissance Rome* (Princeton, 1979), p.256; Andrea Gáldy, 'Lost in antiquities: Cardinal Giovanni de' Medici (1543–1562)', in Mary Hollingsworth and Carol M. Richardson (eds), *The Possessions of a Cardinal: Politics, Piety, and Art 1450–1700* (University Park, 2010), pp.156–8.

42 Hollingsworth, 'A cardinal in Rome', p.86.

43 Hollingsworth, *Conclave 1559*, p.243.

44 Hollingsworth, 'A cardinal in Rome', pp.86–7.

45 William Stenhouse, 'Visitors, display and reception in the antiquity collections of late-Renaissance Rome', *Renaissance Quarterly*, 58 (2005), p.414.

46 Michel de Montaigne, *The Complete Works. Essays, Travel Journal and Letters* (London, 2003), p.1135.

47 Ibid., p.1174.

48 On the visit, see Hollingsworth, 'A cardinal in Rome', pp.87–8.

49 Robert Williams, 'The Sala Grande in the Palazzo Vecchio and the precedence controversy between Florence and Ferrara', in Philip Jacks (ed.), *Vasari's Florence. Artists and Literati at the Medicean Court* (Cambridge, 1998), pp.166–9.

50 Tristano, 'The precedence controversy', p.688.

51 Pacifici, *Ippolito d'Este*, pp.302–4 n.1.

52 Williams, 'The Sala Grande in the Palazzo Vecchio', p.166.

53 Ibid., pp.176–7.

54 Robertson, *Il Gran Cardinale*, p.161.

55 Pastor, *History of the Popes*, 17:100.

56 Ibid., 17:55, 57.

57 Ibid., 17:86–97, 101.

58 David Quint, 'Political allegory in the *Gerusalemme Liberata*', *Renaissance Quarterly*, 43 (1990), p.12.

59 Ibid., pp.13, 14 n.19.

60 Lapini, *Diario Fiorentino*, p.152.

61 Ibid., p.156.

62 Ibid., pp.157, 160, 164.

63 Ibid., p.162.

64 Ibid., p.168.

65 Christopher F. Black, *The Italian Inquisition* (New Haven and London, 2009), pp.124–5.

66 Lapini, *Diario Fiorentino*, p.165.

CONCLUSION

1 Rebecchini, 'After the Medici', p.164 n.59.

2 Parker, *Emperor*, pp.172–3.

3   Robert J. Knecht, *Renaissance Warrior and Patron: The Reign of Francis I* (Cambridge, 1994), pp.10–11.

4   Benedetti, *Diario de bello Carolino*, p.107.

5   Knecht, *Renaissance Warrior and Patron*, pp.400, 404–5.

6   Vasari, *Le vite de' più eccelenti pittori*, 5:168, 172 n.1.

7   Ibid., 7:407 n.

8   Vasari, *Le vite de' più eccelenti pittori*, 4:31–2.

9   Caroline Elam, 'Art in the service of liberty. Battista della Palla, art agent for Francis I', *I Tatti Studies*, 5 (1993), p.61 n.97.

10 Knecht, *Renaissance Warrior and Patron*, p.425.

11 C. Herrero Carretero, 'Les tapisseries', in *Charles Quint, Tapisseries et armures des collections royales d'Espagne* (Brussels, 1994), pp.97–101; Glenn Richardson, *Renaissance Monarchy* (London, 2002), p.184.

12 Vasari: *Le vite de' più eccelenti pittori*, 7:598–9.

13 Ibid., 6:145.

14 Mary Hollingsworth, 'Coins, cloaks and candlesticks: The economics of extravagance', in Michelle O'Malley and Evelyn Welch (eds), *The Material Renaissance* (Manchester, 2007), p.269.

15 Vasari, *Le vite de' più eccelenti pittori*, 7:106, 407.

16 Ibid., 7:407.

17 Richardson, *Renaissance Monarchy*, p.186.

18 Vasari, *Le vite de' più eccelenti pittori*, 6:61.

19 Elam, 'Art in the service of liberty', pp.47–9 and Appendix 5.

20 Vasari, *Le vite de' più eccelenti pittori*, 6:262–3.

21 Ibid., 6:61.

22 Richardson, *Renaissance Monarchy*, pp.184, 187.

23 Vasari, *Le vite de' più eccelenti pittori*, 5:138.

24 Sanudo, *Diarii*, 52:209–10.

25 Pastor, *History of the Popes*, 11:243–5.

26 Roy Strong, *Art and Power. Renaissance Festivals 1450–1650* (Woodbridge, 1984), pp.88–9.

27 Parker, *Emperor*, p.472.

28 Herrero Carretero, 'Les tapisseries', p.43.

29 Parker, *Emperor*, p.457.

30 Strong, *Art and Power*, p.91; Albert van de Put, 'Two drawings of the fêtes at Binche for Charles V and Philip (II) 1549', *Journal of the Warburg and Courtauld Institutes*, 3 (1939–40), pp.51–2.

31 Van de Put, 'Two drawings of the fêtes', pp.52–3.

32 Vasari, *Le vite de' più eccelenti pittori*, 7:537; Bruce Boucher, 'Leone Leoni and Primaticcio's moulds of antique sculpture', *Burlington Magazine*, 123 (1981), p.24.

33 Francis Haskell and Nicholas Penny, *Taste and the Antique* (New Haven and London, 1981), p.5.

34 Hendrik J. Horn, *Jan Cornelisz Vermeyen, Painter of Charles V and his Conquest of Tunis: Paintings, Etchings, Drawings, Cartoons, Tapestries* (Doornspijk, 1989), p.122.

35 Iain Buchanan, 'Designers, weavers and entrepreneurs: Sixteenth-century Flemish tapestries in the Patrimonio Nacional', *Burlington Magazine*, 134 (1992), p.384; Horn, *Jan Cornelisz Vermeyen*, p.126.

36 Mitchell, *The Majesty of State*, p.136.

37 Gonzaga, *Cronaca del soggiorno di Carlo V in Italia*, p.262.

38 Ibid., p.263.

39 Hope, 'Titian's life and times', p.18.

40 Charles Hope, 'Titian's role as official portrait painter to the Venetian republic', in *Tiziano e Venezia* (Vicenza, 1980), passim.

41 Parker, *Emperor*, p.193; Charles Hope, 'La produzione pittorica di Tiziano per gli Asburgo', in *Venezia e la Spagna* (Milan, 1988), p.49.

42 Joanna Woods-Marsden, 'The sword in Titian's portraits of Emperor Charles V', *Artibus et Historiae*, 34 (2013), pp.202–4.

43 Hope, 'La produzione pittorica di Tiziano per gli Asburgo', p.49.

44 Hope, 'Titian's life and times', p.22.

45 Hope, 'La produzione pittorica di Tiziano per gli Asburgo', p.54.

46 Ibid., p.53.

Image credits

p.3 Wikimedia Commons / Art Gallery of New South Wales, Sydney, Australia; p.13 Kreder Katja / Alamy Stock Photo; pp.14–15 Witold Skrypczak / Alamy Stock Photo; p.17 Patrick Guenette / Alamy Stock Photo; pp.20–1 Wikimedia Commons / The Yorck Project, 2002 / National Gallery London; p.27 Metropolitan Museum of Art, New York / Bequest of Gwynne M. Andrews, 1931; p.27 Metropolitan Museum of Art, New York / Rogers Fund, 1974; pp.32–3 Jack Zhou 2015 / Getty Images; p.40 Dea L. Romano, 2007 / De Agostini / Getty Images; p.50 Nadezhda Bolotina / Alamy Stock Photo; pp.56–7 REDA&CO / Getty Images; p.58 Mondadori Portfolio/Electa/Antonio Quattrone / Bridgeman Images; p.61 Wikimedia Commons / Web Gallery of Art / Pinacoteca di Brera; p.66 Heritage Images / Hulton Fine Art Collection / Getty Images; p.71 Photo Josse/Leemage / Corbis Historical / Getty Images; p.72 Heritage Images, 2000 / Hulton Archive / Getty Images; p.77 Wikimedia Commons / AA.VV., L'opera completa di Pisanello, Rizzoli, Milano 1966 / Louvre Museum; p.78 Shutterstock 1434816479 / Gaia Conventi; p.84 Wikimedia Commons / Samuel H. Kress Collection, 1957 / National Gallery of Art; p.87 Shutterstock 1439339201 / Aliaksandr Antanovich; pp.96–97 Stuart Forster, 2018 / Alamy Stock Photo; p.105 Artexplorer, 2016 / Alamy Stock Photo; p.109 National Gallery, Washington / Samuel H. Kress Collection; p.110 Dea / A. Baguzzi, 2006 / De Agostini / Getty Images; p.115 Fine Art Images / Bridgeman Images; p.116 Dea / A. Dagli Orti, 2003 / De Agostini / Getty Images; pp.118–19 Fine Art Images / Heritage Images / Heritage Image Partnership Ltd / Alamy Stock Photo; p.120 Wikimedia Commons / Web Gallery of Art / Palazzo Ducale Mantua; pp.124–5 Andia, 2015 / Universal Images Group / Getty Images; p.127 Illustration Art, 2017 / Alamy Stock Photo; p.136 De Agostini Picture Library, 2009 / De Agostini / Getty Images; pp.137–8 Dea / Archivio J. Lange, 2015 / De Agostini / Getty Images; p.141 Stefano Ravera, 2018 / Alamy Stock Photo; p.144 Wikimedia Commons / The Yorck Project, 2002 / The Uffizi; p.148 Shutterstock 1090044326 / Stefano_Valeri; pp.150–1 Roberharding, 2019 / Alamy Stock Photo; p.153 Metropolitan Museum of Art / Fletcher Fund, 1952; p.158 Marage Photos / Bridgeman Images; p.166 Dea / L. Romano, 2017 / De Agostini / Getty Images; p.177 Dea Picture Library, 2002 / De Agostini / Getty Images; p.178 Adam Eastland, 2017 / Alamy Stock Photo; p.181 AGF, 2011 / Universal Images Group / Getty Images; p.182 Leemage / Corbis Historical / Getty Images; p.187 FineArt / Alamy Stock Photo; p.190 Alinari Archives, 1992 / Alinari / Getty Images; p.199, pp.200–01 Wikimedia Commons / Santa Maria delle Grazie collection; p.212 Luisa Ricciarini / Bridgeman Images; p.216 akg-images / Erich Lessing; p.221 Shutterstock 1631007619 / Gaia Conventi; p.224 A. Dagli Orti / De Agostini Picture Library / Bridgeman Images; p.228, p.229, pp.230–1 Wikimedia Commons / Royal Collection, Hampton Court Palace; p.233 Dea / A. Dagli Orti, 2016 / De Agostini; p.234 Print Collector, Hulton Archive / Getty Images; p.237 Dea / G. Nimatallah, 2003 / De

Agostini / Getty Images; p.238 Wikimedia Commons / Metropolitan Museum of Art; pp.244–5 National Gallery, Washington / Widener Collection; pp.248–9 GL Archive / Alamy Stock Photo; p.252 Sepia Times / Universal Images Group / Getty Images; p.253 Munsey Fund, 1927 / Metropolitan Museum of Art; p.262 Picturenow, 2018 / Universal Images Group Editorial / Getty Images; p.269 Wikimedia Commons / Museo del Prado; pp280–1 Shutterstock 1199013787 / Claudio Zaccherini; p.286 The Picture Art Collection / Alamy Stock Photo; pp.288–9 De Agostini Picture Library / M. Carrieri / Bridgeman Images; pp.209–1 Raffaello Bencini / Bridgeman Images; p.294 Bridgeman Images; p.297 Universal Images Group North America LLC / Alamy Stock Photo; p.299 Dea / M. Borchi, 2018 / Getty Images; p.303 National Gallery, Washington / Samuel H. Kress Collection; pp.306–07 Fine Art Images / Heritage Image Partnership Ltd / Alamy Stock Photo; pp.316–317 Wikimedia Commons / Dorotheum; p.321 AGF / Universal Images Group, 2015 / Getty Images; pp.324–5 StockStudio, 2016 / Alamy Stock Photo; p.327 Peter Delius, 2018 / Alamy Stock Photo; p.328 funkyfood London - Paul Williams, 2018 / Alamy Stock Photo; pp330–1 Wikimedia Commons / National Gallery ; p.333 Bailey-Cooper Photography, 2016 / Alamy Stock Photo; pp.334–5 Art Heritage, 2019 / Alamy Stock Photo; p.336 Jason Knott, 2015 / Alamy Stock Photo; p.338 Panther Media GmbH, 2014 / Alamy Stock Photo; p.341 gardenpics, 2012 / Alamy Stock Photo; p.342 Wikimedia Commons / Museo del Prado; p.349 The Picture Art Collection / Alamy Stock Photo; p.355 Wikimedia Commons / National Museum of Capodimonte; pp.360–361 Wikimedia Commons / Metropolitan Museum of Art; Rogers Fund, transferred from the Library; p.363 The Picture Art Collection / Alamy Stock Photo; p.368 akg-images / Erich Lessing; pp.370–1 Getty 587495004 / Leemage / Corbis Historical / Getty Images; p.373 Heritage Images / Hulton Fine Art Collection; p.374 Fine Art Images/Heritage Images; p.378 Wikimedia Commons / Alessio Damato; p.383 Wikimedia Commons / Art Gallery of New South Wales, Sydney, Australia; p.386 Walker Art Gallery; p.392 The Picture Art Collection / Alamy Stock Photo; p.397 Danita Delimont, 2019 / Alamy Stock Photo; pp.398–9 Sklifas Steven, 2009 / Alamy Stock Photo; p.401 Florian Monheim, 2006 / Bildarchiv Monheim GmbH / Alamy Stock Photo; p.402 Alex Ramsay, 2016 / Alamy Stock Photo; pp.406–07 Wikimedia Commons / National Gallery; pp.410–11 Vyacheslav Lopatin, 2014 / Alamy Stock Photo; p.420 incamerastock, 2020 / Alamy Stock Photo; p.420 Photo Josse / Bridgeman Images; pp.425 akg-images / Erich Lessing; p.428 Ruslan Gilmanshin, 2017 / Alamy Stock Photo; p.433 Bridgeman Images; p.434 Metropolitan Museum of Art; The Milton Weil Collection, 1938; p.437 liz finlayson, 2010 / Alamy Stock Photo; pp.438–9 Shutterstock 1631007619 / Marquez; p.445, pp.446–7 Wikimedia Commons / Museo del Prado; p.449 Bridgeman FIT58817 / Bridgeman Images; p.450, pp.456–7 Wikimedia Commons / Museo del Prado;

Acknowledgements

Among the many people who have been generous in their support, shared their ideas and inspired me with their research, I would like to thank Giles Bancroft, Elisabeth de Bièvre, Sarah Carr-Gomm, Alexander de Chalus, David Chambers, Flora Dennis, Melissa Freeman, Tabitha Goldstaub, Miles Goslett, Charles Handy, Chris Hollingsworth, Rosamund Hollingsworth, Charles Hope, Anna Keay, Amy Kent, Mel Kingsbury, Julian Kliemann, Sally Laurence Smyth, Nigel Llewellyn, Lauro Martines, Michelle O'Malley, Philip Mansel, Ann Matchette, Luca Molà, John Onians, Miles Pattenden, Tim Porter, Clare Reynolds, Nigel Reynolds, Carol Richardson, Glenn Richardson, Nick Ross, Lorna Sage, Henry Saywell, Richard Schofield, Rupert Shepherd, Robin Simon, David Starkey, Terry Sweeney, Thomas Tuohy, Trenham Weatherhead, Evelyn Welch, Geoff Williams and Arno Witte.

I would also like to remember these much-loved friends and colleagues who died during the writing of this book: Suzy Butters, Edward Eden, Liz Handy, David Held, Clare Robertson, David Rowland and Toby Salaman.

It has been a great pleasure to work with the team at Head of Zeus, especially with my ever courteous editor Richard Milbank.

Above all, I owe a huge debt to my agent Andrew Lownie for his unwavering encouragement and support.

Index